Designing Modernity

The Arts of Reform and Persuasion
1885 – 1945

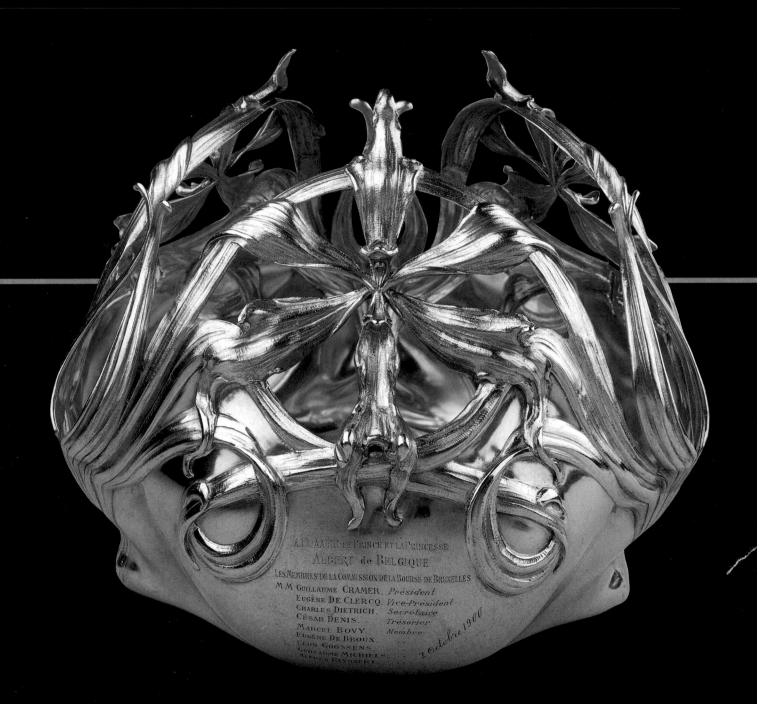

À LL.AA.RR. LE PRINCE ET LA PRINCESSE
ALBERT de BELGIQUE

LES MEMBRES DE LA COMMISSION DE LA BOURSE DE BRUXELLES

M.M. GUILLAUME CRAMER, *Président*
EUGÈNE DE CLERCQ, *Vice-Président*
CHARLES DIETRICH, *Secrétaire*
CÉSAR DENIS, *Trésorier*
MARCEL BOVY, *Membre*
EUGÈNE DE BROUX,
LÉON GOOSSENS
GUILLAUME MICHIELS
ALFRED REYNAERT

2 Octobre 1900

Designing Modernity

The Arts of Reform and Persuasion
1885 – 1945

Selections from the Wolfsonian

Edited by Wendy Kaplan

Thames and Hudson

Previous page
See cat. 44
Centerpiece
Presented to Prince and Princess Albert of Belgium, 1900
Designed by Philippe Wolfers*

* For the explanation of the form and contents of captions and the checklist, see p. 15

Designing Modernity: The Arts of Reform and Persuasion, 1885–1945 was prepared
to accompany the inaugural exhibition of the Wolfsonian, Miami Beach, Florida.

Designed and produced by Thames and Hudson and copublished with the Wolfsonian.

First published in the United States of America in 1995 by Thames and Hudson Inc.,
500 Fifth Avenue, New York, New York 10110

Library of Congress Catalog Card Number 95-60480
ISBN 0-500-23706-9

Printed and bound in Singapore

Exhibition dates for United States tour:

The Wolfsonian, Miami Beach
November 11, 1995 – April 28, 1996

Los Angeles County Museum of Art
July 21 – September 22, 1996

Seattle Art Museum
October 24, 1996 – January 12, 1997

The Carnegie Museum of Art, Pittsburgh
February 22 – May 18, 1997

Lenders

The Art Institute of Chicago
Private Collection, Florence, Italy
Sackner Archive of Concrete and Visual Poetry, Miami
Virginia Museum of Fine Arts, Richmond
John C. Waddell, New York City

Sponsors

The inaugural exhibition of the Wolfsonian was made possible in large part by the National Endowment for the Humanities, a federal agency, and The Chase Manhattan Bank. Further support was received from Alitalia Airlines and Continental Airlines. Generous support for the publication of the catalogue was provided by the Design Program of the National Endowment for the Arts, a federal agency, Reba and Dave Williams, John P. Axelrod, Alfred P. Kennedy, Steven Neckman and Larry Rivero, and the Indian Creek Hotel.

Preface

Peggy Loar, Director

One of the ways in which a civilization defines itself is in its material culture; its infrastructure, architecture, art, furnishings, tools, technologies, ephemera. Through objects, cultures are recorded, providing us with tangible evidence concerning transformations in values and politics. Insights can be garnered on the role of the individual and the family in society, and on the function of art, architecture, and design. In the preservation and study of these objects, we can cast a structured, reflective, and critical eye on the societal shifts and adaptations that have shaped the socio-economic realities of successive eras. Beginning in the eighteenth century and accelerating in the nineteenth, society entered a phase of radical and unprecedented social adjustments as the agrarian basis of Western civilization came to be transformed by industrialization. Indeed, the terms "modern" and "modernity" mark a dramatic break with an agrarian world, and have come to signify a momentous shift in human consciousness as new concepts of time, motion, productivity, and community began to dominate post-agrarian thought in virtually all venues, all forms of expression, and all social transactions.

The reactions to modernity can be characterized in three phases. The first is distinguished by the ambivalence, and often enmity, toward industrialization and the changes it wrought. Those threatened by these changes – for reasons of economic displacement or a clash of values – clung to stability, to certainty, to the mores and cycles of agrarian life, which were perceived as timeless and predictable. The second phase is distinguished by the emergence of a culture of modernity and by its celebration: as society confronted the modern, adjusting to life in a transforming world, a new creative idiom emerged, explosively redefining aesthetics with the images and conceptual implications of the machine, with utopian visions and a redefinition of the individual. A third and concurrent phase is characterized by the exploitation of the modern by governments. With new or refined forms of communication – the poster, radio, journals, textbooks – and new design vocabularies – photomontage, futurism, Neo-Classicism – national leaders became particularly skilled at promoting political goals through aesthetic expression.

These three aspects of modernity, then, are the unifying concepts of this opening exhibition of objects from the Wolfsonian's collection of decorative and propaganda arts. The theme of modernity, the title and focus of these essays – Designing Modernity: The Arts of Reform and Persuasion, 1885–1945 – illuminates one important vein of the Wolfsonian's extensive collections. Headquartered in Miami Beach, the institution is devoted to public education and to a program of research enabling scholars worldwide to explore and interpret its holdings, which encompass but are considerably broader than the themes presented in this opening exhibition.

The Wolfsonian's collection spans the period from 1885 to 1945, beginning with the age of New Imperialism, the peak of Europe's political and economic hegemony over the rest of the world, and ending with the emergence of the Cold War. Its 70,000 objects extend across a singular range of social phenomena and movements in art, design, technology, and politics, including two world wars and the reconstruction of the political boundaries of Europe, Asia, and the Middle East. The collection elucidates the material culture of democracy, capitalism, Socialism, Communism, Nazism and Fascism; it demonstrates how these systems are manifested in both progressive and retardataire styles such as the Arts and Crafts and Art Nouveau movements, Neo-Classicism, Futurism, and Art Moderne.

In the Wolfsonian's collection of design and decorative arts, the U.S.A., Great Britain, Germany, Italy, and the Netherlands are most comprehensively represented, while many other European countries and Russia have a significant presence. The Wolfsonian Library, which forms an important part of the collection, has about 40,000 rare books, periodicals, and ephemera, supported by relevant reference materials. The library has particularly rich holdings of fine press and illustrated books. It includes a superb collection of Italian Futurist books, Dutch Nieuwe Kunst bookbindings, and Czech Constructivist and Surrealist book covers; political propaganda documenting the rise and demise of Nazism and Fascism; and works on world's fairs and expositions; romantic nationalism and modernism in the decorative arts and architecture, transportation, public works and urban planning, and advertising, including a broad selection of sample books and trade catalogues.

More than 20,000 drawings, posters, and prints in the collection reinforce the stylistic, cultural, and political themes represented in the decorative arts and library collections. Strengths in these media consist of political propaganda posters from Germany, Italy, and the U.S.A., including an important group of American WPA prints and mural studies; working drawings for architecture, interiors, and the decorative arts; advertisements and promotional materials from trade fairs and expositions of decorative arts, industry, and architecture; and transportation-related graphic arts.

In Genoa, the Wolfsonian's Italian branch administers an extensive collection of Italian decorative arts, design, architecture, painting, and sculpture of the late-nineteenth through mid-twentieth centuries, and works to realize the restoration of the Castello Mackenzie.

Most civilizations have engaged in the collection and preservation of art and artifacts. One of the most intriguing aspects of this impulse is the phenomenon of the private collector, whose taste, vision, and psyche are indelibly imprinted on some of the most formidable assemblages of art and artifacts in our cultural patrimony. Serious private collectors have, as a result of their highly personal quests, provided the core for many of our major public institutions. Such is the case with the Wolfsonian, which is founded on the prodigious holdings of Mitchell Wolfson, Jr.

How we perceive artifacts and why and what we collect are, consciously or not, governed by the beholder's or the collector's personality. It is a process influenced by intensely individual frames-of-reference, preferences, taste, and motives. In Mitchell Wolfson's case, what began as a self-described "dedication to a sort of aesthetic tourism" soon took on more formal dimensions as a growing commitment to collecting melded with his ardent personal interest in "The social and political drama of the late nineteenth and early twentieth centuries . . . the unification of nations, the dislocation of peoples, the unconscious movements toward self-destruction . . . the turbulent chronicle of Europe and America in the sixty-year period from 1885 to the end of World War II."

It is often the atypical vision evident in private collections that lends institutions based on these collections their uniqueness and distinction. According to Mr. Wolfson's collecting philosophy, objects are significant as much for their meaning as for the caliber of their aesthetics. The focus of the Wolfsonian collection is more on the power of design than on conventional notions of beauty. Collectors typically aspire, foremost, to possess irresistibly attractive objects which, secondarily, awaken curiosity and stimulate the intellect. In the Wolfsonian collection, these priorities are, as often as not, reversed, subverting the notion that art is necessarily beautiful. The quest for Mitchell Wolfson is to understand what he describes as "the interplay – the relation between the created object and its maker or commissioner." Proceeding from this ethos, the 70,000 objects in the collection encompass not just the major political and aesthetic movements of the late nineteenth to mid-twentieth century, but also the ephemeral. The collection embraces the architect-designed masterpiece and the postcard, the furniture that won a gold prize at an international exhibition and the scarf that was a souvenir from it.

This task of making such a vast private collection public is a long and arduous one, and we are very grateful for the assistance provided by individual, government, and corporate sponsors. We especially acknowledge the generous sponsorship of the Chase Manhattan Bank, whose long-standing commitment to the arts continues with its support of "The Arts of Reform and Persuasion."

A rigorous set of professional obligations is borne by those striving to institutionalize collections of the Wolfsonian's magnitude and distinction. The preservation and conservation of the collection and its organization into an orderly, accessible archival system has been a nine-year endeavor. These tasks have given us the necessary tools to research and interpret the collections and make their richness available to the public on many levels – through exhibitions, publications, lectures, and fellowships to scholars.

It is the labors of the talented and uniquely dedicated professional staff whose devotion has made it possible for a singular American institution to come, so auspiciously, into the public eye. Our inaugural exhibition and this book have come together largely due to the efforts of Wolfsonian curator, Wendy Kaplan, who has guided them with grace, flexibility, and professional wisdom. Her combination of intellectual, interpretive, and editorial skills is rare, as is her commitment to the successful realization of this project.

Above all, the highest recognition and praise go to Mitchell Wolfson, Jr. The foundation of the Wolfsonian and the creation of its ambitious programs are a testament to his personal, lifelong commitment to collecting and scholarship. It is his vision and voice, his unique aesthetic and vitality that are, in the last analysis, reflected throughout the extraordinary collection of art and design that has culminated in the establishment of a new museum and research center, an institution devoted to inquiry and education about the world that became modern.

Sponsor's Statement

On behalf of Chase Manhattan, I congratulate the Wolfsonian on the opening of its new headquarters in Miami Beach. More than just a museum of decorative and propaganda arts, it is an important educational center for the humanities.

Chase is delighted to sponsor both the inaugural exhibition, "The Arts of Reform and Persuasion, 1885 – 1945," and the establishment of the permanent galleries. As the exhibition travels across the United States and abroad, we're also pleased to help the Wolfsonian reach a larger audience. In addition, Chase has donated to the Wolfsonian two pieces from our corporate art collection: finials from New York City's majestic Woolworth Building.

Chase is an active member of the Florida business community, a long-time supporter of the state's arts organizations and a contributor to many other local philanthropic efforts. We see our participation in the Wolfsonian as a way to continue our commitment to Florida, its residents and its visitors.

We salute the Wolfsonian for its unique vision in helping nurture fresh, innovative artistic developments.

Thomas G. Labrecque
Chairman
The Chase Manhattan Bank

Acknowledgments

First, I would like to thank Peggy A. Loar, Director, for her extraordinary leadership, encouragement, and expert advice concerning all aspects of the project. Associate director James J. Kamm played an incomparable role in exhibition planning, particularly regarding the installation and the intricacies of establishing the tour.

The exhibition and book would not have been possible without the indispensable efforts of the curatorial staff. Associate curator Marianne Lamonaca provided exemplary supervision of the research on over 400 objects included in this volume, undertaking much of it herself, as well as assuming responsibility for countless other aspects of exhibition planning, including resolution of issues regarding object selection, conservation, and installation. In addition to writing an essay, she carefully evaluated other contributors' essays. Curatorial assistant Donna C. Johnson provided invaluable assistance with research and organization and used her outstanding computer and management skills to ensure that every object could be tracked and all information accurately recorded. The success of the installation and the publication owes a great deal to their determination, commitment, exacting standards, and good humor.

Neither the exhibition nor the publication could have been realized without the contributions and dedication of every member of the Wolfsonian staff. Chief preparator Richard Miltner superbly coordinated the exhibition design and the construction of platforms, cases, and crates: creative solutions to seemingly insurmountable problems were his specialty. Collections manager Anita Gross employed her superlative skills in tireless supervision of all transport and contract issues, photography for the book, and the conservation of works on paper, textiles, and paintings. Because of conservator Gary Stewart's heroic efforts, assisted by intern Deborah Carton, all three-dimensional objects received attentive care. In addition, Gary's expertise about materials and processes elucidated our understanding of how the objects were made. The library staff, particularly James Findlay and Frank Luca, ably assisted in the selection of books and ephemera, as well as producing research for these items. Registration staff members, Mary Hawk, Jacqueline May, and Kimberly Stillwell, and research center coordinator Anne Low also made important contributions to the task of documenting the objects in this volume. Marie Stewart provided matting and framing skills for over 200 works on paper and library items, and Dennis Wilhelm devoted countless hours to the organization and coordination of the myriad details relating to domestic and international shipments for the exhibition. The staff at our Genoa office – assistant director Gianni Franzone, curator Matteo Fochessati, and registrar Silvia Barisioni – provided exceptional research on Italian materials and insightful comments on the Italian design essays. Education curator Lynn Anderson devised innovative programs to make our new research and interpretation accessible to a broad audience. In addition to staff already mentioned, I would like to offer a special thank you to: Stephanie Cox, Judith Dolkart, Pedro Figueredo, Steve Forero-Paz, Maria Gorecki-Nowak, Scott Hartley, Lynn Lambuth, Kelly Mitchell, and Michael Sperow.

Consultant David Kiehl shared his expertise by helping to select and then cataloging the works on paper. Thanks go to interns from the Camberwell College of Art, under the guidance of Mark Sandiford, who carefully conserved and prepared all works on paper for photography and exhibition. Exhibition designer Elroy Quenroe's creativity, sound judgment, and fruitful collaboration with Richard Miltner resulted in a highly successful installation. Claudia and Jacques Auger of Jacques Auger Design Associates were responsible for the exhibition printed materials. We are grateful for their exceptional design skills as well as for the time and advice that they generously donated.

The interdisciplinary skills required to examine the breadth and complexity of the Wolfsonian Collection were provided by a number of outside scholars. In addition to writing essays and critiquing each others' drafts, the consultants were invaluable for their assistance in object selection and developing the themes of the exhibition and book. We extend profound gratitude to these consultants: Ellinoor Bergvelt, Irene de Guttry, Dennis P. Doordan, Paul Greenhalgh, John Heskett, Maria Paola Maino, Jeffery L. Meikle, Bernard F. Reilly, Jr., and Laurie A. Stein. All contributed time and expertise far exceeding the call of duty. Derek Ostergard, Dean of the Bard Graduate Center for Studies in the Decorative Arts, contributed his superb conceptualizing and connoisseurship skills to help formulate the exhibition object list.

The following individuals and colleagues at other institutions are among the many who were generous with their expertise: Marika Hausen, Ålands Konstmuseum; Ian Wardropper, The Art Institute of Chicago; Irmela Franzke, Badisches Landesmuseum,

Karlsruhe; Kevin Stayton, Barry Harwood, Molly Seiler, Elizabeth Reynolds, The Brooklyn Museum; Van Burdick, California College of Arts and Crafts; Wendy Salmond, Chapman University; Marlene Park, C.U.N.Y.; Priska Clerc; Russell Flinchum, Stephen van Dyk, The Cooper-Hewitt Museum; Corigraph, Archivi della Pubblicità, Genoa; Alan Crawford; the staff at Dadart; Jon Catleugh, The De Morgan Foundation; Graham Dry; Beate Dry von Zezschwitz; János Gerle; Jörg Weigelt Auktionen; paintings conservator Patricia Kamm; Marianne Aav and Anna-Lisa Amberg, Konstindustrimuseet, Helsinki; Widar Halén and Anniken Thue, Kunstindustrimuseet, Oslo; Frans Leidelmeijer; Elizabeth McGorty; Tucker Madawick; László Pusztai, Magyar Épitészeti Múzeum; Frederike Huygen, Museum Boymans-van Boyningen, Rotterdam; Ellenor Alcorn and Marianne Carlano, The Museum of Fine Arts, Boston; Tessa Veazey, National Museum of American Art; Annette Carruthers, National Museums of Scotland; Laurin Raiken, New York University; Elisabeth Schmuttermeier, Angela Völker, Christian Witt-Dörring, Österreichisches Museum für Angewandte Kunst, Vienna; Jill Lever, Royal Institute of British Architects; Nancy Valby, San Jose Historical Museum; Maurizio Scudiero; Emily Shapiro; Mark Turner, Silver Studio Collection; Christopher Gow, Sotheby's; Jewel Stern; Terry Keenan, Syracuse University Library; the staff at the Textile Conservation Workshop; Janette R. Athey, Toy Train Collectors Association Library; Mary Ann Bamberger, The University of Illinois, Chicago; Jennifer Opie, Eric Turner and Christopher Wilk, The Victoria and Albert Museum, London; Frederick R. Brandt, Virginia Museum of Fine Arts, Richmond; Jenny Wolfson.

Bruce White brought great skill and rare sensitivity to the photography of the Wolfsonian's objects in this publication. Editor Stanley Baron of Thames and Hudson worked with us on every stage of production; his sage advice and honing skills made this a better book.

Finally, Mitchell Wolfson, Jr.'s profound commitment to making the Wolfsonian Collection accessible to both scholars and the general public has culminated in this exhibition and book. He has fostered a spirit of inquiry, encouraged debate and even contradiction, and insisted on exploring the inter-relationships between objects, their makers and their users in the 1885 to 1945 period.

Wendy Kaplan
Curator

Explanatory Notes for Captions and Checklist

Caption and checklist researched under the direction of Marianne Lamonaca with the assistance of Donna C. Johnson.

1   All objects illustrated in the essays and checklist are part of the Wolfsonian Collection, unless otherwise noted on the credit line.

2   The checklist reflects the order of objects in the exhibition and is organized by its section and subsections.

3   Exhibition objects are given full captions in the checklist; when an object also appears as an essay illustration the captions have been shortened there and the reader is referred to the checklist.

4   Exhibition objects that illustrate essays are not pictured in the checklist; the reader is referred to a corresponding figure number in an essay.

5   The design date appears after the object identification. The production date, when known, is given with the maker or manufacturer information if it is different from the design date.

6   Dimensions in inches precede dimensions in centimeters. Height precedes width and depth.

Confronting Modernity

Traditions Transformed:
Romantic Nationalism in Design, 1890–1920

Wendy Kaplan

Vernacular traditions were updated and redefined throughout Europe at the turn of the century to suit the national interests of individual countries. The Wolfsonian's collections provide a rich source for a comparative analysis. With examples from Britain, Norway, Finland, Russia, and Ireland, this essay will examine a variety of ways that regional design was used to help forge a national identity. In such a limited study comprehensiveness would be an impossible goal; however, the hope is that a careful examination of selected objects will contribute to a better understanding of what they meant to those who designed and used them.

The adaptation of folk and other indigenous cultures to express a country's identity is now known as romantic nationalism or the National Romantic movement. It was a phenomenon in all European countries at the turn of the century, but the shifting geography of Continental borders had much to do with the ways it was manifested and its level of intensity. In all countries, it is characterized by the recasting of traditions for new markets and constituencies. Sometimes nostalgic and resistant to change, at other times progressive and attempting to direct change, designers and promoters of romantic nationalism attest to the complexity of the modern experience.

The late nineteenth century was a period of rapid technological advances, when the development of mass production and new modes of transportation brought about major upheavals in the structure of society. Given the threat to all that was familiar and constant, it is not surprising that the period was also characterized by an intense adherence to a country's heritage. As Marshall Berman has observed: "To be modern is to live a life of paradox and contradiction . . . it is to be both revolutionary and conservative . . . . We might even say that to be fully modern is to be anti-modern [since] it has been impossible to grasp and embrace the modern world's potentialities without loathing and fighting against some of its most palpable realities."[1]

Although Norway, Finland, Russia, and Ireland were not as intensely industrialized as Britain, France, and the newly competitive Germany, all contained articulate groups of intellectuals and artists who were deeply concerned about the negative consequences of modernity. This concern became manifested in a longing for the past, particularly for peasant cultures, which were perceived as unspoiled and as representing the continuity of ancient traditions. As Oscar Falnes pointed out in a perceptive early study of this phenomenon in Norway, romantic nationalists believed that peasants "once had their day of innocence and purity before they became contaminated by foreign contacts . . . . Mindful of the danger to which the Norwegian nationality had been exposed by the official urban and intellectual classes, the romanticists turned eagerly to the peasant to find that in all essentials he had preserved his national identity intact; he had maintained the folk uniqueness with least corruption."[2]

Berman's insight about the simultaneity of modernity and anti-modernity (a seeming oxymoron) is reflected in the romantic nationalist belief that "le style moderne" would encompass traditional styles. In all the countries under discussion, the definition of modern included using native, vernacular architecture and furnishings whose origins were hundreds of years old. For example, in a 1903 lecture, Jens Thiis, the director of the Museum of Applied Art in Trondheim, declared that the objective behind his museum's collecting of folk art was to provide design models "in the service of modern art."[3]

While such usage seems paradoxical to us today, no contradiction was perceived at the time, when to be modern was to be anti-historicist, not anti-historical. What we now term historicist was defined as the arbitrary application of "Louis" styles, or any motifs or forms that had no particular historical resonance in the country's heritage. The vernacular was embraced in the belief that the essence of a culture could be encapsulated and maintained by the continuation of time-honored visual traditions. Such expressions were synthesized with the vocabulary of the "modern" at the turn of the century – symbolism and Art Nouveau.

Berman's definition of modernity epitomizes the fears and aspirations of the romantic nationalists and explains further why to be modern is also to be anti-modern: "It is to be overpowered by the immense bureaucratic organizations that have the power to control and often to destroy all communities, values, lives; and yet to be undeterred in our determination to face these forces, to fight to change their world and make it our own."[4] By distilling the past, romantic nationalists hoped to seize the future – not to be buffeted by overwhelming forces, but to be grounded by the essential nature of what it means to be Norwegian, Finnish, Russian, or Irish.

Analogies for the idealization of folk culture can be found in the eighteenth-century Enlightenment, with its worship of life in a state of nature. Although roots are also evident in early nineteenth-century Romanticism, much of the ideology of European romantic

Fig. 1.01 See Cat. 8
Sideboard, c.1906
Designed by E.W. Gimson

nationalism, as it applies to design, originated in the British Arts and Crafts movement, which in the 1880s had added social issues to the mid-nineteenth-century design agenda. Arts and Crafts reformers believed that the industrial process had stripped craftspeople of their individuality – they vowed to change society through the transformation of the work process. Handcraftsmanship and thus "joy in labor" would be restored; anonymous, shoddy, and excessively decorated work abolished. In their design, Arts and Crafts practitioners turned to solutions that had evolved in response to regional conditions and needs; for example, houses were crafted of local materials and were meant to fit into the landscape and reflect vernacular building traditions.

The influence of the British Arts and Crafts movement protagonists can hardly be overstated. Publishers on the Continent constantly reprinted books by the two most important crusaders, John Ruskin and William Morris (see fig. 3.12 for a translation of Morris into

21

Dutch; see also figs. 3.08 and 3.09 for a translation of a book by the designer and Socialist Walter Crane). Many European design reformers not only read the dictates of the British proselytizers; they traveled to Britain to see the houses of Arts and Crafts architects, to visit utopian communities such as C.R. Ashbee's Guild of Handicraft in Chipping Campden, and to write about the work of leading designers. To cite but a few cases: the pioneer architect of the "Hungarian" style, Ödön Lechner, went to England to study country houses and cottages; co-founder of the Wiener Werkstätte Josef Hoffmann declared in the company's work program its indebtedness to Ruskin and Morris; and the architect and design reform leader Hermann Muthesius's seven years in Britain culminated in a three-volume study, *Das englische Haus* (1904 and 1905), which disseminated a complete examination of British domestic architecture throughout the German-speaking world.

International exhibitions and journals played an essential role in the transmission of British Arts and Crafts ideals. *The Studio*, the leading British periodical of design reform, had a vast readership that extended far beyond the country's borders, and Continental journals often focussed on British works as a model to follow in their own countries. For example, furniture designed by Ernest Gimson, who had retreated to the Cotswolds to pursue the ideal of "the simple life,"[5] was published in a 1903 issue of *Der Moderne Stil*.[6] A sideboard in the Wolfsonian collection, similar to the one illustrated in this German art journal, demonstrates the principles of handwork and vernacular traditions that were adopted on

Fig. 1.02 See Cat. 9
Cabinet, c. 1891
Designed by W. R. Lethaby

the Continent (fig. 1.01). Made using seventeenth-century cabinetmaking techniques, its form evokes cupboards of that era, and the center strut of the back is curved like a plowhandle.[7]

Gimson often worked with W.R. Lethaby, a leading architect, theoretician, and teacher (he was director of the influential Central School of Arts and Crafts in London), whose work provides another example of the British design presence abroad. Muthesius featured Lethaby in *Das englische Haus*, where six illustrations of Lethaby's Avon Tyrell (an 1892 commission with stucco decoration and ceilings executed by Gimson) are included.[8] Gimson and Lethaby were also among the five principals who founded the short-lived Kenton and Co., an early attempt to apply Arts and Crafts ideals to a commercial venture – another important type of endeavor widely imitated on the Continent. A cabinet Lethaby designed while at Kenton and Co. (fig. 1.02) received international exposure when it was published in *The Studio* as part of the journal's review of the 1893 Arts and Crafts exposition.[9] A quote from Muthesius neatly sums up the importance of British precedent: "The whole of our [German] movement is based on the results England achieved from 1860 and up to the middle of the 1890s."[10]

Although deeply influential, the Arts and Crafts movement had different manifestations on the Continent. As suggested earlier, while many were uneasy about the effects of modernity, the repugnance felt by British reformers toward their highly industrialized society could not be fully experienced in nations remaining more largely agrarian. In the countries under discussion here, the issue of national identity was more important. In its service, romantic nationalists in Norway, Finland, and Ireland took from the Arts and Crafts the movement's moral aesthetics, adherence to regionalism, and glorification of "the simple life" and the handmade. These three countries were engaged in a struggle to free themselves from the domination of another and they, as well as Russia, were "peripheral" rather than "core" political and economic powers (in contrast to Britain and France). Norway had been in the shadow of Denmark until 1814, when the country came under Swedish rule; only after years of strenuous effort did it succeed in dissolving that union in 1905. Finland had also been tied to Sweden, but had been ceded to Russia in 1809. With its own constitution, Finland had more autonomy under Russia than it had enjoyed previously; however, these favorable conditions changed in the 1890s. Pressure from the Russian Pan-Slavic movement caused Czar Nicholas II to curtail Finnish freedoms, thus providing more stimulus to the Finnish desire for complete independence, which was achieved in 1917. Ireland had been striving against the British for autonomy – its Home Rule movement, begun in 1870, culminated in the Rebellion of 1916 and finally in the establishment of the Irish Free State in 1921. The situation in Russia, a country long independent, was slightly different. Its Pan-Slavic nationalism developed in reaction to the westernization of Russia first introduced by Peter the Great and then reinforced by the liberal reforms of the 1860s.

In comparison, while nationalism played a critically important role in English design (see Paul Greenhalgh's essay), in such a long-established, powerful, and highly industrialized country it assumed a different character. At the turn of the century, however, all these nations shared a threat to their *status quo*. The attendant features of modernity – mass production, urbanism, new technology, new forms of communication and transportation – irrevocably changed the economy, the pattern of social relations, and the individual's sense of connection with tradition. While modernity itself was integral to the process of becoming a twentieth-century nation, the need for continuity with the past was compelling. The need to modernize was inevitably accompanied by an ambivalence toward modernization. Their combination with the struggle for political independence gave a passionate urgency to the quest for national identity.

In describing how the past has been manipulated, updated, selected, or otherwise reconfigured in order to serve national purposes, the historian Eric Hobsbawm uses the term "the invention of tradition." His work provides a paradigm for understanding how "all invented traditions, so far as possible, use history as a legitimator of action and cement of group cohesion." In this essay, the discussion is limited to the way national characteristics were encoded into *design* for the purpose of creating a shared heritage. Romantic nationalists did not "invent" traditions in the sense of a complete, *sui generis* fabrication. The inventions were all the more powerful for their foundations in documentable culture – in archaeological excavations, folktales, ancient craft techniques, and indigenous building materials. Such traditional practices and their records, as Hobsbawm points out, "were modified, ritualized and institutionalized for the new national purposes."[11]

Norway, Finland, Russia, and Ireland shared many of the processes by which elements of the past were transformed. For example, in all four countries an awakening interest in native language and legends was a prelude to the interest in folk design.

The great Finnish saga *The Kalevala* or *The Land of Heroes* was published for the first time in 1835. This epic poem originated in an ancient oral tradition of story telling in the eastern province of Karelia, a remote, unspoiled wilderness that nationalists regarded as a repository of all that was essentially Finnish. Although the nature of this oral tradition was altered by the act of publication, it was essential to the creation of national identity that these classic tales *were* published and in Finnish – a statement against Swedish, the language of educated and upper-class Finns.

The 1830s also saw the beginning of a new interest in native language and folktales in Norway and Russia. Norwegians embraced the mythology surrounding the Vikings of the Middle Ages – a time when they were the conquerors, well before the union with Denmark in 1384. In post-Napoleonic Russia, where French was the first language of the aristocracy,

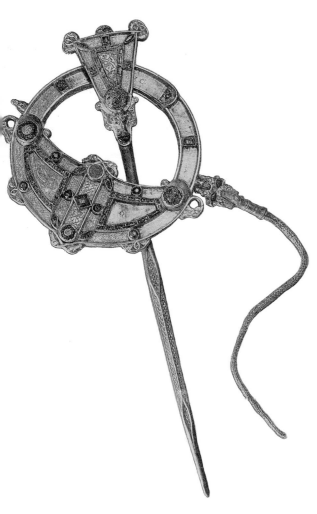

Fig. 1.03
"Tara" Brooch, c.700
Discovered in Ireland, 1850
Bronze overlaid with gold, amber and glass
7 x 4 inches dia. (17.8 x 10.2 cm dia.)
National Museum of Ireland, Dublin

poets such as Aleksandr Sergeyevich Pushkin helped disseminate an indigenous culture by publishing their own renditions of Russian folktales in the native language.

The emphasis on native languages and legends came later to Ireland; but after five hundred years of subjugation by the British, their re-establishment assumed even greater importance. In the late 1880s, nationalists such as Lady Augusta Gregory (co-founder, with William Butler Yeats, of the Abbey Theatre) and Douglas Hyde (president of Gaelic League and later the first President of Ireland) learned Irish in order to publish the country's ancient myths and legends both in that language and in authentic English renderings. Yeats, an equally ardent nationalist, did not read Irish, but published immensely popular versions of Irish folktales derived from English translations.[12] The pre-Gothic period was idealized as a golden age, since it preceded British colonization.

What historian János Gerle terms "the mother-tongue of words" was followed by "the mother-tongue of forms."[13] These were not only three-dimensional; a national vocabulary and grammar of music was developed as well. For example, the composers Edvard Grieg in Norway, Jean Sibelius in Finland, and Nikolai Rimsky-Korsakov in Russia created works inspired by legends and folk music. In their respective countries each belonged to a circle of artists that included most of the painters, architects, and designers discussed here, who all shared a fervent commitment to establishing an aural and visual national identity.

Ireland and Norway had an additional impetus to the growth of national consciousness in design through major new discoveries in archaeology. The "Tara" brooch, uncovered in 1850, and the Ardagh chalice, found eighteen years later, quickly become emblematic of a glorious Irish past. While both were constantly reproduced, the eighth-century "Tara" brooch was particularly influential (fig. 1.03). Its motifs of band and animal interlace, inlaid stones, and filigree scrollwork became the standard design vocabulary of Celtic Revival metalwork.[14]

In Norway, archaeological excavations of Viking ships in Tune (1867) and Gokstad (1880) provided a major stimulus for the Viking revival, also known as "the dragon style." As art historian Widar Halén has pointed out, the Viking revival was also popular in Sweden and Denmark, where, through manifestations in architecture, silver, and furniture, it was used to promote the idea of a unified Scandinavia.[15] At the Paris International Exhibition of 1878, the Swedish-Norwegian pavilion was executed in this style, its gables adorned with dragon heads. Norway was recognized as the source, but Viking culture was presented as a shared Scandinavian heritage. Since such unity was increasingly seen by Norwegians as detrimental to their own interests, the Viking style in Norway became a visual symbol of how its culture *differed* from Sweden's; the same imagery was evoked, but to convey a very different message.

A chair by Lars Kinsarvik exemplifies the Viking revival style (fig. 1.04). Carved dragon heads peer over the back stiles and complicated polychromed interlace patterns adorn every

Fig. 1.04 See Cat. 29
Armchair, c.1899
L.T. Kinsarvik

Fig. 1.05
Tankard, 1899
Designed by Frederik Holm
(Norwegian, dates unknown)
Made by Frederik Holm and Wilhelm Schulze
(Norwegian, dates unknown) for David Andersen, Oslo
Silver, gilt on inside, chased ornaments
10⁷/₁₀ x 8⁷/₁₀ inches (27 x 22 cm)
Kunstindustrimuseet, Oslo

surface except the seat. Decorating one's house with such furniture made a nationalist statement; for example, the homes of Grieg and of the violinist Ole Bull, who was also devoted to the cause of creating an indigenous Norwegian musical language, contain many examples of Viking revival furnishings.[16]

The revival was also well represented in silver. A tankard made in the shop of David Andersen, one of the most renowned silver studios at the turn of the century, not only shows the dragon heads and exuberant interlace decoration that are signatures of the style but also evokes Norse legends central to Norwegian romantic nationalism (fig. 1.05). The chased panels depict the death of Saint Olav, who converted the country to Christianity and was killed for his beliefs in 1060. (Norwegian kings still take his name.) The scenes were adapted from illustrations in a contemporary edition of *Sagas of the Norwegian Kings*, to which the artist Gerhard Munthe contributed many of the renderings.[17]

Munthe's life embodies the commitment to the ideal that native art could serve as a basis for national regeneration. Like other ardent romantic nationalist artists discussed here later (Akseli Gallen-Kallela in Finland, Ivan Bilibin in Russia), Munthe traveled to remote rural cor-

Fig. 1.06. See Cat. 30
Tapestry
The Daughters of the Northern Lights
***(Aurora Borealis)* or *The Suitors*, 1895**
Designed by G. Munthe

ners of his country recording vernacular buildings and furnishings. Already one of Norway's best known painters, Munthe began in the early 1890s to create watercolors whose flat, geometric patterning was well suited for translation into the medium of tapestry. In 1896 he was asked by the director of the Museum für Kunst und Gewerbe in Hamburg to adapt one of these designs. Choosing "Daughters of the Northern Lights," Munthe had the work executed at the tapestry studio of Nordenfjeldske Kunstindustrimuseum (the Trondheim Museum of Applied Art) (fig. 1.06).[18] In 1896, *The Studio* published an appreciative article about Munthe's work which further elucidates how romantic nationalists reinvented the past to serve the intertwined causes of modern art and nationalism. Munthe is quoted as saying: "Each nation must be regarded as an individual whose talents are of a distinct stamp . . . . Tradition is, therefore, not what many believe it to be – viz., ancient romance or history. The first condition demanded of a nation by tradition is that it can be, as it were, digested by it, absorbed by it, and tradition therefore depends largely upon the developing power of the nation itself."[19]

The article goes on to state that Munthe's designs were not derived from specific legends but were imaginative creations inspired by "the spirit and meaning conveyed or transmitted

27

by nations."[20] "The Daughters of the Northern Lights" was not an ancient legend, but all its motifs – polar bears, snow, pine cones, the evocation of the aurora borealis – are imbued with associations that constitute a "science of signs" for national characteristics.[21] The tapestry's continued production for at least thirty years attests to the persistence of such associations. The Wolfsonian's example was woven by Nini Stoltenberg in a colorway characteristic of the 1920s.

Munthe was deeply involved in disseminating the cause of national design. He wrote prolifically about the subject, he decorated the medieval Håkon Hall in Bergen and the Holmenkollen Tourist Hotel in Kristiania (now Oslo) in the Viking revival style, and was on the board of Den norske Husflidsforening (The Norwegian Association of Home Arts and Crafts), whose goal was the revival of indigenous craft techniques and industries.

Similar organizations were established throughout Scandinavia and were particularly rife in Finland. The Suomen Käsityön Ystävät (Friends of Finnish Handicraft) was founded in 1879 to collect and exhibit folk design and to improve modern standards by its own productions. Like the Norwegian Association of Home Arts and Crafts, its focus was on textiles, which were considered a pure peasant art. Just as Munthe had done for the Norwegian organization, so too did leading romantic nationalist artists such as Akseli Gallen-Kallela produce designs for the Friends of Finnish Handicraft.

Born Axel Gallén, he later changed his Swedish-sounding name to one more authentically Finnish. He trained as a painter in Paris, but as an 1897 article in *The Studio* observed, "he delight[ed] in the interpretation of nebulous legends filled with the magic of the ancient Finns."[22] He made many pilgrimages to Karelia and created his own vision of the epic world of *The Kalevala* in his art. In addition to paintings, etchings, and *ryijy* (a traditional Finnish and Swedish knotting technique) rugs for the Friends of Finnish Handicraft, Gallen-Kallela designed posters, bookbindings, jewelry, and furniture. His furniture designs for the Finnish pavilion at the 1900 Exposition Universelle in Paris were executed by the company of his close friend, the artist Louis Sparre. Although a Swede by birth, Sparre shared Gallen-Kallela's passion for native Finnish design, even accompanying him and his bride on their honeymoon to Karelia.

In 1897, Sparre founded the Iris company, an idealistic venture based on the English Arts and Crafts movement model that would eschew "the commercial desire for profit" in favor of a commitment to well-designed furniture and ceramics accessible to a wide audience (fig. 1.07).[23] The first Finnish enterprise devoted to reforming public taste in domestic furnishings, Iris was established in the same year as the Vereinigte Werkstätten für Kunst im Handwerk (United Workshops for Art in Handicraft). In Finland, as in Germany, issues of updating the vernacular, and of modern design and its democratization, were closely tied to the search for a national identity (see Laurie Stein's essay for an extensive analysis of the situation in Germany).

Fig. 1.07
Pitcher, 1897–1902
Designed by Alfred William (Willy) Finch
(British, b. Belgium, 1854–1930)
Made by Iris Factory, Porvoo, Finland
Glazed earthenware
9⅞ x 7½ x 4⅝ inches (23.7 x 19.1 x 10.8 cm)
Marks: underside, incised "A.W.F."/Iris logo/"FINLAND"
85.7.258 a,b

If Gallen-Kallela was, as he has often been called, Finland's "national artist," then Eliel Saarinen was the country's "national architect." He and his partners Herman Gesellius and Armas Lindgren built a home and studio for all of them, Hvitträsk, between 1901 and 1903 (fig. 1.08). It embodies the ideal of design unity, called on the Continent *Gesamtkunstwerk* a total work of art in which the building, its furnishings, and its setting form an environmental whole. Dramatically sited on a ridge above Lake Vitträsk, west of Helsinki, the building seems to grow out of its granite foundation. This stone, a notoriously hard material, had symbolic significance in Finland, not only because it was native but also because it was associated with the strength and durability of the Finnish character. Hvitträsk is actually a series of structures – one free-standing, the others connected with skylighted studios. Faithful to the Arts and Crafts principle of harmony with nature, the building follows the contours of the land. It is tied to its site with stone walls, a series of outdoor terraces, pavilions and porches, and the local materials of which it is made – granite, plaster, and logs, with pantiles and shingles for roofs.[24]

Saarinen's was the dominant hand on the interior, especially after Lindgren left the partnership in 1905 and Gesellius in 1907. (Gesellius, however, continued to live at Hvitträsk until his death in 1916.) The prints Saarinen made of his living room (figs. 1.09

29

and 1.10), which was filled with furnishings of his own design, are studies in the vernacular ideal; they show round log construction, hand-made furniture and metalwork, a *ryijy* rug woven by his wife Loja, and an enormous tiled fireplace that would provide warmth and psychological comfort during the dark, harsh winters.

The *ryijy* rug provided the same physical and psychic qualities. Gallen-Kallela had modernized the traditional *ryijy* design by the application of strong geometric patterns to motifs from the Finnish landscape. The function of these rugs changed as well – they had originally been used as sleeping rugs on boats or as coverlets.[25] After Gallen-Kallela updated its design, the *ryijy* assumed a new function, one particularly suited to the Finnish climate. The lithograph of the living room (fig. 1.10) shows its use as a combination wall, floor, and seat covering, thus providing protection from drafts. The Wolfsonian Collection includes one of Saarinen's *ryijy* masterpieces – a rug that was made as part of a complete boudoir he designed for the twenty-fifth anniversary exhibition of the Friends of Finnish Handicraft in 1904 (fig. 1.11). Here, Saarinen demonstrates his connection to international movements – the abstract geometric patterning and rose motifs are very close to Viennese and Glaswegian design. In light of the previous discussion regarding the comfortable coexistence between the modern and the vernacular, this is not incongruous. Furthermore, the most complete study of Saarinen's work in Finland (he emigrated to the U.S.A. in 1923) points out his development

Fig. 1.09
Print
Saarinen's living room, Hvitträsk
(1901–03; Gesellius, Lindgren, Saarinen,
architects), Kirkkonummi, near Helsinki, 1902
Eliel Saarinen
(Finnish, 1873–1950)
Helsinki
Ink on paper
13½ x 17½ inches (34.3 x 44.5 cm)
Marks: obverse, printed in black, bottom left
"E. SAARINEN A.D. 1902"
XX1990.3390

Fig. 1.10 See Cat. 28
Print
Saarinen's living room, Hvitträsk (1901–03;
Gesellius, Lindgren, Saarinen, architects),
Kirkkonummi, near Helsinki, c. 1905
E. Saarinen

Fig. 1.11 See Cat. 50
Ryijy rug
Ruusu, 1904
Designed by E. Saarinen

Fig. 1.12 See Cat. 27
Design drawing
Bedroom for Villa Bobrinsky
(Gesellius, Lindgren, Saarinen, architects;
unknown if built), Moscow, 1903
E. Saarinen

along more international lines at Hvitträsk: "This personal variation on 'the Finnish style' theme was short-lived, however, and the interiors gradually took on a more international look . . . when Gustav Mahler visited Hvitträsk in 1907, he compared it to the Hohe Warte outside Vienna. Gesellius, in particular, made many changes, covered log walls with plaster and designed new furniture. In Saarinen's quarter the changes came more slowly . . . ."[26]

Despite the political tensions between Russia and Finland, cultural ties were close among progressive circles. The Mir Iskusstva (World of Art) group exhibited and published paintings by Gallen-Kallela, including some of his "Kalevala" subjects. Sparre's Iris company furnishings were popular in St. Petersburg. Saarinen visited that city regularly, and about 1903 his firm received a commission from Count Bobrinsky for a summer villa in Moscow. Although Saarinen's watercolor renderings of the project were published in the German periodical *Moderne Bauformen* in 1904, it is not known if the commission was ever executed. The watercolor of the bedroom (fig. 1.12) demonstrates that although the designs were intended for a villa in Moscow, Saarinen did not adapt his visual language to the different environment. Indeed, the article about the project in *Moderne Bauformen* is entitled "The New Style in Finland" and its author, praising Saarinen's "love of indigenous tradition," notes: "The exterior is purely national in form and material."[27]

Russia, however, did have its own variants of romantic nationalism; objects in the Wolfsonian serve as examples of the forms it took as well as suggest some other paradoxes which emerge in its study. In a 1901 article in *The Studio*, "The New Movement in Russian Decorative Art," Netta Peacock describes the efforts made by artists and their patrons to develop native arts: "they were actuated by two motives – the one a genuine love of their popular art, and the other the fear that the building of manufactories in the large towns would gradually kill the art crafts of the villages."[28] These motivations had led to the creation of two art colonies; the first at Abramtsevo (outside Moscow) in the 1870s, by the railroad magnate Savva Mamontov and his wife Elizaveta and the second, in the 1890s at Talashkino (near Smolensk) by the Princess Maria Tenisheva. Their primary goals were to revive and improve peasant industries by providing training and to encourage the appreciation of traditional crafts. Therefore, both Elizaveta Mamontova and Princess Tenisheva established workshops for crafts such as wood-carving and embroidery and created museums with extensive collections of folk art. Both were passionately concerned with the peasants' plight as well as their art. Mamontova established a hospital for them at Abramtsevo; the Princess, a school for orphans at Talashkino.

The women had just cause for their philanthropic concerns – conditions of peasant life were dire. For hundreds of years, peasants had supplemented their meager incomes from the land with crafts during the long winter months. This rural cottage production, known as the *kustar* (the peasant handcraftman) industries, was being threatened by the emergence of modern industries in Russia. As in the other countries under discussion here, one important manifestation of the protest against industrialization was the idealization of folk cultures. Netta Peacock extols decoration that "seeks its inspiration in the very heart of life – in nature as seen through the eyes of the peasant, who is free from all the conventionalities of civilization, and whose eye is unspoiled by the constant contemplation of the ugliness which is so unsparingly distributed around us."[29] The reality behind the romance was that *kustar* production arose not from harmony with nature but from grim economic necessity, and by the end of the nineteenth century most of its products were ill-made and more expensive than factory goods. Private patronage represented by the art colonies as well as government-sponsored agencies such as the Moscow Kustar Museum recognized the need to improve the quality of *kustar* products, and did so by employing professional artists to upgrade the designs and improve the techniques of manufacture.[30]

Fig. 1.13 See Cat. 33
Mirror, 1903
Made by the furniture workshop at the Talashkino artists'
colony, near Smolensk, Russia

One paradox of the period is that no contradiction was perceived between the preservation of rural traditions and their re-invention by urban artists. Another is the inevitable changes that come to folk cultures once they are institutionalized. The very organizations and museums in Russia (as well as in Norway and Finland) whose mission was to collect and encourage folk craft were responsible for its transformation by their own nationalistic or economic agendas. A third paradox is that no contradiction was seen between the idealization of the peasant's "mentality" and the perception of his desperate circumstances. An article by Aymer Vallance in *The Studio* discusses the widespread famine and misery of the peasant in Russia, only to state a few paragraphs later that "we in England . . . may well envy him." Invoking Ruskin's definition of art as "the expression of man's pleasure in labour," Vallance concludes that if this is true, "then the lot of the Russian peasant cannot be altogether unhappy."[31] Patricia Berman points to an analogous misconception in Norway: "the real basis for folk art in Norway was not an 'instinct toward decoration' as Aubert [the influential turn-of-the-century art historian] suggested, but the economic deprivations of farm life."[32]

The Abramtsevo and Talashkino communities attest to the kind of art-as-philanthropy that was an important component of romantic nationalism. These efforts were frequently characterized by leadership from upper- and upper-middle-class women who were committed to helping peasants upgrade traditional crafts and find new markets for their goods, often on a very large scale. In addition to sponsoring an art school in St. Petersburg and co-funding Russia's most progressive exhibition society and journal, the *World of Art*, Princess Tenisheva established an embroidery workshop at Talashkino, which advertised that "two thousand peasant women and more than fifty villages" were associated with it.[33]

The mirror made at the Talashkino community (fig. 1.13) is dated 1903, the last year that the Moscow painter Sergei Maliutin was in charge of the joinery and woodcarving workshops. His work epitomizes the Russian version of the invention of traditions. He was the creator of the *matrioshka* (nesting dolls) (fig. 1.14). This cliché of Russian design has been presented as an authentic manifestation of folk art ever since its introduction in 1891. Its audience soon became the export market.

The *matrioshka* was marketed by the Moscow Zemstvo (local government), which was pragmatic about the selling points of folk art. In 1909 it stated, "examples of national art interest not so much the Russian consumer as the foreign buyer, therefore the more pronounced their national character, the broader the market they can depend on, including export abroad."[34] The resulting irony is that in this and many other cases, the *kustari* received strict instruction concerning what designs would be made and could not deviate from these mass-produced forms. Therefore, much of their product, even in idealistic workshops such as Maliutin's at Talashkino, was folk industry, not folk art.

Maliutin was a member of the circle of artists that formed the "World of Art" group. Led by the impresario Sergei Diaghilev, who edited its magazine, and the painter and producer Alexander Benois, the group represented the Russian avant garde not only in the visual arts but in opera, theater, and ballet as well. Its goals were "modern" by the turn-of-the-century definition – simultaneously international and national, absorbing cultural influences from Germany, France, and England, as well as idealizing the heritage of medieval and folk Russia. Diaghilev not only produced experimental ballets such as the infamous "L'Après-midi d'un Faune," but also works by nationalist composers whose operas were based on Russian history and folktales (for example, Rimsky-Korsakov's *Ivan the Terrible* and Moussorsky's *Boris Godunov*, for which Ivan Bilibin designed the costumes and sets).

Bilibin's career demonstrates how "le style russe" functioned as part of "le style moderne." While attending Princess Tenisheva's art school in 1899, Bilibin began to receive commissions for drawings from the *World of Art* journal. He wrote in his *Autobiographical Notes*: "I learned a lot from the *World of Art*. Its pages acquainted me with the works of Finnish artists . . . and with the latest developments in Western art. This journal was, as it were, a 'window on Europe' for me."[35] Yet the same year he decided to devote most of his professional life to illustrating Russian folktales in publications and on stage. Bilibin's career

Fig. 1.14
Matrioshka (nesting dolls), 1891
Designed by Sergei Maliutin
(Russian, 1859 – 1937)
Turned wood, oil paint
From *E. Mozhaeva and A. Kheifits, Matrioshka* (n.p., n.d.)
Museum of Folk Art, Moscow

35

also attests to the way romantic nationalism could be allied to both conservative and progressive forces – his two greatest patrons were the Department for the Production of State Documents and the "World of Art." His many government commissions included providing the artwork to accom-pany a series of Pushkin's poems from Russian folktales (fig. 1.15). In 1900 Bilibin became a permanent participant in the "World of Art" exhibitions; he often wrote for the journal as well. His 1904 article, "Folk Arts and Crafts in the North of Russia," was based on numerous trips to rural areas where he collected local crafts and photographed wooden architecture.

This documentation appears in his work – his fantasy illustrations are full of historically accurate details. In an illustration for *The Tale of Tsar Saltan* (fig. 1.15), the church steeple on the left is based on a photograph Bilibin took on one of his journeys. The horse-head eave on the porch of the house is typical of vernacular architecture, as are the diagonal spiral columns. The robe worn by the Tsar and the caftan in a postcard version of an illustration for *Ivan the Tsar's Son, the Firebird and the Gray Wolf* (fig. 1.16) evoke the seventeenth century, Bilibin's favorite period. Medieval Russia is suggested in the latter illustration's borders, which were inspired by illuminated manuscripts first republished in the 1870s.[36]

Fig. 1.15 See Cat. 32
"He had heard the last girl's pledge/ Standing hid behind the hedge" (translation), 1905
From *Skazka otsare Saltane* (The Tale of Tsar Saltan) by Aleksander Sergeyevich Pushkin
Illustrated by I.Y. Bilibin

Another reason folk art was considered a viable "modern" art was that they shared many formal characteristics. The art historian Camilla Gray, discussing the St. Petersburg school and its relation to symbolism, states, "these artists tried to break down the traditional academic methods of picture construction, but their chief stylistic characteristic was the reduction of the human figure to an ornamental-decorative shape which emphasized the two-dimensional quality of the picture-surface and the eloquence of line divorced from colour and modelling."[37] These are all features of folk art, which, predating the Renaissance innovation of three-point perspective and Mannerist *chiaroscuro*, was flat, linear, and abstract in decoration. The qualities of the line were extolled by artists such as Bilibin, who wrote eloquently of its supremacy. Japanese art also shares this aesthetic, which explains its prevalence as a design inspiration during the period. Gerhard Munthe was greatly influenced by Japan, as were British designers such as E.W. Godwin and Christopher Dresser (see figs. 4.07 and 4.08).[38] Bilibin also wrote of his indebtedness to this source and many of his illustrations are directly inspired by Japanese prints.[39]

Fedor Shekhtel is considered to be the most innovative Russian architect at the turn of the century. He built mansions for the emerging class of entrepreneurs in Moscow who demanded a modern expression for their new wealth and status. Shekhtel's work reflects the contribution of the Russian vernacular to the establishment of a new art, and nowhere more clearly than in the four pavilions he designed for the Russian Village at the Glasgow International Exhibition in 1901 (figs. 1.17 and 1.18). The Russian section there was the largest of all the foreign participants. Its purpose was to display national products that would appeal to the British market – 180 carpenters and design students, together with vast quantities of native wood, were sent from Moscow to construct the village.

As historian Catherine Cooke points out, "the form of each pavilion derived from a traditional building type associated with its display function. Thus a North Russian timber church provided the model for the Central ceremonial pavilion . . . . A long low barn was the starting point for the Agricultural Product pavilion . . . ."[40] Shekhtel took these traditional forms and reinterpreted them. They were the basis for developing the anti-classical qualities that rationalist architects from Pugin and Viollet-le-Duc to Otto Wagner had admired in the vernacular. The decoration for the buildings was executed by students from the Stroganov design school with rich polychromatic painting of conventionalized fruits and plants, a folk-inspired style begun at Abramtsevo and continued at Talashkino (seen in fig. 1.13). Shekhtel's later style would be characterized by functionalism and open planning combined with exuberantly organic art nouveau decoration. The Glasgow pavilions, more self-consciously national because of their function, serve as a transition in his work. As Cooke observes, a new synthesis was found there "between the structural forms and aesthetic

Fig. 1.18 (left to right)
Forestry, Mining, Central Ceremonial and Argricultural Pavilions, Russian Village, Glasgow International Exposition, Kelvingrove Park, Scotland, 1901
Fedor Osipovich Shekhtel, architect
(Russian, 1859–1926)
From *The Buildings of Russian Section of International Exhibition in Glasgow – Archit: F. Schechtel in Moscow* (Moscow, 1901), pl. 1
XC1993.2

Fig. 1.17 (left to right)
Mining and Central Ceremonial Pavilions, Russian Village, Glasgow International Exposition, Kelvingrove Park, Scotland, 1901
Fedor Osipovich Shekhtel, architect
(Russian, 1859–1926)
From *The Buildings of Russian Section of International Exhibition in Glasgow – Archit: F. Schechtel in Moscow* (Moscow, 1901), pl. 3
XC1993.2

traditions of Russian building and the line, surface and tensely exaggerated hyper-real proportions characteristic of the International 'new art.'"[41]

The projection of a national identity combined with the promotion of economic interests is nowhere more clearly demonstrated than at World's Fairs. At the 1900 Exposition Universelle in Paris all the Norwegian, Finnish, and Russian designers discussed above were represented. A version of Munthe's "Daughters of the Northern Lights" was shown, as was Andersen's Viking revival tankard. Furnishings by the Iris company and many works by Gallen-Kallela (including his first *ryijy* rugs) were on view in a building designed by Gesellius, Lindgren, and Saarinen – the first time Finnish art was displayed in its own pavilion. As *The Studio* pointed out: "The earliest occasion for the West to become acquainted with the Russian revival was the Paris Exhibition."[42] The *matrioshka* was exported for the first time, Bilibin's illustrations were on display, and balalaikas made at Talashkino were greatly admired. The declaration of national design was intricately linked with its marketing for export abroad.

The four countries whose national consciousness in design is explored here share many similarities in their development. Ireland, however, presents another variant, since it was the only country directly under the control of another power. These special circumstances contribute to a different focus in its national design idiom.

The Celtic Revival, which began in the 1880s, was most profoundly expressed in literature rather than the visual arts. As Jeanne Sheehy explains,

> when the poets and playwrights of the late nineteenth century wished to create a distinctively Irish literature, drawing on native sources, they found an unbroken tradition of folklore, rich in language and literary invention . . . . The people of the Irish-speaking districts, the *Gaeltacht*, had distinctly national music, dancing and storytelling, but no fine art to speak of, and very little appreciation of it. The last great period of Irish art, in the eighteenth century, was associated in people's minds with the Anglo-Irish Protestant Ascendancy, and therefore suspect among Nationalists.[43]

There were no revivals of vernacular building traditions analogous to those in Norway, Finland and Russia, and few attempts to establish a national style in painting.[44]

The Celtic Revival did have some significant manifestations in art. Like Norway, Finland, and Russia, Ireland had a plethora of organizations devoted to the revival of native crafts, particularly textiles. The Arts and Crafts Society of Ireland was founded in 1894, and the Dun Emer Guild in 1902 by Evelyn Gleeson with Susan Mary (Lily) and Elizabeth Corbett Yeats, who shared their brother W.B. Yeats's fervent belief that Irish artists should base their works on their country's own traditions and places. The Dun Emer Guild is a romantic nationalist paradigm for art as philanthropy. Run by women who supervised the production of embroidery, textiles, and handmade books, it combined a passion for an

indigenous Irish culture with a commitment to the production of native crafts as an antidote to rural poverty and unemployment.

Even the crafts organizations had a strong literary component, attesting to the power of words in Irish society. Illuminated manuscripts such as the Book of Kells and the Book of Durrow were among the most important sources for Celtic Revival imagery. Not only were the manuscripts reproduced, but the Donegal Industrial Fund's "Kells" embroidery was based on decorations found in these eighth- to tenth-centuries Gospel books. Desk sets were a popular manifestation in metalwork – the Wolfsonian has one that was given as a wedding present in 1884 (fig. 1.19). Early medieval Ireland is recalled in the Celtic cross-shape of the inkstand and the stationery holder in the form of a reliquary. Both are embellished with interlace-decorated brass mounts.

One of the masterpieces in the Wolfsonian Collection, an eight-panel stained glass window by Harry Clarke, demonstrates how romantic nationalism in Ireland was best expressed in the country's modern literature (fig. 1.20). In 1926 the Irish Free State, eager to assert its new position as an independent country, commissioned Clarke to design a large window as a gift to the League of Nations, to be installed in the International Labor Building in Geneva.

Fig. 1.19
Stationery box and Inkstand, 1884
Manufactured by T.K. Austin & Co., Dublin
Left: Yew, brass, glass, grosgrain
Right: Yew, brass, glass, velvet
Left: 8 7/8 x 11 x 6 1/4 inches (22.5 x 27.9 x 15.9 cm)
Right: 6 1/4 x 13 1/8 x 13 inches (15.9 x 33.3 x 33.0 cm)
Left, marks: interior, impressed on insert, in gold ink, center front "AUSTIN•WESTMORELAND ST DUBLIN"; engraved on brass plate, rear edge "TK AUSTIN & CO/Dublin"
Left, inscription: exterior, top center of lid, engraved on brass medallion "PRESENTED/By the Employees/AT KYLEMORE CASTLE/To Miss Marie Henry/ON THE OCCASION OF HER MARRIAGE/July 1884"
TD1993.77.2 and TD1993.77.1a,b
Note: Desk set includes a blotter pad, TD1993.77.3 [not illustrated]

He decided to depict scenes from the work of fifteen contemporary writers. With the help of W.B. Yeats, whom he described as "wildly enthusiastic" about the project,[45] Clarke selected the following authors (clockwise as their work appears in the panels): George Bernard Shaw, James Stephens, Sean O'Casey, Liam O'Flaherty, Æ [George Russell], Seumas O'Kelly, James Joyce, George Fitzmaurice, Padraic Colum, W.B. Yeats, Lennox Robinson, Seumas O'Sullivan, John Millington Synge, Lady Gregory, and P.H. Pearse. Most of the writers – Yeats, Synge, Æ, and Lady Gregory in particular – identified completely with the Celtic Revival. Some were members of the Gaelic League; others were involved with the Abbey Theatre or the many small presses devoted to promoting a national voice. With a few exceptions (e.g., Shaw), their work was imbued with the Irish experience – plays such as O'Casey's *Juno and the Paycock* (fig. 1.21) and Synge's *Playboy of the Western World* (fig. 1.22) are still considered to be quintessential expressions of Irishness, with all its tragedy, humor, and eloquence.

Clarke was well aware that, although his window would represent the zenith of modern Irish culture, some of his literary choices would be controversial to political and religious leaders. A few had already been banned by the Censorship Board; in addition, the fact that half the writers represented were Protestants and many of the Catholics were not considered devout would be suspect. Clarke tried to be cautious; for example, he avoided an excerpt from *Ulysses*, choosing one of Joyce's poems instead.

All Clarke's prudence came to no avail, since the Irish government rejected the window. The country's President explained in a letter to him, "the inclusion of scenes from certain authors as representative of Irish literature and culture would give grave offense to many of our people."[46] The scene from *Mr. Gilhooley* proved the worst offender (fig. 1.23). Lennox Robinson, one of the authors represented and Clarke's close friend, elaborated: "The Irish Government discovered that the window might conceivably give foreigners a false conception of the Island of Saints. The bottle of Guinness was not seriously objected to but did not the Playboy's tight breeches show him a little too virile, was not the female's clothing in the Gilhooley panel slightly too diaphanous? The window was erected in Government buildings in Merrion Street and could be sniffed over. After many, many months of evasions and half-truths Harry's widow was allowed to buy it back for the price the Government had paid for it."[47] Drunken scenes and implications of sex were not what the Irish government wanted to project about its national identity. The first permanent home for this most powerful portrayal of the Irish literary renaissance has been provided in Miami Beach.

Although by its very nature romantic nationalism was political, involving the appropriation of design to construct a national identity, it was not inherently a conservative or a progressive force. It could be either, depending on what cause it was called upon to serve.

41

Fig. 1.20   See Cat. 175
Stained glass window
For the International Labor Building,
League of Nations, Geneva, commissioned 1926,
completed 1930 (never installed)
H. Clarke

Fig. 1.21
Panel from "Geneva" window (Fig. 1.20)
on left, from: "The Demi-Gods" by James
Stephens, and on right, from: "Juno and the
Paycock" by Sean O'Casey

Fig. 1.22
Panel from "Geneva" window (Fig. 1.20),
on left, from: "Playboy of the Western World"
by J.M. Synge, and on right, from: "The Others"
by Seumas O'Sullivan

Fig. 1.23
Panel from "Geneva" window (Fig. 1.20)
on top, from: "Mr. Gilhooley" by Liam
O'Flaherty, and on bottom, from: "Deirdre"
by George Russell (Æ)

43

In Ireland, it tended to be subversive, establishing solidarity with an oppressed native population and calling for profound social reforms that, ironically, were often modeled on British precedent. In Russia, as Wendy Salmond asserts, it functioned more as "a way of maintaining the social status quo in the countryside, while celebrating indigenous cultural traditions."[48] No movement that had the support of the Imperial family could be considered radical. In Norway and Finland, romantic nationalism could be embraced by either the Left or the Right; it affirmed middle-class values of stability and group cohesion while it challenged the hegemony of non-native powers.

Romantic nationalism was both progressive and conservative, modern and anti-modern; it asserted that art sprang naturally from the soul of the peasant while insisting that it needed to be sifted through the hands of a professional designer. Recent scholarship has exposed its inherent contradictions, but only one generation had to pass before some ominous consequences of romantic nationalism would be revealed. As explored in later essays of this volume, the elevation of earthy, peasant culture as the only true reflection of the national soul could lead to an intolerance of anyone not considered part of the native society.

The draft of this essay was reviewed by scholars specializing in the countries discussed; I am deeply grateful to Anna-Lisa Amberg, Anniken Thue, Widar Halén, Wendy Salmond and Nicola Gordon Bowe for their insightful comments. Gina Maranto and Mark Derr also gave the essay a careful reading; their suggestions helped improve it.

NOTES

1   Marshall Berman, *All That is Solid Melts into Air: The Experience of Modernity* (2nd edition, New York, 1988), pp. 13–14.

2   Oscar J. Falnes, *National Romanticism in Norway* (New York, 1933), pp. 55–6.

3   Quoted in Patricia G. Berman, "Norwegian Craft Theory and National Revival in the 1890s," from Nicola Gordon Bowe, ed., *Art and the National Dream: The Search for Vernacular Expression in Turn-of-the-Century Design* (Dublin, 1993), p. 162.

4   Berman, *All That is Solid Melts into Air*, p. 13.

5   For extended discussion of the Arts and Crafts concepts of "the simple life" see, for example, Wendy Kaplan, *'The Art that is Life': The Arts and Crafts Movement in America, 1875–1920* (Boston: Museum of Fine Arts, 1987), see especially my essay "The Lamp of British Precedent: An Introduction to the Arts and Crafts Movement" and Cheryl Robertson's "House and Home in the Arts and Crafts Era: Reforms for Simpler Living"; Fiona MacCarthy, *The Simple Life: C.R. Ashbee in the Cotswolds* (London, 1981); and David E. Shi, *The Simple Life: Plain Living and High Thinking in American Culture* (New York, 1985).

6   Mary Comino, *Gimson and the Barnsleys: 'Wonderful furniture of a commonplace kind'* (New York, 1980), p. 109.

7   The sideboard was also published in Walter Shaw Sparrow, *The Modern Home* (London, 1906), p. 129, and Sparrow, *Our Homes and How to Make the Best of Them* (London, 1909), p. 197.

8   Hermann Muthesius, *The English House*, ed. Dennis Sharp, translated by Janet Segilman (Oxford, 1987), pp. 38–9. (First published in 3 volumes as *Das englische Haus* by Wasmuth, Berlin, in 1904, 1905.)

9   "The Arts and Crafts Exposition, 1893," *The Studio* 2 (1894): 14.

10   Quoted in Stephan Tschudi Madsen, *Sources of Art Nouveau* (New York, 1975), p. 303. (First published, 1956.)

11   Eric Hobsbawm, "Introduction: Inventing Traditions," in Eric Hobsbawm and Terence Ranger, eds., *The Invention of Tradition* (6th edition, Cambridge, 1988), pp. 1, 12, 6.

12   Lady Gregory published a retelling of the epic saga of Cú Chulainn. As Linda Seidel points out in her essay "Celtic Revivals and Women's Work," "She acquired an English version of the stories, had them put into Irish, and then translated them back into English." (From T.J. Edelstein, ed., *Imagining an Irish Past: The Celtic Revival, 1840–1940* (Chicago, 1992), pp. 23–4. In Frank Kinahan's essay, "Notes on the De-Anglicization of Ireland," from this same exhibition catalogue, the author discusses Douglas Hyde's early collections, *Leabhar Sgeuluigheachta* (Baile Ath Cliath: Clóbhuailte le Gill, 1889) and *Beside the Fire* (London, 1890), and Yeats's early anthologies *Fairy and Folk Tales of the Irish Peasantry* (London, 1888) and *Irish Fairy Tales* (London, 1892). pp. 73–4, 78–9.

13   János Gerle, "What is Vernacular? Or the Search for the 'Mother-Tongue of Forms'" in Bowe, *Art and The National Dream*, pp. 144–5.

14   For more on Celtic Revival metalwork, see Michael Camille, "Domesticating the Dragon: The Rediscovery, Reproduction, and Reinvention of Early Irish Metalwork" in Edelstein, *Imagining an Irish Past*, pp. 22–43.

15   Widar Halén, *Drager: Gullsmedkunsten og drmmen om det nasjionale* (Oslo: Kunstindustrimuseet I, 1992), p. 31.

16   Since Ole Bull died in 1880, much of the Viking revival furnishings might have been brought to Lysøen by his American wife or their daughter, both of whom continued to spend their summers on the estate (on an island near Bergen) until their respective deaths in 1910 and 1911.

17   Snorre Sturlason, *Sagas of the Norwegian Kings* (Oslo, 1896–99). See Halén, *Drager*, p. 34.

18   Sometime earlier (about 1895) Munthe's wife had made the first version of "Daughters of the Northern Lights" as a tapestry. (I am grateful to Anniken Thue, director of the Oslo Museum of Applied Arts, for sharing her research about the tapestry.)

19   K.V. Hammer, "Gerhard Munthe, Decorative Artist," *The Studio* 8 (1896): 222.

20   *Ibid.*

21   For more on this semiological concept, see Roland Barthes, *A Barthes Reader* (New York, 1982).

22   "Studio Talk," *The Studio* 10 (1897): 61. In the best account of Finnish design in this period available in English, John Boulton Smith points out that Louis Sparre must have written this anonymously published article. See John Boulton Smith, *The Golden Age of Finnish Art: Art Nouveau and the national spirit* (2nd ed.; Helsinki, 1985), p. 109.

23   Quoted in Marita Munck and Marketta Tamminen, *Furniture by Louis Sparre: The Iris Works and Louis Sparre's New Style Furniture, 1897–1905; Catalogue of Furniture by Sparre in Porvoo Museum* [English title of book, whose text is also published in Finnish and Swedish] (Porvoo, 1990), p. 60.

24   Most of the information about Hvitträsk was taken from my chapter, "The Arts and Crafts Movement on the Continent" in Elizabeth Cumming and Wendy Kaplan, *The Arts and Crafts Movement* (London and New York, 1991), pp. 182–7. For more on Saarinen's work in Finland see Marika Hausen *et al.*, *Eliel Saarinen: Projects 1896–1923* (Cambridge, MA, 1990); Museum of Finnish Architecture, *Saarinen in Finland* (Helsinki, 1984); Museum of Finnish Architecture, *Saarinen's Interior Design* (Helsinki, 1984); Museum of Finnish Architecture, *Hvitträsk: The Home as a Work of Art* (Helsinki, 1987); for a more general view on Finnish nationalism in design see Smith, *The Golden Age of Finnish Art* and Ritva Toumi, "On the Search for a National Style," *Abacus: Museum of Finnish Architecture Yearbook* (Helsinki, 1979), pp. 57–98. This same author offers a dissenting view on the prevalence of nationalism in Finnish architecture: Ritva Wäre, "How Nationalism was Expressed in Finnish Architecture at the Turn of the Century," in Bowe, *Art and the National Dream*, pp. 169–80.

25   Finnish Society of Crafts and Design and Smithsonian Institution, *Ryijy Rugs from Finland* (Washington, D.C., 1979), pp. 4–7.

26   Hausen *et al.*, *Eliel Saarinen*, p. 116. The Hohe Warte was a fashionable neighborhood where architect Josef Hoffmann built a group of houses and villas.

27   Jac. Ahrenberg, "Der Neue Stil in Finnland," *Moderne Bauformen* 11 (1904): 80.

28   Netta Peacock, "The New Movement in Russian Decorative Art," *The Studio* 22 (1901): 270.

29   *Ibid.*: 268.

30   Information on the *kustar* industries and art education in Russia was derived from Wendy Salmond's pioneering work on the subjects. See the following essays by her: "Reviving Folk Art in Russia: The Moscow Zemstvo and the Kustar Art Industries," in Bowe, *Art and the National Dream*, pp. 81–98; "The Solomenko Embroidery Workshops," *The Journal of Decorative and Propaganda Arts* 5 (summer 1987): 126–43; "Design Education and the Quest for National Identity in Late Imperial Russia: The Case of the Stroganov School," *Studies in Decorative Arts* 1 (spring 1994): 2–24.

31   Aymer Vallance, "Russian Peasant Industries," *The Studio* 37 (1906): 242. Although both British and French sources during the period evoke Morris and Ruskin when describing national design in Russia, according to Wendy Salmond, no mention of the British Arts and Crafts movement leaders is made in Russian sources until about 1902.

32   Berman, "Norwegian Craft Theory . . . ," p. 162. Berman's source for this observation is the Norwegian folk art historian Peter Anker.

33   Quoted in John E. Bowlt, "Two Russian Maecenases: Savva Momontov and Princess Tenisheva," *Apollo* 98 (December 1973): 451.

34   Quoted in Salmond, "Reviving Folk Art in Russia," p. 91. See pp. 88–91 for more on *matrioshka*.

35   Quoted in Sergei Golynets, *Ivan Bilibin* (Leningrad and New York, 1981) (translated by Glenys Ann Kozlov), p. 182. This book is a rich source of Bilibin's own writings.

36   I am grateful to Wendy Salmond for sharing her research and expertise about Bilibin's sources.

37   Camilla Gray (revised by Marian Burleigh-Motley), *The Russian Experiment in Art, 1863–1922* (London and New York, 1986), p. 59.

38   Widar Halén, "Gerhard Munthe and 'The Movement that from Japan is moving across Europe now,'" *Scandinavian Journal of Design History* 4 (1994), pp. 27–47.

39   Golynets, *Ivan Bilibin*, quotes from Bilibin, pp. 9–10.

40   Catherine Cooke, "Fedor Shekhtel: Architect to Moscow's 'Forgotten Class'," in *The Twilight of the Tsars: Russian Art at the Turn of the Century* (catalog, London, 1991), pp. 50–1.

41   *Ibid.*, p. 51. For more detail about Shekhtel and the Russian Village, see Catherine Cooke, "Shekhtel in Kelvingrove and Mackintosh on the Petrovka: Two Russo-Scottish Exhibitions at the Turn of the Century," *Scottish Slavonic Review* 10 (Spring 1988): 177–205.

42   Vallance, "Russian Peasant Industries," p. 241.

43   Jeanne Sheehy, *The Rediscovery of Ireland's Past: The Celtic Revival, 1830–1930* (London, 1980), p. 95.

44   Nicola Gordon Bowe, "A Contextual Introduction to Romantic Nationalism and Vernacular Expression in the Irish Arts and Crafts Movement," in Bowe, *Art and the National Dream*, p. 196. For more on objects produced in Ireland, see Bowe's numerous publications on the subject, among them: "The Arts and Crafts Movement in Ireland," *Antiques* 142 (December 1992): 864–75; "The Irish Arts and Crafts Movement (1886–1925)," *The Irish Arts Review Yearbook* (1990/91): 172–85; "The Arts and Crafts Society of Ireland (1894–1925),"*Journal of the Decorative Arts Society 1850 to the Present* 9 (1985): 29–40; *The Arts and Crafts Movement in Dublin, 1885–1930* (Edinburgh, 1985). See also Paul Lamour, *The Arts and Crafts Movement in Ireland* (Belfast, 1992).

45   Quoted in Michael Laurence Clarke, "The Geneva Window," in The Fine Arts Society, *The Stained Glass of Harry Clarke, 1889–1931* (London, 1988), unpaged. The author is Harry Clarke's son.

46   *Ibid.*

47   Quoted in Nicola Gordon Bowe, *The Life and Work of Harry Clarke* (Dublin, 1989), p. 229.

48   Salmond, "Design Education and the Quest for National Identity . . . ," p. 17.

II. KRAFT- und ARBEITS-MASCHINEN-AUSSTELLUNG MÜNCHEN 1898.

PERMANENTE und PERIODISCHE GARTENBAU-AUSSTELLUNGEN.

11. JUNI — 10. OKTOBER

KARL STÜCKER'S KUNSTANSTALT (G. FALTERMEIER) MÜNCHEN.

German Design and National Identity 1890–1914

Laurie A. Stein

with contributions from Irmela Franzke

German design and architecture from the turn of the century to the founding of the Bauhaus in 1919 are characterized by the conspicuous intention to create a national idiom for modernity. In the late 1890s artists, architects, and critics began to search with almost missionary zeal for a new theoretical and stylistic vocabulary appropriate for modern German design. Munich, Darmstadt, and Dresden were early centers, but after 1900 this quest became a widespread artistic trend throughout the country. It was not a limited rebellion of a small group of social reformers, political Socialists, or elitist aesthetes. The German progressive movement encompassed a sweeping breadth of activity, disseminated through an array of periodicals, exhibitions, arts organizations, and design workshops established in the period 1897–1914. The initial phase of the movement became known as *Jugendstil* after the title of a contemporary Munich-based periodical *Jugend*. Later work lacked one specific identification tag and was generally termed Reform Style or modernist.

Motivation for the national quest in these years was rooted in a complex mixture of utopian goals and cultural patriotism, with pragmatic socio-economic and political elements. German unification in 1871 brought about heightened internal scrutiny of the relationships between regional traditions and national trends, and intensified exploration of pan-Germanic traits. Authors such as Julius Langbehn and Friedrich Nietzsche produced important treatises about the German character and spirit.[1] New financial, trade, and political systems evolved, at the same time that rapid industrialization was under way. This framework generated between 1890 and 1914 a German modernist ideology and iconography which developed in response to the perceived challenge of self-definition and self-determination. Reformist design was employed as a means for solidifying national identity and building cultural self-esteem.

Business and government became active partners with artists and writers in fostering the movement. To a profound degree, the resultant *Kulturpolitik* was actually defined by its

49

competitive and propagandistic stance. In the first issue of *Deutsche Kunst und Dekoration* in 1897, publisher Alexander Koch typified this attitude in claiming that "This undertaking gives itself the mission to bring about a gathering up and fertilization of indigenous arts in all fields, and therefore also wring respect for German art in foreign countries, yes, to help Germany and the German-speaking lands to achieve victory in competition with other nations!"[2] National self-consciousness was the fuel for the evolution and *Qualität* (quality) became its watchword.

In spite of turn-of-the-century discussions about *Formensprache* (language of forms) and a great number of more recent studies devoted to the period, precise codification of overarching aesthetic, formal, and stylistic criteria for German design and architecture between 1890 and 1914 still remains elusive.[3] In-depth review yields the conclusion that *Jugendstil* and modernist idioms encompassed a wide variety of artistic and design tendencies. Three dominant modes overlapped throughout the period: 1) highly ornamented pieces with naturalistic decoration, 2) revival of vernacular folk handicraft traditions adapted through modern styles, materials, and techniques, and 3) restrained decoration in functional or classicist design.

The *Jugendstil* and early modernist collection at the Wolfsonian includes the broad spectrum of media, types, and styles created during the period. The lack of clearcut stylistic unity within the museum's holdings mirrors the nature of the German progressive movement and offers a special reading of the multiple and contradictory design options current in Germany between 1890 and 1914. The scope and the selection of works enables an analysis of the material both as individual objects and as elements in a network of information about the psychic sensibility of a style and an era.

In comparison with contemporaneous trends in Britain, Austria, and France, German efforts were formally more diffuse. The key contribution of the German movement had less to do directly with style or method; the will for stylistic unity was subservient to the will for conceptual unity. Rather, through efforts to determine an articulate national design idiom, Germany achieved one of the first broad-based twentieth-century frameworks for significant debate about design policy. This was supported by the conscious endeavor to foster productive structures for conception, realization, and dissemination of new design.

One general German tendency was experimentation to create unified total works of art, known as *Gesamtkunstwerke*. The concept derived from Wagnerian opera and the British Arts and Crafts movement; German *Gesamtkunstwerk* design variations could range from a single book design to a complete interior, or even to the monumental size of a garden city. In addition, German progressive leaders were preoccupied with the role of the machine and the feasibility of mass-production for good design. They were generally not averse to new technological capabilities. Many artists and manufacturers eagerly embraced the practical possibilities of these options and even became advocates of serial production. Debate about preferences for *Typus* (standardization) versus *Individualität* (individuality) as official design policy eventually exploded in 1914 around the architects Hermann Muthesius and Henry van de Velde during the Deutsche Werkbund exhibition in Cologne.[4] A contemporary satire demonstrates how the respective debate positions encapsulated tensions between democratic and individualistic impulses which marked German design philosophies throughout the pre-war years (fig. 2.01).

The structural underpinnings of the design policy debate were rooted in the German penchant for bureaucracy and voluntary associations. The history of the period is punctuated by the foundation of an enormous number of organizations and companies devoted to furthering the cause of German modernist design. Among the most prominent groups were workshops such as the Vereinigte Werkstätte für Kunst im Handwerk or the Deutsche Werkstätten für Handwerkskunst, artist colonies such as the Künstler-Kolonie in Darmstadt or Worpswede, and advocacy associations such as the Deutsche Werkbund.

Munich was a pioneering center for establishing a characteristic modern German design idiom. The movement had its debut there on June 1, 1897, when two small rooms of *Kleinkunst* (decorative arts) were presented at the international fine arts exhibition held in the Munich Glaspalast. The committee for the decorative arts section noted in the guidelines that it " . . . places the main emphasis on originality of invention and on the perfect artistic and technical execution of such artistic objects as fulfill the requirements of our modern life

Fig. 2.01
Caricature
"Von der Werkbund-Ausstellung"
Karl Arnold Erben
(German, 1883–1953)
From *Simplicissimus*, 19 Jahrg., Nr.18, Munich
(August 3, 1914): 285

Fig. 2.02   See Cat. 74
Vitrine cabinet
Model no. 2616, 1903–04
Designed by B. Paul

Fig. 2.03   See Cat. 75
Side chair
Model no. 1555, from the Hermann Obrist
residence, Munich, 1899
Designed by R. Riemerschmid

. . . it excludes everything that appears as a thoughtless and false copy or imitation of past or foreign styles, that is not abreast of the latest developments in modern technology."[5]

This small section within the larger show was praised as a harbinger of the future for German art. It reflected a recent trend among Munich artists to turn away from painting and sculpture toward applied arts.[6] In *The Studio*, a correspondent observed, "I must, however, draw attention to the couple of small yet capacious rooms in which modern applied art asserts itself publicly and formally for the first time in Munich. These two narrow apartments, decorated with a healthy and refined taste, hold out perhaps more promise for the future than any in the whole exhibition . . . "[7] Organized as unified interiors for a typical bourgeois home, the rooms included contributions such as stained glass by Richard Riemerschmid, tapestries and metalwork by Otto Eckmann, a decorative frieze by August Endell, ceramics by Max Laueger and Theodor Schmuz-Baudiss, and woodcuts by Peter Behrens. Through the installation of complete interiors, close collaboration between artists and producers, and work in multiple media by one artist, the new German progressive movement placed itself securely within the norms of international design reform trends and simultaneously foretold much about the particular character of the German tendencies as it would evolve during the following decades.

In 1898 a limited liability company, the Vereinigte Werkstätten für Kunst im Handwerk (United Workshops for Art in Handicraft), was established in Munich. This was a new type of structure in Germany, developed from reconsideration of the relations of artists with design, production, and marketing. Its principal members, including Riemerschmid, Hermann Obrist, Bruno Paul, Bernhard Pankok, and Paul Schultze-Naumburg, were determined to bring modern decorative arts to the purchasing public and involve artists more directly in the processes from conception to sale.[8] The company planned both to buy and to manufacture works, distribute them under conditions advantageous to the artists, and train workers in craft skills necessary for production. There was no lack of philosophical and social idealism behind the project, but its main organizational aim was to create a profitable, independent distribution system for a flexible range of products in which the aid of the machine was enlisted whenever necessary. Designs produced by the Werkstätten included all manner of decorative arts: for example, furniture such as Bruno Paul's cabinet made around 1903 (fig. 2.02), and such architectural elements as an ornamental radiator screen produced for the Villa Sack in 1908.[9]

The group's members also supported each other's work. For example, Richard Riemerschmid designed several rooms of furniture which were manufactured by the company and included by the Werkstätte supporter Obrist among the furnishings of his house.[10] Surviving pieces from these rooms, such as a side chair (fig. 2.03), demonstrate Riemerschmid's functional design principles of logic, comfort, and honesty of construction. The chair's arched central backsplat derives from quasi-ergonomic considerations, the prominent wood graining differentiates the structural elements of the chair, and simple construction highlights the basic wood as its own natural decorative element.

In 1898–99, Darmstadt emerged as another center of the movement, when Grand Duke Ernst Ludwig von Hessen und bei Rhein invited seven artists, architects, and designers to settle just beyond the city center and establish a Künstler-Kolonie determined by principles of modern artistic production. This project on the Mathildenhöhe site was the first major German undertaking to create a community as *Gesamtkunstwerk*. Ernst Ludwig's motivations for the revolutionary and unprecedented experiment were a complex mixture of nationalistic, financial, and idealistic concerns. Through high-quality work by artists such as Peter Behrens and Joseph Maria Olbrich, he hoped to gain attention to Darmstadt as an artistic center and increase revenues for the state of Hessen. With partial financial support from the Hessian government and encouragement from local industrial and intellectual interests, the artists collaborated on homes, studios, and exhibition spaces. They also participated in outside projects and commercial commissions.

Fig. 2.04
Opening ceremonies
Ein Dokument deutscher Kunst, 15 Mai 1901
From *Katalog, Museum Künstlerkolonie Darmstadt*
(Darmstadt: Institut Mathildenhöhe Darmstadt, 1991), p. XIX
Hessisches Landeshochschule Bibliothek, Darmstadt

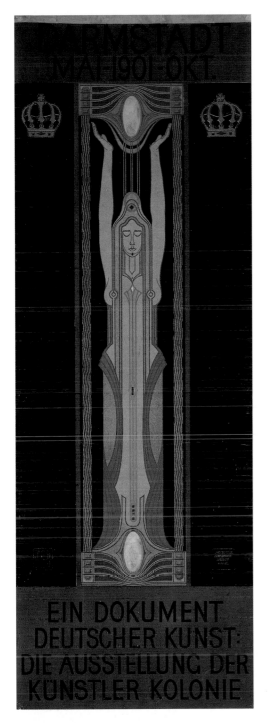

Fig. 2.05 See Cat. 59
Poster
Darmstadt. Ein Dokument deutscher Kunst. Die
Ausstellung der Künstlerkolonie. Mai-Okt. 1901
(Darmstadt. A Document of German Art.
Exhibition of the Artists' Colony . . .), 1901
Designed by P. Behrens

In 1901, the Künstler-Kolonie's achievements were showcased in the exhibition "Ein Dokument deutscher Kunst" (A Document of German Art).[11] The show was the culmination of the first three years of collaborative efforts by the artists. Based on an innovative installation concept, public exhibition spaces included the studio building, salesrooms, temporary edifices, and artists' houses with complete interior decorations. Many of the pieces were available for purchase, whether displayed in settings such as the house-showroom for Julius Glückert (a prominent local manufacturer who produced much of the Kolonie's furniture), or installed within the artists' own houses. The exhibition represented the first large-scale integrated expression of a *Jugendstil Gesamtkunstwerk*.

The opening ceremonies of the exhibition, organized by Peter Behrens, were an occasion of pomp and fanfare (fig. 2.04). The spectators, estimated at ten thousand, watched a performance of *Das Zeichen* (The Sign), a drama by Darmstadt writer Georg Fuchs, in which a crystal was carried down toward them by a messenger intoning, "For you a new life begins . . . "[12] The performance expressed hopes for the Künstler-Kolonie's success; but on a deeper level it was related to Nietzschean philosophical precepts and symbolism, which were potent influences on modern German arts and philosophy. Nietzsche, one of the most influential thinkers in late nineteenth-century Germany, severely criticized ancient Germanic and Christian religious and moral systems, calling for the establishment of a new national culture through unity of thought, will, life, and aesthetics.[13] His numerous theoretical writings, including *The Birth of Tragedy* (1872), *The Use and Abuse of History* (1874), and *Thus Spake Zarathustra* (1883–85), challenged cultural patriotism and probed aesthetic consciousness. They also prompted efforts to create a new symbolic form-language among German artists, writers, and designers. Crystallic and stereometric shapes came to signify spirituality. The ideal of emerging new life was invoked through embryonic egg forms.

Behrens's designs for the 1901 exhibition incorporate symbolic form-language in a powerful fusion of philosophy and ornament. This is particularly evident in his official poster for the exhibition (fig. 2.05), which surpasses surface decorative intent to stand as seminal design. The poster reflected his interest in a new German aesthetic ideology, employing a column-like female as a static icon of Art, reaching up toward a stylized ovoid form from which emanate waves of new life or new style. The formal composition predicts Behrens's later more geometric and classicist style.

Similar symbols reappear as leitmotifs with Nietzschean echoes throughout Behrens's house on the Mathildenhöhe. Built for the 1901 exhibition, it was the only home at the Kolonie not designed by the Austrian architect Olbrich. Behrens had rejected Olbrich and undertook the project himself as his first major three-dimensional endeavor. This initiated a long and successful architectural career for Behrens, whose legacy remained strong through

Fig. 2.06
Dining room
Peter Behrens residence, Darmstadt artists'
colony, 1901
Designed by P. Behrens
From *Katalog, Museum Künstlerkolonie Darmstadt*
(Darmstadt: Institut Mathildenhöhe Darmstadt, 1991), p.7
Hessisches Landeshochschule Bibliothek, Darmstadt

Fig. 2.07 See Cat. 60
Armchair
From the dining room of the Peter Behrens
residence, Darmstadt artists' colony, 1900
Designed by P. Behrens

his work after 1907 as artistic adviser for the A.E.G. and his influence on Ludwig Mies van der Rohe, Le Corbusier, and Walter Gropius, all of whom worked briefly in his Berlin office.

Behrens's Darmstadt house was a bold personal statement, a tightly conceived *Gesamtkunstwerk* of unified interior and exterior design.[14] Most of the interior was steeped in a dark dramatic atmosphere, but the dining room for which this chair was designed was lighter, with white furniture and deep red accents (figs. 2.06 and 2.07). The fluid form and curved linear elements of the chair were related to shapes and decoration found in Behrens-designed porcelain and glassware for the room which were executed by firms such as Gebr. Bauscher and Rheinische Glashütte A.G. Consistent with Kolonie policy to promote sales, many of the artist's designs were produced in quantity and sold commercially.

The Kolonie remained active, with a shifting slate of members, from 1898 to 1914. Though the experiment never proved to be a resounding financial success – the 1901 exhibition actually created a large deficit – the Kolonie continued as a visible forum for *Jugendstil*. Through active cooperation between the artists and commercial firms, the project had significant impact beyond the borders of the Darmstadt region.

Much of the Künstler-Kolonie's influence was due to the presence of Olbrich. As senior member of the Kolonie and the well-known architect of the Vienna Secession building,

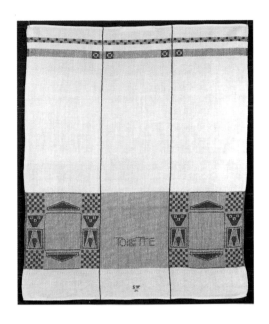

Fig. 2.08 See Cat. 62
Toilette towel, c. 1904
Designed by J.M. Olbrich

Fig. 2.09 See Cat. 63
Sideboard, c. 1902
From the "Hessisches Zimmer"
(also known as the "Blaues Zimmer")
Prima Esposizione Internazionale d'Arte
Decorativa Moderna, Turin, 1902
Designed by J.M. Olbrich

Olbrich exercised a dominant role and was a favorite of the Grand Duke. Beyond his architectural designs for the Wedding Tower, the artists' houses, and the studio building, Olbrich's smaller-scale contributions also included collaborations with commercial firms. Among his many designs available for purchase by the general public were a group of basic household towels designated specifically for furniture, knife, cup, and toilette (fig. 2.08). Produced by the firm Joseph Stade, these towels were included in a show of textiles at the 1904 Künstler-Kolonie exhibition and offered in affordably priced sets of a dozen for 10–14,50 marks.

An Olbrich sideboard (fig. 2.09) is one of the rare furniture designs surviving from the architect's three interiors for the Darmstadt Künstler-Kolonie at the Prima Esposizione Internazionale d'Arte Decorativa Moderna at Turin in 1902.[15] Designed for the "Hessisches Zimmer" (Hessian Room), also known as the "Blaues Zimmer" (Blue Room) because of the distinctive blue-gray tonality of its walls and furnishings, the sideboard was executed by

the Darmstadt firm of Julius Glückert in oak with stained glass panels and copper brass-embossed mounts.

Although Olbrich's designs for Turin won a first prize, much of the critical press about the German section favored Behrens's design for the Hamburg Antechamber. This was an impressive sculptural space in which Behrens's fascination with Nietzsche and the challenge for a new national artistic spirit was made overt through the inclusion of his magnificent binding for Nietzsche's book *Thus Spake Zarathustra* in a specially designed oak-and-glass vitrine. This dramatic presentation, centrally positioned in the space, conferred the status of reliquary and sacred text on the binding and the book. Six years later, the cult of Nietzsche in book design reached its apogee with a masterful collaboration by Henry van de Velde and Georges Lemmen on a special edition of *Thus Spake Zarathustra* (fig. 2.10). Van de Velde's binding and illuminations, with Lemmen's typeface, incorporated powerful cursive ornament reminiscent of medieval illumination. The welter of negative and positive forms was charged with anthropomorphic qualities.[16]

Architecture and design competitions played an increasingly important role in the evolution of the German reform movement. Among these, the Haus eines Kunstfreundes (House for an Art Lover) competition announced in December 1900 by publisher Alexander Koch's *Zeitschrift für Innen-Dekoration* (Journal for Interior Decoration) had an especially deep resonance. International and national entries were encouraged; a distinguished jury

Fig. 2.10 See Cat. 65
Title pages
Also sprach Zarathustra
(Thus Spake Zarathustra) by Friedrich Nietzsche, 1908
Designed by H.C. van de Velde and G. Lemmen

Fig. 2.11 See Cat. 57
"Music Room," 1901
M.H. Baillie Scott

Fig. 2.12 See Cat. 57
"Empfangs Raum und Musik Zimmer"
(Reception Hall and Music Room), 1901
C.R. Mackintosh and M.M. Mackintosh

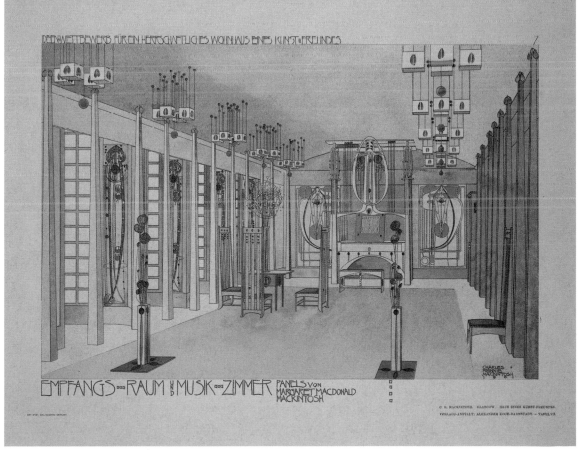

evaluated the thirty-six entries at Darmstadt in May 1901. None was deemed thoroughly successful as a solution to the "important questions within modern architecture," so no first prize was awarded.[17] Second prize went to the English Arts and Crafts architect M.H. Baillie Scott (fig. 2.11), with the remark that this design was outstanding, especially in its interior details, but had not fulfilled the spirit of a fully modern exterior.[18] Three third prizes were awarded for designs by the Austrians Leopold Bauer (see Cat. 57) and Oskar Marmorek, and the German Paul Zeroch. A special purchase prize was given for designs by Charles Rennie and Margaret Macdonald Mackintosh (fig. 2.12). The Scottish couple had transgressed the requirements of the competition by omitting several prescribed interior views, but were praised for "strongly personal coloring, a modern strong design, and cohesiveness of the inner and outer construction."[19]

Through its stated aims and final results, this competition helped to define publicly the German modernist mission and provoke critical assessment of the state of German progress. In the July 1901 edition of *Innen-Dekoration*, Koch criticized the level of quality in the German entries for the House for an Art Lover: "Without the intervention of foreign countries the success of this competition would have been subject to question."[20] He challenged German designers to achieve excellence equal to or exceeding foreign standards. Such sentiments became typical among leading critics, patrons, and artists who urged a German design idiom which could compete successfully with international and especially British trends. The relationship between German design and foreign styles became increasingly complicated – friendly but competitive, interested but defensive.[21] The Germans eagerly embraced other movements and invited foreign participation in projects, but often manipulated them as a measuring stick for their own national aesthetic development.

The British Arts and Crafts movement had gained significant influence in Germany as early as 1897 when Baillie Scott and Charles Robert Ashbee redecorated rooms in the New Palace in Darmstadt for the Grand Duke Ernst Ludwig. Afterwards, Baillie Scott remained on particularly good terms with German colleagues and patrons. In a letter to Muthesius he noted, "I wish we had a Grand Duke in England!" and other correspondence reveals that Baillie Scott was being considered as a candidate for Künstler-Kolonie membership in 1904.[22] This plan was never realized but he was involved in numerous German design and architectural projects for many years. To Muthesius, he explained sympathetic ideals:

> . . . Then there is the question of manufacture. The modern designer is confronted by the fact that he has no workmen that is artist-workmen and he is like a composer who must make music to be rendered on the street organ by machinery. What must he do then. Either he must train a little band of workers of his own or else he must adapt his designs to the machine.[23]

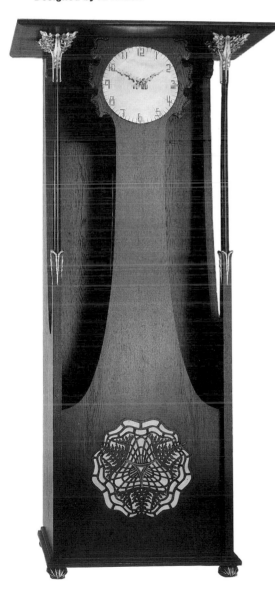

In addition to Koch, other publishers and writers disseminated analysis concerning British and international reform precedents. Under the direction of figures like Harry Graf Kessler in Berlin, Georg Hirth in Munich, and Julius Meier-Graefe in Munich and Paris, periodicals and art publications such as *Pan, Jugend,* and *Dekorative Kunst* became powerful, serving as primary organs for information on international avant-garde movements. Many of these figures also became active patrons. Kessler, for example, gave Henry van de Velde private commissions and promoted the Belgian artist's appointment in 1902 as artistic adviser to the Grand Duchy of Sachsen-Weimar.[24] Soon, Van de Velde was appointed director of the newly founded Kunstgewerbeschule (School of Arts and Crafts) in Weimar, which under Gropius became the Bauhaus in 1919.

Around 1902–05, Dr. Rosenberger, a director of Wasmuth publishers and the periodical *Berliner Architekturwelt,* acquired major suites of domestic furnishings by August Endell for his Berlin apartment. (Since Wasmuth published the landmark portfolio of *Ausgeführte Bauten und Entwürfe von Frank Lloyd Wright* in 1911 [see Cat. 39], it seems that the directors' circles were well informed about international design trends, including North American innovations.) Rosenberger proudly illustrated the Endell furniture in the February issue of *Berliner Architekturwelt.*[25] Many of the pieces are now in the Wolfsonian (fig. 2.13). Decorative ornamentation in the designs reflects Endell's Munich *Jugendstil* roots, and the complex reticulated motifs were profoundly influenced by the zoological illustrations of scientist Ernst Haeckel in his 1899 *Kunstformen der Natur* (Art Forms of Nature).[26] Furthermore, the attenuated pillars in the Rosenberger furniture may have been adapted from British precedents such as designs by C.F.A. Voysey.

Direct interaction with British design precedents was consciously fostered by the German government. From 1896 to 1903, the Prussian Ministry sent Hermann Muthesius to London as a cultural and technical attaché, and while there the Berlin architect embarked on a serious study of modern British architecture, design, and ways of life. He meticulously investigated Arts and Crafts architecture and quickly became the most direct liaison between British and German reform movements. His study culminated in the 1904–05 publication of the three-volume *Das englische Haus.*[27] This was the first comprehensive analysis of the British domestic house movement produced in any language, and served almost as an encyclopedia, explaining the British movement in such detail that the book could be used as a guide for adaptation to a new German design and architecture.

After returning to the Prussian Ministry of Trade in Berlin, Muthesius's ties to Britain remained strong. However, he became increasingly vocal in the burgeoning discourse about national design policy. In an inaugural lecture on "The Significance of Applied Arts" at the Berliner Handelshochschule (Berlin Trade School) in spring 1907, he cited the demoralization

Fig. 2.14
Interior lightwell
Tietz Department Store, Düsseldorf, 1907–09
Designed by Joseph Maria Olbrich
(Austrian, 1876–1908)
Kaiser Wilhelm Museum, Krefeld, Germany

of German producers and consumers through a predominance of shoddy production and historicist styles. He stated, "Here German production has done almost nothing to catch up with the directions of other lands . . . In architecture, we are considered the most backward of all nations, as generally, according to the judgment of foreign countries, German taste stands on the lowest conceivable rung . . . "[28] He pleaded passionately for design reform and urged cooperation between a broad spectrum of German industrial and artistic interests. The speech sparked vehement outrage from the Trade Association to Further the Economic Interests of the Art Industries. During the ensuing controversy, known as the "Fall Muthesius" (Muthesius case), several progressive firms seceded from the Association, joined forces with leaders of the reform movement, and spurred the founding of the Deutsche Werkbund later that year.[29]

The department stores also became central venues for the dissemination of *Jugendstil* and modernist styles to German society. Buildings such as the 1895–97 Wertheim department store, designed on Leipziger Strasse in Berlin by the Darmstadt architect Alfred Messel, or the Tietz department store in Düsseldorf designed by Olbrich in 1907–09 (fig. 2.14),

Fig. 2.15
Dining room
Wertheim Department Store,
Berlin, 1902
Designed by Peter Behrens
(German, 1868–1940)
From *Deutsche Kunst und Dekoration, XI* (March 1903): 291–2
Werkbund-Archiv, Berlin

Fig. 2.16 See Cat. 77
Side chair, 1902–03
Designed by P. Behrens

were monumental modernist structures planned to facilitate the movement of large numbers of customers and display the broad diversity of increased available domestic products. In the case of the Wertheim store the functional pragmatism of industrially made product sales was enhanced through a conscious philosophy for exhibiting and selling decorative arts. Hoping to democratize consumerism, the Wertheim family promoted progressive culture and supported the drive for better quality German goods. In 1902 the Berlin store held an innovative exhibition of modern living spaces which, according to the organizer Curt Stoeving, was intended to " . . . provide the possibility for spectators at every level of education to experience the simple unity of these modern ensembles, to see the practicality of the furnishings, and to purchase such furniture at moderate prices."[30] Twelve prominent designers, including Riemerschmid, Behrens, and Baillie Scott, each created a complete room. The whole was laid out as two contiguous apartments.

The critic Max Osborn declared that, for the first time, the "intrinsically democratic character of the decorative arts movement, which had earlier only been theoretically expressed,

63

had finally gained practical meaning."³¹ The Wertheim rooms, like the earlier Munich Kleinkunst interiors or the Darmstadt Kolonie houses, functioned primarily as didactic model environments, *Gesamtkunstwerke* to elevate public taste. The efficacy of the new style was as legible in the commercial setting of the department store as when installed in fine art exhibitions or utopian colonies.

The dining room by Peter Behrens (fig. 2.15) was praised as a "strong unified creation in which every detail is subordinated to an ordered conception."³² The design scheme was based on a geometrical pattern of regularly recurring rectangles and squares, repeated throughout the individual elements such as the chairs (fig. 2.16), carpet, dinnerware, glassware, and lighting fixtures. Many examples of the porcelain survive and at least two sets of the dining room furniture were known to have been made.

Throughout the period, many German manufacturers initiated reforms to revitalize and update their industries. The move to engage outside artistic contributions by commercial (and often conservative) firms indicated political and economic pressures to update design for the modern taste and insinuate new art into pre-existing export markets.³³ This trend intensified particularly in the stoneware and porcelain industry after the Paris 1900 exhibition when outmoded German designs bearing no reference to contemporary trends were criticized.

The Westerwald region had been a traditional German stoneware center since the Renaissance, but the industry had languished with the advent of the Dresden porcelain

Fig. 2.17 See Cat. 38
Beer stein
Model no. 1757, 1902
Designed by R. Riemerschmid

Fig. 2.18
Vase, 1904–05
Max Laeuger
(German, 1864–1952)
Made by Tonwerke Kandern, Kandern, Germany
Glazed earthenware, glass
10¼ x 7 inches dia. (26.0 x 17.8 cm dia.)
Marks: underside, stamped "323/MUSTER GESETZL. GESCHZT."/artist's monogram/"GESETZL. GESCHZT./H"
87.1635.7.1

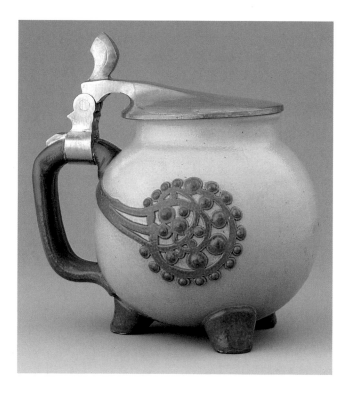

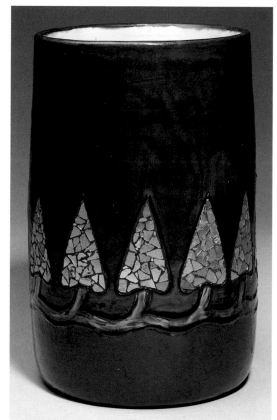

factories in the eighteenth century. During the second half of the nineteenth century, a massive merchant and government initiative sought to rejuvenate the stoneware tradition for household objects by providing funds for training programs, new technology, exhibitions, and museum collections of historic models. By the turn of the century, companies around the country were commissioning *Jugendstil* artists to submit designs for stoneware production.

Reinhold Merkelbach, a new branch of an older Westerwald firm, commissioned designs from architect/designers, including Richard Riemerschmid, from 1901 onwards. Hundreds of pieces are documented in *Price and Model Books* from 1905 to 1929 and cover a wide variety of domestic vessel forms. The Wolfsonian's stein (fig. 2.17) was typical of Riemerschmid's designs for the company. The pieces revive vernacular forms as a reminder of a proud historical past and identification with solid Germanic ancestry, but even as these vessels looked familiar and spoke of traditional Westerwald craftsmanship in both their execution and their decoration, they remained entirely unprecedented creations.

Max Laeuger was also inspired in his career as a ceramic artist by the legacy of German vernacular earthenware.[34] From the early 1890s in Karlsruhe and Kandern, he worked with traditional porous earthenware to create vessels turned and painted according to his own specifications and decorated with colored slips in a technique adapted from Black Forest customs. Laeuger's designs employed simple outlines and stylized plant motifs; the decoration evoked impressions of overgrown vegetation and drooping branches. Designs such as a vase of 1904–05, in which slip is covered with geometric gold inlays worked in mosaic technique with naturalistic references, were limited in number and rather anomalous within his oeuvre (fig. 2.18). They were made during a short period in which the artist also experimented with gold and silver mosaic inlays of fully abstract motifs. After 1905, Laeuger reverted to pure slip decorations with stylized floral forms covering the entire body of the vessel.

Laeuger had been an active presence in the new German movement from its early days in Munich, and in 1899 his design for a tiled fireplace surround was exhibited in Dresden, surmounted by an impressive wall textile by Otto Eckmann (fig. 2.19). Eckmann had been one of the first artists in Munich to abandon fine arts for decorative arts, and he was quickly acclaimed as a pioneer in many areas of *Jugendstil* including metalwork, typography, and textiles.[35] The *Five Swans* tapestry shown above Laeuger's fireplace in Dresden had been designed in 1896–97 and executed in the school and workshop of Scherrebek in Schleswig. It became Eckmann's most famous design, characterized by strong flat colors and undulating lines with an elongated rectangular format related to Japanese scrolls Eckmann had studied in the Museum für Kunst und Gewerbe (Museum of Art and Crafts) in Hamburg (fig. 2.20). The artist's choice of swan imagery (which was common in many of his drawings and prints) was partially drawn from childhood memories of swans on the Alster in Hamburg and also

Fig. 2.19
Installation
Die Deutsche Kunst-Ausstellung zu Dresden
(German Art Exhibition . . .),
May to October 1899.
From *Deutsche Kunst und Dekoration*, IV
(April–September 1899): 517.
XB1990.2171

reflected the swan motifs which permeated much international literature and symbolist art at the time.

The Scherrebek Kunstwebschule (Art Weaving School) had been set up through the encouragement of Justus Brinckmann, Director of the Hamburg museum, and his assistant Friedrich Deneken, later Director of the museum in Krefeld, to revive handloom techniques of northern Germany, Schleswig, and nearby Scandinavian areas.[36] Between 1896 and 1903, some two hundred different wall hangings and cushion covers were made from designs by artists that included Eckmann, Hans Christiansen, Walter Leistikow, Van de Velde, and Heinrich Vogeler.

Vogeler was an artist and graphic designer who expanded into applied arts and architecture around 1898.[37] In 1900 he joined the artists' colony at Worpswede outside Bremen, a rural utopian community of modern artists working closely with northern German vernacular traditions, and eight years later he established the Worpswede Werkstätte Franz Vogeler,

Fig. 2.20
Tapestry
***Five Swans**, 1896–97*
Designed by Otto Eckmann
(German, 1865–1902)
Made by Kunstwebschule, Scherrebek, Germany
Cotton, wool
94 x 29½ inches (238.8 x 74.9 cm)
Marks: obverse, woven in red, bottom left, intertwined "OE"
+ factory mark
TD1989.169.5

which designed interiors for the colony and published a catalogue with individual items or suites of furniture for sale to the public. Derived from local traditions, furniture styles at the workshop expressed the rustic idealism of the group's Lebensreform (lifestyle reform) tenets. Many of the designs adapted shallowly carved owls and flower motifs typical of Lower Saxony country furniture. In a chair designed by Vogeler about 1908, the squared timbers, flat planks, and ladder-type leg construction closely followed traditional German forms (fig. 2.21).

Vogeler's romantic naturalism was mixed with pragmatic modern intentions and a sense of social responsibility. An early member of the Deutsche Werkbund, he attempted for the Worpswede Werkstätte a program consistent with the Werkbund's call for solidarity in handcraftsmanship, effective production methods, and new technology. The firm exhibited in international exhibitions, the furniture carried the proud mark of the artists, and their catalogue explained that the workshop had "the obligation to deliver the furniture through modern quality work."[38] The integration of rural utopian and progressive modern aspects was expressed subtly through details. Vogeler's motifs were mixtures of sources; for example, the red-and-white geometric banding on furniture for the Worpswede train station waiting-room was abstracted from traditional furniture banding but also adapted from new colored machinery markings of locomotive warning signal lamps.[39]

The ideal of artist-craftsmen who were also machine-oriented designers was increasingly heralded by some German progressives as a national goal, and workshops rapidly evolved to encompass larger capabilities for both hand and mechanized production. The most successful fusion of these tendencies on a significant commercial scale occurred at the Deutsche Werkstätten Dresden-Hellerau und München (German Workshops Dresden-Hellerau and Munich). Begun in 1898 as the Dresdner Werkstätten für Handwerkskunst (Dresden Workshops for Handicraft Arts), this firm was founded through the efforts of a carpenter, Karl Schmidt, rather than by a group of artists.[40] A utopian pragmatist with limitless energy and sharp intuition, Schmidt gathered advice and ideas from liberal politicians such as Friedrich Naumann, leading reform advocates such as Muthesius, and designers such as Johann Vincent Cissarz. In 1907 the Dresdner Werkstätten merged with the Münchener Werkstätten für Wohnungseinrichtung (Workshops for Apartment Furnishings) into the Deutsche Werkstätten GmbH Dresden und München. In ten years (1898–1908), the Dresden workshop alone had grown to employ over five hundred workers.

From the start, Schmidt enlisted established artists such as August Endell and Heinrich Vogeler to work with the firm. He created an unusually liberal system in which the furniture was published with the name of the designer mentioned before that of the maker, and the designers retained copyright in their work. He also arranged a cooperative compensation policy whereby the designer received between five and ten percent of the profits of each

Fig. 2.21 See Cat. 37
Armchair
Model no. 864, 1908
Designed by H. Vogeler

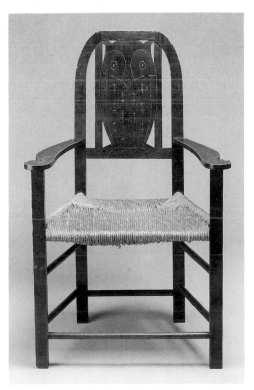

object sold. Following the *Jugendstil* precepts, the Werkstätten encouraged entire rooms rather than single objects.

Schmidt's propagandistic and nationalist tendencies were evident in the 1898 *Opening Prospectus*, in which he said that "people should also consider that our furniture is created on German soil, by German artists, and is the expression of German feelings and sensitivities." However, the savvy businessman soon expanded his network to include foreign designers. When he traveled to the United Kingdom in 1903, Muthesius's introduction eased his approach to architect-designers such as Baillie Scott and Mackintosh for contributions to the company. In a letter to Muthesius, Mackintosh explained, " . . . Herr Schmidt came the day after I returned. I had the pleasure of showing them round . . . .He wants me to do a Bedroom for his Dresden exhibition. He will pay me 10% on all sales, he thinks that is the best arrangement. He thinks he will be able to sell a good many if the price is not too high."[41]

Schmidt believed deeply in the possibilities for betterment of all levels of German society through improvement in the quality of its objects and surroundings. Around 1906–07 he began planning for a new factory and garden city at Hellerau. His aim was to create a full-scale *Gesamtkunstwerk* through the complete integration of social, spiritual, cultural, economic, and architectural plans. His vision for the project included schools, employee housing, and a theater for Emile Jaques-Dalcroze's Institute for eurhythmic dance.[42] The breadth of Schmidt's undertaking differentiated it from other workshops at Munich and Vienna; Hellerau became known equally for the Deutsche Werkstätten, for the social aspect of its architectural and design program, and for avant-garde theater, opera, and dance.

Richard Riemerschmid drew the original plans for the factory, the marketplace, and several streets of homes, using a mixture of vernacular and modern elements. Numerous other architects contributed to the growing scope of the Hellerau colony during 1907–14. As the work evolved, increasingly divergent tendencies emerged between the *Jugendstil*-based styles of Riemerschmid and Muthesius, for example, and the classically proportioned aesthetic of buildings by designers such as Heinrich Tessenow. This reflected shifting developments in attitude among German reform propagandists toward organic and abstract aesthetics, as well as growing divisions within the broader national design forum regarding artistic ideals and mass-production capabilities.

During 1903–06, Schmidt and Riemerschmid began collaborating on the first major line of machine-made mass-produced furniture in the new style. They hoped to challenge the belief that handwork was the only criterion for quality. The furniture, known as *Maschinenmöbel* (Machine furniture), was marketed individually or as unified ensembles in three sales categories from about 500 to 1,500 marks (fig. 2.22).[43] Pieces were serially pro-

Fig. 2.22
Maschinenmöbel ensemble, 1906
Designed by Richard Riemerschmid
(German, 1868–1957)
From Johann Vincenz Cissarz, *Dresdner Hausgerät, Dresden 1906* (Dresden, 1906, first edition), p. 18
Werkbund-Archiv, Berlin

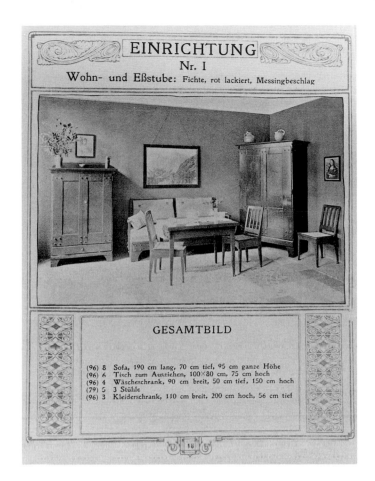

duced and cut by machine, but still required some hand-finishing. Designs were simple and composed of good-quality, durable materials which could be cut to size, planed, incised, and drilled by machine, with details such as hinges providing ornament. Construction elements (e.g., supporting planks or wooden screws) functioned as decorative ornamentation.

The *Maschinenmöbel* were unveiled at the Third German Applied Arts Exhibition in Dresden in 1906. According to the exhibition catalogue, "One of the most significant tasks of our modern civilization will be to guide the creation of such useful objects along healthy lines (objects made with the machine), for by their mass production they will determine the needs and hence the taste of our epoch."[44] Influential figures such as Muthesius and Naumann encouraged the *Maschinenmöbel*, but the designs were not universally accepted as the path for the future by artists or by other visitors to the Dresden exhibition.[45] The designs proved highly controversial. This was partly due to the profound differences among German artists, patrons, and industry about preferences for dynamic aestheticism, geometric classicism, or unadorned functionalism.[46] Disagreement focussed, however, less on the role of stylistic preference as a carrier of design identity than on the issues of mass-production, handcrafts-

69

manship, or individual artistic contribution as the basis for a national design ethic, and on appropriate production means, marketing strategies, and exhibition methods.

Even as Schmidt fulfilled an increasing flow of commissions for *Maschinenmöbel*, he continued to produce handcrafted designs as well. He argued that both the best mass-produced and the best handcrafted work could be realized within the premises of his large workshop-factory setting. To cater to clients "who prize the quality of the work, its simplicity, and its tastefulness,"[47] Schmidt maintained a special workshop within the factory to produce *hand-gearbeitete Möbel* (handcrafted furniture) made with fine materials and according to the newest and best designs. These designs were included in separately published catalogues from 1909.

The Wolfsonian's chair (fig. 2.23), designed by Riemerschmid in 1907–08, was shown in the 1910 catalogue for 62 marks and in the 1912 catalog for 76.[48] Its design is especially interesting; slightly curved elements connecting the back and seat hark back to his early music-room chair executed by the Vereinigte Werkstätten in Munich for the 1900 Paris Exposition, but the simplicity of the design and the construction of the underseat structure are so similar to the *Maschinenmöbel* examples that it has often been mistaken for one of the higher-priced examples in that series.

Amidst the charged atmosphere of style battles, industrial production, political involvement, and large-scale exhibitions, the Deutsche Werkbund (German Work Association) was founded in October 1907. Interest in an advocacy initiative for German design had been discussed by the politician Naumann, the architect Muthesius, and the businessman Schmidt since 1906.[49] When the Werkbund was founded the following year as a joint venture between art, industry, and politics, it aimed to determine the message and criteria for national design, and it defined specific goals to support artistic and crafts production, increase exports, and foster high quality. Founding members included twelve architects and designers, such as Behrens, Laeuger, Olbrich, Paul, Riemerschmid, and Fritz Schumacher, and twelve firms such as the Deutsche Werkstätten, the Vereinigte Werkstätten, Eugen Diederichs publishers, and Bruckmann & Söhne silversmiths. German-speaking Austria and Switzerland participated; the Viennese architect Josef Hoffmann was present at the founding.

The function of the Werkbund was to build and propagandize national design identity. It became the vital German arena for theoretical and practical debate about design policy issues from its founding until the 1930s. Membership grew rapidly, numbering 492 by the first annual meeting in 1908 and 1,870 by 1914. A broad spectrum of the artistic and design community was represented, as well as patrons, industrial leaders, commercial firms, government officials, and special interest groups.

The Werkbund sponsored journals, publications, and exhibitions, and advocated *Reklame Kunst* (advertising design) as a medium which could not only provide numerous

Fig. 2.23 See Cat. 76
Side chair
Model no. 137/2, 1907–08
Designed by R. Riemerschmid

commissions for artists but also promote corporate identities for member firms. Advertising design in the Wolfsonian includes coffee tins for Kaffee Hag (fig. 2.24), and a tobacco box designed by F.H. Ehmcke for Jos. Feinhals (fig. 2.25).

In 1907, the Berlin general electric company A.E.G. appointed Behrens as official artistic adviser. This direct partnership between an artist and a commercial firm was hailed by the Werkbund as the model union for art and industry. Behrens designed the firm's advertisements, products, and even factory architecture.[50] The A.E.G. designs canonized a German idiom of functionalism, machine technology, and serial production in well-designed simple forms for everyday products such as electric fans, lamps, barometers, and tea kettles (figs. 2.26 and 2.27).

At the Werkbund's annual meeting in 1911, Hermann Muthesius posed the question, "Wo stehen wir (Where do we stand)?"[51] The question implied more than a simple résumé of the Werkbund's accomplishments and outline for future plans; from this point until the occasion of the Werkbund's first major exhibition, planned from May to October 1914 in Cologne, the Werkbund and the larger German design movement engaged in a tense and critical self-definition process. During the summer of 1914, the conflict finally erupted. Divisive long-simmering arguments within the group's ranks boiled to the surface and for the annual meeting in Cologne differing positions were codified in opposing theses on the responsibilities and goals of the Werkbund. Debate focussed on the role of standardization versus individuality as an optimal basis for future German design and architecture.[52]

Muthesius represented one opinion emphasizing standardization, with ten theses, including: "Architecture, and with it the whole area of the Werkbund's activities, is pressing

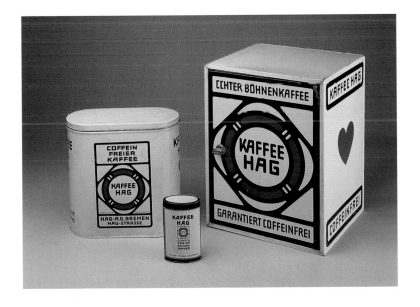

Fig. 2.26
**A.E.G. shop window,
Königgrätzerstrasse, Berlin, 1910
Designed by Peter Behrens**
(German, 1868–1940)
Kaiser Wilhelm Museum, Krefeld, Germany

toward standardization, and only through standardization can it recover the universal significance which was characteristic of it in times of harmonious culture."⁵³ A second circle led by Van de Velde and supported by members such as Gropius, Endell, and Karl Ernst Osthaus, countered with such statements as "So long as there are still artists in the Werkbund and so long as they exercise some influence on its destiny, they will protest against every suggestion for the establishment of a canon and for standardization. By his innermost essence the artist is a burning idealist, a free spontaneous creator."⁵⁴ The heated arguments underlined the tense coexistence of stylistic diversity and contradictory ideological positions within the Werkbund, and illuminated underlying ambiguities in the German design field.

The Cologne show had been planned as a grand showcase of Werkbund firms, products, and architecture. In spite of the debates, this was indeed the seminal presentation of the organization. Landmark buildings created for the temporary show included Gropius and Meyer's model administration building (fig. 2.28), Henry van de Velde's theater, and Bruno Taut's *Glass House*. With the outbreak of World War I, the full effect of this proud undertaking for national and international audiences was cut short. Many Werkbund firms who had donated materials or sponsored promotional pavilions for the exhibition quickly reclaimed material from the buildings, including the glass from the *Glass House*.⁵⁵ The site became a plundered shell and remains of the buildings were eventually auctioned off.

The war postponed any long-term solutions to questions about design identity and most work was scaled down to essential production for the war. The Werkbund continued

Fig. 2.27 See Cat. 81
**Electric kettle
Model no. 3599, 1909
Designed by P. Behrens**

limited activities throughout the war years and reactivated its broader program after the war's end. During 1917–19, however, the focus of design and architecture shifted to immediate concerns for housing and basic domestic goods for the displaced masses of society; the crippled state of the German economy often restricted the scope of realized projects. Significant creative experimentation continued mainly in social housing architecture, within the borders of two-dimensional sketchbooks, and in art school studios.

Walter Gropius took over Van de Velde's directorship of the Weimar school in 1919 (the latter, exiled during the war, did not return afterwards).[56] His early goals for the school, restructured as the Bauhaus, reflected the lingering influence of pre-war discourse about design identity. The Bauhaus manifesto proclaimed, "Architects, sculptors, painters, we must all return to the crafts! . . . Together let us desire, conceive, and create the new structure of the future, which will embrace architecture and sculpture and painting in one unity and which will one day rise towards heaven from the hands of a million workers like the crystal symbol of a new faith."[57] The dilemmas of German design between 1890 and 1914 had been left unresolved on the occasion of the Werkbund Exhibition in Cologne; a gap remained between rhetoric and formal realization of the reform idiom. The history of the Bauhaus, particularly in the years up to its move to Dessau, is emblematic of a continuing struggle with these issues. The legacy of the pre-war dialogue continued to shape the direction of German design and architecture throughout the 1920s and 1930s.

I wish to thank Brigitte Leonhardt, Albrecht Pyritz, Angelika Thiekötter, Debbie Wilkens, and Rüdiger Joppien for their contributions.

Fig. 2.28

Model Administration Building (Walter Gropius [American, b. Germany, 1883–1969] and Adolf Meyer [German, 1881–1929], architects) Deutsche Werkbund Exhibition, Cologne, 1914

From *Deutsche Form im Kriegsjahr, Die Ausstellung Köln 1914, Jahrbuch des Deutschen Werkbundes* (Munich, 1915), p. 140
Werkbund-Archiv, Berlin

NOTES

1   See Fritz Stern, *The Politics of Cultural Despair, a study in the Rise of Germanic Ideology* (Berkeley, 1961).

2   Alexander Koch, "An die deutschen Künstler und Kunstfreunde," *Deutsche Kunst und Dekoration* 1 (October 1897): 11.

3   A summary of some important stylistic and art historical studies includes Fritz Schmalenbach, *Jugendstil. Ein Beitrag zu Theorie und Geschichte der Flächenkunst* (Würzburg, 1935); Nikolaus Pevsner, *Pioneers of the Modern Movement* (London, 3rd ed. 1936; Harmondsworth, 1975); Reyner Banham, *Theory and Design in the First Machine Age* (Cambridge, MA, 2nd ed., 1960); Klaus-Jürgen Sembach, ed., *1910 Halbzeit der Moderne, van de Velde, Behrens, Hoffmann, und die Anderen* (Stuttgart, 1992). Key studies which explore *Jugendstil* and Werkbund relationships to bourgeois political developments (which are only touched on in this essay) include Julius Posener, *Anfänge des Funktionalismus: von Arts and Crafts zum Deutschen Werkbund* (Berlin, 1964); Gert Selle, *Jugendstil und Kunstindustrie, zur Ökonomie und Aesthetik des Kunstgewerbes um 1900* (Ravensburg, 1974); dissertation by Frederic Schwarz, Columbia U., 1994.

4   Anna-Christa Funk, *Karl Ernst Osthaus gegen Hermann Muthesius, Der Werkbundstreit im Spiegel der im Karl Ernst Osthaus Archiv erhaltenen Briefe* (Hagen: Karl Ernst Osthaus Museum, 1978).

5   Quoted and translated in Kathryn B. Hiesinger, *Art Nouveau in Munich, Masters of Jugendstil* (Munich, 1988) p. 12.

6   Maria Makela, "Munich's Design for Living," *Art in America* (February 1989): 145 ff.

7   G. Keyssner, "The Munich International Art Exhibition," *The Studio* (1897): 193.

8   See Sonja Guenther, *Interieurs um 1900. Bernhard Pankok, Bruno Paul und Richard Riemerschmid als Mitarbeiter der Vereinigten Werkstätten für Kunst im Handwerk* (Munich, 1971). Dr. Alfred Ziffer of Munich is currently researching in the firm's archives and preparing a major publication.

9   See Wolfsonian Collection TD1990.295.1.

10   Winfried Nerdinger, ed. *Richard Riemerschmid vom Jugendstil zum Werkbund, Werke und Dokumente* (Munich, 1982), p. 146.

11   *Ein Dokument Deutscher Kunst, Die Ausstellung der Künstler-Kolonie in Darmstadt* (Munich, 1901); also *Ein Dokument Deutscher Kunst, 1901–1976* (5 vols.; Darmstadt: Hessisches Landesmuseum und Kunsthalle, 1976–77); *Museum Künstlerkolonie* (Darmstadt, 1990).

12   For an English discussion on Behrens and theater, including this opening, see Alan Windsor, *Peter Behrens, Architect and Designer 1868–1940* (New York, 1981), pp. 27–37.

13   Jürgen Krause, *"Märtyrer" und "Prophet" Studien zum Nietzsche-Kult in der bildenden Kunst der Jahrhundertwende* (Berlin/New York, 1984); Paul Fechter, "Nietzsches Bildwelt und der Jugendstil," *Deutsche Rundschau,* Bd. 243 (1935), reprint in Jost Hermand, ed., *Jugendstil* (Darmstadt, 1971).

14   For information on the house, its origins, interiors, and meaning, see Tilman Buddensieg, "Das Wohnhaus als Kultbau: Zum Darmstädter Haus von Behrens," in *Peter Behrens und Nürnberg, Geschmackswandel in Deutschland, Historismus, Jugendstil und die Anfänge der Industriereform* (Munich, 1980), pp. 37–47.

15   Drawings for the interior are held in the Olbrich Estate in the Kunstbibliothek in Berlin. Another extant piece is discussed in Torsten Bröhan and Thomas Berg, *Avantgarde Design 1880–1930* (Cologne, 1994), pp. 54–5. Also comments from Dr. Renate Ulmer, Darmstadt, 1994.

16   This information derives from Irmela Franzke's study of the subject. See also Jane Block, "The Insel-Verlag 'Zarathustra': An Untold Tale of Art and Printing," *Pantheon* 45 (1987): 129–37.

17   See "Entscheidung des Wettbewerbes zur Erlangung von Entwürfen für ein herrschaftliches Wohnhaus eines Kunst-freundes. Protokoll," *Innen-Dekoration* (June 1900): 109–10.

18   *Ibid.*

19   *Ibid.*: 110.

20   Alexander Koch, "Unser Wettbewerb: Wohnhaus eines Kunst-freundes," *Innen-Dekoration* XII (July 1901): 111.

21   For example, Hermann Muthesius, "A German View of British Art," *The Standard* (March 20, 1897), n.p. See also forthcoming dissertation by Laurie A. Stein, *Germany and the British Arts and Crafts Movement, 1898-1914* (University of Chicago).

22   M.H. Baillie Scott to Hermann Muthesius, undated (c. 1902–3), Muthesius Estate, Werkbund-Archiv, Berlin,; M.H. Baillie Scott to Hermann Muthesius, May 30, 1904, Muthesius Estate, Werkbund-Archiv, Berlin.

23   M.H. Baillie Scott to Hermann Muthesius, undated letter (c. 1904), Muthesius Estate, Werkbund-Archiv, Berlin.

24   The newest major work on van de Velde is Klaus-Jürgen Sembach and Brigit Schulte, eds., *Henry van de Velde: Ein europäischer Künstler seiner Zeit* (Cologne, 1992).

25   Illustrated in "Wohnung Dr. Rosenberger, Lietzenburger Strasse 2," *Berliner Architekturwelt* (1905): 420–8; a discussion by anonymous author in *Kunst und Künstler* III (1905): 176, may also have to do with the Endell Rosenberger furniture, with wonderful descriptions: "kräuselndes, zuckendes, vibrierendes Oberflächenspiel auf unerschütterlichem Grunde . . . "

26   Ernst Haeckel, *Kunstformen der Natur* (Leipzig, 1899). Haeckel's book had great influence at the turn of the century on progressive designers as divergent as Endell, Friedrich Adler, and Bruno Taut.

27   Hermann Muthesius, *Das englische Haus*, 3 vols. (Berlin, 1904–05).

28   Hermann Muthesius, "Die Bedeutung des Kunstgewerbes," *Dekorative Kunst* XV (1907): 177ff., cited in Kurt Junghanns, *Der Deutsche Werkbund, sein erstes Jahrzehnt* (Berlin, 1982), p. 140.

29   Joan Campbell, *The German Werkbund. The Politics of Reform in the Applied Arts* (Princeton, 1978); *Hermann Muthesius im Werkbund-Archiv* (Berlin, 1990); and Stein's forthcoming dissertation.

30   Curt Stoeving, "Kunst dem Volke," *Deutsche Kunst und Dekoration* IV (March 1903): 257.

31   Max Osborn, "Die modernen Wohn-Raume im Waren-Haus von A. Wertheim zu Berlin," *Deutsche Kunst und Dekoration* IV (March 1903): 259.

32   *Ibid.*: 263.

33   See Beate Dry-v. Zezschwitz, *R. Merkelbach Spezialpreisliste 1905* (reprint Munich, 1981); Jürgen Erlebach and Jürgen Schimanski, *Westerwälder Steinzeug, Die Neue Ära 1900–1930, Jugendstil und Werkbund* (Düsseldorf, 1987–88); and Judy Rudoe, "Aspects of Design Reform in the German Ceramic Industry around 1900, as Illustrated by the British Museum Collection," *Decorative Arts Society Journal, 1850 to Present* 14 (1992): 24–33. See also Irmela Franzke, *Bestandskatalog, Jugendstil, Glas, Graphik, Keramik, Metall, Möbel, Skulpturen und Textilen von 1880 bis 1945* (Karlsruhe: Badisches Landesmuseum, 1987).

34 Comments from Irmela Franzke, Karlsruhe, 1994. See also Elisabeth Kessler-Slotta, *Max Laeuger, 1864–1952, Sein graphisches, kunsthandwerkliches und keramisches Oeuvre* (Saarbrücken, 1985).

35 Dr. E. Zimmermann, "Prof. Otto Eckmann, I. Die Jahre künstlerischer Entwicklung," and Dr. Max Osborn, "Prof. Otto Eckmann, II. Seine kunstgewerbliche Thätigkeit," *Deutsche Kunst und Dekoration* VI (April–September 1900): 305–32; G. Fiedler-Bender, *Otto Eckmann (1865–1902). Ein Hauptmeister des Jugendstils* (Krefeld: Kaiser Wilhelm Museum, 1977–78).

36 Rüdiger Joppien, "Departure towards Modernism, Justus Brinckmann as Director of the Museum für Kunst und Gewerbe," in *Europäischer Jugendstil* (Hamburg: Museum für Kunst und Gewerbe, 1991), p. 27.

37 Neue Gesellschaft für Bildende Kunst, ed., *Heinrich Vogeler: Kunstwerke, Gebrauchsgegenstände, Dokumente* (Berlin, 1983); Karl Veit Riedel, "Worpswede im Teufelsmoor bei Bremen," in Gerhard Wietek, ed., *Deutsche Künstlerkolonien und Künstlerorte* (Munich, 1976), pp.100–13.

38 Franz Vogeler, ed., *Worpswede Sitzmöbel* (Worpswede bei Bremen, n.d.), p. 1. TD1989.183.1.

39 Observations from Angelika Thiekötter, Werkbund-Archiv, Berlin.

40 Nerdinger, *Richard Riemerschmid vom Jugendstil zum Werkbund*, pp. 194–205, 476–90; Klaus-Peter Arnold, *Vom Sofakissen zum Städtebau, Die Geschichte der Deutschen Werkstätten und der Gartenstadt Hellerau* (Dresden and Basel, 1993).

41 Charles Rennie Mackintosh to Hermann Muthesius, May 27, 1903, Muthesius Estate, Werkbund-Archiv, Berlin.

42 Wolf Dohrn, *Die Gartenstadt Hellerau, ein Bericht* (Jena, 1908); Kristiana Hartmann, *Deutsche Gartenstadtbewegung; Kulturpolitik und Gesellschaftsreform* (Munich, 1976).

43 Arnold, *Vom Sofakissen zum Städtebau*, pp.180–262; Nerdinger, *Richard Riemerschmid vom Jugendstil zum Werkbund*, pp. 194–205; Hans Wichmann, *Aufbruch zum neuen Wohnen* (Basel and Stuttgart, 1978), pp. 59–75.

44 Fritz Schumacher, *Dritte Deutsche Kunstgewerbe-Ausstellung, Dresden 1906. Offizieller Katalog. Illustrierte Ausgabe* (Dresden, 1906).

45 "Der Geist im Hausgestühl. Ausstattungsbriefe," cited in Arnold, *Vom Sofakissen zum Städtebau*, p. 180. Among Naumann's many related writings around the period was "Die Kunst im Zeitalter der Machine" (Art in the Machine Age) *Kunstwart* (1904).

46 For discussions about Classicism in the period around 1900 see "Die Jahre neben dem Jugendstil," and "Die Wende 1906," in Heinrich Kreisel/Georg Himmelheber, *Die Kunst des deutschen Möbel*, Vol. 3: *Klassizimus, Historismus, Jugendstil* (Munich, 1973, 1983); Hans Ottomeyer, "Der Jugendstil und die Stile," in *Jugendstil-möbel: Katalog der Möbelsammlung des Münchener Stadtmuseums* (Munich, 1988), pp. 8–9.

47 Arnold, *Vom Sofakissen zum Städtebau*, p. 139.

48 *Ibid.*, p. 466.

49 *Hermann Muthesius in Werkbund-Archiv*, pp. 32-57.

50 Tilmann Buddensieg in collaboration with Henning Rogge, *Industriekultur: Peter Behrens und die AEG, 1907–1914* (Berlin, 1979).

51 The lecture was published in Hermann Muthesius, "Wo Stehen Wir?," *Die Durchgeistigung der deutschen Arbeit, Wege und Ziele in Zusammenhang von Industrie/Handwerk und Kunst, Jahrbuch des Deutschen Werkbundes* (Jena, 1912): 11–26.

52   Funk, *Karl Ernst Osthaus gegen Hermann Muthesius;* and *Hermann Muthesius im Werkbund-Archiv*, pp. 89–98.

53   In Ulrich Conrads, *Programs and Manifestoes on 20th-Century Architecture* (Cambridge, MA, 1964), pp. 28-9.

54   Angelika Thiekötter, ed., *Kristallisationen, Splitterungen, Bruno Tauts Glashaus Köln 1914* (Basel and Stuttgart, 1993).

55   During the war, Van de Velde recommended several potential successors, of whom Gropius was a leading candidate. Relevant correspondence is held in the Walter Gropius Estate at the Bauhaus-Archiv, Berlin, and also at the Karl Ernst Osthaus Museum's Archive in Hagen. See Klaus Weber, "Wir haben viel an Ihnen gut zu machen. Einige Dokumente zum Verhältnis von Henry van de Velde und Walter Gropius," in Sembach and Schulte, eds., *Henry van de Velde. Ein europäischer Künstler seiner Zeit*, p. 360.

56   Conrads, *Programs and Manifestoes on 20th-Century Architecture*, p. 49.

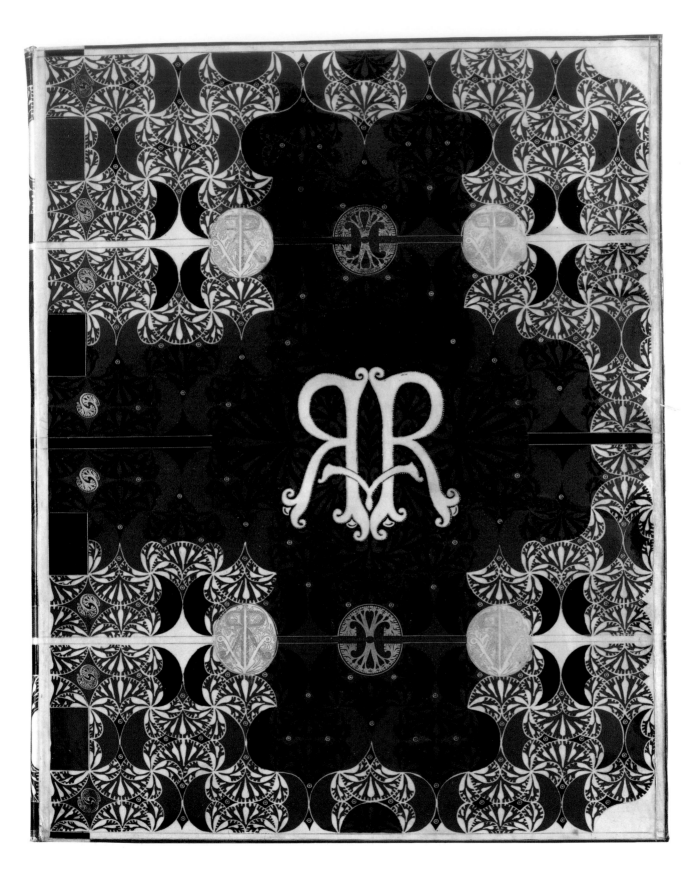

The Decorative Arts in Amsterdam 1890–1930

Ellinoor Bergvelt

Introduction

In 1898 the Amsterdam publishing house and bookstore Scheltema & Holkema issued a very expensive and beautifully designed portfolio with a batik cover, known as the Rembrandt portfolio (fig. 3.01). It contained reproductions of paintings by Rembrandt that had been displayed in Amsterdam and London in the first of a long series of exhibitions devoted to the artist.[1] The Amsterdam exhibition was one of the festive events organized on the occasion of the inauguration of Queen Wilhelmina in the same year.

What does this portfolio tell us about Dutch design and the role of the decorative arts at the time? Immediately noticeable is the discrepancy between its exterior and its contents. Designed by Carel Adolph Lion Cachet, the avant garde batik cover contrasts sharply with the illustrations in heliogravure, an advanced method of mechanical reproduction, and the traditional typography of the text pages. This inconsistency between exterior and interior is characteristic of Dutch book art of this period. Artists made the covers and sometimes the illustrations for such books, whereas the typography of the text pages was left to someone else, generally not an artist. Only later did the typography become the point of departure for book design (fig. 3.12).[2]

Since the beginning of the 1890s there had been an interest in expressing visually the structure of a book or portfolio, and this is certainly the case with the Rembrandt portfolio, which creates the illusion of being secured with three linen bands. By the same token, the bands only appear to be affixed with stickers, round shapes containing either Rembrandt's monogram or the publisher's logo. The patron's initials or coat of arms were meant to appear at the middle of the back cover.[3] For his avant-garde design, Lion Cachet devised a pattern of horizontal lines and circles containing a stylized "claw" fern motif. Rembrandt's monogram – also surrounded by claw ferns, though in a less geometric and severe pattern – appears at

79

the center of the front cover. This combination of a free design with a geometric structure was characteristic of Nieuwe Kunst (the Dutch variant of Art Nouveau) in this period. Geometric figures increasingly served as the basis for decorative designs after 1895, and stylized elements from nature were replaced by more abstract forms towards the end of the 1890s.[4] Within this rationalistic context, Lion Cachet displayed a sumptuous, almost Oriental approach to color: dark red, black, and gold against a white background.

Interestingly, the cover gives no indication whatsoever of the portfolio's contents. The expression of the autonomous genius of the artist was evidently more important than making historical or patriotic allusions. It was typical of Dutch society that avant-garde artists such as Lion Cachet received commissions to add luster to this sort of national event, but at the same time these artists showed a lack of concern with the Dutch past. Thus Rembrandt, considered since the 1880s the seventeenth-century Dutchman par excellence, did not inspire Lion Cachet in terms of either content or style. Although it would have been appropriate for the portfolio to express the nationalistic and monarchist emotions that swept the Netherlands in 1898, the year of the inauguration,[5] Lion Cachet opted for something quite different.

The *new* style sought by architects such as Hendrik P. Berlage and designers such as Lion Cachet and Gerrit W. Dijsselhof since the beginning of the 1890s is part of a larger story. After decades of heated debates concerning what exactly the national style should be, provoked in part by the need to choose a style for the Amsterdam Rijksmuseum (completed in 1885) (fig. 3.02), the problem became the search for a new style suitable for the twentieth century. From the beginning of the 1890s, renewal was no longer sought in the Dutch past, but primarily in the East: inspiration was found not in the Dutch collections of the Rijksmuseum, but rather in the ethnographic collections of Artis, the Amsterdam zoo; the Koloniaal Museum in Haarlem; and the collections of Eastern art in the museums in Leiden.

As everywhere else in Europe, the new style was expected to come out of a renewal of the crafts. Thus, there was a revival of old Dutch cabinetmaking techniques;[6] and batik, which originated in Java, one of the Dutch East Indies (now Indonesia), also became a Dutch specialty.[7] Originally batik was a process for ornamenting lengths of cotton which served as garments. The design is first painted on the fabric in wax, so that when the fabric is dyed these parts do not absorb the color. This technique was adjusted to the northern Dutch climate and applied to all sorts of other materials, such as silk, and parchment as in the Rembrandt portfolio. In the Netherlands, batik was used not only for clothing, but also for bookbindings and furniture decoration.[8]

All things considered, this portfolio, designed by a leading artist, is a superb example of Amsterdam Nieuwe Kunst. Lion Cachet also designed for the portfolio an elaborate stand in expensive woods bearing the Rembrandt monogram. This object, like the portfolio, also did

Fig. 3.02
Rijksmuseum
(1877–85; Pierre Joseph Hubert Cuypers
[Dutch, 1827–1921], architect), Amsterdam
From Victor de Stuers, *Le Musée National à Amsterdam*
(Amsterdam, 1897), pl. 27
Copy inscribed by P. J. H. Cuypers
XC1992.790***

not include references to the Dutch seventeenth century.[9] It was made by the furniture workshop of E.J. van Wisselingh & Co., art dealers in Amsterdam and London who specialized in modern Dutch, French, and sometimes even American painting (for example, they sold works by Whistler).[10] Scheltema & Holkema were connected with Van Wisselingh through K. Groesbeek, a director of both firms. In 1898 Groesbeek also established the exclusive furniture works for which Lion Cachet and his friends, Dijsselhof and Theo W. Nieuwenhuis, provided designs. These firms offered the Dutch elite a complete, deluxe package, including books (bound in leather or parchment and provided with embossed initials or family coats of arms), portfolio stands, and bookcases. The paintings could be displayed on easels, also made of precious woods. The extremely well-to-do could even order a complete Van Wisselingh interior to accommodate their collections of paintings and books. The products of the Van Wisselingh firm, such as the Rembrandt portfolio, were contemporary collectors' items destined for the wealthiest of Dutch patrons.

The designers working for Van Wisselingh represented one of the two avant-garde currents in Amsterdam at the turn of the century: the one which emphasized the reform of craftsmanship and artistic renewal. The other direction was taken by Berlage and his friend Joris Johannes Christiaan (Chris) Lebeau, socially committed artists who wanted to create simple designs that a far broader audience could afford, and were later to be involved in industrial design.

Regardless of the differences in the look of their products and their intended clienteles, these two currents in Amsterdam Nieuwe Kunst had much in common. Both attached great importance to the role of the artist who, through expressing his genius in works of art, could help create a better society. Both groups also believed in nature, combined with a rational point of departure, as the basis for the design of decorative arts: in their view, decoration would flow naturally from the structure of an object or a building.[11]

Some of these ideas also underlay totally different visual styles in the following period in the Netherlands. The Amsterdam School and De Stijl movements both held that the therapeutic influence of art would improve society; anyone coming into contact with their art would be the better for it. The genius of the artist was central for both movements.[12] These ideals, originally those of the Arts and Crafts movement, were tenacious. In the Netherlands it was not only artists, but also idealistic manufacturers, civil servants, and city councilors, who promoted good design, primarily in the 1920s and 1930s. It was typically Dutch, however, that since the 1890s the seventeenth century – the zenith of Dutch culture – hardly played a role in the renewal of craftsmanship. Even when seventeenth-century subjects were illustrated, there was no attempt to make them look like seventeenth-century works of art.

A Second Golden Age

There is some justification in calling the period from around 1870 to 1930 the Netherlands' "second Golden Age." It was the time of such painters as Vincent van Gogh and Piet Mondriaan, and in architecture Berlage, Gerrit Rietveld, and Michel de Klerk. Granted, in the nineteenth century the Netherlands was not the world power it had been 200 years earlier. However, a protracted period of economic stagnation, which began in the mid-eighteenth century and lasted until the first half of the nineteenth century, was followed by a tremendous economic, scientific, and cultural rebirth. A significant share of this new prosperity from 1870 on was derived from the exploitation of the colonies in the East Indies. The tiny Netherlands had developed into a colonial empire, colonial wars and all! A drawing by Jan Toorop (fig. 3.03) illustrates the impact of this on Dutch society; it was made for a publication to raise money for the next of kin of Dutch soldiers killed while quelling tribal warfare in Lombok Island.[13]

The Industrial Revolution gained momentum in the Netherlands around 1870, and just as elsewhere in Europe, the deplorable living and working conditions that ensued led to the formation of political parties and labor unions. Thus, the Sociaal Democratische Arbeiders Partij (S.D.A.P.; Social Democratic Workers Party) was founded in 1894. Among the first points on its agenda in the Amsterdam city council was the improvement of the appalling housing conditions of the masses: town planning and low-income housing were the most important Social Democratic themes at the municipal level. The Party leaders, however, were concerned not only with improving the immediate living, working and housing conditions of the working classes, but also with preserving the fabric of the urban experience and sometimes of the natural landscape.[14]

The solution to the ever-increasing traffic in the cities was filling up some of the seventeenth-century canals, whereas that of overpopulation was sought in city expansion, with disastrous consequences for the landscape. Traditional buildings, landscape, and regional costume rapidly vanished in an increasingly industrialized society.

The notion that the beauty of the traditional town and countryside (including folk art) was threatened was a central theme of the Arts and Crafts movement, which greatly influenced the cultural ideals of the Dutch Social Democrats. Naturally, preservation of the countryside and nature was not limited to these circles. More conservative proponents of art, history, and nature joined forces in various organizations dedicated to preserving local history and nature, some of which had a decidedly nationalistic cast.[15]

The last years of the nineteenth century saw the rise of the feminist movement which strove for the improvement of the working conditions of the female labor force and the right

Fig. 3.03

Preparatory drawing for an illustration in
***Nederland-Lombok* (Rotterdam, [1894]),**
c. 1894

Jan Theodoor Toorop

(Dutch, 1858–1928)

Netherlands

Graphite on paper

7⅛ x 9 inches (18.1 x 22.9 cm)

Marks: obverse, in pencil, bottom center "TOOROP"

TD1989.317.53

Fig. 3.04 See Cat. 237

Poster

***Loten van de Nationale Tentoonstelling van
Vrouwenarbeid* (Lottery of the National
Exhibition of Women's Work), 1898**

Designed by J. Th. Toorop

LOTEN VAN DE NATIONALE TENTOONSTELLING VAN VROUWENARBEID à 50 CENTS OP HET TERREIN EN IN DE DEPÔTS VERKRIJGBAAR. EERSTE PRIJS EEN JUWEELEN SIERAAD TER WAARDE VAN f.1000.

83

Fig. 3.05
**Stedelijk Museum
(1892–95; Adriaan Willem Weissman
[Dutch, 1858–1923], architect), Amsterdam**
Gemeentelijke Archiefdienst Amsterdam

of women to seek independence through education and employment. This cause was championed at an exhibition in 1898, also held on the occasion of Wilhelmina's inauguration (fig. 3.04). Not only was work by women presented, but also women working – for example, great interest was aroused by Indonesian women demonstrating batik.[16]

In Search of a National Style

The controversy over the national style began shortly before the economic boom of the 1870s, sparked by the national jubilee in 1863. In that year, celebrations were held commemorating the 50th anniversary of the House of Orange's return to the Netherlands in 1813, after Napoleon's defeat. It was natural that monuments should be erected to honor this event – but in what style? Detailed discussions in numerous newspapers and professional journals queried whether the national style should be Neo-Classical or Neo-Gothic. As part of the festivities, a private committee organized a competition for the design of a new national museum to house the collection of the Rijksmuseum, which until then had been in the Trippenhuis, Amsterdam's largest canal house. The prerequisite was that the style had to be in keeping with the core of the collection, namely Dutch seventeenth-century paintings.

Adversaries of the Neo-Gothic argued that this style did not suit the Baroque paintings. Moreover, it was too Roman Catholic, as Gothic was the style of the Roman Catholic

Middle Ages, before Protestantism gained ascendancy in the Netherlands in the second half of the sixteenth century. In 1863 the Protestants opted for Neo-Classicism. Plans to build a new museum, however, failed because of insufficient funds and because the liberal government, out of principle, did not subsidize art and culture.

The debate was resumed in the late 1870s, and opinions changed. The Protestants forswore Neo-Classicism and determined that the national style could only be that which had blossomed after Protestantism prevailed. In their eyes this was the colorful Renaissance style current at the beginning of the seventeenth century, the dawn of the Dutch Republic, with its alternating red brick and yellow-gray natural stone. Roman Catholics continued to favor the Neo-Gothic because of its association with the heyday of the Middle Ages, when a single indivisible faith reigned as yet unchallenged by Protestant heretics.

Only after the Roman Catholic lawyer Victor de Stuers came to power as a high ranking official in the Ministry of the Interior did the government become genuinely interested in cultural affairs. De Stuers saw to it that his brother-in-law, the architect P.J.H. Cuypers, also a Roman Catholic, was commissioned to build the Rijksmuseum. After studying under the French architect E.-E. Viollet-le-Duc, Cuypers had developed into a sober, rationalistic designer utterly devoted to the Neo-Gothic. He became the most important Dutch architect of the nineteenth century. Designed around Rembrandt's *Nightwatch* (fig. 3.02), his museum was a Neo-Gothic structure incorporating some Renaissance elements in deference to his opponents.[17]

Not surprisingly, the Rijksmuseum was subject to great criticism; with its numerous references to Gothic medieval architecture it was considered too Catholic. Rising virtually next door was the Amsterdam Stedelijk Museum (fig. 3.03), which would open its doors to the public ten years later in 1895. It embodied the Protestant vision and was modeled on early seventeenth-century architecture, such as the Haarlem Meat Market with its alternating red brick and natural yellow-gray stone.[18] To this day the architectural debate between Catholics and Protestants, both viewpoints firmly anchored in the soft Amsterdam soil, can be seen in the Museumplein.

In addition to his significance for the realization of the new Rijksmuseum, De Stuers also played a crucial role in the reform of arts and crafts education.[19] In his view, the art industry needed improvement, and how better to achieve this than by changing the educational program and establishing an applied arts collection? The combination of a collection and training in the applied arts, following the London South Kensington system, was prevalent in Europe in the second half of the nineteenth century. The Dutch collection that would serve as an example to aspiring applied artists and craftsmen was established in the Rijksmuseum, together with two of the new schools.

The necessity to train craftsmen became painfully clear during construction of the Rijksmuseum: all manner of specialized workers had to be recruited from abroad as they were not to be found in the Netherlands.

Training at the two Rijksmuseum schools was based on rationalist, Neo-Gothic principles (the subject being taught by the architect of the Rijksmuseum himself), following the tenets of Viollet-le-Duc. The pupils had to draw after nature, and those natural forms then had to be stylized and incorporated into rationalist designs. Important decorative artists such as Lion Cachet, Dijsselhof and Theo W. Nieuwenhuis were trained at the Rijksmuseum. As all three were in search of a new style in the 1890s, one could even argue that Nieuwe Kunst was the result of a new interpretation of Neo-Gothic principles.[20]

It is somewhat ironic that the Rijksmuseum, whose purpose was partly to exhibit traditional Dutch applied arts in order to serve as an example for the modern Dutch art industry, did not have the effect its makers had in mind. By the time the museum opened in 1885, it appeared that architects and applied artists had lost interest in their own Dutch past. Rather than being a beginning, the Rijksmuseum – at least with regard to architecture and the applied arts – proved to be an end. Evidently, its construction had so definitively concluded this struggle that the younger generation turned its back on the Dutch past and set out in quest of something new.

In Search of a New Style

At the turn of the century, artists were engaged in a widespread search for renewal in painting, architecture, sculpture, and the applied arts. Painters were the first to formulate the ideals of *gemeenschapskunst* (community art), or art inspired by the medieval past which expressed the highest sentiments and ideals of future society or "community." They were opposed to the impressionism of the painters of "Tachtig" (artists active in the 1880s), with their accidental, anecdotal, and personal art. The artist was considered a visionary seer or prophet who had to enlighten his own generation by making art that foreshadowed the future, ideal society.[21] A moderate Socialist variant of community art can be detected in the Amsterdam Beurs or Exchange building (1898–1903; fig. 3.06). Just as in the Middle Ages, as it was perceived, a real *Gesamtkunstwerk* came into being under the supervision of the architect Berlage; sculptures subordinate to the architecture were made by Lambertus Zijl, wall decorations were provided by Jan Toorop and Richard Roland Holst, and stained glass by Antoon Derkinderen.[22] The theme of the iconographic program is the development of the bad, capitalistic society into a good, collectivist one. Originally man lived in paradise, but since then civilization was perceived to be in a state of decay. Through trade, however – most appropriate for an exchange – the utopian ideal of a collective world community could be achieved.

Compared with Cuypers's Rijksmuseum, for example, the Exchange building was inordinately severe and, like the Rijksmuseum, it was showered with criticism. In this case, however, the building was judged to be either too bare or too Socialist.[23] Still, the Beurs was not really a twentieth-century building devoid of all references to preceding styles. Compared with earlier structures, including some by Berlage himself, the references were better incorporated here. Inspiration was derived from Italian fourteenth-century city walls and Romanesque churches. The focus was on construction, not on decoration, which was subordinated to the architecture. The material had to be "honest," that is, faithful to its intrinsic characteristics and not used unnaturally, in imitation of other materials. Like so many other architects of his generation who followed these principles, Berlage also designed furniture and light fixtures for his Beurs. During work on the building, he started a furniture workshop called 't Binnenhuis with a group of kindred spirits to make good and simple furniture for low-income groups; a worthy ambition which, however, would prove unrealizable.[24]

Thus, in Amsterdam at the turn of the century, in addition to the more usual, commercially oriented businesses, there were two fairly different avant-garde furniture workshops: 't Binnenhuis and Van Wisselingh & Co. Both made products that were austere and reserved

Fig. 3.06

**Amsterdam Exchange
(1898–1903; Hendrik Petrus Berlage
[Dutch, 1856–1934], architect), Amsterdam**

Gemeentelijke Archiefdienst Amsterdam

– even Calvinistic. This sobriety may well have been caused by the virtual absence in nineteenth-century Holland of the Neo-Baroque and Neo-Rococo, with their asymmetric ornamentation.[25]

Book Decoration and Designs on Paper

Renewal of the applied arts was ushered in by designs on paper and book decoration.[26] Decisive in this respect was an initiative by K. Groesbeek of Scheltema & Holkema's Boekhandel, who organized a competition for the design of diplomas to be awarded to the winners at the great book trade exhibition held in Amsterdam in 1892. The competition was limited to three former pupils of the Rijksmuseum schools: Nieuwenhuis, Dijsselhof, and Lion Cachet. The diplomas were carved in wood by the artists themselves as a conscious break with the division of labor in the more traditional wood engraving. That the three artists had not fully mastered the finer art of woodcutting can be seen from their somewhat roughly finished forms. They were far more concerned with demonstrating their "handwriting".[27]

Lion Cachet indulged in various kinds of typeface, such as Greek, Persian, Arabic, and Hebrew, most appropriate for a diploma in the book trade (fig. 3.07). His undulating lines

Fig. 3.07
Diploma
***Vereeniging ter Bevordering van de Belangen des Boekhandels* (Association for the Advancement of the Book Trade), 1892**
Carel Adolph Lion Cachet
(Dutch, 1864–1945)
Amsterdam
Woodcut
17½ x 28 inches (44.0 x 71.5 cm)
XA1993.294

are somewhat Expressionistic and the alternation of black and white in the sound waves coming from the bell at the upper left evinces his delight at the possibilities afforded by this – for him new – technique. His models are quite clear: at the left is a monogram by Albrecht Dürer, the sixteenth-century German great master of woodcutting, and at the right that of Dijsselhof. Lion Cachet and Nieuwenhuis greatly admired Dijsselhof, who can be considered their artistic mentor in these years.[28] Dijsselhof had completed his training as a painter at the Hague Academy and was well informed about developments abroad.

At the time, he made the decorations for the Dutch translation of a book by the English Socialist artist Walter Crane, *Kunst en Samenleving* (English title: *Claims of Decorative Art*). This publication served as the textbook for Dutch Nieuwe Kunst in terms of both content and design.[29] According to Crane, art evolved in a harmonious society from the most fundamental manifestations, such as folk art, to the most refined. However, the links between art and society had been severed, so that this natural development could not take place. There were two ways of healing the breach: one was to create a better, Socialist society through political action. In such a society, good art would emerge again in and of itself. The other possibility lay in the hands of the artist: he could contribute to the realization of the new society by creating the image of future beauty. This corresponded with the ideas of

Fig. 3.08 See Cat. 21
Cover
Kunst en samenleving. naar Walter Crane . . .
(translation of *Claims of Decorative Art*
by Walter Crane), 1894
Designed by G.W. Dijsselhof

Fig. 3.10 See Cat. 22
Cover
***De Stille Kracht* (The Hidden Force)**
by Louis Couperus, 1900
Designed by C. Lebeau

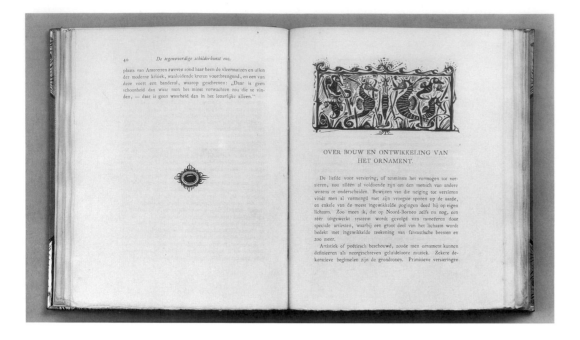

Fig. 3.09 See Cat. 21
Pages 40–41
Kunst en samenleving. naar Walter Crane . . .
(translation of *Claims of Decorative Art*
by Walter Crane), 1894
Illustrated by G.W. Dijsselhof

Dutch community art. Art had to reveal the artist's personality, which relied on a manual process. Moreover, according to this book, industrial design was still far away.

Dijsselhof designed the covers of both the simple, stitched edition and the expensive, bound edition of Crane's book (fig. 3.08).[30] Heavy, sturdy materials (such as leather) were used to reinforce the back and the four corners of the binding and the decoration was embossed with gold. For the interior, thick, handmade paper was used to underscore once again the book's anti-mechanical tenets. Dijsselhof only provided the woodcut illustrations and was not involved with the typography or the visual coherence between typography and ornament. The decoration of the binding reiterates its function: the five gathered lines on the spine represent the sewing cords, which continue over the front and back, ending in five lobster tail motifs on each side. They symbolize the function of the binding: to protect and hold the book together.[31] For the front cover Dijsselhof made a woodcut of a diamond-shaped vignette with a fern motif sprouting leafy twigs. Around the vignette are traces of uncut wood – a deliberate primitivism. The same combination of refined design and references to simple folk art is also found inside the book in the woodcuts marking the beginning of each chapter: unity of style does not appear to have been Dijsselhof's point of departure. Most of the subjects portrayed are derived from the fauna prevalent in the Dutch countryside – mosquitoes, frogs, and ladybugs – but he also included jet peasant jewelry, a feature of various Dutch regional costumes (fig. 3.09). The connection with folk art was obvious, certainly given Crane's writing, in which vernacular art was considered the basis of all the arts.[32]

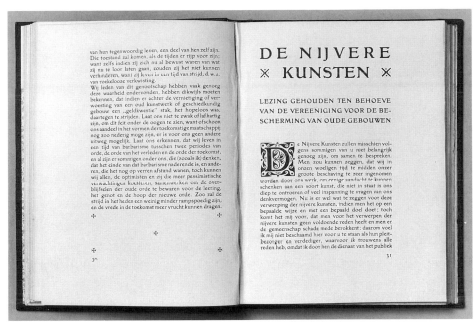

Fig. 3.11 See Cat. 54
Napkin
No. 505, *Vlinder* (Butterfly), c. 1906
Designed by C. Lebeau

Fig. 3.12
Pages 30–31
Kunst en Maatschappij. Lezingen van William
***Morris* (Art and Society. Lectures by William**
Morris), 1903
Designed by Sjoerd Hendrik de Roos
(Dutch, 1877–1962)
Translated by M. Hugenholtz-Zeeven
(Dutch, dates unknown)
Printed by Ipenbuur & van Seldam, Amsterdam
Published by A.B. Soep, Amsterdam
8¾ x 6⅝ inches (22.2 x 16.8 cm)
XA1993.3

The following phase in the development of book art is reflected in the work of Chris Lebeau. He too had been trained at the Rijksmuseum schools, but as an anarchist his vision of the applied arts differed radically from that of Lion Cachet and his circle, who considered themselves artists *pur sang*. This difference is not yet visible in Lebeau's early book designs. For example, around 1900 he was involved in experiments with the batik technique in the Koloniaal Museum in Haarlem. In November of that year his batik cover for *De Stille Kracht* (fig. 3.10), a novel set in the East Indies by the famous writer Louis Couperus, was published in several variations.[33] Because batik is a craft, batik book covers were primarily made at the request of individuals, as was the case with the Rembrandt portfolio. This is one of the few published batiked editions.[34]

Its decoration consists of a diamond pattern with plant-like motifs in a more abstract and less free design than that in Lion Cachet's portfolio. As with Dijsselhof's design, lines extend over the spine connecting the front and back covers, thus emphasizing the book's actual construction,[35] though Lebeau had nothing to do with its typography. This cover is one of the many batik designs Lebeau executed from 1900 until around 1906. Because his involvement with batik was regarded by Socialist critics and by Lebeau himself as elitist, he later turned to designing textiles which could be machine-made, such as table linen (fig. 3.11).[36]

These book designs by Lion Cachet, Dijsselhof, and Lebeau have several features in common. For one thing, the artists limited themselves to the cover; only Dijsselhof also made illustrations. Moreover, all three stressed the actual construction, just as a rationalist architect did when designing a building. This is hardly surprising given their training under Cuypers and, through him, Viollet-le-Duc.

The next step in the development of book art was taken by a designer who had a completely different education. From his beginnings as a simple lithographer, Sjoerd H. de Roos slowly evolved into the premier Dutch typographer of his time. Unlike his immediate predecessors, he had little ambition in the area of artistic expression.[37] His first important book design was for the Dutch translation of William Morris's essays, published in 1903 under the title *Kunst en Maatschappij* (Art and Society). For the first time, typography and not the cover was the starting point. De Roos began with the page spread, as can be seen from, among other things, the small Maltese crosses filling in the residual blank space. The text was compactly contained in a straight-edge block without paragraph indentations and the lines of text were justified at the right (fig. 3.12). This book heralded the dawn of twentieth-century Dutch typography and the extinction of book embellishers.

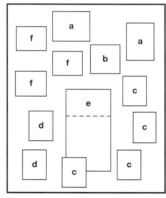

Fig. 3.13 See Cat. 90
Group of Postage stamps
a) *Nederland 2 cent; Nederland 4 cent*
Designed by P. Koch, 1943–44
b) *Nederland: Luchtpost 40 cent*
Designed by C. Lebeau, 1928
c) *Nederland 1 1/2 cent; Nederland 5 cent;*
Nederland 6 cent; Nederland 12 1/2 cent
Designed by G. Kiljan, 1931
d) *Nederland 2 cent*
Designed by J.Th. Toorop, 1923
e) *Nederland 1 cent; Nederland 2 cent*
Designed by M. de Klerk, 1923
f) *Nederland 1 cent; Nederland 1 1/2 cent;*
Nederland 2 1/2 cent
Designed by C. Lebeau, 1926

The publication of both Morris's and Crane's writings were crucial for the evolution of ideas on the role of art and design in Dutch society, primarily in Social Democratic circles. Generally speaking, Morris and Crane espoused the same ideas. Morris too wanted a return to medieval craftsmanship, the principles of which he adopted in his own company. Morris's social concerns led to his involvement with the Socialist movement, for which he frequently proselytized through lectures that were later published.

Crane and Morris, the latter partly through his political activities, were seen by the Dutch Social Democrats more as political thinkers than as design philosophers.[38] Moreover, the ideology of this English pair was shared by other Dutch idealists of all persuasions who were not necessarily politically active.

The idea that beauty contributes to human happiness did not only stimulate artists in the Netherlands, but also all kinds of non-artists. For instance, in 1924 the Bond voor Kunst in Industrie (Association for Art in Industry) was established by idealistic manufacturers. Membership was restricted to businesses which sold quality products designed by artists.[39] This idea was also behind a new design policy for postage stamps at the Nederlandse Posterijen (P.T.T.; Dutch Postal Services).[40] In fig. 3.13 stamps designed by Toorop, De Klerk, and Lebeau share space with some by far more modern designers, such as Gerard Kiljan, who employed the photomontage technique in the 1930s. The man responsible for involving artists in stamp design was J.F. van Royen, general secretary of the P.T.T.'s board of directors.[41] Morris's ideals were also behind Van Royen's efforts to provide beauty for everyone. Sharing Morris's deep appreciation of craftsmanship, he even had his own printing press.

Interiors

For interior designs by Lion Cachet and his circle we have to go back several years in time and briefly look at the above-mentioned furniture workshop of E.J. van Wisselingh & Co., whose furniture and interiors, generally for the canal houses in Amsterdam, are among the most luxurious ever produced in the Netherlands.[42] Founded in 1898, the firm's workshop was headed by Dijsselhof, Lion Cachet, and Nieuwenhuis. Dijsselhof left in 1903; but Lion Cachet continued until 1906, after which he worked for various shipping companies designing a series of spectacular, luxurious ship interiors, characterized by their use of dark and exotic materials.[43] Nieuwenhuis continued to direct the workshop until it closed in 1924.[44]

The Wolfsonian Collection includes the woodwork and fireplace from one of Nieuwenhuis's most important early interiors (figs. 3.14–3.16), a study for the Amsterdam lawyer F. Kranenburg. From archival documents we know that Kranenburg also purchased modern art from Van Wisselingh. It appears that the commission was carried out in stages, as

Fig. 3.14
Oak bookcase with batik curtains
From the study of the Ferdinand Kranenburg
residence, Keizersgracht, Amsterdam, c. 1900
Designed by Theodoor Willem Nieuwenhuis
(Dutch, 1866–1951)
From *Afbeeldingen van werken naar ontwerpen*
van T. Nieuwenhuis (Amsterdam, 1912): pl. 15
83.2.2070.2

Fig. 3.15 See Cat. 53
Door
From the study of the Ferdinand Kranenburg
residence, Keizersgracht, Amsterdam, c. 1900
Designed by Th. W. Nieuwenhuis

payment for this room was made in installments from 1899 to 1905. This is supported by the fact that the room does not seem to have been designed as an entity.

Nieuwenhuis favored flower and plant motifs, which he used to create a sense of unity in his interiors. His particular genius manifested itself not so much in the area of furniture construction or spatial concepts, as in the kind of flat surface decoration seen in one of the room's doors (fig. 3.15). The oak and maple ceiling and paneling, the marble slabs and the brightly colored marble mosaic on the mantlepiece, contributed to the overall impression of light and color (fig. 3.16).

Inspiration for this room was certainly not derived from the Dutch past. For example, Japanese influences can be detected in the marble etched panels of the chimneypiece, elements of Classical antiquity in the ladies adorning the sides, and Oriental textiles clearly served as inspiration for the flower decorations. This interior can only be characterized as an extremely eclectic manifestation of Nieuwe Kunst. Nieuwenhuis's later interiors, several of which are in the Rijksmuseum, generally have a greater sense of unity and are much darker, like the ship interiors of Lion Cachet.

Fig. 3.16
Chimneypiece
From the study of the Ferdinand Kranenburg
residence, Keizersgracht, Amsterdam, c.1900
Designed by Theodoor Willem Nieuwenhuis
(Dutch, 1866–1951)
From *Kunstnijverheid. Ontwerpen van G.W. Dijsselhof, C.A.*
Lion Cachet en T. Nieuwenhuis (Amsterdam, [1904]), pl. 4
83.2.2071
Note: Chimneypiece, TD1990.235.1

Fig. 3.17
Boudoir
Th.G. Dentz von Schaick residence,
Frederiksplein, Amsterdam, c. 1911–12
Designed by Carel Adolph Lion Cachet
(Dutch, 1864–1945).
From R.W.P. de Vries, Jr., "C.A. Lion Cachet,"
Elsevier's Geïllustreerd Maandschrift 22 (1912): 201
Amsterdam Historical Museum

Equally dark were the interiors designed for the lawyer Th.G. Dentz van Schaick and his wife, owners of an extensive and varied collection of art. They lived on the Frederiksplein in Amsterdam in a double house dating from the 1860s. Its interior was totally redone by Van Wisselingh after designs by Nieuwenhuis and Lion Cachet.[45] The wife's boudoir, after a design by Lion Cachet (fig. 3.17), had dark calamander wood and rosewood paneling, with panels of etched asbestos and cement serving as a light accent.[46] Inspiration for the iconography and style came from varied sources; Italian Renaissance-inspired decorations grace the panels above the built-in settee and Assyrian lion motifs the ceiling.

Lambertus Zijl, also trained in the Rijksmuseum schools, was responsible for the woodcarving here and also in other areas of the house. In the boudoir, he decorated the cabinet facing the settee with reindeer and a Viking ship, referring to the lady of the house's Scandinavian heritage.

For the fireplace (fig. 3.18), Lion Cachet devised a strikingly novel design: splendid wrought-iron filigree grilles with a stylized floral motif. This originally Oriental technique is usually used on a much smaller scale for works in precious metals. Lion Cachet enlivened the

parallel bands in the middle of the filigree curls with red copper. A hand-welded plaque with a representation of two buffaloes by Zijl is set into the fireplace. There appears to be an almost deliberate stylistic discrepancy between the "coarse" Expressionistic plaque and its refined framework. This may well reflect the notion that every artist had the right to display his "signature." Moreover, unity of style may not have been as important to these particular artists as it was to others at the time. This notwithstanding, the interior of the Dentz van Schaick house must have made a dark, Oriental and above all opulent first impression. The stylistic and iconographic idiosyncrasies become apparent only upon closer inspection.

Though the Van Wisselingh group were not necessarily adherents of Protestant sobriety and restraint, as shown in their exuberant and luxurious use of materials, the structure of their furniture and ornaments follows the rationalist principles they had learned. Serenity and classical uniformity are the key concepts; there is absolutely no question of asymmetry.

Fig. 3.18 See Cat. 55
Fireplace
From the boudoir of the Th. G. Dentz von Schaick residence, Frederiksplein, Amsterdam, c. 1911–12
Designed by C. A. Lion Cachet
Relief designed by L. Zijl

A passion for the arts of the Orient is a constant in Dutch interiors. Already in the seventeenth century the Dutch adorned their houses with Japanese and Chinese porcelain, and carpets from the Middle East. This concern continued unabated in the following century and even intensified by around 1900, extending to Egypt, Persia, Assyria, India, and the East Indies.

The Amsterdam School

The interest in the Orient, as well as eclecticism among the applied artists of the Nieuwe Kunst, recurred in the following generation of Amsterdam School artists, whose training was generally in architecture. Some of the most important of them had worked in the office of Eduard Cuypers, a cousin of P.J.H. Cuypers, where they had been exposed to diverse vocabularies. Ed. Cuypers could supply structures in any desired style. In this respect, nothing much had changed since the heyday of the historicizing neo-styles. They could find all manner of inspiration in Cuypers's large, internationally oriented library, ranging from modern designs from Glasgow, Scandinavia, and Vienna to traditional architecture from India or the East Indies. Still, the Amsterdam School was not a neo-style, but a distinct twentieth-century movement. A variety of influences had been forged into something unique, best described as "expressionistic" in comparison with Nieuwe Kunst. The Amsterdam School took the older concept of the artist as prophet or seer and transformed it into the notion of individualistic expressionism: a work of art could only be conceived after a deep, inner struggle.[47] What was important now was that a building or object should express the artist's emotions.

Other Nieuwe Kunst principles can be found virtually unaltered in the Amsterdam School: like Nieuwe Kunst, the Amsterdam School strove for the improvement of society through the curative power of art. And, like the previous generation, Amsterdam School artists considered nature as their guiding principle. However, rather than incorporating natural forms within rational ornamental designs, the buildings and furniture themselves had to look alive, as if they had grown up from the soil or emerged from the depths of the ocean.

The architecture of the Amsterdam School was certainly not functional in the sense that "form follows function." The architects began with the exterior, often first modeling the design into which the houses had to fit. For example, the block of low-income housing that Michel de Klerk designed for the Spaarndammerbuurt (Spaarndammer neighborhood; 1917–21) had to incorporate fifteen different types of dwelling in order to conform to the curvature of the exterior.[48]

The architectural journal *Wendingen* (1918–31) is a testament to the opinions and sources of inspiration of the Amsterdam School.[49] Its layout, for which the editor H.Th. Wijdeveld used blocks of type-setting material, was distinctive. It covered and illustrated a

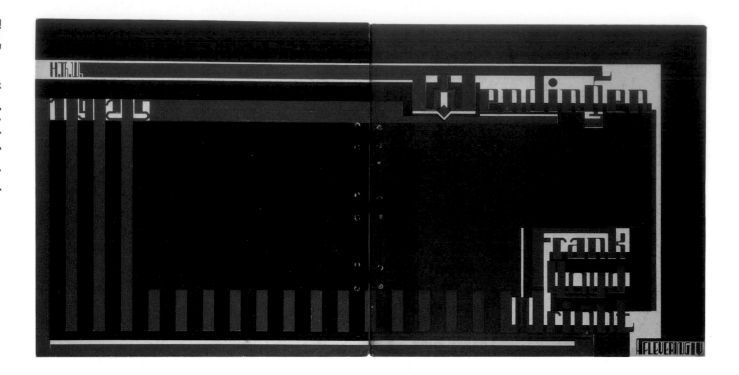

wide range of subjects. Much space was reserved for national and foreign architecture; for example, seven issues were devoted to Frank Lloyd Wright (fig. 3.19). In addition, attention was paid to Oriental art and ethnographic objects such as masks. Natural shapes were highlighted in special crystal and shell issues. An issue was even devoted to Technology and Art, despite the hostile attitude displayed by most Amsterdam School designers in 1917, when an inquiry was conducted into the desirability of permanent collaboration between industry, trade, and art. At the time, De Klerk was one of the antagonists of industrial design. He was against mass-production because the designer had no control over the end result. In his experience, control was possible only for a series of six or seven variants at most.[50]

Architecture

The Scheepvaarthuis (Shipping Building; 1912–16), a joint commission from the six Amsterdam shipping companies, can be considered the first structure built in the Amsterdam School style. It was located close to P.J.H. Cuypers's Central Station, on the quay from which ships had set sail for the East Indies in the seventeenth century. It was designed by J.M. van der Mey, with the assistance of Michel de Klerk and P.L. Kramer, all three of whom had recently left the office of Ed. Cuypers. It consists of a concrete skeleton sheathed in brick, around which a second layer seems to have grown up, namely the web of intricate and delicate wrought-iron metalwork covering the facade.[51]

Fig. 3.19
Cover
***Wendingen*, "Frank Lloyd Wright, Aflevering IV," series 7, 1926**
Designed and edited
by Hendrikus Theodorus Wijdeveld
(Dutch, 1885–1987)
Published by C.A. Mees, Santpoort, Netherlands
Printed by Joh. Enschedé & Zonen, Haarlem, Netherlands
13½ x 13⅜ inches (34.3 x 34.0 cm)
XB1990.2025

Fig. 3.20
Interior
Scheepvaarthuis (Shipping Building)
(1912–16; Johan Melchior van der Mey [Dutch,
1878–1949], Michel de Klerk [Dutch, 1884–1923],
and Piet L. Kramer [Dutch, 1881–1961], architects),
Amsterdam, 1916
Stained glass by Willem Bogtman
(Dutch, 1882–1955)
Gemeentelijke Archiefdienst Amsterdam

Fig. 3.21
Chandelier
From a secretary's office of the Scheepvaarthuis
(Shipping Building), Amsterdam, c. 1915
Designed by Michel de Klerk
(Dutch, 1884–1923)
Manufacture attributed to H.J. Winkelman
& Van der Bijl, Amsterdam
Iron, glass
58 x 23½ x 22 inches (147.2 x 59.7 x 55.9 cm)
TD1989.328.16

Fig. 3.22 See Cat. 179
Shelf clock and incense burners, c. 1920
Designed by H. Krop

The building's numerous decorative features (fig. 3.20) in the form of sculpture, metal-work, stained glass, textiles, and woodwork contain references to shipping and navigation – for instance, the sculpted portraits of seventeenth-century Dutch naval heroes. With regard to style, however, at the time neither the building nor its decoration had anything to do with existing Dutch architecture or design. It comes closest to the Expressionistic architectural style that had originated somewhat earlier in Germany.[52]

De Klerk designed at least two executive office suites for the Scheepvaarthuis. The lamp in the Wolfsonian (fig. 3.21) is from a secretary's room adjoining one of the offices. Here too are found maritime references, in this case relatively aggressive inhabitants of the sea.[53]

The most important interior, however, the meeting room (1917–21), was the creation of a member of the previous generation: Nieuwenhuis. While De Klerk's contribution to the realization of the Scheepvaarthuis must have been considerable, it has proven impossible to establish precisely what he did.[54]

Dutch architects became interested in low-income housing only in the early years of the twentieth century. An example of this is De Klerk's housing project at the Spaardammerplantsoen (1913–20). City expansions also evolved around the same time. Berlage's 1917 plan for the southern expansion of Amsterdam (Plan-Zuid) was fleshed out with low-income housing by Amsterdam School architects, such as the housing blocks in P. L. Takstraat (1919–21) designed by De Klerk and Kramer.[55] Seminal for the unity of the architectural style of Plan-Zuid was the municipal Schoonheidscommissie (a committee to regulate the design and appearance of buildings), which vetted all building plans and whose members were mostly ardent supporters of the Amsterdam School.

It is somewhat paradoxical that the Amsterdam School style, which was so explicitly anti-modern, anti-industrial, and even elitist, was so strongly supported by the Social Democrats in the Amsterdam city council. This support arose from the primarily Morrisian conviction that workers were entitled to beauty in their daily surroundings. This beauty could be expressed in low-income housing or bridges – of which Amsterdam has many – and in the sculptures embellishing the new bridges, schools, and housing estates. The most important sculptor was Hildo Krop, who also designed furnishings with a strong sculptural presence (fig. 3.22). Even the typographical design of municipal publications was in the Amsterdam School style. As mentioned above, these city councilors had grown up with the Socialist ideals of Nieuwe Kunst – Morris and Crane had been their mentors – and their craft-oriented principles were still best advanced by the Amsterdam School. Only a subsequent generation of Socialist city councilors would embrace the ideals of the functionalist architecture of the Nieuwe Bouwen, as the Modern Movement was called in the Netherlands.[56]

Furniture

Although famous mainly for his low-income housing, De Klerk did not design inexpensive furniture for the masses, as did his colleague Kramer.[57] De Klerk's furniture was luxurious, unsuitable for industrial production, and would never have fit into his small dwellings. Unlike Lion Cachet, he did not take the material as his point of departure – De Klerk was first and foremost a draftsman. His working drawings could only be executed by "the most skilled cabinetmakers."[58]

Of the approximately two hundred pieces of furniture that were made, about twenty-five still exist, the majority of them now in the Wolfsonian Collection. That so few pieces have been preserved can perhaps be attributed to their emphatic "presence," which quickly went out of fashion. In 1915 De Klerk made numerous sketches for furniture for the Amsterdam firm 't Woonhuys,[59] which seems somewhat incongruous as this firm actually specialized in historicist styles, like Queen Anne. The furniture for the dining and living rooms in various types of wood was not made before the beginning of 1917 (fig. 3.23).

The furniture exudes an unmistakable Oriental aura – for example, the supports of the armchairs and the sofa are reminiscent of a pasha's slippers.[60] The hanging tassels also appear to be derived from Oriental clothing. The carved heads of fish and frogs on the armchairs (fig. 3.24) were inspired by Hindu sea monsters; the tortoises crawling up the armrests of the

Fig. 3.23   See Cat. 177
Furniture suite
Exposition Internationale des Arts Décoratifs
et Industriels Modernes, Paris, 1925
Designed by M. de Klerk
From *Wendingen*, series 7, vol. 10 (1925), p. 8
XB1990.2025

Fig. 3.24
Detail of armchairs, 1915–16
Designed by Michel de Klerk
(Dutch, 1884–1923)
Commissioned by F.J. Zeegers for 't Woonhuys
(The Dwelling), Amsterdam
Manufactured and retailed by 't Woonhuys, Amsterdam, c.1917
Mahogany, velvet, brass
Left: 39¼ x 33⅜ x 32⅞ inches (99.7 x 84.8 x 83.5 cm)
Right: 39¼ x 33½ x 33¼ inches (99.7 x 85.1 x 84.5 cm)
TD1989.328.2 a,b and TD1989.328.3 a–c

Fig. 3.25   See Cat. 178
Dining chair with armrests, 1915–16
Designed by M. de Klerk

Fig. 3.26   See Cat. 56
Platter
Model no. 25, commemorating the twenty-fifth
year of the reign of Queen Wilhelmina, 1923
Designed by Th. A. C. Colenbrander

sofa refer to the Chinese symbol for a long and happy life.[61] The striking parabolic form here, as in many Amsterdam School designs, is partly derived from Indian temple architecture.[62]

As is often the case with De Klerk, not all the references are so cheerful. Mushrooms, hopefully not poisonous, sprout on the armrests of the dining room furniture (fig. 3.25). More disturbing are the remains of a vertebral motif in the supports of the chairs. De Klerk initially intended to use a spine made of wood for the back of the chairs, but because no armrest could be connected to it and also perhaps because of the somewhat macabre associations it evoked, this design was never executed.[63]

De Klerk's untimely death in 1923 was considered a serious blow to Dutch architecture, and *Wendingen* dedicated no fewer than six special issues to his work.

Conclusion

This study ends, as it began, with a royal celebration, in this case Queen Wilhelmina's 25th jubilee in 1923. One of the many objects commemorating that event was a dish designed by Theodoor A.C. Colenbrander (fig. 3.26).[64] Since the Rembrandt portfolio not much had changed in the way of design inspiration. Colenbrander, who was older than Lion Cachet, belonged to the same group that had aspired to a new art at the turn of the century. It is

therefore not surprising to find similar principles in his work: here too are floral decorations without a trace of preceding styles. Equally absent are depictions of historical events, which might have been most appropriate for a 25th anniversary. Looking closely, we can just distinguish the word "Oranje" on the edge of the dish and only expert flower connoisseurs would know that the three round shapes in the middle are meant to represent oranges – the symbol of the Dutch Royal House.

For Nieuwe Kunst and Amsterdam School artists, indigenous Dutch art barely served as a source of inspiration. Even when seventeenth-century subjects were illustrated, as in the sculptures of the Scheepvaarthuis or in ship interiors by Lion Cachet, there were virtually no stylistic references to the past. It is characteristic of this period in the Netherlands that the commissioners found it more important to allow a famous decorative artist to make a splendid object than to make a historically coherent iconographic statement.[65] The fine and the applied arts were subservient only to the genius of the artist. In Amsterdam and elsewhere in this period it was considered wrong for patrons to impose restrictions on Dutch applied artists with regard to content, let alone to allow the process of machine production to place demands on artists' designs.

At the 1925 Exposition Internationale des Arts Décoratifs et Industriels Modernes in Paris, virtually all the artists mentioned in this essay were represented in the Dutch section, from Lion Cachet with his Rembrandt portfolio to De Klerk with his living room furnishings. The Dutch selection committee appears to have completely ignored the avant-garde of that time, for the De Stijl group was not even invited to participate. Ironically, the attention that the now internationally famous De Stijl artists and Berlage and his followers later garnered precisely for having blazed the trail to modernity through their industrial designs long obscured appreciation of the Van Wisselingh group and the Amsterdam School.

Only recently has interest been revived in these two groups, which generally placed their extravagant creativity at the service of the elite, yet in the time of the Amsterdam School also produced art for the general public, and served the cause of social housing under Amsterdam's Social Democratic city council.

(Translated from the Dutch by Kist & Kilian, Amsterdam)

NOTES

1 The illustrated example contains the supplement with 26 heliogravures. On the publication in various languages and in various designs, see P.J.J. van Thiel, "De Rembrandt-tentoonstelling van 1898," *Bulletin van het Rijksmuseum* 40 (1992): 54–56. The standard edition in half parchment with batik cost 300 guilders, the deluxe edition in full parchment 600 guilders. At the time, the latter amount was more than the average yearly income of a craftsman.

2 On Dutch book art in the time, see Ernst Braches, *Het boek als Nieuwe Kunst 1892–1903. Een studie in Art Nouveau* (Utrecht, 1973).

3 This concerns one-off books, as they were only produced on commission. The book compiled by Hijner, unpaginated, contains illustrations of the stamps used for clients' monograms and coats of arms. See C.J.A. Hijner, ed., *Catalogus van de werken uitgegeven door Scheltema & Holkema's Boekhandel te Amsterdam en verzorgd door K. Groesbeek. 1882–Januari–1922* (Amsterdam, 1922–23). The copies in the Wolfsonian were made for the still unidentified ELA (TD1989.317.111) and NMvG (TD1990.340.132). Several other copies are in the Veeze Collection – the largest assemblage of turn-of-the-century book bindings, now part of the Wolfsonian's holdings. There are also two portfolios in full parchment in the Royal Collection in The Hague, one for Queen Wilhelmina (G 35.45) and one for the Queen Mother Emma (G 35.46). See Jacobine E. Huisken and Friso Lammertse, *Koninklijke geschenken: Traditie en vernieuwing rond de eeuwwisseling* (Amsterdam: Koninklijk Paleis op de Dam, 1988), p. 25 and Van Thiel, "De Rembrandt-tentoonstelling," p. 55 and fn. 99. Copies in half parchment are also in the Royal Collection. In the recent Lion Cachet exhibition, it appeared that not only the monograms and colors of the portfolios differed, but also that Lion Cachet included variations in the free-hand and geometric ornamentation. For the objects Lion Cachet made for the celebration, see Marion Duijsman, with the assistance of Mienke Simon Thomas, "Batikwerk," in *C.A. Lion Cachet 1864–1945*, Mechteld de Bois, ed. (Assen: Drents Museum, and Rotterdam: Museum Boymans-van Beuningen, 1994), pp. 37–40.

4 In the 1890s, K.P.C. de Bazel and J.L.M. Lauweriks played a leading role in the introduction of mathematics as a guiding principle in architectural as well as ornamental design. See Braches, *Het boek als Nieuwe Kunst*, pp. 105–15; Ype Koopmans, "In het voetspoor van Pythagoras. Kosmische symboliek in de Nederlandse architectuur tussen 1900 en 1940," *Jong Holland* 5. no. 5 (1989): 23–34; Marty Bax, "Het 'Sfeeren'systeem 1898–1900. Berlage, Van den Bosch, De Groot, Lauweriks en Walenkamp," *Jong Holland* 6, no. 4 (1990): 17–29.

5 Henk te Velde, *Gemeenschapszin en plichtsbesef. Liberalisme en Nationalisme in Nederland, 1870–1918* (The Hague, 1992), pp. 148–53.

6 It seems that in the Netherlands, regionalism and the vernacular were not as important as, for instance, in the English Arts and Crafts movement. See Elizabeth Cumming and Wendy Kaplan, *The Arts and Crafts Movement* (London and New York, 1991), pp. 31–65. Research in the field of Dutch architecture and design concerning nationalism and regionalism has not yet begun.

7 To such an extent that Madsen calls his chapter on Dutch Art Nouveau "Books and Batiks," see Stephan Tschudi Madsen, *Sources of Art Nouveau* (1956; reprint, New York, 1976), pp. 387–98.

8 Lion Cachet used batik for decorative textiles and on parchment with various functions. See Duijsman and Simon Thomas, "Batikwerk," pp. 28–51.

9 The publisher issued this portfolio stand after the second portfolio was ready. It cost an additional 275 guilders. One specimen, made in 1903, is in the Amsterdam Rijksmuseum (RBK 1970–96); there are

two others in a private collection in Bussum (see fig. 104 and 105 in De Bois, *C.A. Lion Cachet 1864–1945*, p. 84). The Wolfsonian owns one less elaborate portfolio stand of this type (TD1991.152.1). Judging by the absence of the initials RvR, this one was not made specially for the Rembrandt portfolio.

10 On Van Wisselingh & Co., see Richard Bionda, "De afzet van eigentijdse kunst in Nederland," in Richard Bionda and Carel Blotkamp, eds., *De schilders van Tachtig. Nederlandse schilderkunst 1880–1895* (Zwolle and Amsterdam: Rijksmuseum Vincent van Gogh, 1991), pp. 59–62.

11 On the ideology of New Art, see Braches, *Het boek als Nieuwe Kunst*, pp. 24–131. A far more international version of Art Nouveau could be found in The Hague with artists like Jan Toorop and Rozenburg pottery. On the Rozenburg factory, see Marjan Boot, *et al.*, *Rozenburg 1883–1917. Geschiedenis van een Haagse fabriek* (The Hague: Haags Gemeentemuseum, 1983).

12 Wim de Wit, ed., *The Amsterdam School. Dutch expressionist architecture, 1915–1930* (New York and Cambridge, MA, 1983), pp. 32–7.

13 On the drawing, see Bettina Polak, *Het fin-de-siècle in de Nederlandse schilderkunst. De symbolistische beweging 1890–1900* (The Hague: Martinus Nijhoff, 1955), pp. 364–5, no. 72. The publication itself is also in the Wolfsonian, TD 1989.317.54, *Nederland-Lombok* (Rotterdam, [1894]).

14 A book about the beauty of Dutch cities and landscapes was written by a leading figure of the trade union of laborers in the diamond industry, Henri Polak, *Het kleine land en zijn grote schoonheid* (The Small Country and its Great Beauty) (Amsterdam: Algemeene Coöperatieve Verbruiks- en Productievereeniging "Samenwerking" U.A, 1929).

15 Te Velde, *Gemeenschapszin en plichtsbesef*, pp. 207–12.

16 For more on the National Exhibition of Women's Work see W.H. Postumus-van der Goot and Anna de Waal, eds., *Van moeder op dochter. De maatschappelijke positie van de vrouw in Nederland vanaf de Franse tijd* (Nijmegen, 1977), pp. 109–28 and Liesbeth Brandt Corstius and Cora Hollema, eds., *De kunst van het moederschap. Leven en werk van Nederlandse vrouwen in de 19e eeuw* (Nijmegen, 1982), pp. 89–91.

17 Aart Oxenaar, *Het Rijksmuseum, schetsen en tekeningen (1863–1908) van P.J.H. Cuypers* (Rotterdam, 1993).

18 Michiel Jonker, "Het Stedelijk Museum," *Museumjournaal* 24 (1979): 197–200; and Joost Braat, "De bouw van het Stedelijk Museum (1892–1895)," in *Amsterdam het beschouwen waard* (Amsterdam: Stadsuitgeverij Amsterdam/Gemeentelijk bureau Monumentenzorg Amsterdam, 1993), pp. 145–53.

19 On De Stuers's art reforms, see Jan Alexander Martis, "Voor de kunst en voor de nijverheid. Het ontstaan van het kunstnijverheidsonderwijs in Nederland" (dissertation, University of Amsterdam, 1990).

20 Braches, *Het boek als Nieuwe Kunst*, p. 19, fn. 44.

21 A Roman-Catholic "gemeenschapskunst," first developed in the highly stylized wall paintings by Antoon J. Derkinderen, in which the Middle Ages were idealized. See Braches, *Het boek als Nieuwe Kunst*, pp. 24–9. On community art in general, see Caroline Boot and Marijke van der Heijden, "Gemeenschapskunst," in Carel Blotkamp, *et al.*, *Kunstenaren der Idee. Symbolistische tendenzen in Nederland, ca. 1880–1930* (The Hague: Haags Gemeentemuseum en Staatsuitgeverij, 1978), pp. 36–47. On Derkinderen, see Roos Verheyen, *et al.*, *Antoon Derkinderen, 1859–1925* ('s-Hertogenbosch: Noordbrabants Museum, 1980).

22   Pieter Singelenberg, *H.P. Berlage. Idea and Style. The quest for modern architecture* (Utrecht, 1972), pp. 80–138.

23   On the criticism, see A. W. Reinink, *Amsterdam en de Beurs van Berlage. Reacties van tijdgenoten* (The Hague, 1975; with an abridged text in English). The stockbrokers were so dissatisfied with Berlage's Exchange building (which originally included the Stock Exchange as well) that they decided to build, very near Berlage's, their own, more traditional Stock Exchange (1909–12) – another example of an architectural discussion still to be seen in Amsterdam. The architect was Joseph Th.J. Cuypers, a son of P.J.H. Cuypers.

24   For various reasons the furniture never reached the people it was meant for, see for instance Marjan Boot, "Klandizie van 't Binnenhuis," in *Jac. van den Bosch en de vernieuwing van het Binnenhuis* (Haarlem: Frans Hals Museum, 1976), pp. 19–25.

25   As suggested by Madsen. He states that in the nineteenth century the New Art had only Neo-Classicism, Neo-Gothic, and the Dutch variant of Neo-Renaissance (sometimes in eclectic combinations), to look back on. See Madsen, *Sources*, pp. 387–98. Madsen based his views mainly on developments in architecture. Nineteenth-century Dutch silver, for instance, does include Neo-Baroque and Neo-Rococo elements.

26   The theoretical change had set in earlier. See Mienke Simon Thomas, "Het Ornament, het Verleden en de Natuur," *Nederlands Kunsthistorisch Jaarboek* 39 (1988): 27–60.

27   Braches, *Het boek als Nieuwe Kunst*, pp. 76–7. In addition to the three woodcuts, a lithographed diploma designed by Nieuwenhuis has survived and is in the Wolfsonian (Veeze collection).

28   Walter Crane's monogram is also faintly visible above Dijsselhof's. The same combination appears on the cover of *Kunst en Samenleving*, which Dijsselhof was working on at the time (see fig. 3.8).

29   Braches, *Het boek als Nieuwe Kunst*, pp. 69–70.

30   *Ibid.*, pp. 289–92.

31   *Ibid.*, pp. 289–92.

32   *Ibid.*, p. 290.

33   The author was delighted with the covers. See Mechteld de Bois, *Chris Lebeau 1878–1945* (Assen, 1987), p. 66.

34   The total number of those bindings is not known, but probably no more than a few hundred. The publisher was L.J. Veen in Amsterdam, a literary house which had several other covers for Couperus's novels designed by Toorop.

35   Braches, *Het boek als Nieuwe Kunst*, pp. 374–5.

36   Initially, however, his designs for damask could only be woven by hand. See De Bois, *Lebeau*, pp. 84–85.

37   Braches, *Het boek als Nieuwe Kunst*, pp. 380–1. From 1907 on, De Roos worked for Lettergieterij Amsterdam; he designed a whole series of new typefaces, starting with his highly successful "Hollandse Mediaeval" in 1912.

38   See Lieske Tibbe, "Theorie versus praktijk. De invloed van Engelse socialistische idealen op de Nederlandse kunstnijverheidsbeweging," in *Industrie & Vormgeving in Nederland 1850–1950*, eds. Ellinoor Bergvelt, *et al.* (Amsterdam, 1985), pp. 31–43.

39   On the Association for Art in Industry, see Renny Ramakers, *Tussen kunstnijverheid en industriële vormgeving. De Nederlandsche Bond voor Kunst in Industrie* (Utrecht, 1985). Members included the Brusse publishing house in Rotterdam, the Leerdam glass factory, Lettergieterij Amsterdam, Metz & Co. and pottery workshop Ram in Arnhem.

40   Paul Hefting, "De Dienst voor Esthetische Vormgeving van de PTT," *Kunst en beleid in Nederland* 2 (1986): 85–124.

41   Paul Hefting, "Weldadigheid in 1923," *Jong Holland* 5, no. 1 (1989): 19.

42   On the study day devoted to Lion Cachet held on 10 June 1994 in the Museum Boymans-van Beuningen, the furniture conservator Pol Bruijs recounted that the use of material at the Van Wisselingh furniture atelier was extraordinarily extravagant; for example, in some instances even the interiors of the drawers were made of the same deluxe wood as the exterior of the piece of furniture. This waste of material did not occur in the seventeenth century.

43   On Lion Cachet's interiors, see Ir.S. van Ravesteyn, *De sierkunst op Nederlandsche passagiersschepen* (Rotterdam, 1924); Elsja Lewin, "Interieursculptuur," in *Lambertus Zijl 1866–1947*, Jan Jaap Heij, ed., (Assen, Eindhoven and Dordrecht, 1990), pp. 89–119; and Elsja Lewin, "De scheepsinterieurs," in *C.A. Lion Cachet 1864–1945*, Mechteld de Bois, ed., (Assen and Rotterdam, 1994), pp. 120–63.

44   On Nieuwenhuis, see Hanneke Olyslager, *Theo Nieuwenhuis. Sierkunstenaar en meubelontwerper (1866–1951)* (Rotterdam, 1991).

45   It is not certain, however, whether Lion Cachet's designs were executed by Van Wisselingh & Co.

46   The boudoir was the back room on the first floor of no. 50, Frederiksplein. See R.W.P. de Vries Jr., "C.A. Lion Cachet," *Elsevier's Geïllustreerd Maandschrift* 22 (1912): 206–7. No traces of gilding are left on the eternite panels mentioned by de Vries. After demolition of the houses in the 1950s, this room was transferred to Berlage's Exchange.

47   De Wit, *The Amsterdam School*, pp. 35–7.

48   *Ibid.*, pp. 37–41.

49   Jeroen Schilt and Jouke van der Werf, *Genootschap Architectura et Amicitia 1855–1990* (Rotterdam, 1992), pp. 234–5; *Wendingen 1918–1931. Documenti dell'arte olandese del Novecento* (Florence, 1982) – partly translated into Dutch: *Wendingen 1918–1931* (Leeuwarden: Gemeentelijk Museum Het Princessehof, 1982).

50   M. de Klerk, "De arbeid van den Driebond in verband met het meubel," *Architectura* 25 (1917): 298. See also Frans van Burkom, "Kunstvormgeving in Nederland," *Amsterdamse School 1910–1930* (Amsterdam: Stedelijk Museum, 1975), pp. 71–2.

51   Van Burkom, "Kunstvormgeving," p. 94.

52   Clear similarities with the Scheepvaarthuis can be seen in the Chilehaus (1923–24) in Hamburg, by Fritz Höger. The Dutch and German movements showed parallel tendencies.

53   The lamp resembles the one shown in figs. 115 and 116 in Helen Boterenbrood and Jürgen Prang, *Van der Mey en het Scheepvaarthuis* (The Hague, 1989), p. 99. In the drawing illustrated in fig. 115 a starfish can also be seen.

54   It is known, however, that De Klerk made rough sketches to indicate to the sculptors what kind of carvings the architects had in mind. See E.J. Lagerweij-Polak, *Hildo Krop: beeldhouwer* (The Hague, 1992), p. 25. De Klerk's contacts with the sculptors inspired him to start applying sculpted elements

to his furniture and buildings (for his architecture he often engaged Hildo Krop). See Frans van Burkom, *Michel de Klerk, 1884–1923: bouw- en meubelkunstenaar* (Rotterdam, 1990), p. 21.

55   Karin Gaillard and Betsy Dokter, eds., *Berlage en Amsterdam Zuid* (Amsterdam and Rotterdam, 1992).

56   W. Hartman, *et al.*, eds., *Algemeen Uitbreidingsplan Amsterdam 50 jaar* (Amsterdam, 1985).

57   Van Burkom, *Michel de Klerk*, p. 3.

58   From De Klerk's obituary by F.J. Zeegers, November 1923, quoted in van Burkom, *Michel de Klerk*, p. 7.

59   *Ibid.*, p. 23.

60   They have also been compared to more Dutch objects, such as skates or sleds. Comparable curls can be found in the copper ashpan of the fireplace by Lion Cachet discussed above. The relationship between Lion Cachet and De Klerk deserves further study.

61   Van Burkom, *Michel de Klerk*, p. 27. See also Hanneke Olyslager, "Indische invloed op het werk van Michel de Klerk," *Jong Holland* 4, no. 4 (1988): 21–31.

62   Olyslager, "Indische invloed," p. 28.

63   Van Burkom, *Michel de Klerk*, p. 27.

64   Although his official name was Theodoor Christiaan Adriaan, he used the initials T.A.C., and is commonly known as T.A.C. Colenbrander. See Boot, *Rozenburg*, pp. 24–5; see also Riet Neerincx, ed., *T.A.C. Colenbrander (1884–1930). Plateelbakkerij "Ram" te Arnhem (1921–1935)* (Arnhem, 1986), pp. 70–1. One hundred plates must have been made. Several copies are kept in Dutch museums, painted by different painters: Antoon Muller; no 18/100 (Gemeentemuseum, Arnhem). Identical copies are found in the Haags Gemeentemuseum: 36/100; Rijksmuseum, Amsterdam: 48/100 (painted by a certain B S); Museum Boymans-van Beuningen, Rotterdam: 87/100 (painted by Willem Elstrodt).

65   The Plateelbakkerij Ram was founded in 1921 by a group of Colenbrander's admirers, primarily for the execution of designs in decorative earthenware by Colenbrander – proof that he was considered to be an exceptional artist. A substantial number of designs and sketches from this period have been preserved and can be found in the Wolfsonian Collection (T.A.C. Colenbrander, TD1991.151.14–60) among others.

The English Compromise:
Modern Design and National Consciousness 1870-1940

Paul Greenhalgh

"The art of any country is the exponent of its social and political virtues . . . The art, or general productive and formative energy . . . is an exact exponent of its ethical life."

W.G. Collingwood, from *The Philosophy of Ornament*, 1883

In 1897, when Queen Victoria celebrated her Diamond Jubilee, she received many hundreds of gifts from her subjects. A large, lidded ceramic casket made by the firm of Della Robbia was among these (figs. 4.01 and 4.02).[1] Squat and octagonal, it stands ponderously on eight legs. Modeled in low relief, the eight sides are divided by caryatids bearing the names of the four nations which comprise the United Kingdom, interspersed with the four largest imperial possessions; England, India, Wales, Australia, Scotland, British Africa, Ireland and Canada. On the panels, sailing ships from a previous age bounce on turbulent seas, and each panel has a line from Shakespeare's *Richard II*:

> This Royal Throne of kings, this sceptered Isle,
>
> This fortress built by nature for herself,
>
> This happy breed of men, this little world,
>
> This precious stone set in the silver sea,
>
> Which serves it in the office of a wall,
>
> Or as a moat defensive to a house
>
> Against the envy of less happier lands.
>
> This blessed plot, this earth, this realm, this England.

Tudor roses embellish the upper rim,[2] and on the lid, St. George stands amid the coils of the serpent he has just vanquished. The object is a concentrated site of signs of English nationalism.

However, the meanings of the casket are not as obvious as they might at first seem. While the iconography was a strident and reactionary appraisal of the English heritage, the

111

manufacture of the casket was adventurous and experimental. In both the modeling and the application of glaze, there is a fluidity which was typical only of the more advanced, design-conscious potteries. Indeed, the freedom in the execution reflected a broadly humanitarian ethos which emanated from the radical end of English intellectual life.[3]

The Della Robbia Pottery was a progressive company founded largely on the principles of the Arts and Crafts movement and the Pre-Raphaelite Brotherhood.[4] Opened in 1894 in Birkenhead, Liverpool, it embraced the idea of design as a force for qualitative, moral change, using historical styles not only for aesthetic, but also for ideological meanings. The company was an innovative force in English design; its directors espoused a material and intellectual approach broadly similar to those of individuals and movements in Europe and the U.S.A. who are now identified as being pioneers on the road to modernism.

The casket thus appears now to be held in tension between the messages it conveys and the means by which it conveys them. It seems to contain two quite different personalities, which reside together in uncomfortable truce. Its consciously humble modeling and glazing and its Arts and Crafts heritage contradict the pomposity of its boasting, and subvert its imperial pretensions. It has an eccentric individualism about it which belies its public function. In the way it is made, it signals the future; its symbolism, however, celebrates the past. Such paradoxical combinations are often found in fin-de-siècle England.

At the turn of the century, Britain as a whole, and England in particular, visibly began the traumatic shift from being a dominant world force in the imperial and economic spheres, to being one nation among others.[5] As W.G. Collingwood suggests above, the arts of a culture mirror its condition in a wider sense. The Della Robbia casket, along with thousands of other decorative objects, encapsulated the socio-cultural climate of late Victorian and Edwardian England. Its apparent contrariness was derived from the world around it. J.B. Priestley described the period as "A time when a lot of people are trying to cling to the past while many others are trying to hurry themselves and everybody else into a future of their own devising. Most of the adjectives tacked onto this age – spacious, leisurely, and the rest – seem to me quite wrong. It was an era of tensions between extremes."[6]

These "tensions between extremes" developed first in the political, economic, and social spheres, but they soon surfaced in design, and especially in work which attempted to deal with the contemporary world. Designers were pulled simultaneously by sets of opposing factors; between the past and the future, the Left and the Right, and nationalism and internationalism. From the end of the nineteenth century until World War II, whenever designers wrestled with modernity, these factors entered into consideration. The forms and images they used would continually change, but these larger, ideological issues would affect them just as they had the designers of the Della Robbia casket. Modernism implied the

Fig. 4.03

The Crystal Palace (1850 – 51; Joseph Paxton [British, 1801–65], architect), London

From *Tallis's History and Description of the Crystal Palace and the Exhibition of the World's Industry in 1851*
Illustrated by Beard, Mayall, et al.
Printed and published by John Tallis & Co.,
London and New York, [1852]
10⅞ x 8⅝ x 1⅝ inches (27.6 x 21.9 x 4.5 cm)
85.2.140.1

future, and the future had to be characterized in a very particular way for a nation which believed its greatest successes to be behind it.

The material essence of English life as it existed in 1870 owed everything to the size and scope of industry and empire. On an ever-increasing basis from that date, however, the country's industries faced daunting rivals.[7] By 1900, the voracious laissez-faire Liberalism which was the driving force behind the material success of England in the middle decades of the nineteenth century was no longer the confident force it had been. Free trade and industrial advance had made possible the Great Exhibition of 1851, the shimmering glass of the Crystal Palace representing in itself the first phase of modernization which would eventually transform the world (fig. 4.03). By 1900, however, many nations had built Crystal Palaces of their own, supported by growing national economies.[8] Britain also felt threatened by the developing desires of other nations to acquire overseas empires, demonstrated most brutally by "the scramble for Africa" of the 1880s.[9] Still a dominant world power with vast resources at its disposal, Britain was nevertheless in relative decline from the last years of the century. Edward VII's Britain (1901–10) was a far less self-assured one than Victoria's had been.

Thus the economic and imperial rise of the U.S.A., Japan, and various mainland European nations corresponded with Britain's slide from grace; from the beginning of the twentieth century, the space between Britain and these nations grew. With some justification therefore, the English related industrial modernization abroad to their own decline. They also tended to connect the cultural manifestations of this larger process of modernization – the modern movements in the arts – with their demise.[10] Modernism, especially Continental and American versions of it, heralded a new world in which the English were by no means sure they wished to participate. This is the context within which English modern design is best understood.

Concern with national identity grew significantly in this atmosphere of uncertainty. Nations which are politically and economically stable tend to be less overtly concerned with national identity than less stable ones. Rapidly ascending or declining nations, or those suffering coercive threats from outside, often become involved in the attempt to characterize collectively the peoples within their boundaries. Nationalism is, among other things, a defense mechanism against the outside world.[11]

Thus, the late Victorian and Edwardian eras were crucial for the formation of what we might refer to as "Englishness." The English fashioned themselves for the new century, surrounding themselves with ideas and objects which allowed them best to cope with the daunting prospect of the modern world. As the laissez-faire advance became a protectionist siege, the question of what it was to be an Englishman became all the more important. As Richard Shannon has noted: "The quip that all the oldest English traditions were invented in the last quarter of the nineteenth century has great point."[12]

In 1909, the writer Stewart Dick acknowledged the need to reappraise the way in which English traditions were personified. "John Bull," the legendary symbol of Englishness, could not, for him, continue to stand for the nation, "for, representing as he does the bluff farmer of Georgian days, he belongs to the old era of agriculture and hand-labour, which has passed away. But in these shifting and transitory times we have not been able to evolve a new type to take his place."[13] Rather than engaging with these "transitory times," however, Dick recommended a vision of England built around "the old English cottage."[14] History was used as a support by writers who were interested in the collective characteristics of England's inhabitants. The historian Henry Thomas Buckle set this trend by being one of the first to suggest that historic events affected traits in the personality: "As early as the eleventh century [circumstances] began to affect our national character, and had assisted in imparting to it that sturdy boldness . . . those habits of foresight, and of cautious reserve, to which the English mind owes its leading peculiarities."[15]

Such a cultural environment was bound to impinge upon the design world. One of the first and most interesting aspects of this was, from around 1890, a rise in consumer concern for history. This was evident not so much through the taste for previous styles – this was far

114

from new — but as a celebration of the past in and for itself. It was expressed particularly through a growth of interest in antiques. In 1908, the entrepreneur and critic H.C. Marillier observed that "The craze is all for that is old and rare — not necessarily for what is beautiful, but simply for what is old."[16]

From 1890, English sections at national and international exhibitions began to contain far larger sections devoted to historical examples, the number of private galleries specializing in antiques grew steadily, and a sizable literature developed to support the prospective patron (fig. 4.04).[17] The love of antiques was symptomatic of attitudes toward design. Alongside other sections of English society, consumers of the decorative arts began to seek solace in the past.

The preference for antiques had not always been a feature of either English designers or their patrons. Between 1840 and 1900, English contemporary design was extremely healthy, and a major influence in many areas of the world. Two main sources can be credited with forming the basis of this influence. The first was what might be loosely termed "Mediaevalism." This implies the range of activity emanating from the Gothic Revival, including those designers and writers connected with the Pre-Raphaelite Brotherhood and the Arts and Crafts movement. The second was the Design Reform movement, which contained within it a wide range of critics and designers who were committed to raising the standard of design practice in Britain, principally through the connection of art with industry. The former was essentially a romantic response to the condition of the world, the latter was a rationalist one. Both

Fig. 4.04
William and Mary Room
Historic Loan Collection of British Furniture
Section, Franco-British Exhibition, London, 1908
From F.G. Dumas, *Franco-British Exhibition: Illustrated Review* (London, 1908), p. 255
Paul Greenhalgh

enjoyed international success largely through the trade base which the British had built up, and the influence of English as a key language for the dissemination of ideas. The most marked success of the rationalist reformers was in the realm of institutions; the Royal Society of Arts, the great international exhibitions, the schools of design, and several of Britain's national museums owe their foundation to the reformers' pressure.[18]

Designers associated with the Arts and Crafts movement are important principally for the way they moved away from this historical eclecticism. The use of motifs derived from nature, in conjunction with vernacular and non-European (especially Japanese) forms, allowed them to develop decidedly new shapes. C.F.A. Voysey (fig. 4.05), W.A.S. Benson (fig. 4.06), and E.W. Godwin, for example, effectively made nature into a convention capable of replacing previous styles.

Godwin's furniture is especially innovative. He was one of the first furniture designers to understand the compositional potential of Japanese art and design. The prototype for his sideboard of 1876 (fig. 4.07) was made for his own use in 1867, little more than a decade after Japan had been opened to the West. Japanese art gave him the stimulus to expand his formal and symbolic range beyond accepted conventions for English furniture. He manipulated planes rather than masses, the cupboards themselves "hanging," as it were, within a linear scaffold, allowing him to create a free-form arrangement of open and closed spaces. The domination of horizontal and vertical lines reveals a formal rigor which anticipates later movements in the history of furniture. The designer shows his knowledge of European conventions, yet the ambiance of his sideboard is one of unfettered, sophisticated play.[19]

Fig. 4.06 See Cat. 14
Chandelier, c. 1909
Designed by W.A.S. Benson

Fig. 4.05
Furnishing textile
From the W. Ward Higgs residence, London, 1896
Designed by Charles Francis Annesley Voysey
(British, 1857–1941)
Manufactured by Alexander Morton & Co., Darvel, Scotland
Retailed by Liberty & Co. Ltd., London
Cotton
31 x 34 inches (78.7 x 86.4 cm)
85.14.2

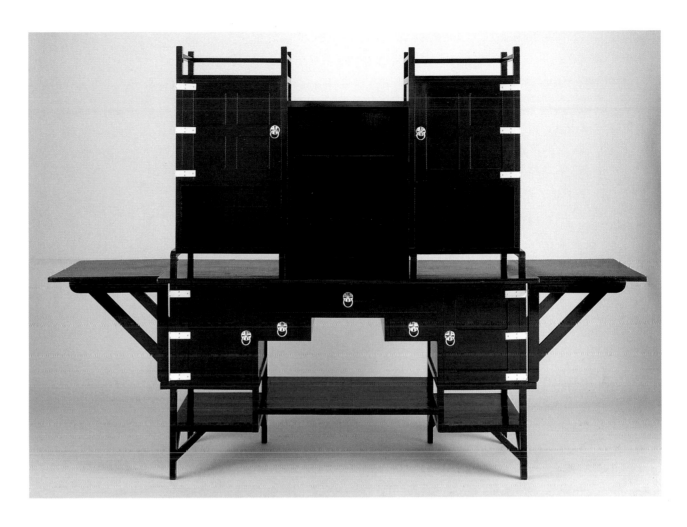

Fig. 4.07 See Cat. 4
Sideboard, c.1867
Designed by E.W. Godwin

If anything, design reformer Christopher Dresser was even more daring in his willingness to utilize new sources. Professionally qualified as a botanist, he applied biological principles to design, creating organic forms of a simple yet powerful intensity. As did Godwin, he owed a considerable debt to Japanese art. Indeed, he was one of the most important of European designers in this regard. He visited Japan in 1876 and wrote extensively about Japanese art and culture, eventually acting in a quasi-official capacity for the Japanese government itself.[20]

Perhaps Dresser's main contribution was his commitment to designing for industry. Believing that innovation was the key to industrial success, he insisted throughout his life that "the beautiful has a commercial or money value."[21] One of the most prolific of his generation, he produced thousands of novel shapes and patterns. Of all the materials he designed in, his metalwork remains his most remarkable achievement (fig. 4.08). The elimination of surface decoration, and the use of rigorously simplified profiles, have led many historians to position this work at the beginnings of the modern movement in design.

While this is rather an anachronistic thing to do, the visual reasoning is clear enough. The abstract, pod-like forms do not appear to be of the nineteenth century.[22]

The perceived strength of English design is evident in contemporary arts magazines throughout the world. At home, design innovation was enthusiastically backed by a specialist literature; starting from the mid-century, there was an extraordinary expansion in the publication of books. By 1880, several publishing houses focussed almost completely on the history and theory of design. B.T. Batsford, for example, boasted a list of 103 books on the subject, and Chapman and Hall had fifty-seven titles available by the turn of the century.[23]

Taken collectively, this activity constituted a major development in the visual arts. Perhaps the most impressive feature of it was its lack of parochialism; the products have a determined sense of liberal cosmopolitanism. The designers believed themselves to be at the center of an international arena, and it showed in their work.

Innovative design can prosper only if it is supported by speculative and informed patronage. In the nineteenth century, such patronage came almost exclusively from the upper middle class. The wealth this class enjoyed also gave it the confidence to allow, and even encourage, that most important of ingredients in advanced art of any kind: critique. This partly explains the comfort of those who had their raison d'être in industry and capital supporting movements which openly criticized industry and the economy. Similarly, only those who had nothing to fear from the outside world could easily accept the notion of internationalism.

Innovative design also demands a certain cultural and demographic flux. It occurs most frequently when economies are expanding, continually developing and changing the socio-cultural picture. At least, this is the case with designs which are actually realized rather than remaining on the drawing board. The conditions in Britain for adventurous designers were thus ideal up to the last decade of the century. Laissez-faire economics, coupled with industrial and imperial advance, simultaneously provided stability and change. But alongside the confident experimentation which was the final flowering of advanced English design grew the shrill jingoism which was not only a dominant feature of English national life into the new century, but came to play its part in the reorientation of English design. At first, the appearance of things was not affected as much as the ideas which underpinned them.

Through much of the nineteenth century, the main intellectual driving force behind Mediaevalism was a moral idealism, which is usually identified as broadly being on the political Left. Inspired principally by the ideas of A.W.N. Pugin, and later by John Ruskin and William Morris, the "Pugin-Morris Line" provided an alternative socio-cultural outlook to the one which celebrated mechanized, rationalist, capitalist modes of behavior.[24]

Progress was the key concept which stood against the Pugin-Morris Line, providing philosophical (and moral) justification for the voracious material activities of the British.

Fig. 4.08 See Cat. 3
Soup tureen
Model no. 12780, 1885–86
Designed by C. Dresser

Progress implied an evolutionist, deterministic solution to society's ills, one which suggested that civilization, through the use of its ingenuity, was capable of infinite improvement.[25] The aforementioned Crystal Palace was its citadel; and progress was the raison d'être of the Design Reform movement.

Outside the rarefied atmosphere of high intellectual circles, however, Mediaevalism and progress did not always appear to be quite so incompatible. Among the industrial middle classes, a popular version of Mediaevalism had existed since the early nineteenth century. This was essentially an unstructured version of the romantic idea, based on an imagined vision of the age of chivalry. It was not an alternative to progressive capitalism, so much as a weekend rest from it. It provided a fictional purity for its patrons, a purity which was, despite its unreality, psychologically important in times of unbridled aggression and pressure in business life. In their patronage, these classes often went beyond superficial interest. They bought some of the most significant products of the Gothic Revival, Pre-Raphaelite, and Arts and Crafts movements. It is no coincidence that many of the best collections of these movements are in the industrial north.[26]

Indeed, these movements in themselves were not constructed solely around the idea of *opposition*, but contained also the idea of *alternative* lifestyle.[27] They were thus deeply attractive to those who wished to construct alternative environments to the ones they normally inhabited. Ironically, therefore, Mediaevalists found themselves simultaneously attacking industrial rationalism, and providing an escape from it, for those who had helped create and maintain it.

In the closing decade of the nineteenth century, both "popular" and "high" Mediaevalism received a boost. *Progress* began to lose its charm for those in government who had previously espoused it, as other nations began to progress faster than the British. The falling on hard times of laissez-faire economics thus led to the further strengthening of the traditionalist lobby in the cultural sphere. The popular historian George Sturt was particularly eloquent in joining the theme of anti-industrialism to those of race and the past: "For England is – what shall I say? The stream, the tradition, the living continuity of public opinion, public conduct, public intercourse and behaviour of English people towards one another and towards hills and valleys, and waving trees and the fair sunshine of this island."[28]

Mediaevalism derived much of its imagery from the Tudor Age, as this was identified as the one in which the foundations of English culture were laid: the Empire, the Royal Navy, the United Kingdom, the Church of England, the language (epitomized by Shakespeare).[29] The "Hearts of Oak" mentality took center stage, and God's Englishmen once again braced themselves against adversity.

The Design Reform movement, which had valiantly introduced art to industry during the nineteenth century, was ominously quiet in the first decade of the twentieth by virtue of its unfashionable "progressiveness." Christopher Dresser was still alive, but his lessons were being emphatically ignored. His cosmopolitanism and commitment to industry were out of keeping with the new climate.

Well-established critics openly referred to the Arts and Crafts movement in nationalistic terms in the early years of the new century. A two-stage process facilitated this approach. The Art and Crafts movement, and all the major makers associated with it, were first de-politicized. Then their products were effectively re-politicized on the nationalist Right. The fact that such sentiments were always present in parts of the Mediaevalist camp made the process so much the easier. Indeed, some makers had never been on the left; C.F.A. Voysey, for example, was not at all uncomfortable with this new visage for English design.

It would be wrong, however, to suggest that the morality of the Pugin-Morris Line was ever eliminated. Oppositions and confusions accepted, it still provided the single strongest intellectual thrust of the late Victorian Age: Utopian Socialism with a conservative agenda. By 1900, therefore, the Arts and Crafts movement could cast its light in two directions at once, and indeed, its survival as a force in British design was based on this ability. It had legitimate claims on the one hand to being an idealist, radical, Left-wing response to society's ills which had inspired innovative design all over Europe, and on the other to being a traditionalist, vernacular representation of the national temperament. Conservative critics, a few years into the new century, thus had the double advantage of being able to attack the current European modernism (Art Nouveau), while proudly claiming that the English provided the initial inspiration for it:

> The great "revival" in Germany, in Belgium, and other countries, based on the artistic conscience that was first awakened by our Arts and Crafts Society, soon to be developed abroad into the amazing and generally distressing examples of the so-called "New-Art", has left England practically untouched and untainted. The art-at-any-price that has made the chaste modern dwelling of the German aesthete a place of exquisite and elaborately contrived discomfort and, usually, of ugliness, has practically no counter-part in Great Britain.[30]

Hatred of Art Nouveau was often more shrill than this; it was variously portrayed as "effeminate,"[31] decadent and foreign, a "delirious art of men raring to do something new, oblivious in their rage alike of use and beauty."[32] The critic Aymer Vallance, writing in 1903, thought it was no less than a "disastrous epidemic," and hoped only that "our British stolidity and self-sufficiency can save us as a nation from this foreign contagion."[33] If Art Nouveau had ever really stood much chance of success in England, its association with decadence (as exemplified by Oscar Wilde and Aubrey Beardsley, both of whom were understood to be associated with it) finished it off.[34]

Fig. 4.09
**The King and Queen Public House, Brighton,
Sussex, England, c. 1925**
Zul, Sussex

Through a process of elimination then, during the Edwardian years, the Arts and Crafts movement was the only force in the English design world which could begin to carry the label "modern." Indeed, some of the purest Arts and Crafts episodes still had to be enacted, and purveyors of the original ethic were productive and vocal as late as 1940. In other parts of the market, however, ethics were not high on the agenda and interest in modernity less so. At the cheaper end, for example, Mock-Tudor began to invade middle-class housing estates all over England, and became the accepted architectural style for pubs and hotels (fig. 4.09). Here, the appropriation was complete; any vestige of moral idealism had gone, leaving a generalized, mostly benign, nationalism.

The complication of meanings was thus at its most emphatic at the time when the nature of modernism became a subject of feverish debate all over Europe and the U.S.A. But the issue in England by now had less to do with the control of the new, as with who controlled the meanings of the old. In literature, the "thees" and "thous" of Socialists abounded, as Utopias were dredged from the past to serve as templates for a better future. At the same time, the chivalric heritage served nationalists and imperialists who could take heart in what Kipling called the "land of our birth, our faith, our pride."

Fig. 4.10 See Cat. 184
"The Party Fight and the New Party or
Liberalism and Toryism disturbed by the
appearance of Socialism," 1894
W. Crane

In the Edwardian world of things, the Della Robbia casket comes to make sense; its contrariness is explicable as a container of opposing ideologies which had come to share the same cultural idiom (figs. 4.01 and 4.02). The crude directness of the subject matter – St. George, the Navy, Shakespeare, roses, the Empire – shroud the casket in propaganda and lend it a distinctive loudness. The former cultural confidence which had reduced the need to proclaim the national heritage, and which had induced a toleration of experimentation, had given way to a nervous boasting of past glories. The nostalgia for a more benevolent Mediaevalism can still be perceived in the casket, however, as can a sense of freedom in the technical treatment. This duality makes it an exemplar of the way the English would deal with modernism in the future.

The combination of values contained in objects could occasionally be witnessed in the designers who made them. Walter Crane, a seminal figure in English design, provides an especially good example in this regard. He disliked what he understood to be the "strange and weird combinations of line"[35] of Art Nouveau, and openly expressed his unsureness of the internationalist stance of many Art Nouveau designers. His influence in major institutional circles contributed to the retardation of that movement, and consequently of the modern movement, in England.[36] He was sympathetic to the cause of Empire, participated in various openly imperial cultural events, and was a founder member of the Imperial Arts League. Yet in his political life he was an international Socialist, and made this plain in much of his graphic work (fig. 4.10). He was against what he considered to be the misuse of history, and was heavily committed to the idea of strong design for the contemporary world. He believed, however, that this was best achieved through an ethnically based historicism. Both in his intellectual outlook and in his design work, he offers a fascinating example of a man caught between different worlds.

A more renowned example will make the point better. William Morris was reinvented after his death in 1896 by, among others, his own company, which received the ultimate establishment accolade, when it was asked to decorate the British Pavilion at the Paris exhibition of 1900.[37] More than anything, this was a sign of the complete acceptability of the Morris style and idiom in the nationalist context. The Company was further celebrated with an entire section to itself at the Franco-British Exhibition of 1908 (fig. 4.11). His politics trimmed away, Morris himself was fêted as "the new Chippendale."[38] In 1911 his official

Fig. 4.11
Morris & Company installation
Franco-British Exhibition, London, 1908
From F.G. Dumas, *Franco-British Exhibition: Illustrated Review* (London, 1908), p. 203
Paul Greenhalgh

Fig. 4.12

Mahogany inlaid commode with brass mountings
Franco-British Exhibition, London, 1908
Designed by William Arthur Smith Benson
(British, 1854–1924)
Made by Morris & Company, London, England
From F.G. Dumas, *Franco-British Exhibition: Illustrated Review*
(London, 1908), p. 206
Paul Greenhalgh

biography, published by the Company, also ignored his Socialist affiliations, referring only to his idealism, which, it claimed, was the cause of his death.[39]

After 1900, the products of Morris & Company became examples of competing world views. Previous ideals were evident in the surfaces and work methods; the bold simplicity and attention to detail in, for example, furniture designed for the Company by W.A.S. Benson or M.E. McCartney were as impressive as ever (fig. 4.12). This was tempered, however, in the same pieces by a luxurious eclecticism which puts them closer in spirit to the extravagance of Art Moderne than to the heritage of Pugin. Individual objects were now struggling to combine the elements of the Right and the Left, the old and the new.

The Great War brought an end to the "Long Nineteenth Century."[40] The situation after then was even more complex, when ideas from the modern movement in design began to drift slowly across the English Channel. European moderns had largely inherited the moral theories of Ruskin and Morris, but had determined to dispense with the past, the vernacular, and the hand-made, in favor of internationalism, humane factory production, and (usually) Socialism. This agenda caused suspicion and outrage across the English design spectrum. All aesthetic and political sects – Left, Center, and Right – could effortlessly find fault with such a combination, discovering their bêtes noires in different parts of the modernist conception and process. The English had reached that xenophobic point in their intellectual evolution where they found themselves united only in what they disliked.

English modern design was never going to form an unswaying march toward Futuropolis. Just as Britain's economic and political roles came into question, so in the design world, manufacturers continuously responded to the changing conditions in society in general and the marketplace in particular, paying due regard to issues beyond modernist idealism.

Since few people in the relevant governmental circles, or in quasi-official bodies such as the Chambers of Commerce or the Schools of Art and Design, had any real ideas regarding the meaning and implications of modern design, the potential for direct leadership on the matter was lost. Especially in the inter-war years, when the Modern Movement came to maturity in Europe and the U.S.A., the British government, when it was concerned with design at all, tended to attach it rather crudely to its agencies involved with selling or with propaganda. Therefore, when design was an official issue, one of two motives was present. First, it might have a role in the promotion of goodwill toward Britain in the international arena. Especially at expositions and trade fairs, objects were selected for their ability to suggest Britishness. Second, design sold things. If either of these criteria was met by a design idiom, it might be used.[41]

The first of these left its mark most powerfully on the imagery which became internationally associated with English design in these years. During the 1930s, the Department of Overseas Trade actively worked at constructing the iconography of quintessential Englishness, both to sell goods and to respond to the increasing amounts of hostile propaganda emanating from Europe's totalitarian regimes. An extraordinary document entitled *The National Projection*, written by Stephen Tallents in 1932, actually went as far as to produce a list of things which could be used to illustrate the idea of Englishness.[42] He included the monarchy, Parliamentary institutions, the Royal Navy, the English Bible, the works of Shakespeare, the Derby, the Grand National, Henley, the Boat Race, Test Matches, the Trooping of the Colour, the Lord Mayor of London, Piccadilly, Bond Street, Big Ben, Oxford, *The Times*, *Punch*, the English countryside, English villages, fox-hunting, English servants, English bloodstock, pedigree stock, gardening, tailoring. These symbols of England later formed the core of the propaganda effort during World War II. They projected a nation of stable, rural charms, of stiff upper lips, chivalry, sound values, and ancient institutions. Much of this imagery had been in general circulation since 1890.

To be fair to the English, however, they were not alone in their incomprehension of the underlying principles of modernism. Most Europeans in the inter-war period had neither an understanding of, nor use for, the Modern Movement in design. This was dramatically demonstrated by the Paris Exposition des Arts Décoratifs et Industriels Modernes of 1925, the famous Art Deco show, at which the organizers made "modern inspiration" a condition of entry, and affirmed in the requirements that "copies, imitations and counterfeits of antique styles are rigorously excluded."[43] The Americans modestly decided that they had no modernism to offer and so did not participate. They need not have worried. Most other nations, companies, and individuals invented styles which showed just how widely the term could be interpreted. Few, however, were as bizarre in their logic as the British.

They built a pavilion in the Indian style, or at least what they thought was the Indian style (fig. 4.13).[44] The architects Easton and Robertson, one imagines, were following the well-established principle of using exoticism to denote the modern. The strategy had been used by avant-gardistes for fifty years. Since Africa, Japan, and Oceania had all contributed to various modernisms, the British could feel confident in using India in the same way. They believed that they were shrewdly killing two birds with one stone; their pavilion was simultaneously celebrating modernity and presenting the nation's greatest imperial prize.

If modernism is exclusively identified with the purest products of the various European modern movements, the English design world produced very little. Rather, it generated a series of responses to the call of the modern. The handful of buildings and products devised in England which were examples of unadulterated modern movement design were invariably made by émigrés, or those directly under their tutelage. Berthold Lubetkin, Walter Gropius, Serge Chermayeff, and Piet Mondrian were all resident at one time or another, and all were notable for being outsiders. They inspired the production of

Fig. 4.13
British Pavilion
(Easton & Robertson, architects)
Exposition Internationale des Arts Décoratif
et Industriels Modernes, Paris, 1925
From *Encyclopédie des arts décoratifs et industriels modernes au XXème siècle*, vol. 2 (Paris: Imprimerie Nationale, Office Central d'Éditions et de Librairie, [1927]), pl. LXXVII
XB1990.35

designs, books, and manifestoes by various splinter groups, such as M.A.R.S. (Modern Architecture Research Group) (fig. 4.14), but this indigenous activity was negligible. When the English attempted to look modern, they did not usually feel obliged to cling too faithfully to the ideological rigor of the Bauhaus.

The earlier, international standing of English advanced design had been shattered, first by the general loss of confidence in establishment circles in the idea of progressive design reform, and second, by the shuffling of the Arts and Crafts movement from the Left to the Right. This shuffling was the more significant factor, as it introduced into the core of advanced design thinking the idea that the meaning of a thing can be transformed without changing its form.

Two broad approaches to modern design in England between the wars can be discerned. The first and more obvious of these was the one which simply attempted to preserve Arts and Crafts values into the new century. Invariably, those who harbored these values with any strictness considered themselves to be moderns, and some looked positively on developments on the Continent.

Perhaps the two purest examples of the preservation of this spirit are Bernard Leach and Eric Gill. Having spent many years in Japan, Leach founded a pottery in St. Ives in 1930. In 1940 he published his seminal work, *A Potter's Book*, which not only outlined the

Fig. 4.14
Cover
New Architecture . . . , 1938
Designed by Edward McKnight Kauffer
(American, 1890–1954)
Published by MARS (Modern Architecture Research Group)
and New Burlington Galleries, London
7½ x 11 inches (19.1 x 27.9 cm)
83.2.1021

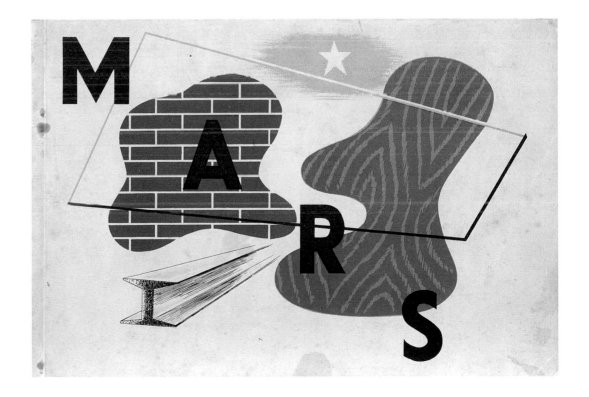

appropriate way to design and make pottery, but was also a philosophical treatise on how to live one's life in relation to the work process. By using the term "artist-craftsman," he sought to shift the status of the crafts much in the way that his Arts and Crafts forebears had done. His pots, his book, and his chosen lifestyle have been the single most important influence on twentieth-century studio ceramics (fig. 4.15).[45]

Eric Gill, in his multi-disciplinary approach to art practice, in his bohemian, rural existence, and in his very public antagonism toward modern urban life, went further than most Arts and Crafts thinkers. Perhaps the only element which lifts him out of the nineteenth century – and this would apply to Leach also – was his interest in, and use of, formal modernist strategies in his work. His conscious archaism was combined with a radical twentieth-century aesthetic (fig. 4.16). Included in a list he drew up of things he approved of were Plain Song, Folk Songs, tools, beer, animals, calligraphy and "most moderns."[46] The combination is starkly revealing: rurality, tradition, the vernacular, and modernism.

As well as being celebrated in this overt way, Arts and Crafts values permeated the oeuvres of designers in more indirect, though no less fundamental ways. In 1915, the Design in Industries Association was formed with a view to improving the quality of design in contemporary industry. A pressure group with an initial membership of 199 members, it

soon became a major force in British design. But despite the fact that its raison d'être was the improvement of industry, it was largely dominated by what was, to all intents and purposes, a craft ethic. By insisting that the production process involved ethical as well as practical decision-making, and by associating good design with the moral well-being of the workforce, the D.I.A. inevitably found itself disproportionately supportive of hand-made and short-run products.

The life and work of Gordon Russell exemplifies English high design through this period. Influential enough to dominate the Royal College of Art and to be selected by the British government as adviser to the Wartime Utility Furniture scheme, Russell was remarkably close to the Arts and Crafts movement in most aspects of his outlook. In an article of 1946, while advocating the need for better industrial designers, he reaffirmed his lifelong belief "that it is essential for [the designer] to have been able to use hand-tools, as in no other way can he get into intimate contact with his material. Use a hand-plane or an adze on various woods and the special qualities of each one become apparent to you."[47] His blanket chest of 1927 is a prime study in nineteenth-century ethical aesthetics (fig. 4.17). In the form of a sea chest, the whole is constructed, following Pugin's lead, without the use of glue for the joints – it is pegged. Made of simple oak planks, its lid is attached by Tudoresque

Fig. 4.17 See Cat. 26
Blanket chest
Design no. 503, 1927
Designed by G. Russell

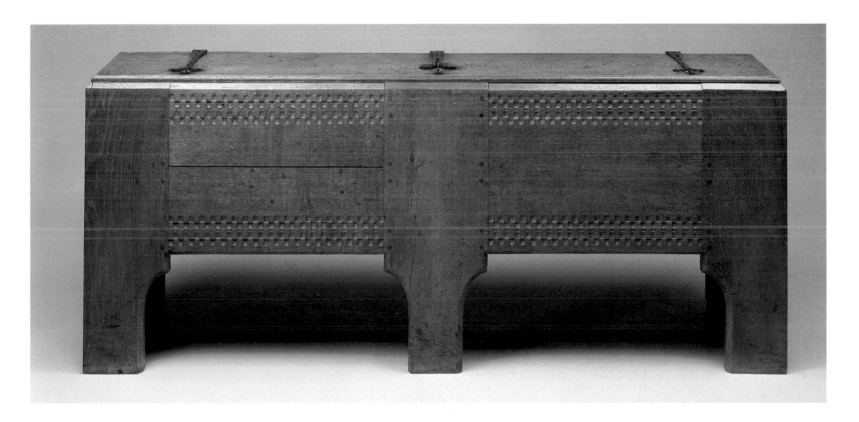

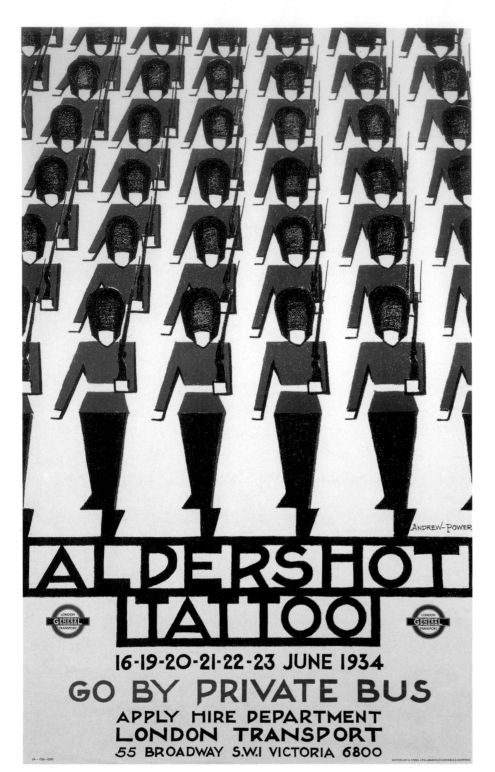

Fig. 4.18

Poster

Aldershot Tattoo. June 1934.

Go By Private Bus, 1934

Designed by Sybil Andrews

(British, b. Canada, 1898–1992)

and Cyril Power (British, 1872–1951)

Printed by Waterlow & Sons, Ltd., London
Published by London General Transport, London
Commercial color lithograph
39¹⁵⁄₁₆ x 24¹³⁄₁₆ inches (101.3 x 63.0 cm)
Marks: obverse, printed in black, center right "ANDREW-POWER."
84.4.610

Fig. 4.19

Mug

Commemorating the coronation

of Edward VIII, 1936

Designed by Eric William Ravilious

(British, 1903–42)
Made by Josiah Wedgwood & Sons Ltd., Etruria,
Staffordshire, England, 1937
Glazed earthenware
4 x 5¾ x 4⅜ inches (10.2 x 14.6 x 11.1 cm)
Marks: underside, printed underglaze in black crown mark/
"TO COMMEMORATE/THE CORONATION/OF HIS MAJESTY/
KING EDWARD VIII/1937/WEDGWOOD/MADE IN ENGLAND/
DESIGNED BY RAVILIOUS"; painted in red "CL6203H";
painted in green "H" and "1"
XX1991.590

Fig. 4.20

"Burslem" vase

Boat Race Day, **1938**

Designed by Eric William Ravilious

(British, 1903–42)
Made by Josiah Wedgwood & Sons Ltd., Etruria,
Staffordshire, England
Glazed earthenware
10¼ x 8½ x 8½ inches (26.0 x 21.6 x 21.6 cm)
Marks: underside, printed underglaze in black square
"Designed/by Eric/Ravilious"; impressed outside of square
"WEDGWOOD/MADE IN ENGLAND/H"
85.7.187

hinges, hammered on with brad nails. Oak, wooden pegs, Tudor England, the sea: the addition of these elements makes the chest into a piece of self-consciously English design.

Russell, however, would have been equally conscious of another aspect to this object. The form is simple and plain, having a functional clarity which is very much of the modern period, and lines of checkered carving on the front that could only have been of the "Deco" years. The designer has thus gently coaxed his object into the twentieth century. The chest would be less remarkable if Russell and his oeuvre were not so closely associated with design innovation in England.

The second way to achieve a modern style was to appropriate it. This usually entailed the borrowing of the formal language of one of the European modernisms widely available after World War I. Cubism, Futurism, and the De Stijl group were frequent models. An interesting feature of this kind of activity was the clear dominance of the two-dimensional arts, and especially painting, as sources. For many, the design process seemed to entail no more than the application of two-dimensional images to the surfaces of three-dimensional objects.

With impressive confidence, designers ignored and removed the theories which originally accompanied the forms they borrowed. Not for the English were the violence of Marinetti, the anarchism of Van Doesburg, or the poignant musings of Apollinaire. The shapes were the thing. A broad acceptance existed among those interested in modernity that form and narrative could be mutually exclusive, an acceptance that had been in evidence since the original principles of the Arts and Crafts movement had been distanced from its styles. The appropriation of modernist forms and their combination with English symbolism was essentially the same process: progressive form used to contain a regressive content.

Often, the messages flatly contradicted, rather than merely ignored, the formal and ethical intent of the artist/designer who had invented the original style, and were frequently close to the ones suggested by Stephen Tallents in his list. The graphic designers Sybil Andrews and Cyril Power, for example, were prone to use modernist formalism for imagery which often had little to do with the modern. In their poster *Go by Private Bus* (fig. 4.18), the Queen's Guards, the traditional pride of Britain's army, are arranged into a geometricized grid which was learned from post-Cubist exponents of abstraction.

Eric Ravilious, the celebrated illustrator and graphic artist, produced a number of ceramic decorations in the inter-war period for the Wedgwood Company. His formal approach was influenced by Cubism, Vorticism, and the various schools of abstract art then current. His lightness of touch imbued his work with a light *joie de vivre* not unlike the decorative work of Dufy. Yet he used this lyrical and eclectic style to depict the most staid and traditional of scenes. Among other things, he produced decorations depicting the 1937

131

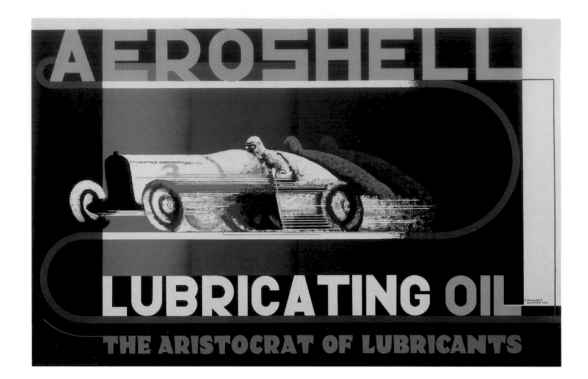

Fig. 4.21 See Cat. 105
Poster
*Aeroshell Lubricating Oil: The
Aristocrat of Lubricants*, 1932
Designed by E. McKnight Kauffer

Coronation on a tea mug (fig. 4.19) and the Oxford-Cambridge University Boat Race on a vase (fig. 4.20). The shapes of the vessels are direct derivations from standard traditional forms, the events depicted are the mythic stuff of English life, but the style is post-Fauvist Ecole de Paris.

In similar fashion, Edward McKnight Kauffer used a lyrical post-Cubism to serve various purposes within the world of commercial posters.[48] The angular, flat, geometric forms which characterize his style are in the spirit of Section d'Or Cubists such as Amédée Ozenfant and Jacques Villon. When he used combinations of illustration, photographs, and words, he divided the picture plane with lines and geometric "frames" which created a complex, shallow space. This structure allowed him to integrate the disparate pieces of text and image into a whole (fig. 4.21). Masterly as these compositions could be, however, the disjuncture between subject matter and formal values was often as wide in his work as it was elsewhere in the English design world.

In Bloomsbury, where the avant garde was more usually associated with the fine arts, a powerful formalism evolved which enabled practitioners to dissociate absolutely their work from the immediacy of politics and society. Duncan Grant and Vanessa Bell, working for the Omega Workshops, espoused an asocial universalism which largely came out of the ideas of Roger Fry and Clive Bell.[49] This allowed them to put a space between form and meaning which few European moderns attempted or believed to be desirable. Bell and Fry's theory of "significant form" was, in effect, a strategy for the decontextualization of art objects, to allow them to affect the intellectual sensibilities via the retina alone.[50] To suggest merely that they absorbed the influence of Paris would understate the case; rather, they attempted to philosophically dislodge it from events in the social world.

Grant and Bell applied the painterly language of French Cubism to domestic interiors and objects (fig. 4.22). They were influenced by the work of Robert and Sonia Delaunay, both in the color range and form the Delaunays used, and in the directness with which they applied these to objects of everyday use (fig. 4.23).

Keith Murray's ceramic designs for Wedgwood were seen at the time, and have been presented subsequently, as being examples of modernist thinking in Britain in the 1930s. Indeed, his designs are probably the only readily acknowledged modernism to have come out of the Staffordshire pottery industry before World War II. The sleek, clean forms he devised imply the precision and finish of machine work, with colors which are deliberately synthetic. There is a certain purity about the designs which reveals a knowledge of the Modern Movement (fig. 4.24).[51] Yet, some of the objects in the range contain narratives which evoke the mythology of English national life. The form of his tankard, for example, is quasi-Tudor, and its principal association is with the non-urban drinking tavern (fig. 4.25). It is further immersed in English myth through the common association of tankards with the idea of commemoration, especially of events surrounding the Royal Family. Indeed, with added inscriptions, this was a role that the Murray tankard later came to fulfill.[52] It embodies the "Hearts of Oak" mentality, a looking back to a halcyon past which was always one step beyond empirical testing.

If the strategy of the designers was to combine opposing narratives and forms, supportive critics dealt with modernism in much the same way, although the lack of need to face up to the production process meant that criticism had a greater potential for novelty. English modernist writing on design was almost exclusively revisionist.[53] Few writers doubted that there was a significant distance between England and the rest of Europe; as the architect Sir Reginald Blomfield unambiguously put it, "As an Englishman and proud of his country, I despise and

Fig. 4.22
Box, c. 1913; and Box, given to Pamela Fry, daughter of Omega Workshops co-founder Roger Fry, Christmas 1917, c. 1913
Designed by Duncan Grant
(Scottish, 1885–1978)
Made by Omega Workshops, London
Painted wood
Left: 3¼ x 13¼ x 5¼ inches (8.3 x 33.7 x 13.3 cm) *Right:* 3 x 12½ x 4 ⅜ inches (7.6 x 31.8 x 11.1 cm)
Left, marks: underside, on green ground, painted blue omega within blue square
Right, marks: underside, painted black omega within black square
85.10.2; 85.10.3

Et le monde comme l'horloge du quartier juif de Prague tourne éperdument à rebours
Effeuille la rose des vents
Voici que bruissent les orages déchaînés
Les trains roulent en tourbillon sur les réseaux enchevêtrés
Bilboquets diaboliques
Il y a des trains qui ne se rencontrent jamais
D'autres se perdent en route
Les chefs de gare jouent aux échecs

Tric-trac
Billard
Caramboles
PARABOLES
La voie ferrée est une nouvelle géométrie
SYRACUSE
ARCHIMÈDE
Et les soldats qui l'égorgèrent
Et les galères
Et les vaisseaux
Et les engins prodigieux qu'il inventa
Et toutes les tueries
L'histoire antique
L'histoire moderne
Les tourbillons
Les naufrages

Même celui du Titanic que j'ai lu dans le journal
Autant d'images associations que je ne peux pas développer dans mes vers
Car je suis encore fort mauvais poète
Car l'univers me déborde
Et j'ai négligé de m'assurer contre les accidents de chemin de fer
Car je ne sais pas aller jusqu'au bout
Et j'ai peur.

J'ai peur
Je ne sais pas aller jusqu'au bout
Comme mon ami Chagall je pourrais faire une série de tableaux déments
Mais je n'ai pas pris de notes en voyage

« Pardonnez-moi mon ignorance
« Pardonnez-moi de ne plus connaître l'ancien jeu des vers »
Comme dit Guillaume Apollinaire
Tout ce qui concerne la guerre on peut le lire dans les Mémoires de Kouropatkine
Ou dans les journaux japonais qui sont aussi cruellement illustrés
A quoi bon me documenter
Je m'abandonne
Aux sursauts de ma mémoire.

A partir d'Irkoutsk le voyage devint beaucoup trop lent
Beaucoup trop long
Nous étions dans le premier train qui contournait le lac Baïkal
On avait orné la locomotive de drapeaux et de lampions
Et nous avions quitté la gare aux accents tristes de l'hymne au Tsar
Si j'étais peintre je déverserais beaucoup de rouge, beaucoup de jaune sur la fin de ce voyage
Car je crois bien que nous étions tous un peu fous
Et qu'un délire immense ensanglantait les faces énervées de mes compagnons de voyage
Comme nous approchions de la Mongolie
Qui ronflait comme un incendie.
Le train avait ralenti son allure
Et je percevais dans le grincement perpétuel des roues
Les accents fous et les sanglots
D'une éternelle liturgie

J'ai vu
J'ai vu les trains silencieux les trains noirs qui revenaient de l'Extrême-Orient et qui passaient en fantômes
Et mon œil, comme le fanal d'arrière, court encore derrière ces trains
A Talga 100 000 blessés agonisaient faute de soin
J'ai visité les hôpitaux de Krasnoïarsk
Et à Khilok nous avons croisé un long convoi de soldats fous
J'ai vu dans les lazarets des plaies béantes des blessures qui saignaient à pleines orgues
Et les membres amputés dansaient autour ou s'envolaient dans l'air rauque
L'incendie était sur toutes les faces dans tous les cœurs
Des doigts idiots tambourinaient sur toutes les vitres
Et sous la pression de la peur les regards crevaient comme des abcès
Dans toutes les gares on brûlait tous les wagons
Et j'ai vu
J'ai vu des trains de 60 locomotives qui s'enfuyaient à toute vapeur pourchassées par les horizons en rut et des
bandes de corbeaux qui s'envolaient désespérément après

Disparaître
Dans la direction de Port-Arthur

A Tchita nous eûmes quelques jours de répit.
Arrêt de cinq jours vu l'encombrement de la voie
Nous les passâmes chez Monsieur Iankéléwitch qui voulut me donner sa fille unique en mariage
Puis le train repartit.
Maintenant c'était moi qui avais pris place au piano et j'avais mal aux dents
Je revois quand je veux cet intérieur si calme le magasin et les yeux de la fille qui venait le soir dans mon lit
Moussorgsky
Et les lieder de Hugo Wolf
Et les sables du Gobi
Et à Khaïlar une caravane de chameaux blancs
Je crois bien que j'étais ivre durant plus de 500 kilomètres

Mais j'étais au piano et c'est tout ce que je vis
Quand on voyage on devrait fermer les yeux
Dormir
J'aurais tant voulu dormir
Je reconnais tous les pays les yeux fermés à leur odeur
Et je reconnais tous les trains au bruit qu'ils font

Les trains d'Europe sont à quatre temps tandis que ceux d'Asie sont à cinq ou sept temps
D'autres vont en sourdine sont des berceuses
Et il y en a qui dans le bruit monotone des roues me rappellent la prose lourde de Maeterlinck
J'ai déchiffré tous les textes confus des roues et j'ai rassemblé les éléments épars d'une violente beauté
Que je possède
Et qui me force

Tsitsika et Kharbine
Je ne vais pas plus loin
C'est la dernière station
Je débarquai à Kharbine comme on venait de mettre le feu aux bureaux de la
Croix-Rouge

O Paris
Grand foyer chaleureux avec les tisons entrecroisés de tes rues et tes vieilles maisons qui se penchent au-dessus et se réchauffent
Comme des aïeules
Et voici des affiches du rouge du vert multicolores comme mon passé bref du jaune
Jaune la fière couleur des romans de la France
J'aime me frotter dans les grandes villes aux autobus en marche
Ceux de la ligne Saint-Germain–Montmartre m'emportent à l'assaut de la Butte
Les moteurs beuglent comme les taureaux d'or
Les vaches du crépuscule broutent le Sacré-Cœur

O Paris
Gare centrale débarcadère des volontés carrefour des inquiétudes
Seuls les marchands de couleur ont encore un peu de lumière sur leur porte
La Compagnie Internationale des Wagons-Lits et des Grands Express Européens m'a envoyé son prospectus
C'est la plus belle église du monde
J'ai des amis qui m'entourent comme des garde-fous
Ils ont peur quand je pars que je ne revienne plus
Toutes les femmes que j'ai rencontrées se dressent aux horizons
Avec les gestes piteux et les regards tristes des sémaphores sous la pluie
Bella, Agnès, Catherine et la mère de mon fils en Italie
Et celle, la mère de mon amour en Amérique
Il y a des cris de sirène qui me déchirent l'âme
Là-bas en Mandchourie un ventre tressaille encore comme dans un accouchement
Je voudrais
Je voudrais n'avoir jamais fait mes voyages
Ce soir un grand amour me tourmente
Et malgré moi je pense à la petite Jehanne de France.
C'est par un soir de tristesse que j'ai écrit ce poème en son honneur
La petite prostituée
Je suis triste je suis triste
J'irai au Lapin agile me ressouvenir de ma jeunesse perdue
Et boire des petits verres
Puis je rentrerai seul

Paris
Ville de la Tour unique du grand Gibet et de la Roue
Paris 1913

Fig. 4.23   See Cat. 92
Book (detail)
*La Prose du Transsibérien et de la
Petite Jehanne de France*, 1913
S. Delaunay

Fig. 4.24 See Cat. 152
Coffee service, c. 1934
Designed by K.D.P. Murray

Fig. 4.25
Mugs, c. 1933
Mug on left commemorates coronation
of Edward VIII, 1937
Designed by Keith Day Pearce Murray
(British, b. New Zealand, 1892–1981)
Made by Josiah Wedgwood & Sons Ltd., Etruria,
Staffordshire, England
Glazed earthenware
Left: 4⅞ x 5½ x 3⅞ inches (12.4 x 14.0 x 9.8 cm)
Center: 5 x 4⅞ x 3⅝ inches (12.7 x 12.4 x 9.2 cm)
Right: 5 x 51/8 x 35/8 inches (12.7 x 13.0 x 9.2 cm)
Left, marks: underside, printed underglaze in blue crown
mark/"TO COMMEMORATE/THE CORONATION/OF HIS
MAJESTY/KING EDWARD VIII/1937"; printed in green with
facsimile signature "Keith Murray/WEDGWOOD/MADE IN
ENGLAND"
Center, marks: underside, printed overglaze in green with
facsimile signature "Keith Murray/WEDGWOOD/MADE IN
ENGLAND"
Right, marks: underside, printed overglaze in green with
facsimile signature "Keith Murray/WEDGWOOD/MADE IN
ENGLAND"
85.7.1; 85.7.3; 85.7.4

detest cosmopolitanism."[54] Having accepted the essential separation, pro modernists used one of two strategies. They either showed that modernist forms were compatible with English life and customs, or, second and more daringly, that indigenous design had had all the basic ingredients of modern design for several hundred years, well before its advent in Europe.

One of the most important writers in the inter-war period, for example, was John Gloag. A confirmed modernist revisionist, his many publications enjoyed an audience well beyond the specialist confines of the design industries.[55] He very much encouraged the view that the English way of life and English traditions were compatible with modern design. Typically, his written oeuvre demonstrates an anxiety to sever social theory – whether it be of the Left or the Right – from the aesthetic dimension: "The something safe to sell spirit is as dangerously stupid and unconstructive as the red hot air of communism; it is the enemy of industrial design."[56] In his most complete statement on English modernism, *The English Tradition in Design* (1947), he developed a dialectical model which showed English culture moving through history in waves of action and reaction. Having endured chaos in design through the dreaded Victorian period, he suggests, modernism will usher in a new golden age, reminiscent of past glories such as the Medieval and Georgian eras.

J.M. Richards, editor of the *Architectural Review* and a champion of modern architecture, came up with a novel, not to say extraordinary incentive to embrace modernity, in his article "Black and White" of 1937:

135

This article is an attempt to isolate an idiom of decoration and design peculiar to this country. This idiom may be described as one that gets its architectural effect through the disposition of contrasted areas of black and white, applied to the surface of an object. . . . White boats tarred below the waterline, with clear white lettering on a black gunwale, provide a starting point. And on the quayside, the nautical paraphernalia, posts, bollards, capstans, rails, show the translation of tradition into rudimentary architectural form. Against a rotting barge, white seagulls play counterchange with this pattern, or a slim white flagpole picks itself out against a hut or boatshed tarred as black as your hat.[57]

He reasoned from this that, as white and black patterns were indigenous to English culture and also amenable to modern, international-style architecture, English modernist architects should decorate their buildings with black and white, to make them feel more English. Tudor mansions and the naval tradition thus meet Le Corbusier halfway. No substantial evidence has emerged to gauge the extent to which patriotic English modernists responded.

Design movements do not usually disappear with suddenness. They are normally absorbed into causes that are not necessarily their own, whether aesthetic, economic, social, or political, which undermine and eventually obliterate them. Often all that remains of a movement once it has been appropriated are its stylistic mannerisms. This process has to be understood before the changes which took place in English design from the mid-nineteenth to the mid-twentieth century can be charted.

Narrative was used in a very particular way within the English modern matrix; modernism was all about rephrasing the stereotypical narratives of English life. It was about new ways of telling old stories, or at least new ways of telling stories which had pretensions to being old. It aimed to put a stable, better past into the future tense.

The key feature in English modern design was the space between form and content, a gap which was first opened up at the end of the nineteenth century. It would be a mistake to attribute this simply to aesthetic failure on the part of the designers. Indeed, many of them showed great ingenuity in responding to the briefs they were faced with. Perhaps *structured compromise* is a more accurate way of describing their approach. This suggests that the bringing together of progressive form with regressive content was not a fault of incompetence but an inevitable expedient in an ideological climate which rendered any other approach to modernism economically, politically, and even socially unacceptable. This particular *English compromise* did not come about by accident.

NOTES

1   One of two made. The other is in Osborne House, England.

2   An unintended irony, as Richard was a Plantagenet, whose dynasty was brought to a close by the Tudor House of Lancaster.

3   Experimentation in all the arts tended to be connected to liberal and Left-wing thought, overtly so in the cases of Bloomsbury and the Fabian Society.

4   Williamson Art Gallery and Museum, Birkenhead, *Della Robbia Pottery Birkenhead, 1894–1906, An Interim Report* (Liverpool, c. 1980).

5   The essay is about English, not British nationalism. I refer to Britain with regard to economic conditions, when they pertain to the United Kingdom. For the politico-economic condition of Britain see the following: François Crouzet, *The Victorian Economy* (London, 1982); George Dangerfield, *The Strange Death of Liberal England* (London, 1935); Paul Thompson, *The Edwardians: The Remaking of British Society* (London, 1975); and Guy Routh, *Occupations of the People of Great Britain 1801–1981*.

6   J.B. Priestley, *The Edwardians* (London, 1970), p. 84.

7   Especially the U.S.A. and Germany. See Sir Robert Ensor, *England 1870–1914*, (Oxford, 1985), pp. 498–526.

8   See Paul Greenhalgh, *Ephemeral Vistas: Expositions Universelles, Great Exhibitions and Worlds Fairs 1851–1939* (Manchester, 1988), pp. 3–51.

9   See Thomas Pakenham, *The Scramble for Africa* (London, 1992). For more general reading on the condition of the Empire, see Winfried Baumgart, *Imperialism: The Idea and Reality of British and French Colonial Expansion 1880–1914* (Oxford, 1982); C.C. Eldridge (ed.), *British Imperialism in the Nineteenth Century* (London, 1984).

10 For discussion of the wider implications of modernization, see Marshall Berman, *All that is Solid Melts into Air: The Experience of Modernity* (London, 1983).

11 For discussion of nationalism in this regard see E.J. Hobsbawm, *The Age of Imperialism 1875–1914* (London, 1987), pp. 142–64.

12 Richard Shannon, *The Crisis of Imperialism 1865–1915* (St. Albans, 1976), pp. 12–13.

13 Stewart Dick and Helen Allingham, *The Cottage Homes of England* (London, 1909), p. 2.

14 *Ibid.*

15 H.T. Buckle, *History of Civilization in England*, vol. 1 (London, 1902), p. 501. Buckle was first published surprisingly early, in 1862. The book was constantly reprinted, and was at its most influential, however, in the Edwardian period.

16 Quoted from the *Official Souvenir Album of the Franco-British Exhibition* (London, 1908), p. 246.

17 See Stefan Muthesius, "Why do we Buy Old Furniture? Aspects of the Authentic Antique in Britain 1870–1910," *Art History*, 11, no. 2 (June, 1988).

18 See Barbara Morris, *Inspiration for Design: The Influence of the Victoria and Albert Museum* (London,1986).

19 See E.W. Godwin, *Art Furniture, from Designs by E.W. Godwin and Others* (London, 1877).

20 See Widar Halén, *Christopher Dresser* (London, 1990), pp. 33–77.

21 Christopher Dresser, *The Principles of Decorative Design* (London, 1873), p. 21.

22 Nikolaus Pevsner, in his *Pioneers of Modern Design* (London, 1936), was one of the first to cite Dresser as a precursor of future modernisms. Many others have since followed suit. See also Halén, *Christopher Dresser*.

23 The holdings of the National Art Library (Victoria and Albert Museum) include several hundred books and specialist journals on the theory and practice of British design, published between 1870 and 1914.

24 Ruskin was not a Socialist, but favored a return to a version of feudalism. Nevertheless, his writings were vital for the Labour Movement in Britain. In 1906, when the Labour Party made its major break-through by sending fifty-two MPs to Parliament, the majority claimed Ruskin's *Nature of the Gothic* as their political inspiration.

25 See P.J. Bowler, *The Invention of Progress: The Victorians and the Past* (London, 1989).

26 Museums benefited from this patronage, as collections were given over to the public domain. Particularly fine gatherings of Pre-Raphaelite work can be found in Birmingham and Manchester City Art Galleries, and the Lady Lever Art Gallery, Port Sunlight, Liverpool.

27 See Mark Girouard, *The Return to Camelot: Chivalry and the English Gentlemen* (Yale, 1981). I am also responding here in part to the argument put forward by Martin Wiener in his *English Culture and the Decline of the English Industrial Spirit, 1850–1980* (Cambridge, 1981), that the love of rural and ancient imagery was partly symptomatic of a shift away from industry during the second half of the nineteenth century. Wiener argues that a psychological shift among the English made them "embarrassed" by industry, and led to the "adopting [of] a conception of Englishness that virtually excluded industrialism." I would argue that the psychological condition of the English, and the cultural forms they developed are a result of the perception of decline, not a cause of it.

28 Written in 1916. See E.D. Mackerness, ed., *The Journals of George Sturt 1890–1927* (Cambridge, 1967), p. 767.

29 See Sir John Seeley's *The Expansion of England* (London, 1883), widely read at the close of the century, which proposed the idea of English history effectively beginning with the successes of Tudor England.

30 M.H. Spielmann, *Official Souvenir of the Fine Art Section, Franco-British Exposition 1908* (London, 1908), p. 69.

31 *Ibid.*

32 Lewis F. Day, quoted from Elizabeth Aslim, "Sir George Donaldson and 'Art Nouveau' at South Kensington," *The Journal of the Decorative Arts Society*, no. 7.

33 Aymer Vallance, "The British Arts and Crafts in 1903," *Magazine of Art* (1903): 169.

34 The later erotic works of Beardsley and the trial of Wilde (1895) had a more significant effect of the progress of the Aesthetic Movement and Art Nouveau in Britain than is generally acknowledged. For Wilde's views of visual culture, see Richard Ellman, *Oscar Wilde* (London, 1987).

35 Walter Crane, "Modern Decorative Art at Turin: General Impressions," *Magazine of Art*, 1902. Quoted from E.G. Holt, *The Expanding World of Art 1874–1902* (New Haven, 1988), p. 147.

36 Crane was frequently a judge on committees which decided the contributions of Britain to international exhibitions. He was the dominant voice, for example, at the Franco-British Exhibition (1908).

37 Greenhalgh, *Ephemeral Vistas: Expositions Universelles, Great Exhibitions and Worlds Fairs 1851–1939*, pp. 122–3.

38   Anon., *The Franco-British Exhibition Illustrated Review* (London, 1908).

39   *William Morris: Life and Work* (London, 1911), pp. 5 – 6.

40   The most eloquent development of the idea of the "long nineteenth century" can be found in Hobsbawn, *The Age of Imperialism 1975–1914*.

41   See Greenhalgh, *Ephemeral Vistas: Expositions Universelles, Great Exhibitions and Worlds Fairs 1851–1939*, and P.M. Taylor, *The Projection of Britain: British Overseas Propaganda 1919–1939* (Cambridge, 1981).

42   Taylor, *The Projection of Britain: British Overseas Propaganda 1919–1939*.

43   Department of Overseas Trade, *International Exhibition of Modern Decorative and Industrial Art, Paris 1925* (London, 1925).

44   See *Encyclopédia des Arts Décoratifs et Industriels Modernes, Paris 1925*, volume II of XII (Paris, 1925).

45   See Bernard Leach, *A Potter's Book* (London, 1941).

46   Fiona MacCarthy, *Eric Gill* (London, 1989).

47   Gordon Russell, "The Industrial Designer," *Art in Industry Magazine*, December 1946.

48   McKnight Kauffer was an American living in London. This does not alter the discussion of nationalism in this context.

49   Crafts Council, *The Omega Workshops 1913–1919, Decorative Arts of Bloomsbury* (London, 1983).

50   Fry and Bell's concept of "significant form," expressed most clearly in Bell's *Art* (London, 1911), pp. 9 – 22, was essentially a universalist formalism. Fry himself was wary of any theoretical position which injected social or political meaning into art.

51   Murray's ceramics were widely illustrated both at the time and subsequently in texts which used them as examples of modernism. Murray was born in New Zealand and a resident of Britain.

52   Wedgwood was using the shape with a range of different glazes and decorations for many years after their association with Murray finished.

53   There were exceptions to this revisionism. Le Corbusier's key writings were translated rapidly, for example. There are other instances, and *Architectural Review*, especially during the 1930s, had spurts of modernist lucidity. An interesting text in this light is Raymond McGrath, *Twentieth Century Houses* (London, 1934).

54   Sir Reginald Blomfield, "Is Modern Architecture on the Right Track?," *The Listener* X (1933). Quoted from William Curtis, "The English Tradition and Modern Architecture," in *The History of Architecture and Design 1890–1939* (Milton Keyes, 1975), pp. 54 – 81.

55   Gloag was editor of *The Cabinet Maker*; he was deeply involved with the Design in Industries Association, contributing to several of their publications, and made many public broadcasts for the B.B.C. He wrote a large number of books during the period, including *Design in Modern Life* (London,1934), *English Furniture* (London, 1934), *The Englishman's Castle* (London, 1944), *Men and Buildings* (London, 1936), *Industrial Art Explained* (before 1944). He continued to publish prolifically after the War.

56   John Gloag, *Word Warfare* (London, 1939), p. 47.

57   J.M. Richards, "Black and White: An Introductory Study of a National Design Idiom," *Architectural Review*, 1937. Richards was a key figure for the exposure of European ideas in Britain.

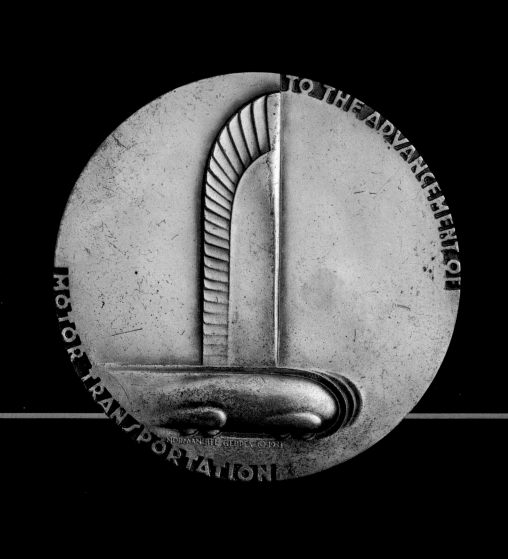

Celebrating Modernity

Domesticating Modernity:
Ambivalence and Appropriation, 1920–40

Jeffrey L. Meikle

Fig. 5.04 See Cat. 96
Print
Whence and Whither?, c.1932
C.E. Power

Recent historians have emphasized modernity as a disjunctive experience. Marshall Berman, for example, borrowing a phrase from Marx, has argued that accelerating urbanization and industrialization in Europe and the U.S.A. stimulated a perception that "all that is solid melts into air." No sooner was a new invention, process, or structure established than it was swept away by a dynamic capitalist system that fostered continuous innovation and obsolescence even as its managers tried to escape the flux.[1] Some modernist artists and writers, such as the Italian Futurists, celebrated the resulting vertigo. But perpetual revolution did not appeal to governments and corporations seeking stability; nor did it appeal to ordinary people who sought the familiar comforts of traditional life. In democratic and totalitarian societies alike, those with power and influence realized they had to domesticate the disruptive experience of modernity. They had to persuade ambivalent populations that new modes of living retained or promoted traditional values. The situation reached a crisis point during the 1920s and 1930s. As social and economic chaos overtook both Europe and the U.S.A., it became necessary to construct reassuring narratives and iconographies – in other words, to insist on the paradox that a self-conscious machine age retained stability even as it celebrated technological change.[2]

This essay focusses on three modes of domesticating modernity during the inter-war years. The first approach situated modernity in a historical continuum linking past, present, and future. This strategy suggested an evolution from past to future, thereby naturalizing modernity and neutralizing its strangeness. The second mode involved limiting modernity in space to a discrete zone – the modern city. Its cosmopolitan inhabitant could leave the zone of modernity as a traveler to explore a larger outside world that remained timelessly whole and reassuringly traditional. If perspectives of time or space did not overcome modernity's vertigo, a third mode of domestication remained. By directly appropriating and

Previous page
See Cat. 114
Medal
To the Advancement of Motor Transportation.
Commemorating the 25th anniversary of
General Motors, 1933
Designed by Norman Bel Geddes

143

Fig. 5.01
Print
Aero Plane, c. 1932
Angelo Raphael Pinto
(American, b. Italy, 1908–94)
Wood engraving
Philadelphia
9¾ x 12 inches (24.8 x 30.5 cm)
Marks: obverse, in pencil, lower left corner "30 'Aero Plane'";
lower right corner "Angelo Pinto"
XX1990.3631

incorporating icons of the modern into one's own personal environment, their threatening aspects could be neutralized. These three responses to the ambivalence of modernity comprise a tentative typology. What follows is a sampling from the scores of images and artifacts in the Wolfsonian Collection that support this typology as indicative of responses to modernity in Europe and the U.S.A. in the years between the wars. Before considering variations on these modes of response, however, one must understand the anxiety that motivated those whose business was making people comfortable with the machine age.

Representations of doubt about the future rarely appeared in official or corporate propaganda. Instead, anxiety emerged in works by individual artists with limited audiences. That uncertainty, however, spoke to urbanites who should have been at home with modernity if anyone was – suggesting that a wider public shared their fears. Of dozens of such expressions among the Wolfsonian Collection's prints and drawings, Angelo Pinto's *Aero Plane* (fig. 5.01) distilled the modern experience of disorientation. The engraving portrayed an airplane skewed across a dark landscape. Each of its elements – hangars, harbor, ocean liner, factories, clumps of skyscrapers, even a tiny squadron of planes flying below – existed in a separate plane of reference, violating the conflicting perspectives of the others. The stylized image afforded no hint of pilot or cockpit to suggest human control, but instead expressed the vertigo of a depersonalized machine in a fractured landscape. Pinto's engraving

Fig. 5.02 See Cat. 133
Print
New York Breadline, c. 1932
C.V.H. Leighton

New York Breadline

contained three elements that recurred in other depictions of modernity: presence of the machine, absence or insignificance of human beings, and the urban landscape itself, typically an aggregation of crystalline monoliths.

During the 1920s and 1930s, a genre of urban representation was popularized by Hugh Ferriss, an American architectural renderer who portrayed the city as a vast heavy mass of forms tending toward a single pyramidal structure.[3] This gravitational presence over-whelmed the insignificant ciphers who typically appeared below, as in Clare Leighton's engraving *Skyscrapers*,[4] with its gnomic construction workers laboring to obscure the sky, or the same artist's *New York Breadline* (fig. 5.02), with its huddled masses, shoulders rounded and faces averted, vanishing to infinity at the base of towering structures. More often, people simply vanished. Borrowing from Ferriss, a gloomy charcoal drawing by Edmond van Dooren, *City with Machines* (fig. 5.03), portrayed a view through a girdered archway at an urbanization of such scale that its towers vanished above and elevated roadways appeared

Fig. 5.03 See Cat. 134
Drawing
***City with Machines*, c. 1930**
E. van Dooren

indistinctly below. Many structures resembled vast dynamos and machines whose architectural scale rendered humanity obsolete.

Many artists did include human figures in representations of urban life. Even in WPA prints, however, people sometimes did not appear as independent subjects but instead suffered modernity – either with passive resignation or as a result of direct repression. Charles Turzak's woodcut *Man with Drill*[5] translated a jackhammer's bone-splitting rhythm into images of pedestrians and skyscrapers splintering into painful semi-Cubist fractures. More evocative was Carl Hoeckner's engraving *Machine Fodder*,[6] depicting ranks of workers, brutal overseers, and a surreal conflation of mechanized industry and industrialized warfare. Loss of human control was fully realized in a linocut by Cyril Power (fig. 5.04), one in a series of renderings of the London Underground, which depicted a sinuous line of faceless figures, more a single organism than a collection of individuals, sweeping down an escalator in dynamic motion – thereby posing the unanswerable question of all these representations: *Whence and Whither?* At least privately, however, Power thought he knew the answer. One of his preliminary drawings of a similar scene bore the unequivocal title, *Robottomless Pit, Homo Mechaniens.*[7] Such views obviously claimed no place in government propaganda and corporate advertising. But with economies collapsing around the globe and a nearly universal sense of loss of control, it was hard to convince weary populations on either side of the Atlantic to be comfortable with modernity.

The concept of time was central to modern experience. Faced with a wealth of new products, consumers wanted to be "up to the minute" – or, as an advertising agent expressed it in 1929, to keep up with a "new American tempo."[8] Among new appliances, the electric clock most quickly yielded to the modernizing touch of the industrial designer. The Zephyr clock (fig. 5.05), designed by Kem Weber for a firm calling itself the Lawson Time Company as if it had cornered the market on time itself, was one of many clocks of metal, plastic, or wraparound wood veneer whose streamlined forms promised to keep people "in touch with the times." It became a cliché that Mussolini "made the trains run on time." Indeed, a German poster from the 1930s (fig. 5.06) promised "ever faster" travel on state railways – supporting the claim with a track-level perspective in the style of Cassandre showing a stylized passenger train and a red lightning bolt rushing into infinity as a superimposed speedometer pushed the 150-kilometer limit. Emphasis on speed for its own sake stimulated insecurity as events moved so rapidly that the past was left behind or, in Berman's metaphor, melted away. Despite continuing celebration of machine-age progress evidenced by the popularity of streamlining in both Europe and the U.S.A., many people feared the disappearance of the past or a melting away of tradition. Denial of a clear distinction between past and future, gained by situating both on an unbroken time line, became a common way of domesticating

147

modernity. Disjunctive experiences thereby disappeared in a comfortingly natural process of evolution.

This first mode of domestication, through neutralizing of time's frightful annihilation, often appeared in posters devoted to transportation – the very process whose speed implicated it in destroying the past. Rediscovery of Cassandre's work has wrongly fostered a notion that transportation images typically represented neverending flight into the future. In fact, by juxtaposing past and present, European posters often implied that the present had not broken with the past but instead would supply better versions of experiences similar to those of the past. A poster for an exhibition commemorating the centennial of German railroads in 1935 (fig. 5.07) portrayed a blurred streamliner streaking across a colossal bridge (between past and future) formed out of the numerals "100." At the bridge's base idled an 1830s locomotive and carriage, with sentimental renderings of passengers, crew, and observers (including a

Fig. 5.05 See Cat. 106
Digital clock
Model no. 304–P40, *Zephyr*, 1934
Designed by K. Weber

Fig. 5.06 See Cat. 97
Poster
Immer Schneller. Deutsche Reichsbahn
(Always Faster. German State Railroad), c. 1935
Designed by H.J. Barschel

Fig. 5.07 See Cat. 98
Poster
100 Jahre Deutsche Eisenbahnen Ausstellung,
Nürnberg, 1935
(Centennial Exhibition of the German State
Railroad . . .), 1935
Designed by J. Wiertz

Fig. 5.08
Postcard
Deutsche Lufthansa, c. 1940
Designed by Max Ullmann
(German, dates unknown)
Published by Deutsche Lufthansa, Germany
4⅛ x 5⅞ inches (10.5 x 14.9 cm)
XC1991.900

woman and her son) providing a human interest lacking in futuristic images of transportation. This convention of representing traditional past and futuristic present in a single frame of reference also appeared in a postcard for Deutsche Lufthansa (fig. 5.08). In this example, a horse-drawn post coach accompanied by a greyhound careened gaily along while an attractive young woman strained from the window to glimpse an airliner overhead with the Nazi swastika on its tail.[9] The viewer was again invited to assume the perspective of a female figure whose position in the past enabled a bridging of past and future. These female figures humanized an otherwise dehumanized portrayal of machine transportation and thus indicated modernity's literal domestication.

Other representations in transportation posters of the continuity of traditional past and futuristic present seemed less innocent. In 1927, for example, the Italian steamship company Lloyd Sabaudo displayed stylized moderne renderings of four ocean liners referred

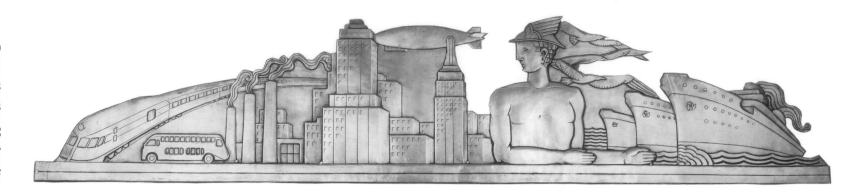

Fig. 5.09
Relief
From the Hotel St. George,
Brooklyn, NY, c. 1930
U.S.A.
Chrome-plated metal
17⅞ x 83⅞ x ⅝ inches (45.4 x 213.0 x 1.6 cm)
TD1989.13.1

to as "the four counts" after the fourteenth-century leaders of the House of Savoy, whose descendant King Victor Emmanuel III had acquiesced in Mussolini's rise to power. Above the four ocean liners towered the figures of four galloping knights portrayed romantically with a hint of futurist dynamism as they cantered across the sky.[10] In similar fashion, but even more ominously, the image of a helmeted knight, hands on the hilt of a heavy sword, rose above a liner of the Seedienst Ostpreussen in a travel schedule of 1939.[11] Evoking nationalisms whose legitimacy rested on claims of continuity with past traditions and military glory, these posters differed little from frequent Italian illustrations of airliners flying over classical ruins, often in the North African desert, suggesting the grandeur that was Rome continuing on into the future. The most advanced transportation machines became weapons for realizing national aspirations as old as history itself.

Domesticating modernity by bridging past, present, and future seemed especially popular in the U.S.A., partly because the social upheavals of the Depression years called into question the validity of the American experiment and led Americans to seek grounding in the sort of historical traditions that European cultures both glorified and took for granted. Unlike European examples of the genre, which typically referred back to a single past moment, American versions often portrayed history's entire panoramic sweep – and, in doing so, mingled past, present, and implicit future in a sometimes surrealist medley. The panorama was already a familiar technique in more simple, unconflicted celebrations of modernity. During the 1930s, for example, Brooklyn's modernistic Hotel St. George boasted a frieze (fig. 5.09) whose panorama of New York City encompassed the Empire State Building, an airship, factories, ocean liners, a streamlined double-decker bus, a streamlined passenger train, and an image of the hotel itself – all overseen by a rather smug-looking Mercury. Such images of dynamic modernity proved so seductive that a Baptist Young Peoples convention at Detroit in 1929 promoted itself with stickers depicting an urban silhouette complete with massed skyscrapers, dramatically skewed suspension bridge, airplane, airship, and wisps of smoke blowing from smokestacks.[12] Despite this approval of undiluted modernity by religious fundamentalists, examples in the Collection suggest that most American panoramas grounded modernity in a simple past from which present multiplicity had developed. Especially convincing for its naïveté was Adelaide Zitella Philips's study for an Alabama post office mural (fig. 5.10). Her design portrayed a pioneer in coonskin cap shaking hands with an Indian before a grove of trees. In the distance to the left appeared a stockade and evidence of cultivation; to the right a plantation house, a large farm, and a modern highway with speeding cars and trucks. The purity of this vision, with a handshake bridging a frontier past and a modern future that remained partially agrarian, marked it as almost unique, but similar themes echoed through more complex panoramas.

The most complex of these panoramas was life-sized – the Chicago Century of Progress Exposition, opening in 1933 on the shore of Lake Michigan. Celebrating the centennial of America's brashest city, this world's fair boasted an architecture of "modernistic cubistic extravagances," as a hostile critic observed.[13] Over a two-year period, such technological wonders as Buckminster Fuller's three-wheeled Dymaxion car, the first Burlington Zephyr streamliner, and the Goodyear blimp added dynamic presence to the futuristic architecture. Even so, the fair also possessed both an "exact replica" of Fort Dearborn as it appeared in 1833 and an "actual replica" of Lincoln's log-cabin birthplace. Fort Dearborn, according to a viewbook, "breathe[d] the romance of frontier days amid startling modernistic surroundings."[14] Often ignored by historians tracing utopian visions, the reconstructed fort was essential to the fair's panoramic effect. The official guidebook counseled visitors to look back and "scan" the fair's architecture and the city's own "towering skyscrapers" before entering Fort Dearborn to be "carried back a hundred years and more." The contrast was "almost

Fig. 5.10
Study
For the Eutaw, AL, Post Office
mural competition, 1939
Adelaide Zitella Philips
(American, dates unknown)
U.S.A.
Tempera over graphite on paper
13½ x 39 inches (34.3 x 99.1 cm)
Marks: obverse, in black ink, lower left corner "Zitella/.39"
84.5.113

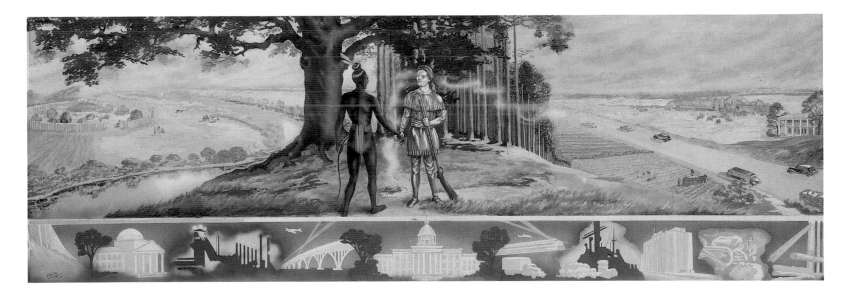

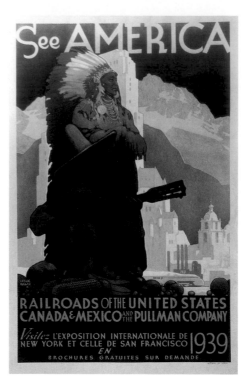

Fig. 5.11
Poster
Mexico, c. 1935
Published by Departamento de Turismo, Secretaria de
Gobernacion and Asociacion Mexicana de Turismo, Mexico
Commercial color lithograph
36 9/16 x 27 5/16 inches (92.9 x 69.4 cm)
XX1992.224

Fig. 5.13
Poster
See America. Railroads of the United States,
Canada, and Mexico and the Pullman Company,
1939
Designed by Leslie Darrell Ragan
(American, b. 1897)
Publisher attributed to Pullman Palace Car Company,
Chicago
Commercial color lithograph
40 1/16 x 26 15/16 inches (103.3 x 68.4 cm)
Marks: obverse, printed in yellow, lower left "LESLIE/RAGAN"
TD1989.240.1

breathtaking," but it was also comforting to realize that everything outside had sprung from pioneer origins.[15] Even the American Indian appeared in the fair's official iconography as a figure on a white horse releasing an invisible arrow from an invisible bow in a gesture emblematic of the hidden potential of 1833. Despite the exposition's aspiring to modernity, Fort Dearborn and the American Indian remained central to a panorama that suggested effortless progress without loss of a comforting past.

Few American celebrations of progress during the 1930s were complete without its representation in a historical panorama. When the city of Buffalo celebrated its centennial in 1932, for example, a commemorative medallion depicted the ever-present Indian, grain elevators at his back, gazing eastward from a hillock toward factories, high-tension wires, and a speeding locomotive, as an airplane flew overhead.[16] The logic of the panoramic form proved so compelling that the Asociacion Mexicana de Turismo employed a surrealist variant in a poster promoting *Mexico* (fig. 5.11) as a realm of Art Moderne towers, fast cars, trains and planes, baroque colonial churches, and mystical Aztec pyramids hovering in the sky. By 1947, the historical panorama was so familiar that printmaker Ralph Fabri could satirize it with a wickedly inventive etching entitled *Americana* (fig. 5.12). Shortly before this lampoon, the panoramic form attained a straight-faced culmination in a romantic poster issued by American railroads exhorting foreigners to *See America* when traveling to the 1939 expositions at New York and San Francisco (fig. 5.13). Leslie Ragan's richly colored illustration reduced modernity to glowing but indistinct images of skyscraper, factory, and streamliner. The poster not only granted visual equality to indistinct images of Quebec's Chateau Frontenac and Mexico City's cathedral

Fig. 5.12
Print
Americana, 1947
Ralph Fabri
(American, 1894–1975)
Published by the Society of American Etchers, New York
Etching
11 ¹/₁₆ x 14 ¼ inches (28.1 x 36.2 cm)
Marks: obverse, in pencil, lower left corner "Americana";
lower right corner "Ralph Fabri"; lower right corner of margin "5"
84.4.639

but also obscured modernity by emphasizing traditional images of the land and its people – an Indian chief in full regalia, a Mexican playing a guitar, a woman of color (possibly Asian rather than Hispanic), all posed against the rugged towering peaks of the Rockies with an abundance of agricultural produce scattered across the foreground. The wealth of the American land and people so overwhelmed modernity that it shrank to something taken for granted. Americans might not escape the modern age in their own cities, and had to accommodate it by denying any break with the past, but foreigners could escape modernity, in the perspective of Ragan's poster, by fleeing to America as to some unchanging colonial land. If history offered no escape from modern anxieties, then geography promised a way out. Ragan's poster leads through a near inversion or reversal of the panoramic form to the second mode of domesticating modernity – by escape to pristine realms untouched by the disjunctive modern experience of continuous change.

A map of the world displayed at the Century of Progress affords an introduction to this strategy. Appearing as one of four murals in Westinghouse Electric's exhibit, the map offered insight into modernity's effect on world geography. It was composed of anodized aluminum in silver and copper hues inlaid in glossy black Micarta plastic laminate, part of a triptych celebrating *Radio Broadcasting* (fig. 5.14). Concentric circles indicated radio waves emanating to the entire world from Pittsburgh, site of stations KDKA and W8XK, while side panels depicted broadcasting of music and sports. Although the map conveyed the central message that radio possessed power to "bind the whole world together" into one "neighborhood," even this precisely machined display of new materials in the service of a revolutionary form of communication reinforced comforting notions of traditional stability.[17] Along with representations of modern travel (steamships, a zeppelin, and Richard E. Byrd's plane over Antarctica), the map included small iconic representations of various regions. With the exception of a bulldozer for Russia and grain elevators and smokestacks for the U.S.A., these icons referred to natural or traditional attributes – a Roman arch and Gothic cathedral for Europe, the Taj Mahal for India, the Egyptian pyramids, an African elephant, an Australian kangaroo, and so on. The world might be shrinking through technologies that annihilated time and space, but modern travelers found that most destinations fitted into stable clichés. They sought to discover in exotic locales that most of the world continued on as if preserved in amber, eternally protected against modernity.

Even so, most travelers enjoyed modern comforts. The train, steamship, airplane, or zeppelin became an extension of the cosmopolitan zone from which they had set out. Images of travel often focussed on the comfort of the vehicle itself – portrayed as so abstracted from the outside world as to suggest lack of change even in the act of motion. A postcard for the

Fig. 5.14   See Cat. 111
Panel
***Radio Broadcasting*, from the Westinghouse Pavilion, "A Century of Progress" exposition, Chicago, IL, 1933**
Made by Westinghouse Electric and Manufacturing Company, Pittsburgh, PA

German national railway (fig. 5.15) represented a "comfortable railway journey" by showing an elegant couple lounging side-by-side on an upholstered seat superimposed over a stylized track in an otherwise black void. Less surreal, another German poster[18] portrayed a stylish young woman in bright yellow pajamas sitting on her railway berth, enjoying a civilized breakfast of poached egg and croissant, her face averted and gazing at an indistinct blue landscape. Even zeppelin travel, now regarded as emblematic of a cult of technology, evoked a tranquil air of domesticity in a leaflet whose photographs revealed cozy rooms with frilly curtains, fresh-cut flowers, and female travelers writing letters or entertaining children. For airplane travel – with its noise, turbulence, temperature extremes, and odors of airsickness – it was misleading to refer, as Lufthansa did, to "the comfort of home."[19] Ocean travel, however, did offer "safety, pleasure and comfort" in "spacious and comfortable" surroundings with "smart, modern furniture, hot and cold running water, and beds that woo even insomniacs," as claimed by the Holland-America Line. In other words, whatever it actually delivered,

Fig. 5.15
Postcard
Die bequeme Eisenbahnreise
(The Comfortable Railroad Journey), c. 1935
Designed by Friede
(German, dates unknown)
Printed by Julius Beltz, Germany
4⅛ x 5⅞ inches (10.5 x 14.9 cm)
86.19.981

Fig. 5.16
Advertisement
Winterreisen in den Tropenfrühling
***Mittelamerikas* (Winter travel in Central**
America's tropical springtime), c. 1935
Designed by Ottomar Anton
(German, 1895–1976)
Published by Hamburg-Amerika Linie, Hamburg, Germany
8⅜ x 5⅞ inches (21.3 x 14.9 cm)
XB1992.1

modern travel promised "absolute security."[20] Equally important, it promised to reveal a non-modern world that remained in its traditional place. That was the point of an illustration published by an Italian steamship line that showed European sophisticates relaxing in a moderne bar, being served by an African waiter against the backdrop of a mural depicting natives hunting gazelle on an African plain.[21]

Judging from the Collection's posters, one motive for travel between the wars involved confirming the existence of the Other (in late twentieth-century critical jargon) – a process that indicated modernity's superiority but also established that most of the world remained untouched by modernity's troubling ambiguities. Images of primitive and colonial realms suggested simple lives of natural harmony. Always exploitative, sometimes racist, these images indicated romantic identification with people who had escaped machine-age tensions. The cover of a booklet promoting a Hamburg-Amerika winter cruise to the Caribbean (fig. 5.16) portrayed three Central American Indian women and a child in vibrant colors. Flanked by lush vegetation, they appeared on a sun-drenched landing amidst oranges, melons, and clay urns whose forms and colors evoked the organic. Blue sea and sky formed an undifferentiated field on which a stylized steamship floated in the distance – sole reminder of the modern world its passengers had left behind. Deferential, eyes downcast or obscured, these natives posed no threat to any established order. They existed as reminders of the reassuring presence of their vast geographic realm, serene and unchanging. Such images, of which there were many,

Fig. 5.17
Poster
Complete Map of the Airlines of K.N.I.L.M.,
Royal Netherlands Indies Airways, **c. 1935**
Designed by Jan Wijga
(Dutch, 1902–78)
Printed by J.A. Luii & Co., Amsterdam
Published by K.L.M. and Nepon, Amsterdam
Commercial color lithograph
23 5/8 x 31 1/2 inches (60.0 x 80.0 cm)
Marks: obverse, printed in blue, upper right corner
"JAN WIJGA"
TD1990.335.15

Fig. 5.18
Schedule
Norway by Airway, **1939**
Designed by Thau
(Norwegian, dates unknown)
Printed by Wittusen & Jensen A/s, Oslo
Published by Det Norske Luftfartselskap, Oslo
7 1/8 x 13 3/4 inches (18.1 x 34.9 cm)
TD1988.154.22

assumed civilized superiority to native peoples whose full absorption into nature marked them not only as inferior but also as paradoxically desirable and absolutely essential to the survival of a fully balanced world in which modernity marked only one pole of experience.

European colonial powers proved most obsessive about this theme. The Dutch emphasized the timeless beauty and escapism of their East Indian empire, whose islands were linked during the late 1930s by KLM's subsidiary, Royal Netherlands Indies Airways (KNILM) (fig. 5.17). The cover of a typical KLM brochure illustrated a plane flying from a landscape of polder and windmill into an East Indian scene with a native plowing a field against a backdrop of grass hut and palm tree.[22] Inside, next to a timetable, a photograph depicted a native boy on a palm-fringed coast drinking from a clay vessel. A more ambitious forty-page booklet offered a breathless account of *Touring the Tropics at Top Speed.* Although the airline's machines penetrated to "the remotest parts of the Netherlands East Indies' archipelago," a traveler could still experience a "primitive society of natives not as yet come within the compass of our culture and civilization." On the "unspoilt" island of Bali, "far from the din and glamour of modern life," one could meet "a people whose fame has spread far and wide" – a people described so glowingly that modern civilization seemed incomplete. Their "stalwart" men exhibited a "walk and gaze" revealing a "spirited and independent nature." Their women possessed a "rhythmic gait" that enhanced "the beauty of their goddesslike forms" – a quality revealed in a bare-breasted woman posing respectfully with other natives behind a white hunter leaning against the jaw of a dead elephant. The irony of gaining easy access to such unspoiled wonders by means of the most modern transportation machines became evident only decades later, long after men and women in London and New York, in Manchester and Detroit, had used the Dutch airline's booklet to fuel romantic fantasies of temporary respite from the dull routine of modern times.[23]

Colonial lands were not alone, however, in offering geographical realms where time stood still. The Holland-America Line, for example, invited American tourists to a Mediterranean cruise in 1933 by promising "unfading memories of an exotic, pulsating life that has flourished since biblical days" in a land "replete with ancient and sacred treasures."[24] The Continent itself contained pockets of tradition, places where the landscape and its inhabitants had changed little for decades, even centuries – except for the intrusion of transportation machines that brought urban sophisticates to enjoy their attractions. A poster for Britain's Southern Railway[25] promoted the Channel service with a luminous pastiche of German landscape, its craggy peaks crowned with a stylized Neuschwanstein towering over a Rhine Valley dotted with picturesque villages – the only modern note being a powerful steam locomotive and train of passenger cars in the foreground. Sometimes not even the *people* of Europe escaped colonization. The cover of a schedule published in English by the

157

Norwegian Airlines Inland Service (fig. 5.18) depicted a seaplane flying over a couple in traditional costume rendered in near-parody of folk styles of illustration. Viewed from behind, their faces invisible, they became, as fully as any Caribbean or East Indian natives, objectified elements of a desirable non-modern landscape.

Even Americans unable to travel to Europe or the East Indies could escape for brief moments into zones of history or of primitivism at the world's fairs of the 1930s. As a view-book from the Century of Progress explained, an international exposition functioned as "the focus, the concentration, the miniature, of the world today and the world tomorrow."[26] Because such a microcosm represented culturally mediated perceptions of reality, it revealed many of society's vital concerns. For the most part, interpreting the modernistic and streamlined architecture of the expositions at Chicago in 1933 and New York in 1939, historians have described them as celebrations of modernity – from which, in the awkward phrases of yet another viewbook, visitors took an "impression of newness, of modernity, of progress of the new tomorrow," an impression of "something altogether new and at variance with the traditions of other days."[27] In fact, however, Chicago's Century of Progress encompassed both modernity's accelerating pace and the desire to escape from it. As a folder promoting travel to the fair by Greyhound Bus asserted, anyone could "enjoy a veritable trip abroad at the heart of your own country" replete with "picturesque rickshaws" and "real Venetian gondolas."[28]

While planning the fair, officials hoped to persuade European nations to celebrate their traditions by building official pavilions in historical styles and mounting handicraft displays.[29] But the Europeans balked at presenting themselves as backward, preferring instead to embrace modernity. As a result, the exposition made do with such synthetic commercial attractions as the Streets of Paris and the Old Heidelberg Inn. During the fair's two-year run there were "villages" devoted to Belgium, Spain, Germany, Switzerland, Italy, Tunisia, Ireland, and Merrie England, as well as to a colony of midgets incongruously installed in a mock-medieval village. Other such pastiches included a replica of a Mayan temple at Uxmal and an "exact replica" of the Golden Temple of Jehol. The latter was "built in Inner Mongolia by skilled native artisans, shipped to Chicago in 28,000 pieces and reconstructed on the Exposition grounds by Chinese workmen."[30] Its ancient-looking facade, suggesting the patina of a varnished painting, peered out from the modernistic frame of a souvenir plaque (fig. 5.19). The juxtaposition indicated just how conflicted the Century of Progress remained about its trajectory into the future.

Although such expositions as the Chicago fair offered a microcosm of the contemporary world, visitors could not comprehend its complexities instantaneously. But there was indeed a way to experience the world at a glance. Modern air travel promised an all-encompassing perspective on the world – not by conquering time or space but by miniaturizing

reality. A Deutsche Lufthansa booklet described the experience of flight as that of the flying carpet, a long-standing dream made reality. The hidden logic binding all human constructions – towns and farms, highways and factories – sprang into consciousness with a directness impossible to achieve from the ground. The past came to life again as one looked out over an old village whose houses, town hall, and church were scattered like toys across the landscape.[31] The experience seemed innocent enough as portrayed by Deutsche Lufthansa, but it also supported destructive fantasies of possession and control – soon realized as military pilots took to the air to bomb and strafe. But a lesser variety of miniaturization also made it possible to domesticate modernity by isolating representative aspects of it, abstracting them from their usual environments, assimilating them into the traditional surroundings of one's own home, and thereby both possessing them and neutralizing their potential for arousing anxiety.

This third mode of domestication was the most direct because it did not depend on situating modernity within larger historical or geographical constructs. Instead, it relied on an implosion that eliminated rational contexts of time or space. The domesticated object existed alone, an icon of modernity divorced from any context other than the personal. At its simplest, the assimilated object was actually a child's toy, often as crude as Midgetoy's tiny spaceship but sometimes as impressive as American Flyer's detailed version of the Burlington Zephyr (fig. 5.20). The Metalcraft Zeppelin Construction Set invited boys to bolt metal

159

Fig. 5.20 See Cat. 99
Toy
Burlington Zephyr, 1934
Manufactured by American Flyer, Chicago, IL
and
Toy spaceship, c. 1934
Manufactured by Midgetoy, Rockford, IL
Metal, rubber, paint
1½ x 1¾ x 3½ inches (3.8 x 4.5 x 8.9 cm)
Marks: underside, raised "MIDGETOY ROCKFORD ILL."
83.18.1

Fig. 5.21 See Cat. 100
Toy
Graf Zeppelin, 1928
Manufactured by Metalcraft Corporation, St. Louis, MO
and
Cover
Instruction Book Zeppelin Construction Set,
1928
Published by Metalcraft Corporation, St. Louis, MO

Fig. 5.22
Souvenir ashtray of the Tower of Empire,
Empire Exhibition, Glasgow, Scotland, 1938
Great Britain
Plastic
4 x 5 inches dia. (10.2 x 1.3 cm dia.)
85.19.223

plates together to construct models of various airships (fig. 5.21). Its instruction manual included a drawing depicting a father looking in on four boys at play, three of them with model airplanes, the fourth with a Metalcraft zeppelin attached fore and aft to a pulley on a string stretched across the front porch.[32] This construction set worked in complex ways, both trivializing a frightening new technology by turning it into child's play and neutralizing it by putting it under the control of an industrious all-American boy. Modernity would hold no surprises for this particular chip off the old block.

Another type of miniaturization – a sort of toy for adults – enabled an exposition visitor to distill its microcosm further through a single souvenir representing the whole in a model of one of its most distinctive parts. At Chicago, for example, one could purchase a thermometer in a plastic stand five inches high[33] – a model of the Havoline tower, the building most visible against the skyline of the Century of Progress and itself intended as a giant representation of a standard thermometer. The drastic reduction rendered even more graspable an iconic form whose originally vast enlargement over its real-world inspiration had also aimed at immediate comprehension of potentially complex technical or scientific concepts. Another example of the souvenir miniature sought not to render modern technology assimilable by trivializing it but to do the same for modernist architecture. The original form in this case was the central tower of the Empire Exhibition at Glasgow in 1938, an uncompromising geometric arrangement of shapes echoing Russian Constructivism. When miniaturized as a plastic ashtray (fig. 5.22),

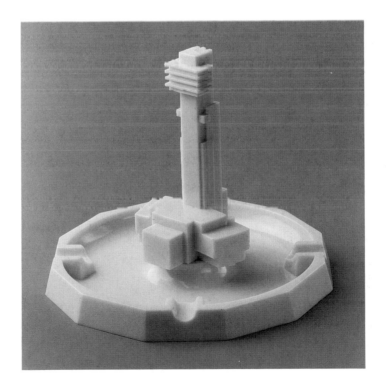

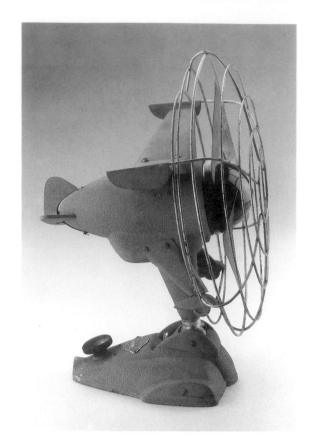

it suggested familiarity bordering on amiable contempt. Casually flicking cigarette ash into it indicated that one had brought the incomprehensible down to size and did not need to ponder its violation of everyday norms.

The most significant category of miniaturization did not express contempt but instead revealed optimistic celebration of a modernity brought under control through domestic assimilation. Industrial designers who gave shape to consumer products of the 1930s often took inspiration from larger forms of a mechanized society. The era witnessed everything from the Ronson Touch-Tip lighter – resembling a moderne steam engine with its solid metal construction, black enamel and chrome finish, and built-in clock echoing a steam gauge – to the more expressive Silvertone Turbine radio with smooth black phenolic plastic finish, cooling fins molded in, and end-mounted semi-spherical dial echoing a turbine's rotor housing.[34] Most such products drew inspiration from streamlined transportation machines. Some, such as the die-cast Aeros fan manufactured in Germany (fig. 5.23), revealed considerable humor. Its designer, working from the similarity of a household fan's blades to an airplane propeller, gave its motor housing the shape of the stubby airplanes of animated cartoons, complete with ornamental wings, tailfins, and shrouded wheels. Most designers avoided humor, however, preferring an elegance that idealized the machines it borrowed from. Two electric travel irons exemplified streamlined design (fig. 5.24). The

162

Fig. 5.23

Fan, c. 1935

Manufactured by Aeros, Germany
Wrinkle-painted iron, steel, plastic
13½ x 12¾ x 11½ inches (34.3 x 32.4 x 29.2 cm)
Marks: on base, red metal plate "AEROS/VOLT PER. WATT
TYPE/ 220 50 50 OW30/ NR. 852395/ D.G.M./ MADE IN
GERMANY"
TD1990.323.1

Fig. 5.24

Travel iron, 1941
Designed by Richard Spencer
(American, dates unknown)
Manufactured by General Electric Company, Bridgeport, CT,
c. 1944
Chrome-plated steel, plastic, fabric, rubber
3½ x 7⅜ x 3¾ inches (8.9 x 18.7 x 9.5 cm)
Marks: underside "CAT. NO. 119F 18W. 375 V. 115 UNITED
STATES PATENTS 2339744 GENERAL ELECTRIC CO.
BRIDGEPORT, CONN. ONTARIO, CALIF. MADE IN U.S.A."
XX1990.511
and
Travel Iron *(See Cat. 153)*
Smoothie, 1946
Designed by C. Kerr, N.H. Lucas, E. Lucas,
and H.T. Holder

Fig. 5.25
Plaque, c. 1925
Designed by Mario Moschi
(Italian, b. 1896)
Italy
Brass
30 x 18 x 2 inches (76.2 x 45.7 x 5.1 cm)
84.9.20.1

more representational, a British product called the Smoothie, looked like an aerodynamic locomotive with lines slightly softened, while a General Electric model presented a sculptural abstraction of speed with a form as attractive to the hand as to the eye. These irons functioned, as did other applications of machine forms to household appliances, by enabling people to assimilate them into everyday surroundings. Beyond that, both these appliances domesticated modernity by putting it into the hands of women – and, as travel irons, they did so inside the very transportation machines that defined modern experience.

A complex relationship between woman and machine lay at the heart of the third mode. Images like that of the young woman in a post coach used by Deutsche Lufthansa to humanize the airplane (fig. 5.08) appeared frequently – but usually without complicating historical references. Postcards portraying stylish women posing in front of trains and planes were common. The German railways published a card for distribution in France that bore a foreground image of a haughty young woman with a bouquet of yellow carnations over her arm and a powerful steam locomotive filling the background.[35] A similar image distributed by the Società Aerea Mediterranea of Rome depicted two young women languidly posed in conversation below the wing and propeller of a passenger plane.[36] These views were intended to be posted by female travelers, perhaps to indicate that modern travel held no terrors for them.

Fig. 5.26
Schedule
SABENA Timetable and Fares: 28.3 to 1.10.1938,
Shell Aviation News supplement, April 1938
Designed by M. Cros
(Belgian, dates unknown)
Printed by Th. Dewarichet, Brussels
9 ⅛ x 7 ½ inches (23.2 x 19.1 cm)
TD1988.154.12

Two other representations of woman and machine offered paradigmatic examples of domestication working to assimilate modernity into more traditional ways of perceiving reality. In each case, isolation of woman and machine from any extraneous context allowed the significance of their joining to emerge with relative purity. The first was an Italian bronze relief from the 1920s (fig. 5.25). Nearly three feet high, it depicted a female nude seated casually at the top of a semi-Corinthian capital, a biplane resting on her outstretched hand. Reputedly intended to ornament an automobile showroom, the sculpture suggested progress could indeed be assimilated. Whimsical details – a string of pearls and a stylish wave in her hair – indicated that here was a goddess of progress. But the classical pose firmly situated the modern era within a historical continuum that encompassed the glories of ancient Rome.

Quite different in effect was an illustration on a 1938 timetable for the Belgian airline Sabena (fig. 5.26). It portrayed a vibrant woman waving a handkerchief and smiling exuberantly. Above her loomed the nose, propeller, and cockpit of an airliner with the Belgian flag waving from it. A violation of perspective allowed one wing and its engine to extend to the frame's right edge. This pliancy of representation suggested a humanizing of the airplane. Its somewhat anthropomorphic nose and cockpit echoed the young woman's face, while the crook of engine and wing echoed that of her elbow. Both woman and plane were rendered in soft rounded forms with a similar warmth of hue. Whether assimilated to the organic, as in this case, or to the traditional, as in the Italian relief, the machine was domesticated by a woman's presence. Or had the machine enticed woman into its domain? Henry Adams's haunting pronouncement several decades earlier that modern woman "must, like the man, marry machinery," seemed a distant threat or a prophecy fulfilled, depending on one's perspective.[37]

One final Wolfsonian artifact concludes this discussion of domestication by means of assimilation. It comes from a huge collection of matchbook covers assembled during the late 1930s and early 1940s by King Farouk of Egypt, a notorious playboy and a source whose improbability reminds us of our tenuous grasp on the past's ephemera. One particular advertising matchbook (fig. 5.27) bore an image of the New York Central Railroad's most famous train, the 20th Century Limited, designed by Henry Dreyfuss in 1938. The image came directly from Leslie Ragan's poster illustration of the locomotive,[38] which, like that of the Belgian airliner, used a softness of shape and hue to render as feminine an object usually perceived as masculine. The locomotive's general outline also suggested mixed associations. If its thrusting tubular form, ending in the circular eye of a single headlight, seemed so phallic as to suggest a grand jest, then its broad front, read vertically as a human figure, assumed the form of a vigorous, large-breasted woman whose amply rounded skirt suggested the possibility of a swelling pregnancy. The image promised a rapprochement of the male realm of technology with the female realm of nature – but with no hint of the result. The matchbook on which this image appeared became a kind of second-generation miniature, approaching the limits of miniaturization, so tiny it could be shoved into a pocket or purse. This appearance on a matchbook both trivialized the locomotive and rendered it a familiar object, thereby neutralizing any ambivalence about its contributions to modernity.

Ultimately it made little difference whether one situated modernity in a smooth historical continuum, or located it in a discrete geographic zone, or packaged its forms for assimilation to the natural or the domestic. Promoters of modernity no doubt used other strategies as well – though the images and artifacts of the Wolfsonian Collection do support this tentative typology. In the final analysis, however, the sheer multiplication of countless representations of modern life, more than any particular type of representation, made people comfortable with modernity. All such images became part of a vast cultural environment of representation – of which the Wolfsonian's provocative collection of thousands of artifacts constitutes a partial and imperfect microcosm. Collected and analyzed in the late twentieth century, they reveal as much about our own needs and desires as about those of the years between the wars. Even in postmodern times we are still engaged in domesticating modernity.

Fig. 5.27
Matchbook cover
***The 20th Century Limited*, c.1940**
Published by New York Central System,
New York
3¾ x 1½ inches (3.9 x 9.5 cm)
XB1992.240 (v.2)

NOTES

1   Marshall Berman, *All That Is Solid Melts into Air: The Experience of Modernity* (New York, 1982).

2   The concept of domesticating modernity as used here owes much to William H. Jordy, *American Buildings and Their Architects: The Impact of European Modernism in the Mid-Twentieth Century* (New York, 1972), especially the chapter on "The Domestication of Modern: Marcel Breuer's Ferry Co-operative Dormitory at Vassar College," pp. 165–219; to Roland Marchand, *Advertising the American Dream: Making Way for Modernity, 1920–1940* (Berkeley, 1985); and to John Hewitt, "The 'Nature' and 'Art' of Shell Advertising in the Early 1930s," *Journal of Design History* 5, no. 2 (1992): 121–39.

3   See Hugh Ferriss, *The Metropolis of Tomorrow* (New York, 1929).

4   See Wolfsonian Collection 83.4.27.

5   See Wolfsonian Collection TD1991.170.1.

6   See Wolfsonian Collection 86.4.76.

7   See Wolfsonian Collection TD1994.18.4.

8   Robert R. Updegraff, *The New American Tempo: And the Stream of Life* (Chicago, 1929).

9   This image exists in the Wolfsonian as a postcard, as a timetable cover, and as an imperforate sticker; presumably it also appeared in full-sized poster form.

10 See Wolfsonian Collection XX1992.132.

11 See Wolfsonian Collection XC1991.476.

12 See Wolfsonian Collection XB1992.733.

13 Eugen Neuhaus, *The Art of Treasure Island: First-Hand Impressions of the Architecture, Sculpture, Landscape Design, Color Effects, Mural Decorations, Illumination, and Other Artistic Aspects of the Golden Gate International Exposition of 1939* (Berkeley, 1939), p. 16.

14 *Color Beauties of a Century of Progress: Chicago 1933* (Chicago: Exposition Publications and Novelties, 1933).

15 *Official Guide Book of the Fair* (Chicago: A Century of Progress, 1933), p. 128. I am indebted to Dennis P. Doordan for pointing out this reference. For an excellent discussion of contrasting representations in advertisements of future cities and traditional villages see Marchand, *Advertising the American Dream*, pp. 255–64.

16 See Wolfsonian Collection XX1991.582.

17 Quotations are from a typescript, probably a draft of a contemporary publicity release, that was conveyed to a researcher by Joseph F. Rishel of Westinghouse Electric Corporation on January 12, 1983.

18 See Wolfsonian Collection TD1991.95.8.

19 *Ihr Flugschein…Ein Mittler für Schnelles, Genußvolles und Sicheres Reisen!* (Berlin: Deutsche Lufthansa, March 1938), p. 7.

20 *Luxury Cruise to the Romantic Borderlands of the Mediterranean* (Holland-America Line, 1932) TD1990.64.29.

21 Illustration by Frantz Leubart in booklet *Conte di Savoia* (Genoa: Flotte Riunite, n.d.).

22 See Wolfsonian Collection TD1988.154.14.

23   *Touring the Tropics at Top Speed* (Royal Netherlands Indies Airways), pp. 2, 32, 37 TD1990.335.1.

24   *Luxury Cruise to the Romantic Borderlands of the Mediterranean.*

25   See Wolfsonian Collection XX1990.2812.

26   *The Official Pictures of A Century of Progress Exposition Chicago 1933* (Chicago, 1933), p. 5.

27   Allen D. Albert, *Official View Book: A Century of Progress Exposition* (Chicago, 1933).

28   *1934 Chicago: World's Fair* (Greyhound Lines). On the obsession of exposition organizers with synthetic preserves devoted to the primitive and the traditional see Paul Greenhalgh, *Ephemeral Vistas: The Expositions Universelles, Great Exhibitions and World's Fairs, 1851–1939* (Manchester, 1988), pp. 82–111; and two volumes by Robert W. Rydell: *All the World's a Fair: Visions of Empire at American International Expositions, 1876–1916* (Chicago, 1984); *World of Fairs: The Century-of-Progress Expositions* (Chicago, 1993).

29   See memoranda by John S. Sewell, director of the exposition's Exhibits Department, to Henry Cole, director of its London office, February 20 and 24, 1931, Century of Progress Archive, Foreign Participation Series, Folder 11–144, University of Illinois at Chicago. I am indebted for these documents to Dennis P. Doordan.

30   *Color Beauties of a Century of Progress: Chicago 1933.*

31   Paraphrased from *Ihr Flugschein...Ein Mittler für Schnelles, Genußvolles und Sicheres Reisen!*, pp. 7, 10, 12–13.

32   *The Metalcraft Zeppelin Construction Set: Interesting History of Airships and an Elementary Course in Their Construction* (St. Louis: Metalcraft Corporation, 1928), p. 17.

33   See Wolfsonian Collection 86.19.112.

34   See Wolfsonian Collection 83.15.26 and XX1990.578.

35   See Wolfsonian Collection TD1990.191.7.

36   See Wolfsonian Collection XB1992.1459.

37   Henry Adams, *The Education of Henry Adams* (Boston, 1961; orig. 1907), p. 447.

38   See Wolfsonian Collection XX1990.2120.

Forging Modern Italy:
from Wrought Iron to Aluminum

Irene de Guttry & Maria Paola Maino

The Italian works in metal in the extensive Wolfsonian Collection are both numerous and particularly significant, as they illustrate the difficult and delicate passage from an artisan to an industrial era. In tracing the course of this development, it seems logical to examine the period covered in the Collection (1885–1945) by decades, with attention focussed on certain emblematic figures (for example, Coppedè, Mazzucotelli, Bellotto, Rizzarda, and Thayaht), each of whom, while advancing his art, was also representative of his epoch.

The Era of Gothic Revival

In 1860, the year when Italy achieved political unification, the process of industrialization had barely begun.[1] The Italian population, which was seventy-five percent illiterate, lived for the most part in the countryside. The social classes were still very much separate and distinct. Artisan workshops were an essential element of the cities, both large and small, and in both the cities and in the countryside, working at home was extremely common. Moreover, a shortage of easily usable roads and an inadequate number of railroad lines kept the rural areas isolated from the cities and from each other.

The new kingdom had to confront many daunting tasks in order to try to attain the level of the more advanced countries. It had to develop industries, create schools, build hospitals and roads, and try to overcome the gap between the north, where industrialization was already under way, and the undeveloped south. It also had to unify into a single national style the many different regional cultures, which combined age-old traditions with the inheritance of cultures brought to Italy by foreign rulers. Whether in architecture or applied arts, the tendency in Italy was to recapture the past through historicist styles rather than to look to the future. Given the heterogeneous nature of the cultures of the new nation, the image that was created in this way was (more than elsewhere in Europe) extremely fragmentary.

The first step toward artistic unity was the creation, in all the major Italian cities, of schools of applied industrial arts, as well as related teaching museums that contained either originals or copies of exemplary works of the past found in Italian churches and palaces. These museums formed collections of models that cabinet-makers, goldsmiths, ceramists, and glass-makers copied in an attempt to learn the techniques of the masters.

The great international exhibitions held in London in 1851 and 1862, in Paris in 1867 and 1878, in Vienna in 1873, and in Philadelphia in 1876, were testing grounds for industrial production. The matchless manual virtuosity of the Italian artisans who took part in these exhibitions contrasted with the more advanced technologies and mechanized production of the other countries. The Italians' works were either faithful copies or eclectic combinations of historical models. Evocations of the Renaissance dominated, for that was the historical style most widely studied in the Italian schools and seemed to confer a national identity. Needing to establish the importance of its heritage, the young Italian state understandably advanced the image of a period when Italy had been the undisputed center of European culture.

Italy, enhanced by a romantic vision of its past, was the destination of artists and intellectuals from all over Europe. Throughout the nineteenth century, cultural pilgrimages continued in a steady stream to Florence, the cradle of the Renaissance and the birthplace of Dante. The cult of this poet had spread throughout the West, but was particularly strong in England. In 1848 – the year in which the Pre-Raphaelite painter Dante Gabriel Rossetti translated Dante's *Vita Nova* into English – the poets Elizabeth and Robert Browning moved to Florence. They were among the first of a thriving international colony of intellectuals and wealthy members of the bourgeoisie who chose to live in the Tuscan capital.

A large villa in Genoa that Evan Mackenzie commissioned the architect Gino Coppedè to remodel in 1896 serves as a model for many of the issues under discussion. (Today this building and its grounds are part of the Wolfsonian and will be a museum and research center of Italian design, decorative arts, and architecture of the 1885–1945 period.) First, the "Castello" exemplifies the revival of the Florentine Renaissance style. Born in Italy but of Scottish descent, Mackenzie was a highly successful agent for several insurance companies. He was also a humanist, bibliophile, and collector of rare editions of Dante's *Divine Comedy*. He chose Coppedè (at that time just beginning his career) because the architect shared his passion for Florentine art and history. Together, they designed a medieval/Renaissance castle, a "Tuscan" interpretation of the Gothic Revival (fig. 6.01). Coppedè was occupied for ten years in the design and construction of this building, which resembled a complex stage mechanism in which modern technology and evidence of modern comforts remained hidden. Drawbridges, loggias, watchtowers, grottoes, and underground passageways created a spectacular, dramatic effect.

Fig. 6.01
Castello Mackenzie, Genoa, Italy (1897–1906)
Gino Coppedè, architect
(Italian, 1866–1927)

Fig. 6.01
Castello Mackenzie, Genoa, Italy (1897–1906)
Gino Coppedè, architect
(Italian, 1866–1927)

Second, the castle shows the renewed interest in wrought iron, a craft that had been in decline as a result of competition from the considerably less expensive cast iron. In the Castello Mackenzie, the vast design repertory of this revived material was on display – ranging from Gothic ornamental grates (with the traditional decorative motif of four lobes inscribed in a square) to Renaissance grilles, gates, well-curbs, hitching rings for horses, candlesticks, spikes, standard-bearers, lanterns, and lamps. Coppedè either reinvented or copied these forms from historical precedents.

The lamp-bearing chimera which was located at the head of the main staircase, however, stands in contrast, being made of cast iron (fig. 6.02). In its vocabulary of the Florentine Renaissance it is, however, the embodiment of Italian late nineteenth-century revivalism. It

171

Fig. 6.02
Lighting fixture
Model no. 106, used as newel post lamp,
Castello Mackenzie, Genoa, Italy, c. 1895
Manufactured by Officina Michelucci, Pistoia, Italy
Iron, metal, cloth, wire
46¼ x 13½ x 16½ inches (117.5 x 34.3 x 41.9 cm)
TD1993.96.1

is an extremely faithful cast-iron reproduction by the Michelucci foundry of the chimera that serves as a standard-bearer on the facade of the fifteenth-century Palazzo Strozzi in Florence.

Design Reform in Italy

By the end of the nineteenth century, when the process of industrialization was gathering pace in North Italy, considerable development took place not only in textiles, but also in the manufacture of chemicals and machines. The social and economic transformations that followed were also reflected in the arts. In Lombardy, painters known as the "Divisionists" – Angelo Morbelli, Gaetano Previati, and Giuseppe Pellizza da Volpedo – addressed social issues and denounced the inhuman conditions in which both factory and farm hands worked. In these years, characterized by mass emigration, by the first efforts to organize workers into unions, and by the establishment of anarchist movements, the Divisionists represented the toil and protests of the workers in their paintings.

At the same time, the entrepreneurial bourgeoisie welcomed the innovations that were reaching Italy from abroad. This was in part because they believed themselves to be allied to the bourgeoisie of the more advanced European countries, but also because this class glimpsed in the new trends the possibility of important developments in Italy for production, consumption, and commerce.

Through the Arts and Crafts movement in the decorative arts, the principles of the new aesthetic of simplicity of line, functionality, and honest materials began to spread throughout Europe. Whereas in Great Britain reform was manifested as a reaction against the Industrial Revolution, in less-industrialized Italy it took the form of a reaction against over-decoration and eclectic disorder. In 1889, the critic Alfredo Melani wrote in a popular manual: "Art in the home is the product of the rational use of material and form in accordance with need," and "art in a decorative object is not the result of complicated decoration, which is often only a detraction."[2] In a rejection of academicism and excessive attachment to the historical, which occurred a few years later than it did in the northern European countries, the direct study of nature was proposed as a source of inspiration. Camillo Boito, the director of the monthly journal, *Arte italiana decorativa e industriale*, which was subsidized by the Ministry of Agriculture, Industry, and Commerce and was distributed in the schools, wrote in an 1898 article that "the young artisan should live among plants and flowers, fall in love with them, entering deeply in them until he succeeds in extracting their decorative essence."[3]

The articles and essays of the art critics Melani, Enrico Thovez and Vittorio Pica, who published in influential journals such as *Arte italiana decorativa e industriale* and *Emporium*, kept the Italian public informed of what was happening abroad. Those articles, generously illustrated with drawings and photographs, explained the *Arte Nuova*. They provided the theory which the artists/artisans put into practice.

One of the principal ideals of design reform – to unite in a single individual the roles of designer and producer – was in Italy virtually taken for granted. The most ambitious and gifted artisans had probably completed their apprenticeship in evening or weekend courses in schools of applied industrial arts, where drawing was a fundamental and required subject. Having learnt drawing, they used it not only to copy, but also to express their own creativity. They knew, in other words, how to work as designers. Moreover, the Arts and Crafts principle of valuing the decorative and the fine arts equally favored talented artisans who were thereby elevated to the status of artist, while many artists abandoned painting and sculpture to take up applied art.

The International Exhibition of Modern Decorative Arts, held in Turin in 1902, was the official act of recognition of imported Modernism. Only works in the Modern style were accepted, and the fact that this "Stile Liberty" was of foreign origin was obvious not only in the name (taken from the London department store) but also in the inspiration that the Italian participants drew from models and formulas already widespread abroad.

Some of them looked to France, with its "whiplash" and naturalistic floral decorations, and others to the austerity of the Arts and Crafts movement. Still others, like the Milanese Carlo Bugatti, invented an original and autonomous artistic vocabulary of Oriental motifs.

Artisan workshops, small, medium, and large companies, as well as individual artists, all participated in the Turin exhibition. The huge effort at organization was undertaken in view of the potential return in business and publicity. Exhibiting alongside already established artistic industries, such as Ducrot, Richard-Ginori, Carlo Zen, and V. Valabrega, were artisans or artists (painters and sculptors) who handcrafted their own designs.[4] The innovative energy they demonstrated guaranteed their success, and their increased commissions transformed them into entrepreneurs. It was these artists/craftspeople, and not (as in the rest of Europe) the architects, who gave impetus to the reform in the applied arts. In Turin, the Italian artists who met the challenge of the architects Mackintosh, Behrens, Olbrich, Baumann and Horta, were, among others, the Turinese sculptor Giacomo Cometti and the Genoese painter Alberto Issel (both of whom had become cabinet-makers), the Florentine painter and ceramist Galileo Chini, and the well-known Milanese artist Giovanni Beltrami, who had abandoned painting to take up the art of stained glass. Two of the protagonists in Turin were artisans: the cabinet-maker Eugenio Quarti and Alessandro Mazzucotelli, who worked in wrought iron, the former the son of a carpenter, and the latter the son of a dealer in iron agricultural equipment.

Mazzucotelli was eighteen years old when he was employed as an apprentice worker in the workshop of the Milanese smith Defendente Oriani, which he took over in 1891 and soon enlarged.[5] At the Exposition Universelle in Paris in 1900, the floral decoration of the gates he exhibited attracted much attention and admiration.[6] He was by then a well-known artist, friend and collaborator of artists and architects, and a standard-bearer of design reform.[7] He already had to his credit executed prestigious commissions in Italy and abroad, restoring dignity and vitality to iron working, which had previously seemed condemned to the reproduction of past models. At the Turin Exposition, where his works were presented in a stand decorated by Carlo Bugatti, he reaffirmed his adherence to the new style, as well as an artistic maturity, in his "iron works full of flowers."[8]

Alessandro Mazzucotelli and the Società Umanitaria

In 1903, Mazzucotelli was asked to direct the department of decorative iron-workers in the workshop-school of applied industrial art founded that same year by the Humanitarian Society. Created in Milan in 1893 with the aim of "enabling the disinherited, without distinction, to help themselves back up again, by finding them housing, work and educational opportunities,"[9] this society was the brainchild of Prospero Moisè Loria, one of the most interesting figures in the Milanese bourgeoisie of the period, who came from a humble background and had become wealthy through skillful commercial operations. In order to allow even the poorest of individuals to receive an education, he left his fortune to the Humanitarian Society.

The Humanitarian Society was a lay Socialist organization, unlike other charitable institutions which tended to be authoritarian and hierarchical. It was run by a members' council and by the public administration of the city of Milan. During the first decade of the twentieth century, as Loria had envisioned, it established employment offices, professional schools for both sexes, institutions for social security and social legislation, schools for children (under the direction of Maria Montessori), libraries, and even a theater.[10] The work of the Society was in the forefront in all areas of social reform, and even included the construction of workers' housing, which was among the very first to have modern plumbing. The Society also provided assistance when emigration was at its height: between 1900 and 1914, eight million Italians – or one-fifth of the entire population – emigrated, for the most part to North and South America.

The aim of the workshop-schools for industrial art was to renew the traditional criteria for teaching according to the values of the British Arts and Crafts movement. Students were encouraged to develop their talents freely, taking their inspiration from nature. That approach represented a considerable qualitative leap, compared to that of the state schools, where students were still expected to copy the established styles of the past.

All the teachers were artists/artisans of considerable fame, and the commitment expected of them was as demanding as it was poorly recompensed. Few managed to continue for long, but Mazzucotelli was one of the most steadfast. Between 1903 and 1924, he trained an entire generation of decorative iron-smiths, and subsequently became the director of the University of Decorative Arts in Monza, another offshoot of the Humanitarian Society.[11] Mazzucotelli considered teaching a form of social service, as well as an opportunity to increase his knowledge through study. He taught others an art that was supposed to be –in accordance with Arts and Crafts tenets – "for everyone," but that instead, as the names of the wealthy northern industrialists who gave him commissions amply demonstrate, was an art "for the few." A gruff but generous teacher, this artist of the people (Mazzucotelli always spoke in the Milanese dialect) was also a cultured man. All of this, combined with a massive physique, made him the symbol of the "self-made man" who was the embodiment of humanitarian Socialism.

The art of wrought iron was traditionally associated with architecture, and the Liberty period was its new golden age. The windows and balconies on the exteriors of villas and apartment buildings alike were decorated with wrought-iron balustrades, while the interiors boasted wrought-iron stairway railings, wrought-iron cages for the new elevators and lamps and chandeliers celebrating the advent of electricity.

Mazzucotelli's presence in modern architecture was considerable. The most famous architects of Milan and Turin – Rigotti, Sommaruga, Campanini, Mazzocchi, Conconi, Stacchini – considered him an equal partner in the creation of their buildings, making use of the incisive effect of his sinuous wrought-iron works to integrate and embellish stone, brick, and cement.

Added to his extraordinary mastery of his material was an inexhaustible creative vitality. Taking his inspiration from nature, he transformed static iron into a lively and expressive material. He modeled it into plastic forms, sensual flowers, plants, and leaves, entwined among flowing ribbons and knots – designs manifested in grilles and gates, balustrades, lamps, and street lamps, where insects or small animals posed, as though the breath of life were still present in them.

Mazzucotelli included in his decorative repertory freely interpreted themes and subjects of the period; the dragonflies, for example, a typical decorative motif of the Liberty style, which he must have noticed at the Paris and Turin Exhibitions, as stylized silhouettes in Carlo Bugatti's furniture as well as in naturalistic representations in the vases of Gallé, the

Fig. 6.03
Lamp stand (Torch holder), c. 1910
Designed by Alessandro Mazzucotelli
(Italian, 1865–1938)
Made by A. Mazzucotelli & C., Milan
Wrought iron
46 $\frac{2}{5}$ x 68 $\frac{5}{8}$ x 14 $\frac{11}{12}$ inches (118.0 x 174.3 x 38.0 cm)
87.905.11.1

Fig. 6.04
Photograph stand, c. 1905
Designed by Alessandro Mazzucotelli
(Italian, 1865–1938)
Made by A. Mazzucotelli & C., Milan
Wrought iron, glass photographic plate
73 1/8 x 27 11/12 x 20 7/8 inches (186.0 x 71.0 x 53.0 cm)
GX1993.61

jewelry of Lalique or the lamps of Louis Comfort Tiffany. He placed them magnified and still vibrant on torch holders, lamps, and gates (fig. 6.03).[12]

His innovation included the re-design of domestic objects, adapting traditional forms to modern uses and taste. To support a photographic plate – virtually the symbol of modernity – he used a classic model for the design of the stand; its high pedestal with its vertical, twisted rods with curled feet, interrupted by four-lobed connecting circles, was still inspired by the Renaissance (fig. 6.04). The plate itself, however, has a Liberty-style frame: it is crowned by a large flower, and its lateral supports move upward, terminating in the form of a stylized tree.

Sensitive to changes in taste, Mazzucotelli was among the first in Italy to become aware of the reform movement of the Viennese Secession. Shortly after the turn of the century, he abandoned fluid, sinuous forms and naturalistic representation of flowers, plants, and animals, for clean geometric forms and stylized ornament. One example of this rapid evolution is a bed, from about 1905 (fig. 6.05). While the form is inspired by the ancient Roman triclinium, the decoration is characterized by the abstract motifs favored by late nineteenth-century design reformers. The sides of the bed, decorated with the same glass cabochons used by his friend Eugenio Quarti in his furniture, were attached to the feet with expressive bolts; bolting was for years a favorite decorative element of Mazzucotelli (fig. 6.06).

The *de luxe* monograph-catalog edited in 1911 by Ugo Ojetti, the most authoritative Italian critic of that period, illustrates the great diversity of Mazzucotelli's artistic repertory, as well as the esteem he enjoyed in artistic circles.[13] In addition, with his successes and an increasingly demanding set of commissions (e.g., the Kursaal at San Pellegrino Terme, the National Theater of Mexico City), Mazzucotelli's catalytic role as a guide for other decorative iron-smiths became clearly visible.[14] Large and small workshops scattered across Italy imitated his designs, and he served as a constant point of reference even for those who had begun to work in the field before he did.

A Discovery of the Second Decade of the Century: Umberto Bellotto

Working as an iron-smith requires great strength; beating iron on an anvil with a heavy hammer is physically demanding. It also requires humility, because it is dirty work. Smiths have traditionally come from humble backgrounds. Those fortunate enough to be born at a time when craftsmanship was appreciated had the possibility of becoming famous artists and seeing their talents offer the means for social advancement.

Contrary to events in the rest of Europe, where the most important works in iron were designed by architects and executed by smiths who remained anonymous (examples of this are the iron works of Guimard, Horta, and Gaudi), in Italy the protagonists of the renewal of wrought-iron art were themselves smiths. Of equal importance to Mazzucotelli as an artist

177

Fig. 6.05
Bed, c. 1905
Designed by Alessandro Mazzucotelli
(Italian, 1865–1938)
Made by A. Mazzucotelli & C., Milan
Wrought iron, glass paste
62³⁄₄ x 82¹⁄₂ x 60¹⁄₂ inches (159.4 x 209.6 x 153.7 cm)
XX1991.463

Fig. 6.06
Detail of Bed with cabochons (Fig. 6.05)

Fig. 6.09
Flower stand, c. 1920
Metalwork by Umberto Bellotto
(Italian, 1882–1940)
Glass vase by Artisti Barovier, Venice
Wrought iron, glass
28¹⁄₃ inches ht. (72.0 cm ht.)
Museo Vetrario, Murano, Italy

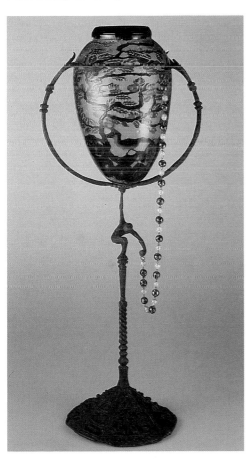

who designed the works he executed was the Venetian Umberto Bellotto, who became prominent about a decade later. The son of a modest iron-smith, Bellotto learned his craft in his father's workshop. In 1903, when he was twenty-one years old, he executed the railings for the restaurant at the International Exposition of Art in Venice (the Biennale). Through this work, he became known to the circle of Venetian artists and architects who, in the years that followed, commissioned works from him and helped him gain access to the Biennale as an artist rather than an artisan.[15]

In fact, from the very beginning, the Biennale included works of applied art, considering them to be equal in value to the fine arts. The promotional role of this exhibition was decisive, and participating in it meant recognition as an artist. Bellotto made a first, modest appearance at the Biennale in 1909, exhibiting two tripods. That debut occurred during a time of great stylistic uncertainty. As the turn-of-the-century wave of renewal had lost its vigor, and the Liberty style had run its course, the only valid point of reference seemed, once more, the past.

The time was ripe for the emergence of an original talent. In the Biennale of 1914, Bellotto succeeded in obtaining a room to himself. He set it up in a brilliantly theatrical manner, filling it with iron-bound chests, gilded iron and velvet caskets, and benches in metal and leather (fig. 6.07). The impression was one of decadence, the atmosphere of Venice immortalized by the poet Gabriele d'Annunzio and the painters Mario de Maria (known as Marius Pictor) and Mariano Fortuny, champions of a refined and sensual aestheticism, which was undiluted nostalgia for the past.

Bellotto also looked back to the Middle Ages – not to the period of Dante and the austere stones of Florence, but to that of Marco Polo, who imported the Orient to a city floating on and reflected by the waters of its lagoon. It is from the ancient Venetian tradition that Bellotto drew his taste for the sumptuous, and at the same time the light and transparent.

His Moorish grilles evoke the delicate lace-work of Burano, and his tripods and burners have slender legs reminiscent of the stems of the blown wine-glasses of Murano. Bellotto strained his material, as though attempting to bring out simultaneously the strong, pliable, and malleable character of iron and its capacity to be reduced to very slender threads and almost insubstantial sheets. His models were so captivating that other craftsmen soon imitated his work, witness the incense burners realized in the small workshop of the Demenego brothers in Cortina d'Ampezzo (fig. 6.08). Bellotto experimented in the uses of iron with the curiosity of an alchemist, seeking to combine it with other materials such as wood and leather, and, above all, ceramics and glass, in an "attractive alliance of strength and fragility."[16] (fig. 6.09)

World War I was by then imminent. In May 1915, Italy declared war on the Austro-Hungarian Empire, and before long advances in the applied arts ground to a halt, as workshops closed and workers were called to the front.

The Nineteen-Twenties: Apotheosis and Decline of Wrought Iron

Although victorious, Italy emerged from the war damaged and impoverished. Inflation triggered a wave of strikes by factory employees and protests by farm workers. Heightened social tensions weakened the position of the liberal ruling class, which proved incapable of stemming the rapid rise of the Fascist movement, founded in 1919 by Benito Mussolini upon the principles of passionate nationalism and violent anti-Socialism. The 1922 "March on Rome" ended with Mussolini's power established; the Fascists instituted an authoritarian, repressive regime which prohibited worker protest or any other form of opposition. Censorship imposed consensus and propaganda furthered the Fascist cause via the mass media, including the press (newspapers, magazines, school textbooks, and advertising) and, eventually, radio and cinema. In the arts and architecture, however, Mussolini did not mandate any one aesthetic, but instead pragmatically included various and even contradictory styles under the common denominator of the Fascist revolution, which claimed to be dynamic and innovative.

Fig. 6.08   See Cat. 47
Incense burners, c.1925
M. and U. Demenego

The 1920s were characterized by rapid and profound transformations in the decorative arts. The cult of decoration performed its last rites. Wrought iron became less frequently used on building exteriors but even more frequently in interiors. It reflected the styles of the decade: executed with medieval, archaic motifs such as torches and lanterns, it echoed the desire for vernacular expression; gilded and painted in Venetian green (in reference to patinated bronze Roman forms), it reinforced the Neo-Classicism in the general "call to order" (see Marianne Lamonaca's essay). With angles and curls, it suited the Art Moderne imported from France.

The First International Exhibition of Decorative Arts was inaugurated in Monza in May 1923.[17] This was a biannual exhibition which, together with the Venice Biennale, was intended to stimulate and document the post-war renewal of artistic activity in Italy. There the protagonists of the first two decades of the new century – Mazzucotelli and Bellotto – were joined by Carlo Rizzarda.

Mazzucotelli's style had evolved towards more rigid, harsh silhouettes, as he worked primarily in curled and drilled sheet metal cut-outs. In his rigorously geometrical grilles and

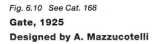

Fig. 6.10 See Cat. 168
Gate, 1925
Designed by A. Mazzucotelli

balustrades, he reintroduced the theme of the iron bar knot. That knot, which during the Liberty period had been a softer version, imitating cloth, was now a rigid knot repeated and greatly magnified. Mazzucotelli used it in works exhibited in two of the most symbolic sites of that decade; a gate exhibited in Paris at the International Exposition of Modern Decorative and Industrial Art in 1925 (fig. 6.10), and a grille executed in 1927 for d'Annunzio's residence, the Vittoriale.[18]

Bellotto's success during that period was astonishing. His works were included in most exhibitions, and he was awarded first prize at the 1923 Monza exhibition. His workshop, which produced large and small objects in iron, glass, and ceramic, had become a large-scale commercial enterprise. At the 1924 Venice Biennale, in a radically new setting, luminous and stylized – a play on the contrast between the light-colored walls and show cases and the black of the iron – he exhibited fifty-two pieces. They included wrought-iron screens, gates, lamps and tripods, ceramic plates, goblets and vases of iron and glass, and small "barbaric" sculptures.[19] An "iron trophy for rowing regattas" made of sheet metal, folded and drilled as if it were paper, demonstrated his virtuosity.[20] It was a ship model, many versions of which were created by Bellotto (fig. 6.11).

In 1928, he was summoned to Rome by his fellow Venetian, Giovanni Giuriati, then Minister of Public Works, who commissioned him to execute not only wrought-iron works, but also all the other furnishings for some of the regime's most prestigious buildings.[21] These commissions earned him the epithet of "Mussolini's iron-smith." Mussolini was credited with the "rare intuition" and "lucid discernment" of having understood early on Bellotto's value as an artist.[22] Bellotto had forged a "cup of wheat" and a sword of honor, both presents for Mussolini from the Minister of Public Works. His work in Rome was characterized by the Neo-Renaissance style, which was still practically obligatory for public buildings; although of impeccable workmanship, it is conventional and pedantic. His appearance at the Venice Biennale in 1932 was his swan song. His iron urns, powerful and sculptural, admirable for their archaic and almost Etruscan sensibility, once more illustrated his ability to combine the modern with the ancient (fig. 6.12).

With the advent of Fascism, the figure of the iron-worker assumed other connotations – no longer only the symbol of the man who forges his own destiny, but also representative of Italian industriousness. Mussolini was himself the son of a smith and particularly proud of his humble origins.[23] Undoubtedly, for him, all the qualities and the symbolism connected with forging iron had strongly positive connotations. In his speeches, the verb "to forge" appears continuously. "We will *forge* a great, superb and majestic Italy . . . " or "Fascism has *forged* the new Italian . . . "[24] Also, the adjective "iron-like" is always used to describe discipline, and the noun "iron" is often used as a synonym for dagger.

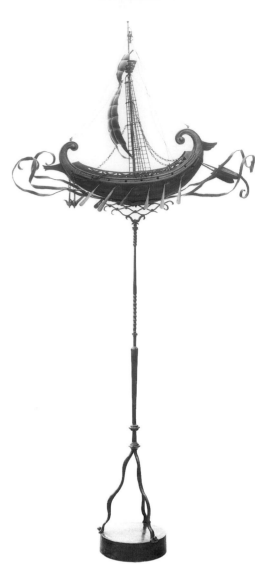

Fig. 6.11
Trophy cup for rowing regattas, c. 1925
Designed by Umberto Bellotto
(Italian, 1882–1940)
Venice
Wrought iron
92 1/8 x 45 2/7 inches (234.0 x 115.0 cm)
GX1993.323

Corresponding to Bellotto's success in Venice was the success of Carlo Rizzarda in Milan. Trained from boyhood as a smith, Rizzarda moved at the age of twenty-one from his native Feltre to Milan in order to join the workshop of Alessandro Mazzucotelli. He remained there from 1904 to 1911, when he opened his own workshop. By the time the war broke out and he enlisted, Rizzarda's work was already well known and admired. Upon his return at the end of the war, the pace of his activity – which had never been slow – became frenetic. He worked in collaboration with prominent architects for a large and wealthy group of clients. Aware of his own worth as an artist, he bought a *palazzo* in Feltre with the intention of using it in future as a museum for his works.[25]

Rizzarda understood and interpreted the fashions of the 1920s, including stylized graphic forms, while following a Neo-Classical order. He freely borrowed motifs from the Art Moderne repertory, of which one important example is his "flowing fountain" (fig.

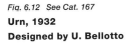

Fig. 6.12 See Cat. 167
Urn, 1932
Designed by U. Bellotto

6.13). Adhering to a typical schema of the new style, Rizzarda enclosed decoration within definite frames – oval, round, oblong – at the center of the grille, while masking his modest material with gilding and green patina. His origins in the Venetian region were also revealed by his use of gossamer eighteenth-century-style webs, Byzantine-like arabesques, and thin, delicately colored blown glass (fig. 6.14).

At the 1923 Monza exhibition, Rizzarda had a gallery to himself. On that occasion, Ugo Ojetti declared him to be a revelation.[26] Among other things, Rizzarda exhibited a large panel containing examples of handles, doors, and hinges, as well as decorative elements to be applied to furniture, one of which was a small lictorian fasce, demonstrating that this image had already become familiar.

In the 1925 Exposition in Paris, the industrious Italian iron artists displayed their usual wares, in the ingenuous belief that they still represented a modern Italy. However, they were criticized for being "behind the times," although they were also praised and rewarded once more for their virtuosity.[27] Rizzarda's stand at the Grand Palais was filled with objects of a traditional taste, in sharp contrast with the nearby Futurist stand containing the tapestries of Depero and the decorative panels of Balla and Prampolini. Mazzucotelli's iron works at the Esplanade Gallery (fig. 6.10) provided the framework and elegant support for *de luxe* objects: Capellin-Venini's glass, Ravasi's silks, and Ravasco's jewelry.[28] The days of wrought iron were numbered. The Exposition celebrated the apotheosis of Art Moderne, but at the same time marked the end of an era.

Two ways of defining artistic production confronted each other here. The first exalted refined, luxury objects – unique works that were destined for a wealthy élite and while they updated the past, did not break with it. The second responded to the social transformations of the past fifty years and looked to a future that would include industrial production for a vast new market. The small pavilion of Le Corbusier, although discreetly placed off to the side, introduced a new approach – one where a house was a *machine à habiter* (machine for living), and so became a signpost of the modern movement.

From that point on, the architect Gio Ponti played a major role in the future of Italian applied arts as both a designer and a promoter, through editing publications such as *Domus* and contributing to many others.[29] His Neo-Classical ceramics and porcelain displayed in the Richard-Ginori stand at the Grand Palais had scored a complete triumph. His comment on the Exposition was that "industry is the 'manner' of the twentieth century, its method of creation."[30]

It was clear that Italy, if it was not to be relegated to the sidelines, had to produce more quickly. Thus, artisans – who represented its greatest resource – would be encouraged to restrain their creativity and be content with being mere executors of the projects of architects, who in the role of industrial designers were the new protagonists of artistic renewal in Italy.

Opposite
Fig. 6.13
Fountain, c. 1925
Designed by Carlo Rizzarda
(Italian, 1883–1931)
Milan
Wrought iron
64 $^{11}/_{12}$ x 14 $^{11}/_{12}$ inches (165.0 x 38.0 cm)
GX1993.62

Fig. 6.14
Radiator cover
Designed by Carlo Rizzarda
(Italian, 1883–1931)
From *Enciclopedia delle Moderne Arti Decorative Italiane.*
Ferro Battuto (Milan, 1926), pl. 53

This peaceful revolution was surprisingly brief. The architects, the undisputed lords of the 1930 Monza Exposition, had a new alliance to Italian industry in their role of "designers." The key role of architects is clear from the two most influential movements to emerge in the 1920s – the Novecento italiano (the Italian twentieth century) and Rationalism. Introduced by a group of painters about 1922, the Novecento style soon became an important vehicle for architects to express a modernity appropriate for twentieth-century Italy.[31] In buildings and their furnishings, it was characterized by monumentality achieved through the simplification of classical forms inspired by ancient Roman models. Continuity with the past was considered essential.

The Rationalists shared the Novecento passion for designing a modern age but they emphasized far more the necessity for structural expression. The architects of Gruppo 7, who published a manifesto of Rationalist ideals in 1926, embraced the new building materials of steel, glass, and reinforced concrete and the forms engendered by them.[32] Although Gropius, Mies van der Rohe and Le Corbusier were their heroes, the Gruppo 7 were not pure internationalists; like the Novecento designers, they required specific Italian solutions to problems.

The Novecento love of unfettered monumentality and the Rationalist abhorrence of surface ornamentation both resulted in the rejection of wrought iron. Balconies with railings disappeared from smooth building facades, just as every trace of that opaque, black metal disappeared from the interiors of homes and large buildings.

Thus, the art of the smith, which had been revived with Modernism, concluded its vital cycle in the space of a single generation.

The Nineteen-Thirties: Aluminum, the Metal of National Economic Autonomy

By the beginning of the new decade, the "official" image of Italy was for the most part a nation converted to Fascism. Portraits of Mussolini hung in offices and schools, and the fasces (of the Roman lictors) were a ubiquitous decorative element on public buildings and monuments. Huge propaganda posters proclaimed the values of the regime (the nation, the family, the party leadership, the social order) and its aspirations: demographic growth, a return to the countryside, increased agricultural production (known as "the Battle of the Grain"), colonial expansion. And Mussolini ("il Duce" – from the Latin "dux", meaning leader) certainly did intend to expand the Italian empire. However, following the invasion of Ethiopia in 1935, the League of Nations punished Italy with economic sanctions. The economic policy of autarky (self–sufficiency), already started some years before by the Fascist regime, now became a necessity. Fascist propaganda bragged about Italian national autonomy, calling on and exploiting all national resources to the maximum. One of those resources was

Fig. 6.15
Medal
***Prima Adunata Professionisti e Artisti
(First Assembly of Professionals and Artists),
1932***
Thayaht (pseudonym for Ernesto Michahelles)
(Italian, 1863–1959)
Florence
Bronze
2 inches dia. (5.1 cm dia.)
Marks: obverse, in high relief, lower left "THAYAHT/1932"
83.1.192.1

aluminum, a material extracted from bauxite in which Italian soil is very rich. Aluminum had begun to be used in Italy at the end of the nineteenth century; and immediately preceding World War I, the aeronautics industry used it in the construction of dirigibles.[33] Once its properties (high resistance to corrosion, low specific weight) and advantages (low cost) became known, it was used for a vast range of applications in the electrical and mechanical industries, in construction and the production of electric appliances. Experiments were conducted with it in all areas, including the arts. The Futurist artist Thayaht executed his first pieces of sculpture in aluminum in 1927; later he invented an alloy combining aluminum with silicon, tin and nickel – thayahtite – which he used for small castings, sculpture, plates, vases and jewelry.[34]

In 1929 Marinetti, the founder of the Futurist movement, introduced him to Mussolini. Thayaht presented the portrait "Dux," executed in medium hard steel and consisting of a compact head (a medieval helmet of sorts), the features of which were obscured, creating a profile which pressed forward like the bow of a ship. The effect is one of warrior strength, and Mussolini, after examining the sculpture, exclaimed: "Yes, I like it. It is me, it is how I see myself."[35] From then on, in Thayaht's sculpture, paintings, or medals, Mussolini would always be represented in this way (fig. 6.15). Like many other Futurist artists, Thayaht had enthusiastically embraced Fascism. In fact, the ideologies of the two movements – Fascist and Futurist – have many points in common; their shared revolutionary fervor is explored in Dennis Doordan's essay.

Fig. 6.16
***Trittico dell'Amicizia* (Friendship Triptych), 1932**
Thayaht (pseudonym for Ernesto Michahelles)
(Italian, 1863–1959)
Florence
Exhibited at the XVIII Esposizione Internazionale d'Arte,
Venezia, 1932
Archivio Storico delle Arti Contemporanee,
La Biennale de Venezia
Note: Two of the original plaster molds are in the Wolfsonian
Collection; center panel of triptych, on loan, is exhibited
(see Cat. 200)

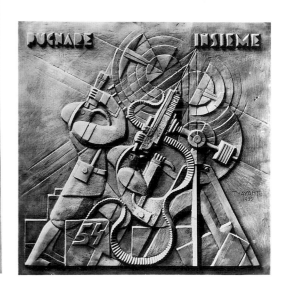

One image of Fascism was the "new man"; healthy, strong, looking to the future, arrogant, and at the same time obedient to his leader and ready to fight for the glory of the nation. The Futurist movement also proposed a "new man," dynamic and aggressive, and driven by an overwhelming desire for power. Nationalistic and violent, this new man saw art as action, had contempt for conventions and academies, and adored machines and progress.

In this sense, Thayaht's *Trittico dell'Amicizia* (Friendship Triptych) is an emblematic work (fig. 6.16). An explicit expression of Fascist propaganda, at the fall of the regime it was buried in his garden by its scared and disillusioned creator. It can, however, be viewed today with that detachment which time permits. Its three, low-relief panels exalt the friendship between two "new men"; the Futurist artist and the Fascist, who together scale a mountain (in celebration of sport and competition), make a film (in celebration of the most modern of the arts), and load a machine-gun (in celebration of machines and war). Thayaht represents the duo as stylized "mechanical" figures, in a vertiginous interplay of straight line and circle. The Triptych was exhibited at the Venice Biennale of 1932.

Aluminum, whose bright silver color was considered more appropriate for the architectural aesthetic of the time, had by then replaced iron in the production of gates, window

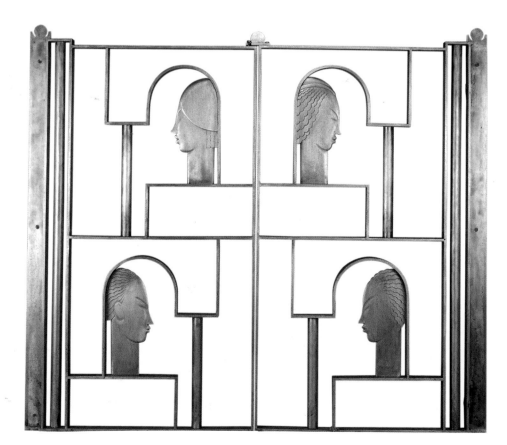

Fig. 6.17
Gate, 1933
Designed by Ernesto Puppo
(Italian, 1904–87)
Manufactured by Officina Matteucci, Faenza, Italy
Exhibited in the E.N.A.P.I. installation, Terza Fiera Nazionale dell'Artigianato (Third National Handicraft Fair), Florence, 1933
Aluminum
46 1/2 x 20 1/4 x 2 3/8 inches (118.1 x 51.4 x 6.0 cm)
87.1569.17.2.1

and door frames, either alone or in the form of alloys (anticorodal, aluminum chrome, aluman, xantal, etc.) (fig. 6.17). Architects also used it for furnishings. They designed prototypes to be produced industrially; however, they did not always succeed in finding companies willing to duplicate them. One example of this is the office furniture designed by the Roman architect Clemente Busiri Vici in aluminum, glass, and fiberglass which was executed only as prototypes (fig. 6.18).[36] The pieces are functional, solid, light, and simple in design, achieving the effect of great elegance with their silver/white contrast. Paradoxically, aluminum, which was the expression of a restrictive nationalist economic policy, assumed the forms of the International Style.

In 1936, Ponti designed in Milan the headquarters of Montecatini, the largest Italian mineral and chemical industry, as well as the principal producer of aluminum. The roof and large gates were made of aluminum, as was the office furniture. Even the archetypical chair of the decade, usually made of tubular chrome-plated steel (following the lead of Breuer, Mies van der Rohe, and Le Corbusier), was executed in aluminum by Ponti. He designed various models for desks and typists' tables, which with slight modifications were subsequently produced industrially (fig. 6.19). The Montecatini building as a whole is practically

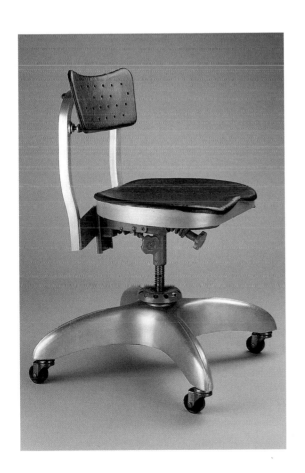

Fig. 6.19
Chair
From the Montecatini Headquarters, Milan, 1938
Designed by Giò (Giovanni) Ponti
(Italian, 1891–1979)
Manufactured by Kardex Italiano, Italy
Aluminum, painted steel, padded leatherette
30¼ x 18½ x 18½ inches (76.8 x 47.0 x 47.0 cm)
Marks: underside of seat "KARDEX ITALIANO, MONTECATINI
S.A. MODELLO 1938"
XX1990.815

Fig. 6.18 See Cat. 244
Writing desk, 1935
Designed by C. Busiri Vici

a manifesto for autarky. In the years to follow, aluminum – a "perfectly autarkic product" – would be a conduit for government propaganda.[37] On November 18, 1939, the Exhibition of the Italian Autarkic Metal opened at the Circo Massimo in Rome. Of the twenty-six pavilions dedicated to various aspects of Fascist policy, the most impressive was the autarkic pavilion; a cement and aluminum cube, the front wall of which was entirely taken up by an aluminum low-relief representation of a rapacious eagle. From then on, the use of iron was further discouraged in decoration for utilitarian as well as aesthetic reasons, since it was an essential metal for the war industry. Following the suggestion to collect scrap iron for re-use, many masterpieces of wrought iron of the Liberty period were destroyed in a frenzy of patriotic zeal. Despite this, the images most dear to Fascist iconography continued to be the anvil and the iron-worker, the first being a symbol of strength, and the second the symbol of male virility (figs. 6.20 and 6.21).

(Translated from the Italian by Joan Tambureno)

Fig. 6.20
Design drawing
Monument for the Opera Nazionale Dopolavoro
(National After-work Organization), c. 1940
Mario Messina
(Italian, dates unknown)
Rome
Graphite on paper
17 5/8 x 20 3/4 inches (44.8 x 52.7 cm)
Marks: obverse, stamped in black ink, top center "STUDIO ARCHITETTO/MARIO MESSINA", written in black ink "1940"
XX1990.212.52

Fig. 6.21
Advertisement for FIAT
Vincere **(To Win)**
From *Stile*, no. 15 (March 1942): XIV
83.3.151.14

NOTES

1. Prior to unification, Italy was divided into seven states of varying size and importance: the Kingdom of Sardinia, Lombardy-Venetia, the Duchy of Modena, the Duchy of Parma and Piacenza, the Grand Duchy of Tuscany, the Papal States, and the Kingdom of the Two Sicilies.

2. Alfredo Melani, *Decorazione e industrie artistiche* (Milan, 1899), pp. 220ff. Melani was an architect and art critic who contributed to a number of journals, including *Arte italiana decorativa e industriale*, *Emporium*, and *Per l'Arte*.

3. Camillo Boito, "L'arte italiana e l'ornamento floreale," *Arte italiana decorativa e industriale*, 7, no. 1 (January 1898): 5. Boito was an architect and architectural theorist who taught architecture at the Brera Academy for 48 years, starting in 1859.

4. Vittorio Ducrot transformed the furniture workshop of his stepfather Carlo Golia into a large industrial complex in Palermo. For ten years following 1899, he collaborated with the architect Ernesto Basile to design his modern line of furniture. Richard-Ginori is the largest Italian producer of porcelain and ceramics, with its main offices in Milan and factories in Milan, Florence, and Pisa. The furniture workshop of the Milanese Carlo Zen, who was active from the last quarter of the nineteenth century, employed two hundred workers and produced furniture of a modern line, richly inlaid with copper wire, mother-of-pearl, and various woods. The furniture factory of the Torinese Vittorio Valabrega employed around fifty workers. The Wolfsonian Collection has outstanding examples from all these manufactories.

5. In 1900, sixty workers were employed in his workshop.

6. "The art of wrought iron was very little represented in the Italian sections. That country revealed to us nothing more than its great ability to reproduce period pieces, overloaded with ornaments, in what is often doubtful taste...Mazzucotelli demonstrated a modernism exceptional for that country." Victor Champier, *Les industries d'art à l'exposition universelle de 1900--Tome premier* (Paris, 1902), p. 63.

7. For example, the writer Carlo Pisani Dossi, a member of the Scapigliatura movement of Milan, commissioned a group of artists, including Mazzucotelli, to work on his villa constructed between 1897 and 1907. Working together were the sculptor Cesare Ravasco, the cabinet-maker Eugenio Quarti, the architect Luigi Conconi, and the painter Carlo Agazzi. Mazzucotelli executed the balustrade of the stairway decorated with thistle motifs. See Alvise e Niccolò Reverdini, *Il Dosso Pisani e Carlo Dossi* (Milan, 1989).

8. "The so-called *stile floreale* is Mazzucotelli's passion, and his works in iron are full of flowers. Our decorative smith knows how to impress natural agility onto these flowers while respecting the properties of iron. He thus knows what to select from among the infinite variety of flowers in our fields and gardens". Melani, "Modernità nei lavori in ferro battuto," *L'Arte Decorativa Moderna*, 1, no. 2 (February 1902): 72.

9. From Article 2 of the Società Umanitaria Statute, published in *L'Umanitaria e la sua opera* (Milan, 1922), p. 20.

10. Maria Montessori was an Italian educator. After obtaining a degree in medicine in Rome in 1896, she devoted herself to studying and assisting abnormal children. In 1906, she organized day-care centers for working-class families in Rome and established "children's homes," which were quickly imitated throughout the world. Her revolutionary approach to child-rearing continues to be influential today. During the Fascist period she left Italy and moved to Holland.

11. The University would later be called the Istituto Superiore Industrie Artistiche (I.S.I.A.) = Advanced Institute of Artistic Industries.

12   The decorative motif of the dragonfly appeared for the first time in the chandelier from the Palazzo Castiglioni presented at the International Exposition of Milan of 1906. It was so successful that Mazzucotelli kept it in his repertory for years. It appears again in a drawing of his, dated 1929 (in the Bertarelli Collection in the Castello Sforzesco in Milan).

13   A copy of this volume, Ugo Ojetti, *I ferri battuti di Alessandro Mazzucotelli* (Milan, 1911), is in the library of the Wolfsonian in Miami Beach.

14   Mazzucotelli had already been awarded with the highest form of recognition in exhibitions in Italy and abroad (Honorary Diploma in Turin in 1902, Grand Prix in St. Louis in 1904, in Milan in 1906, and in Brussels in 1910), when he was given the gold medal in London in 1914.

15   The Venice International Art Exposition, which is held on a biannual basis and is thus known as the Biennale, first took place in 1895.

16   Antonio Fradeletto, "Mostra individuale di Umberto Bellotto," in *Catalogo illustrato della XI Esposizione Internazionale d'Arte della Città di Venezia* (Venice, 1914), p. 74.

17   At the end of the War, in 1919, the Humanitarian School organized at its Milan headquarters a regional exhibition of applied arts. This subsequently became an international event and was moved to Monza where, from 1923 on, it was held once every two years. In 1933, the event was transferred to the new Palazzo dell'Arte in Milan, built especially for this purpose in the park of the Castello Sforzesco. It eventually became the Milan Triennial Exhibition.

18   The correspondence between d'Annunzio and Mazzucotelli on this topic is indicative of the fraternal bond between them. The letters – kept at the Vittoriale library – open with "Dear comrade" or "Dearest Gabriele." The Vittoriale degli Italiani is the residence built by d'Annunzio in the hills above Lake Garda during the second half of the 1920s.

19   In the Wolfsonian Collection in Genoa, the documentation on Bellotto's production and his furnishings for restaurants, cinemas, theaters, and clubs includes 183 original photographs.

20   *XVI Esposizione Internazionale d'Arte della Città di Venezia, 1924*, catalogue (Venice, 1924), pp. 60 and 157. The ship model as trophy has illustrious precedents in seventeenth- and eighteenth-century gold-and silver-smithing.

21   For example, the Airport of the Littorio, the Ministry of Justice, the Ministry of the Navy, the State Polygraphic Institute, and the Ministry of Public Works.

22   Giannino Omero Gallo wrote in his article, "Il Fabbro di Mussolini. Il Maestro del ferro e del vetro," which appeared in the daily newspaper *Il Mezzogiorno* on July 5, 1929: "There are many things the smith of Mussolini – as he is called in Rome – needs not ask his destiny; his destiny came holding out to him energy, will, loyalty, genius, imagination; from raw materials, Bellotto has more than once created and recreated his admirable art. He wanted to be himself and find in the crowd of 'producers' his own mark, his own form and color; now this admirable mastery is recognized even by the doubters, the incredulous, the cynics, the amazed. However, the first Italian to understand the artist and encourage him, with rare intuition and discrimination, perfect sensitivity and lucid discernment, which is partly due to his nature and partly his eclectic preparation, but certainly due to his discernment, was Benito Mussolini."

23   In Predappio, a small town in Romagna, the childhood home of Mussolini, with the iron-smith's workshop of his father Alessandro attached, became a shrine in the nineteen-thirties. The young Benito helped his father in the workshop, working the bellows. See Y. de Begnac, *Vita di Mussolini*, vol. I (Milan, 1936). In 1940, on the first page of the first issue of the journal *Cellini*, published by ENAPI (the National Organization for Craftsmanship and Small Industries), was a large photo of the shop of Mussolini's father.

24 From Mussolini's speech in Perugia on October 30, 1923, "Vomere e spada," *Collected thoughts and maxims from the writings and speeches of Benito Mussolini*, ed. Lena Trivulzio della Somaglia (Milan, 1937), pp. 20-1; from Mussolini's speech in Cagli on August 18, 1926 in *Scritti e discorsi di Benito Mussolini*, definitive edition from 1925 to 1926 (Milan, 1934), p. 223.

25 The museum, which is still open in Feltre, contains not only a vast array of works by Rizzarda, but also a collection of paintings and furnishings that belonged to the artist himself and works in iron by Mazzucotelli.

26 Ugo Ojetti, "Gli italiani alla Mostra di Monza," *Il Corriere della Sera*, Milan, June 20, 1923: 3. Ojetti was a very influential writer and journalist who, from 1898 until his death, wrote art criticism for this daily newspaper.

27 Henri Martinie, *Exposition des Arts Décoratifs, Paris 1925 - La Ferronnerie* (Paris, 1925), unpaginated.

28 The gate of the Cappellin-Venini, Ravasi, Ravasco stand, created by Mazzucotelli, is in fact a slightly modified version of the balustrade in the goldsmiths pavilion at the Milan exposition 1906: the palm branch takes here the place of a magnified pansy, but the support structure is still the same (see fig. 6.10).

29 Ponti, a great supporter of artistic artisan production, designed furniture, glass, textiles, porcelain, mosaics, and enamels. During the second post-war period, while continuing his activity as building designer, he also worked often as an industrial designer.

30 Gio Ponti, "Le ragioni dello stile moderno," in *L'Italia alla esposizione internazionale di arti decorative moderne – Parigi 1925* (Roma, [1927]), p. 69.

31 The history of the Novecento is detailed in Rossana Bossaglia, *Il 'Novecento italiano'. Storia, documenti, iconografia* (Milan, 1979). The Sette pittori del Novecento italiano, founded in 1922, had its first exhibition in 1923 at the Galleria Pesaro in Milan, and included the artists Mario Sironi, Achille Funi, Ubaldo Oppi, Anselmo Bucci, Leonardo Dudreville, Emilio Malerba, and Piero Marussig.

32 Luigi Figini, Gino Pollini, Carlo Enrico Rava, Sebastiano Larco, Giuseppe Terragni, Guido Frette, and Adalberto Libera were the seven young architects who formed the group.

33 The cupola of the Church of S. Gioacchino in Rome, which was designed in 1897, is lined with aluminum.

34 Thayaht is the pseudonym assumed by Ernesto Michahelles, a Florentine artist. Son of an English mother and a Swiss father, Thayaht belonged to that international colony of intellectuals and members of the rich bourgeoisie who settled in Florence during the second half of the nineteenth century. Painter, sculptor, decorator, and stage-designer, he was also active in the applied arts, designing textiles, couture, furniture, jewelry, and furnishings. First exhibiting in 1918, he subsequently showed at the Monza Biennale in 1923 and in 1927; during that year, he also became a member of the Futurist movement. He exhibited in the Milan Triennales of 1933 and 1936 and the Venice Biennales of 1930, 1932, 1934, and 1936. In 1931, he became the promoter in Florence of the "Tuscan Futurist Exhibition."

35 F.T. Marinetti, "Lo scultore," in *Ernesto Thayaht* (Florence, 1932), p. 17.

36 Clemente Busiri Vici, engineer and architect, was descended from seven generations of architects. An exponent of neo-classicism in the 1920s, he adhered to Rationalism in the 1930.

37 This regularly appeared from 1939 to 1941 in the advertisements for the L.L.L. (Lavorazione Leghe Leggere S.A. Alluminio, Milano [Lightweight Alloy Works, the Aluminum Corporation, Milan]).

A "Return to Order":
Issues of the Classical and the Vernacular in Italian Inter-War Design

Marianne Lamonaca

Fig. 7.03 See Cat. 219
Vase
Commemorating the twentieth wedding anniversary of Ugo and Fernanda Ojetti, 1926
Designed by G. M. Balsamo Stella

Design in Italy at the end of World War I and in the years immediately following may be characterized by the search for a mode of expression that could be both Italian and modern. Although the issue was tradition versus modernism, the two were not necessarily diametrically opposed. Modernist theory itself is rooted in the celebration of the classical and the traditions of the vernacular. The German architect and design reformer Hermann Muthesius referred to classical precedents in his efforts to define the concepts of type form and standardization.[1]

The aftermath of the War brought about the call for a "return to order" in artistic circles in Italy and elsewhere in Europe.[2] Many artists, architects, and designers adopted a moderate modernism – one based on continuity with the past. This was often accomplished in one of two ways: by embracing a classical vocabulary, or by preserving the best of the past through quotations of regional culture. In Italy where the classical tradition was the country's native tradition – its natural and rightful heritage – design in a classical vein would be the preferred mode of expression.[3] In this complex period of history – colored by the destruction and dislocation of the War and the victory of the Fascist revolution – classical and vernacular Italian traditions tend to converge.[4] The classical ideal was an ambiguous concept encompassing not only the classical, a work of art that transcends its own and every time,[5] but also classicism, a canon of absolute formal values. In Italy it was perceived as an unbroken tradition stretching from antiquity through the centuries to the present. It included the idea of the *stirpe* (or the origins of the Latin race), which was increasingly invoked in the art of the period in archaic or primitive styles, such as Etruscan.[6] It also embraced the myth of the Mediterranean world as Arcadia, which generated recurrent rustic or folk images to support the notion of continuity in peasant life.

The "return to order" in Italy was multifaceted and often ambiguous. Designers, stressing Italy's links with its celebrated past, explored the rich and varied potential of classical and vernacular motifs (see the essays of Doordan and de Guttry/Maino). This essay examines some of the strategies employed by designers in inter-war Italy in their quest to create a modern, Italian style, specifically through the exploration of its manifestations in *Italianità*, *Mediterraneità*, *Latinità*, and *Romanità*.[7]

In Italy in the late nineteenth century, architecture and the applied arts had fallen victim to the vagaries of eclecticism, especially the copying of historical styles.[8] Low-cost industrial production allowed consumer goods to reach the masses in unprecedented quantities. Manufacturers chose a pastiche of historical forms and decorative treatments for their merchandise. According to one Italian critic, "the production of furniture lost every ideal because it passed from the hands of artists to those of speculators," who were no longer interested in the beautifully conceived and executed object. Success for these manufacturers was measured by the number of serially produced "pieces" offered in the marketplace.[9] Turn-of-the-century mail order furniture catalogues attest to the availability of *cinquecento* and other period-style furnishings. The choice of various revival styles to furnish different rooms in the home (for example, Renaissance-inspired dining room suites and Rococo-inspired salon furnishings) was another manifestation of eclectic historicism. Since its introduction in the mid-nineteenth century, it associated certain styles with suitability for use by either men or women.[10] The pale palette and curvilinear forms of rococo-inspired design were deemed appropriate for the salon, a room traditionally associated with female use.

Eclectic historicism in architecture and design exemplified the lack of innovative thinking in Italian artistic circles. Reformers advocated the creation of a modern idiom that would symbolize a new age and a nascent nation (Italy was united as a republic in 1861). According to the influential architect Camillo Boito, a national style would evolve from the study of historical examples.[11] Others, like the critic Alfredo Melani, denounced the connection to history and instead emphasized imagination and originality.[12]

The 1900 Exposition Universelle in Paris was a catalyst for design reform in Italy. Contact with the international community led to new design initiatives that were highlighted two years later at the Prima Esposizione Internazionale d'Arte Decorativa Moderna (First International Exhibition of Modern Decorative Arts) in Turin. There the anti-historicist naturalism of the *stile floreale*, the Italian variant of Art Nouveau, triumphed. According to one writer, it was "the first exposition in Italy free of academic and conventional shackles."[13] Yet many progressive critics at the beginning of the century dismissed Art Nouveau as superficial and overly decorative. *Stile Floreale* quickly lost its primacy and a return to eclectic historicism was emphatically shown at the 1906 Esposizione Internazionale del Sempione (International Simplon Exhibition) in Milan, and at the 1911 exhibitions in Rome and Turin celebrating fifty years of Italian unity.[14]

The need for reform in Italy's small artistic industries was revealed at the Esposizione Regionale Lombarda d'Arte Decorativa (The Lombardy Regional Exhibition of Decorative Art) held in Milan in 1919, the first show of its kind organized after the War.[15] This display of decorative arts demonstrated that artisans and manufacturers persisted in copying historicist styles, although some halting innovations were evident. The forerunner of the Biennale di Monza, it was organized by influential personalities in Italy's artistic community, including the architect Gaetano Moretti, the metalsmith Alessandro Mazzucotelli, and the art critics Alfredo Melani and Guido Marangoni. Their achievement was to focus the debate taking place in Italian cultural circles regarding design reform, the quality of technical and artistic instruction, and the relationship between schools, stores, industry, and the marketplace.

Pedagogical goals were critically important to the organizers. Recognizing that the traditional system of training apprentices within the workshop scarcely existed, they advocated the assumption of this function by public schools. Marangoni wrote that the Academies should be abolished (as had the Futurists in 1909) because they encouraged the "parrot-like reproduction of stereotypical examples especially in the case of decoration."[16] He believed that the schools should encourage students to *see* and to *study* as well as to *create* and to *interpret* according to their personal inclinations.[17]

The new direction in artistic taste is characterized by the choice of a classical vocabulary to represent national unity in the years of renewal after World War I. Not since the years of Napoleonic rule in Italy when Neo-Classicism prevailed had Italian states shared a common language of form. At the 1921 exhibition of the Famiglia Artistica di Milano (Artistic Family of Milan), an organization of architects and artists, "a fasces of architects [De Finetti, Fiocchi, Lancia, Muzio, Ponti] . . . oriented towards a return to the rhythm and equilibrium of the classics," presented their work.[18] Giovanni Muzio was the unofficial leader of this circle of architects who would define a particular genre of Milanese Neo-Classicism in the 1920s. In Muzio's impassioned 1921 article "L'Architettura a Milano intorno all'ottocento" (Milanese Architecture around 1800), he described his work and that of his contemporaries as a reaction against the eclectic and historicist architectural styles that flourished in the late-nineteenth and early-twentieth centuries. Muzio aspired to "re-establish the principle of order" in the fabric of urban architecture. His Ca' Brutta, a large apartment building in Milan, shows a fresh interpretation of classical architectural values.[19]

The calls to classicism which were heard at this time represented a new poetic quite different from academic imitators.[20] The specter of tradition was intrinsic to the modern idiom in Italy. The first Italian art movements of the twentieth century – Futurism and metaphysical painting – defined their modernity in reaction to tradition. Futurism demanded a "rupture with the past" and metaphysical painting proposed "rupturing with progress" to liberate history from the absolute formal values of classicism.[21] The writings of Carlo Carrà, Giorgio de Chirico, and Alberto Savinio among others in journals such as *Valori Plastici, La Ronda*, and *Rete Mediterranea* in the early 1920s were characterized by the vague catchwords: "classicism, craft, and order."[22] Even in 1919 de Chirico wrote about "Il ritorno al mestiere," (Return to craftsmanship) in *Valori Plastici*.[23] An influential painter, de Chirico embodied in his methods and style the revival of the formal and moral lessons of past Italian art.[24] *Italianità* and *Mediterraneità* signified tradition and nationalism for many artists, architects, and designers. Concomitantly, the exaltation of craft stimulated the renewal of vernacular forms and techniques.

The influential Fascist art critic Margherita Sarfatti recognized that Italian artists inspired by the antique could absorb "the ancient Roman tradition with spontaneous freshness, avoiding copy or servile imitation," as they had done during the Renaissance.[25] The seven painters of the Novecento had their first exhibition in Milan in 1923. Mussolini visited the show with Sarfatti, who was the group's mentor and Mussolini's lover. Through her fervent promotion of the Novecento painters as "revolutionaries of the modern restoration," she came closest to defining an official art of the Fascist regime.[26]

During the period of economic struggle following the War, the Fascist government aimed to elevate a united Italy to the political and cultural level of its European competitors.[27] Under state control, a broad range of public works were undertaken, including new highways, improved ports, railroad electrification, and new city planning. New jobs created by the increased industrialization of the north encouraged mass migration from the agrarian south. Northern cities grew and the middle and working classes became more affluent.

The development of viable products for the national and international marketplace was understood as essential for economic survival. The government, on both regional and national levels, participated in the debate concerning Italy's artistic production.[28] In order to bolster the sales of Italian products, the Fascist government stressed the excellence of Italy's *mestiere* (craftsmanship). "In Italy more than in any other country, the small artistic manufactures for the decorative arts can boast glorious traditions of superiority which were kept since the end of the Middle Ages through the triumphs of the Renaissance to the Modern Age, when individual work was overwhelmed by the machine and the technical improvements that favored the huge development of the industry of manufactories."[29]

Officially sponsored exhibitions such as the Prima Mostra Internazionale delle Arti Decorative (The First International Exhibition of Decorative Arts), the first of the Monza Biennale, opened in 1923 with a visit from Mussolini. Both the first and second Biennali and the Exposition Internationale des Arts Décoratifs et Industriels Modernes in Paris confirmed that Italy's decorative arts industries were slow to reform. The criteria for

Fig. 7.01
Studio
Seconda Mostra Internazionale delle Arti
Decorative, Monza, 1925
Designed by Alberto Issel
(Italian, 1848–1926)
From *Opere Scelte. Seconda Mostra Internazionale delle Arti Decorative* (Milan, 1925), pl. 87
XC1993.264

exhibitors were quality craftsmanship and modern design that did not copy historical styles. The changes originally conceived in 1919, however, were yet to be realized.[30] The Italian critical press recognized that disorder and eclectic historicism remained. The applied arts on exhibit displayed a lingering interest in the sinuous curves of Art Nouveau, eclectic historicism, Futurism, regional vernacular, and the first timid stirrings of Milanese Neo-Classicism. At the second Biennale, for example, Alberto Issel, one of the most creative furniture makers in the Italian modern movement at the turn of the century (see cat. 19), exhibited furnishings solely in period style including some Rococo-inspired pieces (fig. 7.01).

In the applied arts, the Richard-Ginori company exemplified the new direction taken by a centuries-old firm. In 1923 it hired the Milanese architect Gio Ponti to be its artistic director and product designer. The goal was to rejuvenate ceramic production in order to promote sales. Ponti wanted above all to reform Italian industry. He wrote, on the occasion of the 1925 Paris exposition, that "To understand what is 'modern' we have to consider . . . only the things that effectively pertain to the market, that harmonize with our customs and everyday environment, and that are made with today's technology, because they are used today."[31] Ponti selected the language of classicism as the formula for harmony with Italy's customs and environment.[32] The results were first publicly exhibited at the first Biennale di

Fig. 7.02 See Cat. 165
Plate
Le attività gentili. I progenitori
**(Noble activities. Our ancestors), 1923
Designed by G. Ponti**

Monza and included a version of the *Le Attività Gentili. I Progenitori* plate in the Wolfsonian collection (fig. 7.02). As a case study of the new classicism, the plate's design convincingly combines formal and symbolic values manifested as *Romanità* and *Latinità*. Formally the design was inspired by both Roman and Etruscan precedents: the compartmentalization echoes the hermetic layout of ancient Roman wall painting and the gold lines that delineate the figures recall the incised decoration of Etruscan bronze vessels. Ponti combined Greco-Roman mythology with archaic (or Italic) representation. Etruscan art represented an original Italian culture independent of the Greek. The growing interest in Etruscan art at this time is reflected in the periodical *Studi Etruschi*, first published in 1927.[33] On a symbolic level the plate's title and the figures representing the arts and industry embody *Italianità* and its basis in the abstract and humanistic constructs of the Italian classical tradition.

Ugo Ojetti, a prolific Fascist art critic and writer, recognized that "the middle class, the lower middle class, workers, and farmers have always desired and always will desire to imitate even in furniture the classes that are socially placed above them and that serve as their models."[34] The expanding market allowed bourgeois consumers to purchase rarefied objects with traditional overtones that had the power, at least metaphorically, to elevate their status. The use of historical forms and images by a designer assumes a degree of recognition by the consumer, and their acceptance may affect the consumer's social status. Richard-Ginori's new products were aimed at, but not limited to, a middle-class clientele able to afford hand-painted and gold-trimmed tableware.

During the first decade of the twentieth century some progressive German, French, and Scandinavian architects also turned away from *Jugendstil* and Art Nouveau influences and returned to a classical vocabulary. An Italian critic, writing on the occasion of the Paris exhibition of 1925, was convinced that "the objects of the most stable and persuasive character to our eyes are those that take their inspiration most directly from neo-classicism," and cited the work of Carl Malmsten in Sweden, Josef Frank in Vienna, and Emile-Jacques Ruhlmann in France as examples.[35] Scandinavian design in particular was lauded by the critic Roberto Papini for pairing "practicality of intent and refined taste."[36]

Guido Balsamo Stella, married to a Swedish painter, was greatly influenced by the modern, yet classicist, glassware produced by Edward Hald and Simon Gate for Orrefors in Sweden. Balsamo Stella worked primarily as a painter and engraver until 1919. He then began to design for Venetian glasswork firms. In 1922, while serving as instructor of book decoration and graphic arts at the Regio Istituto d'Arte di Santa Croce in Florence, he opened his own glass studio. His exquisitely crafted and decorated vase (fig. 7.03) commemorating Ugo and Fernanda Ojetti's twentieth wedding anniversary in 1925 is indebted to Swedish precedent. Classical figures etched into the clear glass float across its icy surface. The mythological characters of Apollo, Icarus, and Dedalus, in conjunction with the words "destruction," "war," and "recovery," represent in this momentous period of Italy's history a "call to arms." For Ojetti, classicism was the only acceptable idiom for modern Italian art. He viewed "rustic art . . . [as] only a pale reflection of the grand artistic currents, that spread from [Italy] around the world."[37] The dialogue with antiquity was only one strategy employed by designers in this period to align tradition and modernity. Because the classical ideal was seen as a living legacy stretching from antiquity to the present, Balsamo Stella, of Venetian heritage, could also choose the refined and elegant forms of eighteenth-century Venetian Rococo to define his aesthetic.[38] His showroom installation for the Paris exposition in 1925 provides a superb example of this tendency (fig. 7.04).

A dinner service designed by architect Guido Andlovitz for the Società Ceramica Italiana in Laveno (fig. 7.05) is also inspired by mid-eighteenth century rococo design. Like Ponti at the Richard-Ginori company, Andlovitz was hired by S.C.I.in 1923 to modernize its line of production. The dinner service demonstrates its modern conception through the conventionalized renderings of the rural genre scenes that decorate it. The motif of the country

Fig. 7.04
Guido and Anna Balsamo Stella installation
Exposition Internationale des Arts Décoratifs
et Industriels Modernes, Paris, 1925
Designed by Guido M. Balsamo Stella
(Italian, 1882–1941)
From *Italia alla Esposizione Internazionale di Arti Decorative*
e Industriali Moderne (n.p., [1925]), pl. LXXVIII
XC1993.112

Fig. 7.05
Tureen and dinner plate, 1923
Designed by Guido Andlovitz
(Italian, 1900–66)
Made by Società Ceramica Italiana, Laveno, Italy
Glazed earthenware
Tureen: 6 x 11 ¾ x 9 inches (15.3 x 29.9 x 22.9 cm)
Plate: 9 ¾ inches dia. (24.8 cm dia.)
Marks: (both) underside, printed underglaze in black "Dec. a
mano" within black rectangle; printed underglaze in green
company logo, "SOCIETÀ/CERAMICA/ITALIANA/LAVENO"
85.7.289.103 a,b and 85.7.289.22

Fig. 7.06
Poster
IInd International Decorative Art Exhibition
***Milan-Monza Royal Palace**, 1925*
Designed by Giovanni Guerrini
(Italian, 1887–1972)
Printed by Ind. Graf. N. Moneta, Milan
Commercial color lithograph
27 ⅜ x 19 ⅜ inches (69.5 x 49.2 cm)
Marks: obverse, printed in gold, center right
"GIOVANNI/ GUERRINI"
85.4.104

squire who lords over his castle and the local peasantry supports a satirical commentary on the urban bourgeoisie. As life in the cities became increasingly mechanized and frenetic (with automobiles, electric trolleys, telephone lines), families increasingly sought respite in weekend homes in the country. The owners would often decorate their rural house in a vernacular or rustic manner antithetical to their everyday urban surroundings. They could also choose casual formality, as this dinner service suggests. The tureen's squat rounded shape, vegetal finial and feet, and decorative images of country life evoke the life of an aristocratic country gentleman. This attitude is confirmed in the premier issue of the influential magazine *Domus,* subtitled "Modern architecture and furnishings for city and country houses."

The cover depicts men and women in eighteenth-century attire with livery in attendance, enjoying themselves at table and at the piano.

The use of a lighter classicism (called the *Spitzbarok* in Austria) was also characteristic of some contemporaneous German and Eastern European design (see cat. 180). More often, as Giovanni Guerrini's poster for the Second International Decorative Art Exhibition in Monza (fig. 7.06) demonstrates, designers combined classicism and exoticism. An attenuated and stylized palm tree at the center of the poster creates a classically balanced composition. The female nude appears both timeless and modern as she pours water from a cornucopia, the symbol of abundance. Its rich saturated color and fine detail would have made it a strong rival of the French Art Moderne posters designed for the Paris exposition of the same year.

The use of vernacular forms and decoration was yet another way of making modern design desirable to the middle-class consumer. The dialogue between the classical and the vernacular is clearly illustrated by Alla Penna d'Oca, a Milanese restaurant run by the Lombard Press Syndicate, furnished and decorated by members of Il Labirinto (fig. 7.07).

Fig. 7.07
Interior
***Alla Penna d'Oca* restaurant, Milan, 1927**
Designed by Il Labirinto, Milan
From *L'Ambiente moderno in Italia* (Milan, 1930), p. 168
TD1990.61.35

The group included the architects Tomaso Buzzi, Emilio Lancia, Michele Marelli, and Ponti and the designers Pietro Chiesa, Paolo Venini, and Contessa Carla Visconti di Modrone Erba.[39]

The Milanese Novecento architect/designers had the advantage of working in the city that was home to the biannual decorative arts exhibitions. Their designs had a great influence, partly as a result of their prominently displayed and well-received installations at the Biennali and also through a great deal of self-promotion.

Il Labirinto evoked vernacular traditions in order to instill an atmosphere of national pride in the restaurant's interior. The walls were painted with "small views of Italian towns (from Soave to Capri) from which famous Italian wines take their names."[40] The restaurant was fitted with cave-like enclosures which highlighted its basement-level location. The furnishings included a long table with monopodium supports based on a fifteenth-century prototype, as well as simple stools and benches. The semicircular bar was designed to resemble a classical architectural balustrade. These folkloric images celebrated an industry and, more importantly, an Italian custom passed through generations. In *Domus* the dining room was described as a "sacellum" an ancient Roman votive chapel.[41] The use of a Latin word immediately elevated an ordinary dining area into a sacred place. This manifestation of *Italianità* merges the perception of Italy as the inheritor of ancient Roman values with the Italy of traditional folk culture.

The conflation of the vernacular and the classical is highlighted in two characteristic works of the Roman artist/designer Duilio Cambellotti. At the beginning of the century, Cambellotti was a leader in the design reform movement in Rome. A devoted Socialist and member of *In Arte Libertas*, he was influenced by the example of Ruskin and Morris. A committed teacher, he was convinced that "art had its roots in school" and that it could elevate the lives of the masses.[42] His interest in the rural societies surrounding Rome influenced his work and served to validate the customs of the communities. A desk exhibited at the first Biennale (fig. 7.08) loosely echoes the form of a Renaissance center table. Its heavy rectangular top rests at each end on massive monopodium supports linked by a stretcher. Its overall shape suggests the sixteenth century, but its linear simplicity and inlaid geometric, floral decoration are purely modern. Two years later at the second Biennale, Cambellotti presented the so-called "La Notte" (Night) cabinet (fig. 7.09). In this work he combined refined cabinetry with very sophisticated applied ivory decoration. Cambellotti's imagery of shepherdesses in traditional headdresses tending sheep may be both a romantic celebration of regionalism – the countryside surrounding Rome – and a not entirely ambiguous statement about current agricultural policy – the Bonifica Integrale (a land reclamation and improvement campaign begun in the 1920s to curtail the mass exodus of rural agricultural workers into the cities).[43] Threatened by an increasingly industrialized society, these communities

Fig. 7.08
Desk, 1923
Designed by Duilio Cambellotti
(Italian, 1876–1960)
Made by Fratelli Nicoletti, Rome
Walnut, maple
37½ x 82 x 34¾ inches (95.3 x 208.3 x 88.3 cm)
87.597.11.1

Fig. 7.09   See Cat. 36
Cabinet, 1925
Designed by D. Cambellotti

Fig. 7.10
Framed tile, c. 1925
Melkiorre Melis
(Italian, 1889–1982)
Rome
Glazed earthenware; wood, stain, metal
14³⁄₈ x 13¹⁄₈ inches (36.5 x 33.3 cm)
Marks: underside, printed underglaze in blue
"MELIS/SARDEGNA"
XX1990.556

held special significance for Cambellotti as representative of the continuity of an archaic, Roman heritage.

For Cambellotti, vernacular design had specific cultural and political implications. For others, regional craftsmanship was seen as a model of superior achievement in a period of shoddy industrial production. In his book *Il Mobile italiano contemporaneo* Marangoni advised manufacturers to "diligently study rustic furniture so varied in line and robustly constructed, and sometimes capable of uniting beauty with practical utility."[44] The Sardinian-born artist Melkiorre Melis, also working in Rome in the 1920s, created furnishings rooted in the forms, materials, and techniques of his native region. Melis presented his rustic models in rarefied gallery settings to a sophisticated Roman audience. As Cambellotti's student, he learned to respect tradition. A black, geometrically carved frame surrounds a tile depicting a Sardinian woman in native dress (fig. 7.10). Noted for surpassing "the old forms and the ornamental repetition of folk arts," Melis's designs were modern interpretations based on historical precedent.[45] The image of the woman hermetically sealed within the thick black frame evokes archaic art forms.

Artists and designers during the inter-war period benefited from government support of the arts. Various design reform initiatives were undertaken to encourage Italian competition in the international marketplace. Committees were organized, for example, to promote

207

Fig. 7.11 See Cat. 164
Vase, c. 1920
Design attributed to V. Zecchin

the small business sector of the national economy.[46] In 1919 the Istituto Veneto per le Piccole Industrie e per il Lavoro (Venetian Institute for Small Industries and Work) was established. Its aim was to promote Venetian small craft enterprises through professional instruction.[47] While it affected all small companies, it had special relevance for Venetian glassworks. The glassmaking process itself, which involved many specialized craftsmen, imposed a certain degree of repetition. Workshops continued to produce seventeenth- and eighteenth-century forms. Following the example of the Deutsche Werkstätten and artist collaboratives such as the Wiener Werkstätte, Italy's artistic industries sought the design contributions of artists and architects. The Cappellin-Venini company, for example, appointed the Venetian painter Vittorio Zecchin as its artistic director in 1921. In a government-sponsored publication he was lauded for having "extended the use of artistic glass to the needs of modern life."[48] A vase attributed to Zecchin from the Barovier workshop (fig. 7.11) shows the extraordinary quality of *murrine* glass. The designer has chosen a traditional bell-like form, masterfully enhanced by the exquisite colors of the material itself. The rather loose geometry of the decoration is influenced by the rich, decorative surfaces of Viennese Secessionist paintings. While Zecchin's elegant designs reflect traditional eighteenth-century models, he was also greatly influenced by Viennese turn-of-the-century art and design.

Two other significant government-sponsored enterprises were the Ente Nazionale per l'Artigianato e le Piccole Industrie (E.N.A.P.I.) (National Organization for Craftsmanship and Small Industries) and the Opera Nazionale Dopolavoro (O.N.D.) (National After-work Organization).[49] Both established community-based programs of craft instruction. The E.N.A.P.I. supported the collaboration between the artist and the artisan by promoting competitions to choose designs to be executed by the craftsmen and small companies in its membership. The products of their collaborative efforts were promoted and sold at exhibitions like the Biennale di Monza and at various trade fairs (fig 7.12).[50] The exigencies of the marketplace no longer made it feasible for artisans, as in the previous decade, to be both design innovator and executor. The making of one-off items was time-consuming and necessitated high prices. The E.N.A.P.I.'s artistic director, Giovanni Guerrini, designed its pavilion at the Turin exhibition of 1928. From the vitrines for the display of objects to the building that housed them, the design was Neo-Classical (fig. 7.13). Guerrini's formula for modern Italian design embraced the classical principles of form, proportion, and linear simplicity.[51]

Fig. 7.12
Poster
O.N.D. Iª Mostra delle Industrie Sicilia Calabria
(. . . First Exhibition of Industries . . .), 1928
Designed by S. Scalia
(Italian, dates unknown)
Printed by Tip. Lit. Cav. A. Nava & C., Rome
Published by Opera Nazionale Dopolavoro (O.N.D.), Rome
Commercial color lithograph
27⁶/₁₁ x 254 inches (70.0 x 100.0 cm)
Marks: obverse, printed, center right "S. SCALIA"
GD1994.65

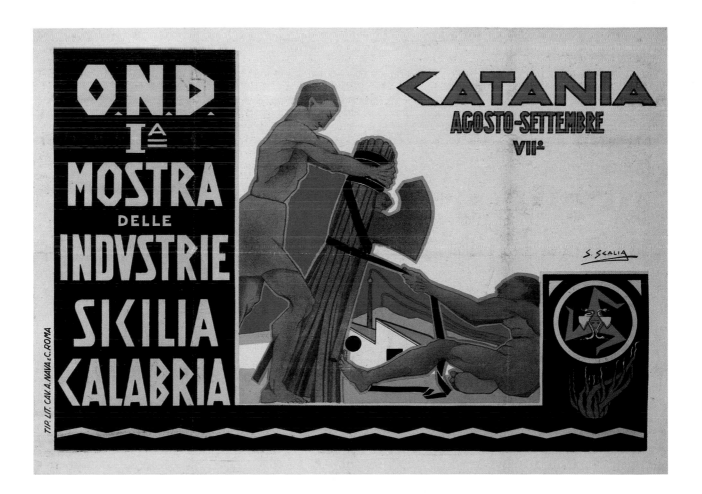

Fig. 7.13
Interior
Ente Nazionale per le Piccole Industrie pavilion, Turin, 1928
Designed by Giovanni Guerrini
(Italian, 1887–1972)
From *Catalogo. Ente Nazionale Piccole Industrie. Esposizione Torino 1928* (Rome, 1928), pl. 6
TD1990.289.23

Fig. 7.14
Ambassador's study
(Tomaso Buzzi [Italian, 1900–81]
and Gio Ponti [Italian, 1891–1979], architects),
1926
From *Architettura e Arti Decorative* (December 1926): 184
83.3.153.11

Fig. 7.15 See Cat. 166
Sideboard
From the Schejola apartment, Milan, c. 1928
Designed by G. Ponti

Fig. 7.16 See Cat. 169
Side chair
From the entrance hall of the Fiammetta Sarfatti and Count Livio Gaetani residence, 1933
Designed by M. Piacentini

Competitions of all kinds sponsored by government organizations and by magazines and newspapers also provided impetus for design reform. *La Rivista Illustrata del "Popolo d'Italia"*, under the direction of Arnaldo Mussolini, brother of Il Duce, announced a competition in January 1926 for the furnishings of an Italian embassy in a foreign country.[52] The competition's goal was to "promote the creation of a modern national style in the art of furniture."[53] The winning entry submitted by Tomaso Buzzi and Ponti was the only one published: "No other project was worthy of a prize or of honorable mention."[54] Classical architectural elements were used to evoke the serenity and grandeur of the past. Robust Renaissance-derived forms were used in the ambassador's study (fig. 7.14), whereas refined and elegant furnishings inspired by the late eighteenth-century were used in the rooms for the ambassador's wife. Ponti and Buzzi's definition of classicism encompassed a wide range of historical interpretations. The designers could safely believe that they were incorporating native Italian vocabulary by creating an interior unified by its frescoed wall and ceiling decorations and furnished with objects mostly of classical derivation, since all these devices could be found in historical Italian interiors.

In the area of home furnishings, magazines such as *Domus* and *La Casa Bella* (both established in 1928) helped to promote throughout Italy the Neo-Classical style later known as the Milanese Novecento. The magazines often juxtaposed articles about Italy's rich historical heritage, especially Palladian and Napoleonic Neo-Classicism, with the work of contemporary Italian architects. This mixture inspired the creation of furniture such as a sideboard designed by Gio Ponti (fig. 7.15), which was inspired by sideboards and pier tables popular in the late eighteenth and early nineteenth centuries. The extreme attenuation of the leg with its tapered line gives the table a crisp, modern shape. Bronze shell decorations, evocative of the Mediterranean and ancient Roman design, functioned as drawer pulls.[55]

In Rome, Marcello Piacentini, the most important architect and urban planner in the Fascist regime, contributed to the formulation of a grand Roman style. A chair designed by him for Margherita Sarfatti's daughter, Fiammetta, on the occasion of her marriage (fig.

Fig. 7.17
Cabinet, 1927
Designed by Gustavo Pulitzer
(Italian, 1887–1967)
Trieste, Italy
Walnut, maple, zebrawood, rosewood, mirrored glass, ivory, silver
70⅛ x 61¼ x 18⅞ inches (178.1 x 154.9 x 47.9 cm)
Marks: obverse, inlaid, bottom left of proper right door "ac"
XX1990.44 a,b

7.16), embodied formal principles of classicism in its linear simplicity and manipulation of simple geometric forms. Piacentini absorbed and re-defined classical values to create an original, modern design. Ponti, on the other hand, emulated a particular historical model and gave it a fresh interpretation.

Metaphysical painters, particularly de Chirico, viewed history with a touch of irony. Carrà added to this his "poetry of ordinary things."[56] This sensibility was also manifested in the applied arts. A jewelry cabinet-on-stand (fig. 7.17) designed by Gustavo Pulitzer for a wealthy Trieste family used both traditional technique (intarsia) and subject matter (Greek mythology) to create a wholly modern work. The inlaid decoration of floating cherubs and a goddess emerging from a shell are clear references to Botticelli's *The Birth of Venus* of 1480. Yet the abstract and generalized rendering of form identifies this design as a work of the 1920s. Similarly, Dante Baldelli's tile depicting Adam and Eve and the serpent (fig. 7.18) and Tullio d'Albisola's maquette for a mural at the sixth Triennale in 1936 (fig. 7.19) expressed the new classicism in a distinctly primitive style. Both Baldelli and d'Albisola were active participants in the avant-garde Italian Futurist movement. Baldelli depicted the temptation scene from Genesis with a childlike simplicity. D'Albisola represented the new Fascist man as a timeless being guided by angels (or muses). His figures, rendered simply and precisely, have an archaic clarity. In 1933 the painter Mario Sironi published his influential "Manifesto della pittura murale" (Manifesto of mural painting), in which he reiterated that no one formula could express the spirit of Fascism. D'Albisola's design, like Sironi's artwork of the period, "embodied the very myth of the eternity of the Italian *stirpe*: powerful hieratic figures set in registers . . . endowed with the weight of history and the authority of the millennia."[57] The mural celebrated art and industry in the Fascist state. Such Fascist

Fig. 7.20 See Cat. 189
Poster
L'Art Italien XIXe-XXe Siècles, Jeu de Paume,
Tuileries, **1935**
Designed by U. Brunelleschi

Fig. 7.21
Sculpture
Paola Ojetti, **1935**
Antonio Berti
(Italian, 1904–99)
Made by Marinelli Foundry, Florence
Bronze
26 ¾ x 18 ⁹⁄₁₀ x 13 ⁷⁄₉ inches (68.0 x 48.0 x 35.0 cm)
Marks: reverse, inscribed, bottom center "Paola Ojetti";
signed, bottom left "ANT.BERTI A. XIII"; stamped, bottom
right "MARINELLI FUSE"
GX1993.212

iconography depicted the "new man" as one whose labor was blessed and whose efforts were equal to those of the ancients.

By the mid-1930s, many designers adopted a stricter "Roman" style. Partially state-driven, the cult of *Romanità* was solidified at the time of the Mostra della Rivoluzione Fascista in 1932 – a celebration of the ten years since the March on Rome. As Fascism profoundly changed the daily reality of life in Italy, the notion of *Italianità* was superseded by that of *Romanità*. In 1937, the Mostra Augustea della Romanità (Exhibition of the Rome of Augustus), on the occasion of the bimillennium of the birth of Augustus, equated classical Roman history with national Italian history.[58] The *L'Art Italien* poster (fig. 7.20) designed by Umberto Brunelleschi for an exhibition in Paris is pure Fascist propaganda. The figure of

liberty stands erect with a large fasces rising up powerfully behind. The cold, marble statue of perfect form both announced and personified the exhibition of Italian art and provided a succinct image of Italy's grandeur. On a more intimate scale, the portrait bust of Paola Ojetti (fig. 7.21), Ugo Ojetti's daughter, exemplified the austere realism popular in the period. The static pose and carefully arranged hair are evocative of early statuary. As historian Romke Visser explains: "[The] elitist cult of the *romanità* is closely linked to a tradition of conservative humanism, characterized by the recognition of the 'universal aesthetic laws' of Hellenistic art."[59] The values associated with ancient Rome appealed to educated Italians and characterized the Ojettis' conservative, Florentine political and cultural milieu.

Fig. 7.22
Dining room
Bedarida residence, Livorno, 1938
Designed by Piero Bottoni
(Italian, 1903–73)
From *Domus*, anno XVII, no. 131 (November 1938): 44
The dining table and chairs are in the Wolfsonian Collection
GX1993.199.1–13

The evolution of the new classicism is powerfully demonstrated by the dining room suite designed by Piero Bottoni, one of the leaders of Italy's Rationalist architectural movement (fig. 7.22). The fundamental lesson of classicism was articulated by Gio Ponti in *Domus* in 1932. Addressing the debate in architecture between the Novecento and the Rationalists, he wrote: "From classicism remains a spiritual, logical, clear, simple, humane lesson, that guides and comforts the architects toward work freely and immediately adhering to the principles of today's uses . . . "[60] Bottoni's arrangement of the dining room has a timeless quality that evokes a ritual meeting place. At the center of the table is an oval crystal plate with internal illumination. Its effect was to pull the family around it, and act, in a symbolic way, as the hearth. The chairs with their ladder backs evoke regional traditions, like those from Chiavari, the renowned chairmaking area of Liguria. Their tall stiles and curving slats seemed to hug the sitter and contributed to the sense of unity around the table. The furniture is simple, linear, and geometric, and enriched by the juxtaposition of materials, not by decoration. Bottoni's design embodied the "classical" as it was understood by Massimo Bontempelli, the influential writer and publisher of the magazine *'900*. "'Classical' is not a temporal choice, it is a spiritual category. In truth, *a work of art is classical when it succeeds in transcending its own and every time.*"[61]

The manifestations of the new classicism were varied but unified by shared concepts concerning tradition. The "return to order" encompassed many aspects of Italy's rich artistic heritage, from the vernacular to the classical. It was, however, only one strategy artists employed in aligning tradition with modernity. In 1939 Giuseppe Bottai, Minister of National Education, declared that no single formula, not even classicism, could represent Italy's artistic heritage. "Instead," he wrote, "it is the unlimited vastness of content and the plurality of forms which give the Italian artistic tradition a universal value and an influence a thousand times larger than its national territory."[62]

NOTES

1   Gillian Naylor, "Swedish Grace . . . or the Acceptable Face of Modernism?" in *Modernism in Design*, ed. Paul Greenhalgh (London, 1990), p. 172.

2   By 1926 when Jean Cocteau's *Le Rappel à l'Ordre* (The Call to Order) was published, the idea of a return to classical ideals was already well established in the European artistic community. Peter Behrens (1869–1940) introduced Neo-Classicism into the vocabulary of the avant-garde in Germany in the early years of the twentieth century with his Art Pavilion at the Oldenburg Exhibition in 1905, the interiors for the Schröder House (1908) and the Wiegand House (1911–13). See N. Pevsner, *Pioneers of Modern Design* (New York, 1960, reprinted 1984), pp. 202–4; and Fritz Hoeder, *Peter Behrens* (Munich, 1913). Moreover, the three founding members of international functionalism, Le Corbusier, Mies van der Rohe and Walter Gropius, all trained under Peter Behrens in Berlin and exhibited in their works aspects of the classical tradition.

3   Elizabeth Cowling, "Introduction" to Elizabeth Cowling and Jennifer Mundy, *On Classic Ground. Picasso, Léger, de Chirico and the New Classicism 1910–1930* (London: Tate Gallery, 1990), p. 11. In this exhibition catalogue the authors make a case for the "avant-garde classicists," stating that one of their achievements was "to have restored to classicism the inexhaustible creative variety, the inherent ambiguity, that had been drained out of it over the years as it was first appropriated, then codified, by academic artists." See also *Les Réalismes 1919–1939* (Paris: Centre Georges Pompidou, 1980).

4   Elena Pontiggia, "L'Idea del Classico. Il Dibattito sulla Classicità in Italia 1916–1932," in *L'Idea del Classico 1916–1932* (Milan, 1992), pp. 17–23.

5   Maurizio Fagiolo dell'Arco, "'Classicismo Pittorico': *Valori Plastici*, Magic Realism and Novecento," in *On Classic Ground*, p. 362.

6   Emily Braun, "Political Rhetoric and Poetic Irony: The Uses of Classicism in the Art of Fascist Italy," in *On Classic Ground*, p. 346.

7   See Braun, pp. 345–58, for the uses of the classical in Fascist art.

8   "For thirty years the dispute between the partisans of antique styles and the champions of the new art have filled pages of magazines and books." S.P., "Omaggio a Tre Artisti," *Le Arti Decorative* (November 1923): 31. *Le Arti Decorative* was founded as the official magazine of the First Exhibition of Decorative Arts in Monza in 1923.

9   Guido Marangoni, *Il mobile italiano contemporaneo* (Milan, 1925), p. 34.

10 Edward Lucie-Smith, *Furniture, A Concise History* (New York/London, 1979), p. 128.

11 Richard A. Etlin, *Modernism in Italian Architecture, 1890–1940* (Cambridge, MA/ London, 1991), p. 19.

12 *Ibid.*, p. 12. Alfredo Melani (1860–1918) was a critic and designer who wrote a series on the decorative arts for Hoepli publishers in Milan beginning in 1907 and founded the magazine *Per l'Arte* (f. 1909).

13 G. Machi, "Esposizione d'Arte Decorativa Moderna, Torino, Italia ed il estero," in *Il Tempo* (Milan, 7 July 1902), as quoted in Gabriel P. Weisberg, *Stile Floreale. The Cult of Nature in Italian Design* (Miami: The Wolfsonian Foundation, 1988), p. 15.

14   de Guttry, Maino, Quesada, *Le Arti minori d'autore in Italia dal 1900 al 1930* (Rome‑Bari, 1985), pp. 51–2

15   The exhibition was organized by the Società Umanitaria (Humanitarian Society) and held at their school. See the essay by de Guttry/Maino for a discussion of this organization.

16   Marangoni, p. 23.

17   Marangoni, p. 21.

18   "La Prima Mostra di Architettura Promossa dalla Famiglia Artistica di Milano," *Architettura e Arti Decorative* (September/October 1921): 298–304; Giovanni Muzio (1893–1982), Emilio Lancia (1890–1973), Mino Fiocchi (1893–1982), Giuseppe De Finetti (1892–1952) and Gio Ponti (1891–1979).

19   Giovanni Muzio, "L'Architettura a Milano intorno all'ottocento," *Emporium* (May 1921): 258. Muzio's Ca' Brutta, an apartment block on Via Moscova in Milan, was built between 1919 and 1923 with P.F. Barelli and V. Colonnese. See Antonio Nezi, "Nostri architetti d'oggi: Giovanni Muzio," *Emporium* (October 1931): 195–212. For additional information about Muzio see G. Gambirasio and B. Minardi, eds., *Giovanni Muzio, Opere e Scritti* (Milan, 1982).

20   Pia Vivarelli, "Classicism and Tradition in Italian Art of the 1920s," in *On Classic Ground*, p. 371.

21   Braun, p. 346.

22   Fagiolo dell'Arco, p. 359.

23   *Valori Plastici*, nos. 11 and 12 (Rome 1919).

24   The writings and paintings of Carrà and de Chirico show a close study of Italian Renaissance painting. See, for instance, Carlo Carrà, "Parlata su Giotto," *La Voce* (31 March 1916); Carlo Carrà, "Paolo Uccello, costruttore," *La Voce* (30 September 1916); Roberto Longhi, "Piero della Francesca e lo sviluppo della pittura veneziana," *L'Arte* (1914).

25   Braun, p. 356, endnote 42.

26   Braun, p. 347 and p. 355, endnote 30. In 1922 the term "novecento," meaning '900, 1900, or twentieth century, was first used by the painter Anselmo Bucci in reference to a "group of seven twentieth-century painters." The seven were Anselmo Bucci, Leonardo Dudreville, Achille Funi, Emilio Malerba, Piero Marussig, Ubaldo Oppi, Mario Sironi. See Rossana Bossaglia, "Il Novecento di Sironi, il Muralismo, il clima novecentista," in *Gli Annitrenta* (Milan, 1982), p. 79.

27   Alexander De Grand, *Italian Fascism. Its Origins & Development* (Lincoln, Nebraska/London, University of Nebraska Press, 1982), p. 5.

28   Vittorio Gregotti, *Il Disegno del Prodotto Industriale. Italia 1860–1980* (Milan, 1980), p. 189.

29   *Catalogo. Ente Nazionale Piccole Industrie Roma. Esposizione Internazionale di Barcellona, 1929* (Rome, E.N.A.P.I., 1929), pp. 5 and 35.

30   Paolo Mezzanotte, "La Prima Mostra Internazionale delle Arti Decorative a Monza," *Architettura e Arti Decorative* (1923): 391ff., 429ff. and 481ff.; "L'Esposizione di Monza," *Dedalo* (September 1923): 263–4; E. Agostinone, "La Prima Biennale delle Arti Decorative," *Emporium* (January 1923): 20–32. For more on Italy's participation at the Paris exposition see Piero Torriano, "L'Arte decorativa

contemporanea e l'Esposizione di Parigi," *Emporium* (January 1926): 38–50; Roberto Papini, "Le Arti a Parigi nel 1925," *Architettura e Arti Decorative* (1926): 345ff.

31   Gio Ponti, "Le Ceramiche," *Italia alla Esposizione Internazionale di Arti Decorative e Industriali Moderne* (n.p., [1927]), p. 71.

32   A notebook dated 1924 in the Archivio Ponti in Milan documents Ponti's visits to public collections in Florence and Rome to sketch antique ceramic vessels.

33   Robin Barber, "Classical Art: Discovery, Research and Presentation, 1890–1930," in *On Classic Ground*, pp. 404–6.

34   Ugo Ojetti, "Lettera a Giovanni Ponti sul lusso necessario," *Pegaso* (January 1933): 97–9.

35   Piero Torriano, "L'Arte Decorativa Contemporanea . . . ": 48.

36   Roberto Papini, "Le Arti a Parigi . . ." : 351.

37   Paolo Mezzanotte, "La Prima Mostra . . ." : 402.

38   A similar manifestation may be seen in the mirrored wall sconce designed by Guido Cadorin and executed by Pasquale Zennaro in the Wolfsonian Collection (84.10.2a,b). It was exhibited in the Venetian salon at the First Biennale in 1923. The overall tone of the room with its mid-eighteenth century furnishings and use of yellow lacquer and gilded surface treatment was purely Venetian Rococo.

39   *Emporium* (August 1927): 116; *Domus* (October 1928): 31; *L'Ambiente Moderno*, p.168; *Domus* (February 1929): 22. For additional information about Il Labirinto see *Emporium* (August 1927): 14–32; *Architettura e Arti Decorative* (March 1928): 300–18; *Catalogo Ufficiale della III Mostra Internazionale delle Arti Decorative*, pp. 28–29, 59; *Il Mobile Moderno*, pp. 35, 89; *Le Arti d'Oggi*, fig. 232.

40   *L'Ambiente Moderno*, p. 168.

41   *Domus* (October 1928): 31.

42   Gianni Piantoni, ed., *Roma 1911* (Rome, 1980), p. 195.

43   Bonifica Integrale, which became one of the central domestic policies of the Fascist regime, was largely the work of Arrigo Serpieri, the Under-Secretary for Integral Land Improvement from 1919 to 1935 (*Dictionary of Italian Fascism*, p. 80).

44   Marangoni, p. 29. See also Alfredo Melani, *Raccolta di mobili moderni d'arte italiana* (Milan, 1913), and Alfredo Melani, *Mobili e ambienti moderni* (Milan, 1923), for the influence in Italy of the English Arts and Crafts movement.

45   de Guttry, Maino, Quesada, *Le Arti minori . . .* , pp. 243–4.

46   Small industries were defined in a 1922 law as "those that are carried on in a home or in a studio of limited importance by virtue of capital employed, by technical means or by self employment": Gregotti, p. 189.

47   *Ibid.*, p. 166.

48   *Catalogo . . . Barcellona, 1929*, p. 37.

49   The Opera Nazionale Dopolavoro was founded in 1925 and brought under Fascist National Party (PNF) control in 1927.

50   *Catalogo . . . Barcellona, 1929*, p. 35.

51   de Guttry, Maino, Quesada *Le Arti minori . . .* , pp. 216–17.

52   In 1914 Benito Mussolini was appointed editor of *Il Popolo d'Italia* and his brother Arnaldo Mussolini was the newspaper's director. *Architettura e Arti Decorative* (December 1926): 181–91; *La Rivista del "Popolo d'Italia"* (January 1927): 43–5.

53   *La Rivista Illustrata del "Popolo d'Italia"*, vol. 4, no. 1 (January 1926): 2.

54   The drawings were signed by Ponti and Buzzi and dated 1926: *La Rivista Illustrata del "Popolo d'Italia"*, vol. 5, no. 1 (January 1927): 44.

55   Compare this work to furnishings for the Contini-Bonacossi residence, the Villa Vittoria, in Florence, designed 1930–31 by Ponti and Buzzi. Two sketchbooks of these designs are in the Wolfsonian Collection (84.2.363** and 84.2.364**).

56   Massimo Carrà, ed., *Metaphysical Painting* (New York, 1971), p. 23.

57   Braun, pp. 353–4.

58   Romke Visser, "Fascist Doctrine and the Cult of the Romanità," *Journal of Contemporary History*, vol. 27, no. 1 (January 1992): 6.

59   *Ibid* · 6, 7

60   Gio Ponti, "Quale sarà la casa, domani?" *Domus* (January 1932): 2.

61   Fagiolo dell'Arco, p. 362

62   Braun, p. 354.

America's answer!

PRODUCTION

JEAN
CARLU

DIVISION OF INFORMATION
OFFICE FOR EMERGENCY MANAGEMENT

Manipulating Modernity:
Political Persuasion

Political Things:
Design in Fascist Italy

Dennis P. Doordan

Introduction

In the modern era, design has been a powerful tool in the hands of political and cultural leaders searching for ways to articulate new systems of belief and promote new patterns of behavior. Although societies have always faced the challenge of explaining themselves to themselves and transmitting from one generation to the next a distinctive sense of identity, common purpose, and shared values, the tumultuous history of the twentieth century has complicated these tasks enormously. Forces unleashed by the process of economic modernization have dramatically transformed the material and cultural framework of society. In the political realm, advocates of revolutionary ideologies have been forced to confront the problem of building popular support for novel political creeds. Leaders of the political left and right have tried to create a nationwide political culture capable of transcending economic, ethnic, regional, or social distinctions in order to effectively harness the energy and talent of an entire population.

The Wolfsonian Collection brings together an extraordinary array of artifacts documenting different design strategies employed to articulate and disseminate the ideological programs of new regimes and create what the historian Victoria de Grazia has described as a "culture of consent."[1] This essay offers a case study of one such historical experience: Italian Fascism. What follows does not pretend to be an encyclopedic account of the individuals and institutions responsible for the production of politically inspired design during the period. It is a review, based on material available in the Wolfsonian Collection, of some of the preeminent themes and imagery typical of Fascism. A survey of Fascist political design serves as an exemplary illustration of the phenomenon of design understood as a tool of political persuasion in an era of revolutionary change.

Founded in March, 1919, Italian Fascism, under the leadership of Benito Mussolini, grew from a small revolutionary clique to a major political force in only a few years. From

Fig. 8.01
Obelisk
Monolito Mussolini, Foro Italico
**(formerly known as Foro Mussolini), Rome,
1932**
Costantino Costantini, architect
(Italian, dates unknown)

the beginning, Fascists accepted violence as a legitimate form of social and political action. The practice of brutally suppressing opposition through beatings, imprisonment, and murder continued throughout the more than two decades of Fascist rule, until Fascism itself was destroyed through the combined efforts of a native resistance movement and foreign armies. But Fascist leaders realized early that violence alone could not insure their hold on power or motivate the various constituencies in Italian society to work together for the common good. Asked by an interviewer how he drew people to him and held their allegiance, Mussolini replied: "I have been able to bind men to me more closely by honour and by persuasion than by money or by force."[2] The club and the rifle were the instruments of suppression; design – in all its varied manifestations – served as the instrument of persuasion.

The category of political design denotes the total set of objects produced during a particular period that address specifically political themes. The category includes everything from ephemeral works on paper to enduring monuments of architecture. The traditional distinctions historians make between the fine and popular arts actually obscure rather than clarify the complex process of translating the abstractions of ideology into the tangible forms of political life. Considered as a whole, the objects that make up the category of political design lack the stylistic unity implied by the art historical concept of *Gesamtkunstwerk.* Instead, political design embraces a messier, more complex array of things created by different designers to convey a variety of messages to different audiences.

How do designers persuade? How do they construct legible and appealing symbolic forms capable of conveying meaning? At times, designers appropriate the traditional and the familiar to introduce new leaders and novel ideologies. In Fascist Italy, historically sanctioned types of architecture were used to evoke the aura of a great civilization. As had emperors and pontiffs before him, Mussolini embellished Rome with major new works of architecture. One of these projects, the obelisk designed by Costantino Costantini and erected in 1932 at the Foro Mussolini (today the Foro Italico), celebrated the Fascist leader in a way that unequivocally associated the Fascist era with previous epochs of Roman grandeur³ (fig. 8.01). On a less monumental scale, the decorative arts could be used to "domesticate" the revolution and introduce a Fascist presence into the routine rhythms of daily life. A majolica bread plate designed about 1927, for example, is decorated with a quotation by Mussolini extolling the simple pleasures of fresh bread (fig. 8.02). Nothing

Fig. 8.02 See Cat. 219
Plate
Amate il Pane Cuore della Casa . . . Mussolini
(Love Bread Heart of the Home . . .), c. 1927
Design attributed to V. Retrosi

could be more reassuring or less suggestive of the specter of revolutionary violence than this paean to the staff of life.

Other designers argued that only radical new design strategies could convey the revolutionary essence of new political systems. Ernesto Rogers summed up the sentiments of an entire generation of modernist architects who supported Fascism: "We based ourselves on a syllogism which went roughly thus: fascism is a revolution, modern architecture is revolutionary, therefore it must be the architecture of fascism."[4] Indeed, some of the finest examples of modern architecture produced in Italy during the Fascist era were sponsored by the Fascist Party or commissioned by government ministries.[5] The Futurist-inspired template for Fascist culture was predicated on radical new treatments for traditional art forms such as portraits. In a portrait bust of Mussolini entitled *Continuous Profile*, the Futurist sculptor R. Bertelli employed the avant-garde concept of simultaneity (fig. 8.03). He multiplied the Duce's image by rotating his stylized profile by 360 degrees. The result is the multiple presentation of a single image rendered simultaneously abstract and representational. Looking more like a machine part than a man's head, this whirling depiction of Mussolini could not be further from the comfortably familiar world of official portraiture.

Futurism

Mussolini and his Fascist cohorts were not the first Italians to realize the power of design to attract attention and animate the process of communication. In 1909, Filippo Tomasso Marinetti published the "Manifesto of Futurism" and launched the Futurist Movement. Marinetti and the Futurists celebrated the technological marvels of the modern era. They argued that technological advances in every sphere of life had altered not only the material but the spiritual and intellectual basis of daily life and political consciousness as well. In dozens of Futurist manifestoes touching on every aspect of the literary, visual, and performing arts, the Futurists outlined their vision of new forms of communication and experience attuned to the new reality of the machine age.[6] In a 1913 manifesto entitled "Destruction of Syntax – Imagination without Strings – Words-In-Freedom," Marinetti wrote:

> Futurism is grounded in the complete renewal of human sensibility brought about by the great discoveries of science. Those people who today make use of the telegraph, the telephone, the phonograph, the train, the bicycle, the motorcycle, the automobile, the oceanliner, the dirigible, the aeroplane, the cinema, the great newspaper (synthesis of a day in the world's life) do not realize that these various means of communication, transportation and information have a decisive influence on their psyches.[7]

Many of the elements of this new sensibility are evident in the Futurist war epic *Zang Tumb Tuuum*, Marinetti's account of the bombardment of Adrianopolis (modern Edirne)

Fig. 8.04 See Cat. 82
Cover
Zang Tumb Tuuum: Adrianopoli, ottobre 1912:
parole in libertà
(Zang Tumb Tuuum: Adrianopolis, October
1912: Words in Freedom), 1914
Designed and written by F.T. Marinetti

during the First Balkan War of 1912–13 (fig. 8.04). From the inception of the movement, the Futurists celebrated all forms of violent struggle, including war. In the Founding Manifesto of 1909, Marinetti hailed war as "the world's only hygiene . . . the destructive gesture of freedom-bringers," and in the manifesto cited above, he described war as "the necessary and bloody test of a people's force." When war erupted in the Balkans between the Ottoman Turks and the forces of the Balkan League (Bulgaria, Serbia, Montenegro, and Greece), Marinetti rushed to the area to cover the conflict as a war correspondent.[8]

Published in 1914, *Zang Tumb Tuuum* offered more than the simple reportage of a distant event, it served as a vivid demonstration of the *ars rhetorica* of Futurism. In the layout of *Zang Tumb Tuuum* Marinetti rejected traditional typographic conventions such as the horizontal alignment of type; instead the graphic design of the book wedded the expressive form of typefaces and literary content in a manner that infused the description of the bombardment with an almost visceral immediacy.[9] The onomatopoetic title of the work captured

Fig. 8.05
Poster
Elezioni Politiche 1924
(Political Elections . . .), 1924
Designed by Filiberto Scarpelli
(Italian, 1870–1933)
Printed by Edizioni Star Officine Impresa Generale d'Affissioni
e Pubblicità, Milan
Published by Partito Nazionale Fascista, Rome
Offset lithograph
39⅝ x 54½ inches (100.6 x 138.4 cm)
Marks: obverse, printed in black, bottom right, designer's
mark of two shoes + "lli"
XX1990.1758

the sounds of the battle: ZANG (the firing of an artillery shell), TUMB (the shell's explosion), TUUUM (the rumbling echo of that explosion). Words appeared to fly across the page like bullets or form up into ranks like soldiers awaiting the order to attack. Many elements of this Futurist *ars rhetorica* would later find their way into Fascist political design.

Fascism

Fascism replaced Italy's multi-party parliamentary system with a one-party dictatorship. Although Mussolini was appointed prime minister in October 1922, the transition from a democratic to a totalitarian state was not finally completed until 1925. One important milestone along the path from the old constitutional system to the new Fascist dictatorship was the election of 1924, the last openly contested election under Fascism.[10] An election poster issued by the Fascist Party and designed by Filiberto Scarpelli presents two views of the Italian peninsula (fig. 8.05). Under the caption, "The liberty which one enjoyed in Italy," Scarpelli depicts a nation in chaos and threatened by Communist agitators waving placards reading "Viva Lenin" and "Down with Italy." The adjacent panel – entitled "The liberty which one enjoys" – shows Italy dispatching the red menace with a sharp kick from the Italian "boot" under the watchful eye of a virile Fascist Party member. This twin-image format was used in other Fascist election posters to contrast the alleged anarchy of civil life before 1922 with the order and harmony of Italy under Fascism.

While Scarpelli's poster clearly conveyed the Fascist interpretation of recent history, nothing about the design of it stamped the form of presentation as Fascist in the way that Marinetti's words-in-freedom format identified *Zang Tumb Tuuum* as undeniably Futurist. As long as the struggle for power was pursued through violent means, the Fascist leadership paid scant attention to matters involving the relationship between visual form and ideological content. The brutal murder of the Socialist deputy Giacomo Matteotti in June, 1924, provoked a political crisis that was not resolved until early 1925 when the Fascists finally eliminated the last vestiges of the old liberal democratic political system.[11] Secure in their control of the machinery of power, the Fascists began to consider the question of a distinctive visual identity for Fascism capable of conveying not only the specifics of a political program but the ethos of an ideological movement as well.

In a major speech delivered at the Academy of Fine Arts in Perugia in October, 1926, Mussolini called for a bold new Fascist art. He offered little, however, in the way of prescriptions or definitions for Fascist art. Mussolini's speech provoked a major debate regarding the form and content of Fascist culture. Some of the most important contributions to this debate appeared in the ideological review *Critica Fascista*.[12] Its editor Giuseppe Bottai invited cultural figures representative of a broad spectrum of contemporary Italian pro-Fascist thought to describe their visions of a truly Fascist art. The responses ranged from ringing endorsements of avant-garde experimentation to conservative appeals on behalf of classical and traditional artistic vocabularies. Rather than resolving Mussolini's call with a definitive articulation of a new Fascist art, the *Critica Fascista* series did little more than establish the parameters for a cultural debate that would continue for the duration of Fascism.

It is important to keep this debate in mind as one reviews political design in Fascist Italy. As Renzo de Felice, one of the preeminent Italian historians of the Fascist era recently noted: "Those who view the connection between fascism and culture in Italy as a simple and/or unitary one, like that which prevailed in Germany during the years of nationalist-socialist power, are making a mistake and denying themselves the possibility of coming to deeper understanding of fascism's peculiar character."[13] An account of Fascist political design cannot be reduced to a simple narrative detailing the triumph of a particular stylistic orientation (such as Socialist Realism in the Soviet Union) accompanying the concomitant suppression of radical modernist alternatives. One historian of the period described Mussolini as "a dictator who did not dictate"; in terms of political design few descriptions of the Duce are more apt.[14]

Despite the lack of consensus on the lineaments of the emerging Fascist culture, most contributors to the *Critica Fascista* debate would have agreed with Massimo Bontempelli's

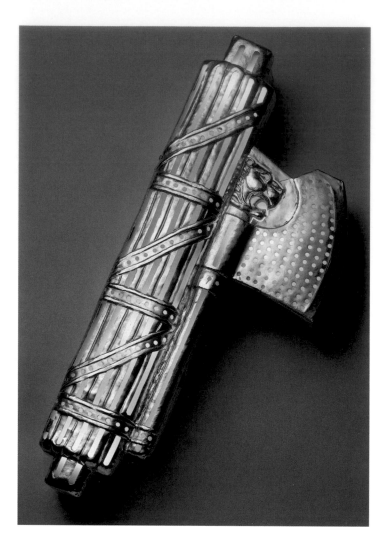

Fig. 8.06 See Cat. 220
Wall lamp
Fascio, c. 1940

argument that Fascism was more than a political program: "But by 'fascism' we mean a whole orientation of life, public and private: a total and perfected order that is at once practical as well as theoretical, intellectual and moral, application and spirit. We all agree on this (and those who do not, simply do not count)."[15] For Bontempelli, the task confronting those committed to the new Fascist order was clear: "Above all we must learn over again how to tell stories, to combine new myths and fables, to invent characters and plots."[16]

Fascist Iconography

Slowly the new stories, myths, and fables of Fascism emerged and a set of distinctive signs identified the Fascist movement. Events such as the founding of the Fascist Party in 1919 or the 1922 Fascist March on Rome that brought Mussolini to power provided the new "creation myths" celebrated by artists and designers. Governmental programs such as the so-called "Battle for Grain" (an effort initiated in 1925 to increase the production of wheat and other cereals), the "Bonifica Integrale" (a major land reclamation program) or the campaign to achieve economic autarky (launched in 1935 following punitive sanctions enacted by the

League of Nations following Italy's invasion of Ethiopia) served as the new "stories" waiting to be told. The bread plate mentioned earlier, for example, acquires a special political relevance when considered in the context of the regime's "Battle for Grain." Side by side with these myths and stories, three signs acquired a particular power to represent Fascism: the fasces, the dagger, and the image of Benito Mussolini.

The fasces – a bundle of reeds bound together with an ax – became one of the most important icons of the new order. It represented the concept of strength through unity and discipline. In antiquity, Roman officials known as lictors carried a fasces as a symbol of authority. In the nineteenth and twentieth centuries, the word fasces was frequently used to describe political groups or associations.[17] In 1926, the *fascio littorio* (fasces) was adopted as the official emblem of the Fascist regime. The fasces combined an overt reference to ancient authority with the modern connotation of a strong political organization. Frequently omitted in party propaganda before 1926,[18] the fasces eventually became ubiquitous in Fascist imagery. Designers incorporated the fasces in the design of anything and everything: jewelry, desk accessories, lighting fixtures, furniture, and architecture (figs. 8.06 and 8.07).

Fig. 8.07
Triumphal Arch
Monumento alla Vittoria
(Monument to Victory) (1925–28;
Marcello Piacentini
[Italian, 1881–1960], architect), Bolzano, Italy
From *Architettura e Arti Decorative*, no. 8
(February 1929), fig. 7
83.3.153.15

233

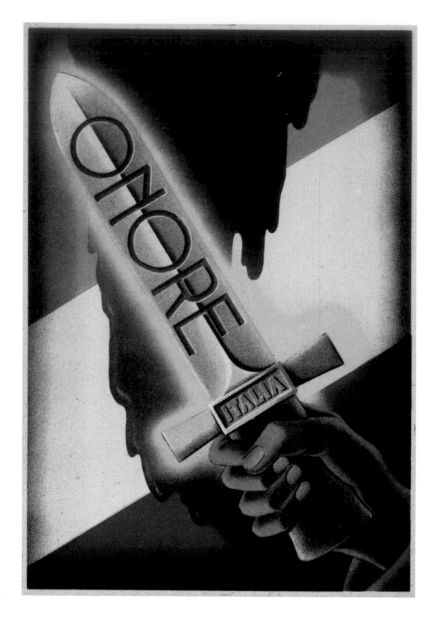

Fig. 8.08
Postcard
Onore. Italia
(Honor. Italy), 1943–45
Published by Repubblica Sociale Italiana, Italy
4 ⅛ x 5 ⅞ inches (10.5 x 14.9 cm)
XB1991.1682

Daggers were another potent symbol of Fascism identified with physical courage and personal honor (fig. 8.08). The fascination with daggers was rooted in their association with the *arditi*, an elite commando corps, whose daring exploits during World War I (including frequent hand-to-hand combat using daggers) captured the popular imagination.[19] Many former *arditi* later joined the ranks of Fascism in search of the same martial spirit and esprit-de-corps that characterized their wartime experience.[20] Daggers, like fetishes, kept the virile spirit of wartime bravery and honor alive in Fascism. Armorers responded to the demand for daggers with models that incorporated the fasces (often clasped in the talons of an eagle) or the letter M (Mussolini's initial) into the design.

The cult of the leader was inextricably woven into the fabric of Fascism. Images of Benito Mussolini, the charismatic Duce (leader; in Latin, "Dux") of Fascism, appeared everywhere. Official portraits and press photos served not only as depictions of the leader but as portraits of Fascism. Dressed in the Fascist black shirt and striking an aggressive pose, he was the epitome of the intense young revolutionary. Mussolini the European statesman appeared in formal dress or a conservative suit. In his military uniform (complete with a dagger at his side) the Duce was the fearless captain of his nation's destiny. Shown bare-chested and harvesting wheat or swinging a pick-ax, Benito was the robust populist laboring side by side with his people. Few modern political leaders can match Mussolini in terms of the shrewd manipulation of his own image.[21]

Fig. 8.09 See Cat. 201
Plate
"Fascismo Futurismo" (Fascism Futurism)
From the *Vita di Marinetti* (Life of Marinetti)
service, 1939
Designed by G. Acquaviva

Futurism and Fascism

In his contribution to the *Critica Fascista* debate regarding the form and character of Fascist art, Marinetti claimed that Futurism alone had the right to portray Fascism: "Futurist art is extremely Italian because it is virile, bellicose, joyous, optimistic, dynamic, synthetic, simultaneous, and colorful . . . . Here is futurist fascist art in perfect harmony with the . . . temperament of Benito Mussolini."[22] Marinetti based his claim for the preeminence of Futurism as the appropriate expression of Fascism on the shared history of the two movements. The links between them extended back into the prehistory of the Fascist Party. Marinetti and Mussolini met during the campaign to force Italy's entry into World War I, and in 1915 the two were arrested together during a political rally in Rome. In March, 1919, Marinetti participated in the founding of the Fascist Party in Milan's Piazza San Sepolcro and, as one of the original "San Sepolcristi," he enjoyed a special status under the Fascist regime.[23]

Fascist and Futurist symbols were often combined in Futurist designs to suggest the two movements were really only two sides of the same revolutionary coin. A 1939 Futurist plate with the legend *"Fascismo Futurismo"* (Fascism Futurism) was part of a set of twelve plates designed by the ceramist Giovanni Acquaviva and produced by the Casa Giuseppe Mazzotti[24] (fig. 8.09). The ax blade projecting from the giant F conflates the *fascio* with the first letter of Futurism and Fascism. A similar fusion of Fascist and Futurist icons characterized Alessandro Bruschetti's 1935 painting *Sintesi Fascista* (Fascist Synthesis)[25] (fig. 8.10). This triptych contains a veritable catalog of Fascist and Futurist images: portraits of the Duce, daggers, an obelisk, sheaves of wheat, ocean liners, aircraft, and radio antennae. Bruschetti rendered his vision of Fascism in a Futurist style that emphasized a sense of movement, the layering of transparent planes, and multiple perspectives. Acquaviva's ceramics and Bruschetti's painting imply a shared ethos between Futurism and Fascism; the recognition and promotion of this common spirit was central to the Futurist redaction of Fascism.

Throughout the course of Fascism, Futurist designers consistently produced the most radical imagery celebrating Mussolini and the Fascist regime. One must be careful, however, to distinguish between private ventures and official commissions when discussing political design. One of the distinguishing features of the Italian Fascist experience was the degree to which market forces played an active role in the evolution of political design. The ceramic industry, for example, offers an excellent example of an economic sector composed of multiple, independent manufacturers producing designs for a consumer market characterized by a broad spectrum of taste.[26] Most of the Futurist ceramics were produced by Casa Giuseppe Mazzotti.[27] Other factories offered stylish but tamer treatments of Fascist themes. Between 1928 and 1930, Ceramiche Rometti commissioned a series of new designs from Corrado Cagli and Dante Baldelli, some of which dealt with political themes (fig. 8.11). The stylized

Fig. 8.10 See Cat. 199
Painting
Sintesi Fascista
(Fascist Synthesis), 1935
A. Bruschetti

figures and vivid color of the ceramic plaque commemorating the 1922 Fascist March on Rome (one of a set devoted to Fascist themes) reveals an Art Moderne sensibility less radical than Futurist ceramics but more "moderne" than the bread plate discussed earlier.[28] Rather than dictate aesthetic norms, the Fascist regime allowed companies to market a wide range of politically inspired images (as long as the inspiration was politically correct). To a surprising degree Italians were free to acquire, literally, their own version of Fascism. As a political doctrine, Fascism proved to be extremely opportunistic, appealing to both modernizing and reactionary elements in Italian society. The variety apparent within the category of political design is one of the most revealing indicators of the polymorphous character of Fascism.

Other Futurists succeeded in securing official support from leading figures of the regime, as the career of the artist and designer Tato demonstrated. Tato was the pseudonym for Guglielmo Sansoni, a native of Bologna and one of the leaders of post-war Futurism in the Emilia-Romagna region. In January, 1924, Tato exhibited a large painting depicting the 1922 Fascist March on Rome and, eventually, donated the work to Mussolini. A color reproduction of the painting appeared in the Fascist monthly *Rinascità*[29] and circulated widely in the form of a postcard (fig. 8.12). Tato's work proved to be very popular with prominent

237

Fascists like Italo Balbo, Ettore Muti, and Nello Quilici. In 1927, Balbo and Quilici commissioned him to decorate the new headquarters of their daily newspaper *Corriere Padano* in Ferrara with a series of murals illustrating various Fascist subjects.[30] Beginning in the early 1930s, Tato's work increasingly dealt with aviation themes. Balbo, then chief of the Ministry of Aeronautics, encouraged Tato's interest in the subject and placed an Air Force aircraft at his disposal so he could personally experience the sensation of flying. The Ministry of Aeronautics acquired works by Tato and other so-called "Aero-Futurists" and displayed them in Ministry reception halls and offices[31] (fig. 8.13).

Ministerial Patronage

Patterns of ministerial patronage remain one of the least explored aspects of political design during the Fascist era. Students of the period err when they limit the scope of their inquiry to the role of Mussolini and the Fascist Party alone. Italo Balbo at the Ministry of Aeronautics, and Costanzo Ciano, head of the Ministry of Communications, for example, were major clients for progressive Italian designers.[32] Other important design clients included various Fascist Party organizations such as the *Opera Nazionale Balilla* (ONB, the youth organization), and the *Opera Nazionale Dopolavoro* (OND, the after-work organization).[33] The paraphernalia of membership in these organizations included pins, badges, certificates, trophies, and souvenirs of all types replete with the full range of Fascist iconography (fig. 8.14).

Fig. 8.11 See Cat. 202
Tile
XXVIII Ottobre
(also known as *La Marcia su Roma*,
The March on Rome), 1931–32
Designed by C. Cagli or D. Baldelli

Fig. 8.12
Postcard
"La Marcia su Roma"
(The March on Rome), no. 226, from the series
***Movimento Futurista Italiano*, 1927**
Designed by Tato
(pseudonym for Guglielmo Sansoni)
(Italian, 1896–1974)
Published by Casa Editrice Ballerini & Fratini, Florence
3½ x 5½ inches (8.9 x 14.0 cm)
XB1992.1190

Government ministries commissioned not only propaganda design but supported basic research and development in science and technology. Italy's impressive achievements in aviation design, for example, were recognized around the world. In response to a request by the Ministry of Aeronautics for a new seaplane, the engineer Alessandro Marchetti developed a radical design. Designated the S.55, the twin-engine, twin-hull seaplane first flew in the summer of 1924.[34] In the late 1920s and early 1930s, the S.55 was involved in a series of epic flights, culminating in the 1933 transatlantic flight of twenty-four S.55's from Rome to Chicago under the personal direction of Italo Balbo[35] (fig. 8.15). What began as an engineering project became one of the most widely recognized images of Fascist modernity. The S.55's

Fig. 8.13 See Cat. 94
Painting
Prima crociera atlantica su Rio de Janeiro
(First Atlantic long-distance flight over
Rio de Janeiro), 1933
A.G. Ambrosi

Fig. 8.14   See Cat. 221
Certificate
Opera Nazionale Balilla, Caposquadra
(National Balilla Organization, Squad Captain),
c. 1935
Designed by A. Calzavara

Fig. 8.15   See Cat. 204
Poster
Crociera Aerea del Decennale 1933
(Decennial of Long-Distance Flight . . .), 1933
Designed by L. Martinati

Fig. 8.16
Medallion
Milizia Volontaria per la Sicurezza Nazionale,
1° Legio Univeristaria "Principe di Piemonte"
(Voluntary Militia for National Security. First
University Legion "Prince of Piedmont"), c. 1922
Pino Stampini
(Italian, b. 1905)
Italy
Bronze
1 ³⁄₄ inches dia. (4.5 cm dia.)
Marks: obverse, in high relief, center right "STAMPINI"
XX1990.1921

distinctive silhouette appeared in countless posters, postcards, paintings, and other forms of propaganda (it appears, for example, in the central panel of Bruschetti's "Fascist Synthesis").

Romanità

Fascism rose to power as a revolutionary political movement, and the spectacle of propagandists for the young regime drawing parallels between contemporary and classical Italy may appear odd at first. But Fascism was perceived as a renaissance as well as a revolution; the regime was quick to cultivate the perception of Fascism as the rebirth of ancient splendor, national unity, and imperial power.[36] In their insightful 1929 study of Fascism, the American scholars Herbert Schneider and Shepard Clough noted: "The feature above all others which singles out Fascism as a unique experiment is that it asserts an ancient ideal to be realized by modern methods: the ends are Roman and the means are up to date."[37] In so doing, the regime was tapping a strong and pervasive sentiment among Italians. Long before Fascism's ascension to power, legions of university scholars and local dilettantes kept a veritable cult of *Romanità* (roman-ness, understood to be the essence of ancient Roman achievements) alive among educated Italians.[38] Ancient Rome was idealized as the repository of universally valid principles of aesthetics and enduring truths about the nature of civilization. Seen through the lens of *Romanità*, Mussolini was the new Caesar. Under his leadership, Rome would assert its millennial claim to cultural and political hegemony in the Mediterranean.

Classical forms and themes pervaded the political designs of the era. A medal struck to honor the Milizia Volontaria per la Sicurezza Nazionale (MVSN, the Voluntary Militia for National Security) depicts three marching militia men with daggers dangling from their belts (fig. 8.16). On the reverse, a rifle together with an open book – the emblem of the Gruppi Universitari Fascisti (GUF, Fascist university groups) – appear before a stylized *fascio*. The design is offset on the bronze medallion, creating an irregular edge. This conscious archaicism evokes the image of ancient coins, thus linking the modern militia men with their forebears in the Roman legions.[39] It is important to recognize that gestures such as the so-called Roman salute to greet Mussolini, the raising of new obelisks, and the striking of medallions "*all'antica*" involved more than facile posturing. The revival of antique forms and customs served as the reification of an almost mystical belief in Fascism as a modern reincarnation of the spirit of ancient Rome.

Ferruccio Ferrazzi's monumental mosaic *The Birth of Rome* captures something of the metahistoricism that proved to be such an important component of the cult of *Romanità* (fig. 8.17). Commissioned in 1938 and executed in 1940–41, *The Birth of Rome* is one of the key images in the decorative program for the new Piazzale Augusto Imperatore in Rome.[40] Created in the 1930s around the newly excavated mausoleum of Augustus, the Piazzale was a centerpiece of Fascist urban planning in Rome.[41] In place of the conventional representation of the Tiber as a mature, bearded man, Ferrazzi depicted the Tiber as a virile youth holding Romulus and Remus and flanked by Roman divinities engaged in various labors. In a style Ferrazzi described as "new mythic naturalism," he tried to evoke the "fantastic reality" of the contemporary renewal of the eternal (and an eternally youthful) spirit of Rome.[42]

While Ferrazzi's iconography may seem obscure, the style is "unmistakably of the thirties."[43] Indeed, some argued that it was through the agency of style itself that the true nature of Fascism could best be revealed. An argument to this effect was advanced in the "Manifesto of Mural Painting" issued by a group of painters, in December, 1933:

> The educational function of painting is above all a question of style. Rather than through the subject (a Communist conception) it is through the suggestion of the ambient, through style, that art will succeed in making a new imprint on the popular consciousness. Questions of "subject matter" are too easily solved to be essential . . . .
>
> To be consonant with the spirit of the Revolution, the style of Fascist painting must be antique and at the same time extremely new.[44]

In the 1930s, many artists began to perceive the spirit of Fascism as something apart from the specifics of ideology. Form gradually took precedence over content until form *became* content. The importance of style in conveying the "essence" of Fascism was not confined to the fine arts.

Information and Exhibition Design

While artists like Ferrazzi depicted the mythic foundation of the Fascist ethos, others grappled with the task of explaining the bureaucratic structure and material accomplishments of the regime. A flood of posters, pamphlets, and government documents appeared describing new economic and political institutions or outlining government programs. Vivid colors and bold graphics rescued facts and figures from the unimaginative treatment too often characteristic of bureaucratic reports. A single dramatic image or a deft manipulation of scale could transform an organizational chart or a compilation of data into the graphic embodiment of Fascist dynamism (fig. 8.18).

The career of Attilio Calzavara is particularly instructive in terms of information design in the Fascist era. Although largely ignored in most accounts of twentieth-century Italian design, Calzavara executed a series of important government commissions for graphic and exhibition designs during the 1930s.[45] In 1932, the Ministry of Public Works headed by Arnaldo di Crollolanza commissioned him to design *Opere pubbliche 1922–1932*, a three-hundred-page report documenting ten years of public works projects sponsored by the regime[46] (fig. 8.19). Calzavara designed the cover, title page, and chapter headings. Similar commissions for ministry reports documenting the construction of a new rail line between

Fig. 8.17
Mural (detail)
***Il Mito di Roma* (The Birth of Rome), Piazzale Augusto Imperatore, Rome, 1940–41**
Designed by Ferruccio Ferrazzi
(Italian, 1891–1978)
From *Stile*, no. 5–6, May-June, vol. XIX (1941): 102
83.3.151.5

Fig. 8.18
Poster
Ordinamento Corporativo dello Stato Fascista
(Corporative Structure of the Fascist State),
c. 1934
Printed by Società Anonima La Presse, Milan
Published by Edizioni di Propaganda Corporativa, for the
Fiera Campionaria, Padua, Italy
Commercial color lithograph
55 3/16 x 39 5/8 inches (140.3 x 100.7 cm)
TD1992.20.2

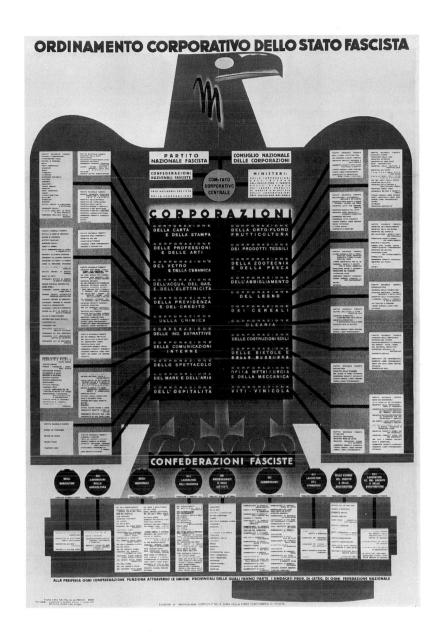

Bologna and Florence and the opening of a new highway through the mountains linking the port of Genoa with the Po valley quickly followed.[47]

Much can be learned by comparing Calzavara's graphic design work on behalf of the regime during the 1930s with Futurists' experiments before World War I. Officially commissioned work was seldom as provocative as pre-war Futurist experiments such as *Zang Tumb Tuuum*. Avant-garde design strategies such as the Futurist words-in-freedom disturbed the bourgeois sensibility of some critics; others were simply baffled and found the Futurist designs incomprehensible. It is the nature of political design to inspire and reassure rather than disturb or confuse its audience. Calzavara excelled at creating slick, attractive designs

that were undeniably modern; but it was a comfortable rather than a provocative modernity. Calzavara is typical of a generation of competent designers who followed in the wake of avant-garde pioneers without ever quite approaching (or being allowed to approach) the risky extremes of Futurism.

Radical designers enjoyed perhaps their greatest "official" successes with ephemeral exhibition design. For a brief period in the mid-1930s it appeared that the regime had accepted the equation of modernism with Fascism. In 1932 the regime sponsored an enormous exhibition celebrating the tenth anniversary of Fascist power (fig. 8.20). The Mostra della Rivoluzione Fascista (Exhibition of the Fascist Revolution) bore an unmistakably modern imprint. As the official guide book noted: "It was in the nature of things that a Revolution which had ushered in a new era, dividing it sharply from the preceding one, should demand a new artistic form of expression, entirely distinct from all previous tendencies and style."[48] The Palazzo dell'Esposizione in Rome was completely transformed as the disparate threads of modernist design were brought together in one of the most important political events of the period.[49] Outside, a new temporary facade, designed by Adalberto Libera and Mario de Renzi, included four huge *fasce* twenty-five meters tall. (This facade appears in the right panel of Bruschetti's "Fascist Synthesis"). Inside, the treatment of the twenty-five individual rooms ranged from Enrico Prampolini's Futurist dynamism to a mytho-heroic monumentality of Mario Sironi (fig. 8.21).

Fig. 8.19 See Cat. 246
Cover
Opere Pubbliche 1922–1932
(Public Works . . .), 1933
Designed by A. Calzavara

Fig. 8.20
Cover
Guida Della Mostra Della Rivoluzione Fascista
(Guide to the Exhibition of the Fascist Revolution), 1932
Designed by Mario Sironi
(Italian, 1885–1961)
Published by Stabilimenti Grafici di A. Vallecchi, Florence, 1933
9⅜ x 6¾ inches (23.8 x 17.2 cm)
83.2.565

The regime exploited every possible device and strategy for promoting the Mostra della Rivoluzione Fascista. Fascist organizations such as the ONB and the OND organized excursions to the exhibition for their members. The state railway offered special discounts for visitors travelling to Rome for the exhibition. Radio and press coverage brought the exhibition to those who could not attend.

The arrangement of the *fascio* as the dominant architectural motif on the exterior was repeated for the Italian pavilions at the 1933 Chicago Century of Progress Exposition[50] and the 1935 International Exposition in Brussels,[51] both designed by Adalberto Libera and Mario de Renzi. In the wake of the Ethiopian war and the proclamation of the new Fascist empire in 1936, however, *Romanità* replaced modernism as the preferred image for Italian participation at international fairs in the late 1930s and early 1940s.

Radio

In February, 1929, Marinetti read "Il bombardamento di Adrianopoli" on Italian radio. This was an adaptation of his book *Zang Tumb Tuuum* published originally in 1914. The onomatopoeia of Futurist words-in-freedom and the emotionally charged character of Marinetti's

Fig. 8.21
Photograph
Galleria dei Fasci, Sala S: L'Italia in Cammino
(Fasces Gallery, Room S: Italy on the Move),
Mostra della Rivoluzione Fascista, Rome, 1932
Designed by Mario Sironi
(Italian, 1885–1961)
Istituto Nazionale Luce, Rome
9 1/16 x 6 7/10 inches (23.0 x 17.0 cm)
GF1993.2.79.17

Fig. 8.22 See Cat. 198
Poster
***Ente Radio Rurale, Radioprogramma Scolastico
N. 67. La Rivoluzione Fascista, no. 14***
**(Rural Radio Corporation, Scholastic Radio
Program N. 67. The Fascist Revolution, no. 14),
1938
Designed by O. Gasperini**

prose translated easily into a dramatic audio presentation. Marinetti quickly emerged as one of Italy's first popular radio personalities.[52] In August, 1933, for example, he broadcast live the return of Italo Balbo from his epic transatlantic flight.[53] That same year Marinetti issued the "Futurist Manifesto of Radio" co-authored with the Futurist playwright Pino Masnata.[54]

While Fascist leaders were always keenly sensitive to the importance of print journalism, they were slow to exploit the potential of the new mass communication medium of radio.[55] It was not until the mid-1930s that the regime seriously tried to promote the use of radio as a significant propaganda tool.[56] The distribution of radio sets among rural populations was subsidized and special programs were produced for use in schools. In June, 1933, the Ministry of Communications created the Ente Radio Rurale and began broadcasting special weekly school programs. Posters illustrating upcoming programs were sent to rural classrooms prior to the broadcasts and served as visual aids. A poster issued in 1938 illustrating a program on the Fascist revolution combined period news photographs with images recycled from the 1932 Mostra della Rivoluzione Fascista (fig. 8.22).

War

In 1920 Mussolini declared: "Strife is the origin of all things . . . the day in which there should be no more strife would be a day of melancholy, of the end of things, of ruin."[57] As one of the most organized and all-encompassing forms of strife, war was held in high esteem by the Fascists. World War I was remembered for the spirit of heroism, self-sacrifice, and fraternal camaraderie it inspired, and gradually what the historian George Mosse has described as the "Myth of the War Experience" replaced the bitter realities of combat in the popular imagination.[58] War was always a privileged metaphor in Fascist propaganda, and domestic programs were often identified in military terms. In the mid-1920s, the campaign to increase agricultural production, for example, was known as the "Battle for Grain." Eventually such symbolic equivalents gave way to the real thing.

In October, 1935, Mussolini launched Fascism's war with the Italian invasion of Ethiopia. By May of the following year the conquest of Ethiopia was completed and the Duce proclaimed the birth of a new Roman empire. The military campaign and the new empire were celebrated with countless souvenirs of all types. Fascist propaganda interpreted the Ethiopian war in a variety of ways: as the revival of ancient Roman imperial glory, as the triumph of a superior white European civilization over an inferior African culture, and as an indication of the invincibility of modern military technology. But efforts to manipulate the impact and significance of the war were not limited to these themes alone.

One of the most intriguing aspects of this process of coming to terms with war is the incorporation of children in war imagery. The equation of war with children's play appears strangely at odds with the heroic themes of so much wartime propaganda. Such an equation serves two purposes: it indoctrinates the child to accept war as natural, and it reassures the adult that war is not as horrible as one might fear. In 1936, the Carlo Erba company, a baby food manufacturer, released a board game entitled "La Conquista dell'Abissinia" (The Conquest of Abyssinia) celebrating the Italian campaign and, at the same time, promoting one of the company's baby food products (fig. 8.23). Superimposed on a map of Ethiopia was a trail marked by 68 numbered squares. Players "marched" from the city of Asmara in Eritrea (one of the starting points for the Italian invasion) to the capital of Addis Ababa. The reduction of war to child's play and the appropriation of the war's popularity to advertise a product inevitably trivialized the entire venture. For our purposes, it is important to note that trivialization is one design strategy for masking the bloody reality of war. As George Mosse has observed: "Trivialization played upon people's immediate reactions without the need for that intellectual mediation, however slight, necessary to properly understand many myths and symbols."[59]

Images of children constituted a recurrent motif in Fascist iconography. Children symbolized innocence, continuity between generations, and unquestioning faith in authority.

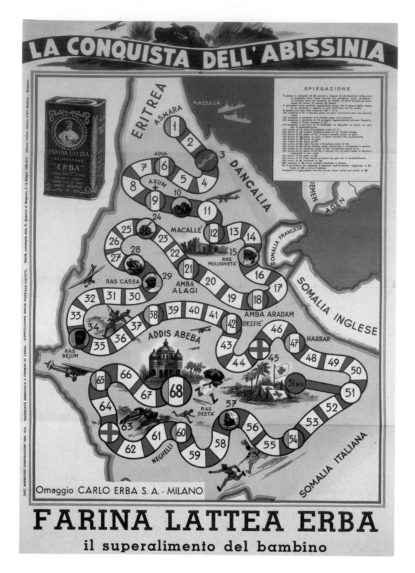

Fig. 8.23 See Cat. 224
Board game
La Conquista dell'Abissinia
(The Conquest of Abyssinia), 1936
Published by Carlo Erba S.A., Milan

Incorporated in wartime propaganda, the motif of children at play rendered war less threatening. Early in World War II, a series of humorous postcards designed by Aurelio Bertiglia were issued depicting Allied and Axis combatants as children. In one, Italian and German "soldiers" roar past their British and Greek adversaries in an automobile shaped like a giant wheeled *fascio*[60] (fig. 8.24). The theme of war as child's play is most persuasive, of course, when the conflict is far away, the casualty rolls are short, and victory seems assured. The reality of global conflict soon robbed World War II of any hint of childhood innocence.

Among those who welcomed the war were the Futurists. Like the Fascists, they had always celebrated war as a purifying experience for nations as well as individuals. During the war years, Mussolini personally subsidized Marinetti's various publishing ventures to insure the steady production of Futurist war propaganda.[61] Marinetti composed Futurist war poems using the words-in-freedom format he had developed three decades earlier. His bellicose rhetoric was the perfect literary complement to Futurist war art depicting the aerial

Fig. 8.25
Poster
Allarme! Cacciabombardieri nemici mitragliano CHE FARE?
(Warning! Enemy fighter-bombers WHAT TO DO!), 1943
Printed by G.E.R.F., Milan. Published by Edizioni Esse, Milan and Rome
Commercial color lithograph
23⅞ x 17⅞ inches (66.7 x 45.4 cm)
XX1990.2249

Fig. 8.24
Postcard
Via della Vittoria: divieto di transito al pedoni
(Victory Road. No Pedestrians), 1941
Designed by Aurelio Bertiglia
(Italian, 1891–1940)
Printed by NMM, Milan
3½ x 5½ inches (8.9 x 14.0 cm)
XB1992.163

Fig. 8.26
Poster
20 Ottobre!
(October 20!), 1944
Designed by Gino Boccasile
(Italian, 1901–52)
Italy
Commercial color lithograph
39¼ x 27⁹⁄₁₆ inches (99.8 x 70.0 cm)
Marks: obverse, printed in black, lower left corner "boccasile"
XX1990.2275

bombardment of cities. In a 1942 essay entitled "The Aesthetics of War," Marinetti claimed that "Bombardment does not frighten the Italians."[62] As the distinction between the battle front and the home front began to erode, however, such bravado gave way to the serious business of staying alive. Broadsides describing how to survive air raids began to appear (fig. 8.25). The straightforwardly didactic character of such information designs contrasted sharply with the lurid style of wartime propaganda designed to arouse support for the war among a populace caught increasingly in the line of fire. No longer depicted as charming substitutes for their fathers and older brothers, children were now portrayed as victims. On October 20, 1944, an Allied air raid on Milan struck a school and left 200 schoolboys between the ages of six and ten dead.[63] Gino Boccasile, one of the most prolific Italian poster designers of the war, created a poster depicting the disaster (the image also circulated in the form of a postcard) (fig. 8.26). With Allied bombers overhead and the spires of Milan Cathedral in the background to identify the place and the event, the skeletal hand of death reaches for the smiling schoolboys. When the enemy acquired a human face, it was one based on frightening racist stereotypes. American soldiers, for example, were usually depicted as brutish Africans eager to rob women of their virtue and the nation of its cultural patrimony[64] (fig. 8.27).

Fig. 8.27
Postcard
Come Ci Vorrebbero
(How They Want Us), 1945
Designed by Dante Coscia
(Italian, active 1940–45)
Published by Repubblica Sociale Italiana, Italy
4 x 5⅞ inches (10.2 x 14.9 cm)
XB1991.1761

Conclusion

The end for Fascism came in April, 1945. War, hailed by Mussolini, Marinetti, and their cohorts as a vital part of the Fascist ethos, brought ruin not glory for Fascism. Although Italian Fascism was destroyed, questions regarding the appeal of Fascism remain. How had this brutal political ideology attracted the undeniable support it enjoyed for more than twenty years among significant sectors of the population? What role did the design arts play in promoting and sustaining Fascist hegemony?

One model for understanding how totalitarian regimes attempt to forge the disparate elements of a nation into a viable "culture of consent" describes a system predicated on 1) the rigid control by the State or the Party of all forms of cultural expression, 2) the single-minded promotion of one (usually realist) style of expression, and 3) the ruthless suppression of alternate formulas.[65] Advocates of this model are forced to admit, however, that it does not apply to the Italian experience.[66] Under Fascism, dramatically different forms of expression conveyed significantly different messages about its nature and direction. Marinetti and his Futurist colleagues argued that the world had irrevocably changed as a result of modern technology and Fascism was the inevitable political manifestation of a new consciousness. Ferruccio Ferrazzi's work, on the other hand, typifies the position of those who maintained that the essence of Rome was eternal and Fascism was the reincarnation of Roman authority and martial virtue.

To appreciate the diversity of political designs assembled in the Wolfsonian Collection requires an alternate model for totalitarian practice, one for which the creation of a mass political culture does not require the same form of expression for every group. Instead, designers are free to select from a set of ideals and symbols and express them in a variety of ways, each one legible and congenial to a different social and political constituency. The result is a political culture suffused with politically "correct" but hardly uniform or consistent messages regarding the essential nature and constituent elements of the dominant ideology. Refining the details of such an alternate interpretive model of totalitarian art and design is a task for future research. How, for example, is the political design agenda established (and later revised)? What is the role of market forces in shaping the production and consumption of political designs? How should one evaluate the relationship between visual style and political content? As the material under review here demonstrates, any authoritative historical analysis of political design must begin by recognizing the complex and multiple design strategies at work in the political culture of Fascism.

NOTES

1   Victoria de Grazia, *The Culture of Consent. Mass Organization of Leisure in Fascist Italy* (Cambridge, 1981), p. 2. Also see Charles S. Maier, *Recasting Bourgeois Europe. Stabilization in France, Germany, and Italy in the Decades after World War I* (Princeton, 1975); Alberto Folin, ed., *Immagine di popolo e organizzazione del consenso in Italia negli anni trenta e quaranta* (Venice, 1979).

2   Emil Ludwig, *Talks With Mussolini* (Boston, 1933), p.108.

3   The obelisk of Carrara marble measured 17.1 meters in height and weighed 770 tons. For an account of the construction of this obelisk see Memmo Caporilli and Franco Simeoni, *Il Foro Italico e Lo Stadio Olimpico* (Rome, 1990), pp. 133–4.

4   Dennis P. Doordan, *Building Modern Italy. Italian Architecture 1914–1936* (New York, 1988), p. 129.

5   Richard Etlin, *Modernism in Italian Architecture, 1890–1940* (Cambridge, MA, 1991).

6   For a collection of Futurist manifestoes see Umbro Apollonio, ed., *Futurist Manifestos* (New York, 1973). For additional information on Futurism see Pontus Hulten, *Futurism and Futurisms* (New York / London, 1986); Caroline Tisdall and Angelo Bozzolla, *Futurism* (New York /London, 1977).

7   Apollonio, *Futurist Manifestos*, p. 96.

8   Gino Agnese, *Marinetti una vita esplosiva* (Milan, 1990), pp. 118–22. This was not Marinetti's first experience as a war correspondent. The previous year he had journeyed to Libya to cover the Italo-Turkish War of 1911–12 (see Agnese, pp. 113–17).

9   For an excellent analysis of this publication see Jeffrey Schnapp, "Politics and Poetics in Marinetti's *Zang Tumb Tuuum*," *Stanford Italian Review* 5 (Spring 1985): 75–92. Also see David Cundy, "Marinetti and Italian Futurist Typography," *Art Journal* 41, no.4 (Winter 1981): 349–52.

10 For an account of the 1924 election see Luigi Salvatorelli and Giovanni Mira, *Storia d'Italia nel periodo fascista* (9th ed., Turin, 1964), pp. 304–18. For a detailed account of the early years of Fascism see Adrian Lyttelton, *The Seizure of Power: Fascism in Italy 1919–1929* (New York, 1973).

11 Lyttelton, *The Seizure of Power*, Chapter Ten, "The Matteotti Crisis"; Salvatorelli and Mira, *Storia d'Italia*, pp. 329–30.

12 For more on the *Critica Fascista* debate see Jeffrey Schnapp and Barbara Spackman, eds., "Selections from the Great Debate on Fascism and Culture: *Critica Fascista* 1926–1927," *Stanford Italian Review* 8, no. 1–2 (1990): 235–72. For more information on Giuseppe Bottai see "Giuseppe Bottai" in Philip V. Cannistraro, ed., *Historical Dictionary of Fascist Italy* (Westport, CT, 1982), pp. 89–91.

13 Renzo de Felice, "Fascism and Culture in Italy: Outlines for Further Study," *Stanford Italian Review* 8, no. 1–2 (1990) : 5.

14 A.J.P. Taylor, review of *Mussolini's Roman Empire*, by Dennis Mack Smith, *The New York Review of Books* (August 5, 1976): 3.

15 Schnapp and Spackman, "Selections from the Great Debate," p. 249.

16 *Ibid.*, p. 250.

17 "Fascio Littorio" in *Historical Dictionary of Fascist Italy*, p. 205. For the specific symbolism of the fasces during the Fascist era see Herbert Schneider and Shepard Clough, *Making Fascists* (Chicago, 1929), p, 190. For architectural uses of the fasces see Etlin, *Modernism in Italian Architecture*, pp. 403–12.

18 The Wolfsonian Collection contains three posters deigned by Filiberto Scarpelli for the 1924 election campaign; only one of the three contains the fasces. This symbol fails to appear in Fascist election posters created by other designers as well.

19 "Arditi" in *Historical Dictionary of Fascist Italy*, pp. 34–5.

20 For more on the role of the *arditi* in the early history of Fascism see Max Gallo, *Mussolini's Italy* (New York, 1973), pp. 53–5; and Schneider and Clough, *Making Fascists*, p. 191.

21 For a discussion of the strict guidelines issued by the regime's press office regarding press descriptions and photographs of Mussolini see Philip Cannistraro, *La fabbrica del consenso. Fascismo e mass media* (Bari, 1975), pp. 80–4. Also see Dino Biondi, *La fabbrica del Duce* (Florence, 1967). For an interesting personal perspective on the evolution of portraits of Mussolini during Fascism see Italo Calvino, "The Dictator's Hats," *Stanford Italian Review* 8, no. 1–2 (1990): 195–210.

22 Schnapp and Spackman, "Selections from The Great Debate," p. 262. Marinetti's essay is also reprinted in Herbert Schneider, *Making the Fascist State* (New York, 1928), pp. 361–2.

23 For the relationship between Mussolini and Marinetti in these years see Renzo de Felice, *Mussolini il rivoluzionario* (Turin, 1965), pp. 474–82.

24 Other designs in this set refer to literary works by Marinetti, *Zang Tumb Tuuum* and his 1909 novel *Mafarka*; one bears the inscription *San Sepolcro*, a reference to the founding of the Fascist Party. For a review of Futurist ceramics and illustrations of the plates see Enrico Crispolti, *La Ceramica futurista da Balla a Tullio D'Albisola* (Florence, 1982). For additional information on the Casa Giuseppe Mazzotti see Carlo de Benedetti, *Il Futurismo in Ligure* (Savona, 1976).

25 "Fascist Synthesis" was illustrated in *Stile Futurista* 2, no. 8–9 (May 1935): 30. For additional information concerning Alessandro Bruschetti see Bruno Mantura, Patrizia Rosazza-Ferraris, Livia Velani, eds., *Futurism in Flight. Aeropittura Paintings and Sculptures of Man's Conquest of Space 1913–1945* (London/Rome, 1990), p. 171; Enrico Crispolti, *Aeropittura Futurista* (Modena, 1985), p. 55.

26 For a discussion of the structure of the Italian ceramic industry during this period see Roberta Fiorini, "Le ceramiche italiane fra le due guerre," in *Cagli e Leoncillo alle Ceramiche Rometti*, eds. Giorgio Cortenova and Enrico Mascelloni (Milan, 1986), pp. 31–43; and M. Cristina Tonelli Michail, *Il design in Italia 1925–1943* (Bari, 1987), pp. 104–7. Also see Fulvio Rosso, *Per virtu del fuoco. Uomini e ceramiche del Novecento italiano* (Aosta, 1983); Pier Giovanni Castagnoli, Fabrizio d'Amico, and Flaminio Gualdoni, *Scultura e ceramica in Italia nel Novecento* (Milan, 1989).

27 The manufacturer Gatti di Faenza produced ceramic designs by the Futurist Giacomo Balla (see Crispolti, *La ceramica futurista*).

28 In addition to "La Marcia su Roma" the set also included plaques entitled "credere, obbedire, combattere," "il silenzio è dura disciplina," and "combattimento." A small ceramic portrait bust of Mussolini completed the set. The pieces are illustrated and discussed in Cortenova and Mascelloni, *Cagli e Leoncillo alle ceramiche Rometti*, pp. 122–3.

29 The Wolfsonian Collection in Genoa, Italy, includes one example of the Rinascità reproduction undated but with the caption "La Marcia su Roma dal N.7 di Rinascità rassegna mensile fascista."

30 The *Corriere Padano* served as an important forum for the progressive, modernizing wing of the Fascist movement; for additional information on Balbo and the *Corriere Padano* see Claudio Segre, *Italo Balbo. A Fascist Life* (Berkeley, 1987), pp. 135–8. For more on the significance of Tato's commission see Claudia Salaris, *Artecrazia. L'avanguardia futurista negli anni del fascismo* (Florence, 1992), p. 82. For an illustration and brief description of the decorative program see Anna Maria Nalini, ed. *Futurismo in Emilia Romagna* (Modena, 1990), p. 51.

31 For Tato's own account of his involvement with Balbo and the Ministry of Aviation see: Tato, *Tato racconTato da Tato: 20 anni di futurismo con scritti poetici* (Milan, 1941), pp. 147–51. For a brief discussion of governmental patronage of Aero-Futurism see: Patrizia Rosazza-Ferraris, "The Aeropainters and the State: Commissions and Acquisitions," in *Futurism in Flight*, eds. Bruno Mantura, Patrizia Rosazza-Ferraris, Livia Velani, pp. 33–6.

32 For a brief account of Costanzo Ciano's efforts at the Ministry of Communications see Cesare Columba, "Architettura e potere nella politica delle Comunicazioni," in *Angiolo Mazzoni (1894–1979): Architetto nell'Italia tra le due guerre*, ed. Anna Maria Matteucci (Bologna, 1984): pp. 73–80.

33 For the O.N.B. see "Youth Organizations," in *Historical Dictionary of Fascist Italy*, pp. 569–73; Michael Ledeen, "Italian Fascism and Youth," *Journal of Contemporary History* 4 (July 1969): 137–14. For the O.N.D. see de Grazia, *The Culture of Consent*.

34 Giovanni Klaus Koenig, "Alessandro Marchetti: idrovolanti come industria," *Rassegna* 18 (June 1984): 34–51.

35 Segre, *Italo Balbo: A Fascist Life*, Chapter Eleven, "Aviator: The Second Atlantic Cruise."

36 For an excellent discussion of the relationship between Fascism and *Romanità* see Romke Visser, "Fascist Doctrine and the Cult of the *Romanità*," *Journal of Contemporary History* 27 (January 1992): 5–21. Also see William MacDonald, "Excavation, Restoration, and Italian Architecture of the 1930s," in *In Search of Modern Architecture. A Tribute to Henry-Russell Hitchcock*, ed. Helen Searing (New York: The Architectural History Foundation, 1982), pp. 298–320; Emily Braun, "Political Rhetoric and Poetic Irony: The Uses of Classicism in the Art of Fascist Italy," in *On Classic Ground, Picasso, Léger, de Chirico and the New Classicism 1910–1930*, ed. Elizabeth Cowling and Jennifer Mundy (London, 1990), pp. 345–38.

37 Schneider and Clough, *Making Fascists*, p. 199.

38 "Romanità" in *Historical Dictionary of Fascist Italy*, pp. 461–3.

39 Another version of this same design, minus the irregular edge, with a ribbon attached is illustrated in Walter Tabacchi, *Medaglie di guerra Italia, 1919–1943* (Carpi, 1990), p. 21. Tabacchi provides no date but the medals were probably struck in the mid-1920s during a period of militia reorganization. For additional information on the M.V.S.N. see "Militia" in *Historical Dictionary of Fascist Italy*, pp. 338–9.

40 The Wolfsonian Collection contains the cartoon for "The Birth of Rome."

41 For a detailed study of the planning and iconography of the site see Spiro Kostof, "The Emperor and the Duce: the Planning of the Piazzale Augusto Imperatore in Rome," in *Art and Architecture in the Service of Politics*, eds. Henry Millon and Linda Nochlin (Cambridge, MA, 1978), pp. 270–325.

42 For Ferrazzi's own description of the mosaic program see Antonio Munoz, "Il mito di Roma. Musaico di Ferruccio Ferrazzi nella Piazza d'Augusto Imperatore," *L'Urbe* 6 (May 1941): 28–30.

43 Kostof, "The Emperor and the Duce," p. 309.

44 Massimo Campigli, Carlo Carrà, Achille Funi, Mario Sironi, "Manifesto della pittura murale," in *Mario Sironi. Scritti editi e inediti*, ed. Ettore Camesasca (Milan, 1980), p. 156.

45 The archive of Attilio Calzavara (1901–51) recently entered the Wolfsonian Collection. For additional information on Calzavara see Enrica Torelli Landini, "Attilio Calzavara: Works and Commissions of an Anti-Fascist Designer," (Miami Beach: The Wolfsonian Foundation; Florence: Amalthea, 1994).

46 Ministero dei Lavori Pubblici, *Opere pubbliche 1922–1932* (Rome, 1933).

47 Ministero dei Lavori Pubblici, *Direttissima Bologna-Firenze 1934-XII* (Rome, 1934). Ministero dei Lavori Pubblici, *Autocamionale Genova-Valle del Po* (Rome, 1935).

48 Dino Alfieri and Luigi Freddi, *Mostra della Rivoluzione Fascista. Guida Storica* (Bergamo: Istituto Italiano d'Arti Grafiche, 1933), English edition, p. 64.

49 Attendance estimates for the exhibition vary between 3.7 and 4 million people. During the two years it remained opened as many as one in eleven Italians attended. For additional discussions of the exhibition see Jeffrey Schnapp, "Epic Demonstrations: Fascist Modernity and the 1932 Exhibition of the Fascist Revolution," in *Fascism, Aesthetics, and Culture,* ed. Richard J. Golson (Hanover, NH: University Press of New England, 1992): pp. 1–32; Libero Andreotti, "The Aesthetics of War: The Exhibition of the Fascist Revolution," *Journal of Architectural Education* 45 (February 1992): 76–86.

50 For a detailed discussion of Italy's participation in the 1933 Chicago Exposition see Dennis P. Doordan, "Exhibiting Progress: Italy's Participation in the Century of Progress Exposition," in *Chicago Architecture and Design 1923–1993,* ed. John Zukowski (Munich/Chicago, 1993).

51 Saverio Muratori, "L'Esposizione Internazionale di Bruxelles," *Architettura* 14 (October 1935): 561–72.

52 Cannistraro, *La fabbrica del consenso,* pp. 231–2; Salaris, *Artecrazia,* pp. 165–8.

53 Segre, *Italo Balbo,* p. 255.

54 Hulten, *Futurism & Futurisms,* p. 546. A year later, the Futurist Fortunato Depero issued a volume of poetry conceived expressly to be read on the radio; see Fortunato Depero, *Liriche radiofoniche* (Milan, 1934).

55 For an account of the development of radio in Italy see Antonio Papa, *Storia politica della radio in Italia,* 2 vols. (Naples, 1978); and David Forgacs, *Italian Culture in the Industrial Era 1880–1980* (Manchester, 1990). For an excellent analysis of the visual imagery associated with broadcasting see Matteo Fochessati, *La Voce del Mondo. L'immagine della radio in Italia fra le due guerre* (Genoa, 1990).

56 Philip Cannistraro, "The Radio in Fascist Italy," *Journal of European Studies* 2, no. 2 (June 1972): 134–6; Folin, ed., *Immagine di popolo,* pp. 47–51.

57 Schneider, *Making the Fascist State,* p. 276.

58 "The Myth of the War Experience was designed to mask war and to legitimize the war experience; it was meant to displace the reality of war." George L. Mosse, *Fallen Soldiers. Reshaping the Memory of the World Wars* (New York, 1990), p. 7.

59 *Ibid.,* p. 147.

60 This series of postcards is illustrated in Furio Arrasich, *Catalogo delle cartoline italiane* (Rome, 1986), p. 17.

61 Salaris, *Artecrazia,* pp. 220–1.

62 F.T. Marinetti, *Esercito italiano: poesia armata* (Rome, 1942), p. 23.

63 Wesley Frank Craven and James Lea Cate, eds., *The Army Air Forces in World War II,* vol. 3, *Europe: Argument to V-E Day January 1944 to May 1945* (Chicago, 1951). The October 20, 1944 raid is mentioned only in passing (pp. 648–9); for a detailed description of the devastation see Luigi Villari, *The Liberation of Italy 1943–1947* (Appleton, WI, 1959), pp. 155–6.

64 For an excellent discussion of Italian wartime propaganda see Mario Isnenghi, *L'Italia in guerra. 1940–1943, Immagini e temi della propaganda fascista,* vol. 1, and *1943–1945, L'immagini della Repubblica Sociale Italiana,* vol. 2 (Brescia: Fondazione Luigi Micheletti, 1989).

65 Igor Golomstock, *Totalitarian Art in the Soviet Union, the Third Reich, Fascist Italy and the People's Republic of China* (New York, 1990), p. xiii.

66 *Ibid.,* p. 121. Forgacs, *Italian Culture in the Industrial Era,* p. 56.

BREMEN

COLUMBUS

EUROPA

Turbinen-
Schnell-
Dampfer
"BREMEN"

NORDDEUTSCHER LLOYD BREMEN

Design in Inter-War Germany

John Heskett

Fig. 9.03

Booklet

Turbinen-Schnell-Dampfer "Bremen"

(Turbine-High Speed-Steamship "Bremen"),

c. 1930

Designed by Bernd Steiner

(Austrian, 1884–1933)

Published by Norddeutscher Lloyd Bremen and Otto Elsner,

Berlin

9⅝ x 7⅞ inches (24.5 x 20.0 cm)

07.1010.19.1

In November, 1918, at the end of World War I, Germany was defeated and exhausted. As the Kaiser abdicated and went into exile, a republic replacing imperial rule was proclaimed in a provincial city, Weimar, since Berlin was engulfed in an attempted revolution. The next fifteen years were similarly volatile and turbulent, a blend of wild utopianism, rampant inflation, brief hope, and bitter disillusion, until the fragile democracy of the Weimar Republic collapsed following the Great Depression.

A second, distinct phase was inaugurated in 1933 with the appointment as Chancellor of Adolf Hitler, the leader of the National Socialists, or Nazis, as they were known. Hitler established a fascist dictatorship, the Third Reich, and harnessed the economy to a program of rearmament and territorial expansion that led directly to World War II in 1939.

Design histories of this period have separated these two phases on a very simplistic basis: the Weimar Republic is depicted as a flowering of modern design that ended when Hitler came to power; the Third Reich is generally ignored. Studies of the period reveal attitudes in modern scholarship that emphasize whatever is radical and avant-garde. The focus, therefore, is overwhelmingly on the Modern Movement (or Modernism, as it is alternatively termed), a grouping of artists, architects, and designers that emerged in the 1920s and vehemently rejected both past society, seen as responsible for the recent war, and the decorative excesses in design associated with it. Instead, they sought to reform society through new design approaches, characterized by abstract geometric forms and primary colors. These were considered to be timeless, the ultimate abstraction that cannot be further reduced, and also synonymous with the nature of machine-produced form. The allure of this theory was that art could harness industrial mass-production to transform every aspect of life.

This essay seeks to explore a wider context of design beyond the artistic theories and practice of modernism in the Weimar period by expanding the discussion to encompass

German design in the inter-war period as a whole. It does so on the basis of four propositions:

1. A greater range of sources and ideas about the forms appropriate to the age existed than was represented by the theories of modernism.

2. Design practice was more diverse than that constituted by the artistic avant garde.

3. Developments in technology, products, and markets decisively influenced design.

4. Continuity existed in design, on many levels, between the Weimar Republic and the Third Reich – in other words, a change of government did not change every aspect of German life.

Firstly, however, it is relevant to ask why such a simplified history came into being and how it endured for so long? Partly, it was due to modernism's being such a compelling idea. Active supporters, among them Herbert Read, Nikolaus Pevsner, and Siegfried Giedion, powerfully articulated its origins and evolution as the standard history of the period, an achievement beyond which further progression was unnecessary.[1] In these histories, the Bauhaus, the teaching institution founded by Walter Gropius in Weimar in 1919, plays a central role and

Fig. 9.01 See Cat. 136
Postcard
Bauhaus Ausstellung: Juli–September 1923
(Bauhaus Exhibition . . .), 1923
Designed by O. Schlemmer

virtually every aspect of its fourteen-year existence has been researched and consistently publicized.[2] It was indeed a remarkable institution, but its considerable achievements do not alone explain this emphasis and positioning.

The explanation to a large extent lies in the history of Germany after World War II, above all in problems of confronting the horrendous legacy of fascism. The Nazis consistently opposed modernism, labelling it *Kunstbolschewismus* (Art Bolshevism), and after 1933 sought to eradicate its influence. Many of its leading figures emigrated or were driven into exile. Basically, therefore, modernism could be detached from Nazism.

Equally significant, the Bauhaus was a constant target of the Nazis and was closed by the police soon after Hitler came to power. For the two German states formed after 1945, the Federal German Republic and the German Democratic Republic, the Bauhaus provided an icon of high aesthetic achievement from the recent past untainted by association with Nazism. Both consistently invoked it for their own purposes. A result of this focus on modernism in general, and the Bauhaus in particular, however, has been the neglect of other relationships between design and society during the inter-war years. This essay is based on a belief that although the consequences of design when used for repugnant political purposes may be discomforting, evading a discussion of them distorts understanding and, above all, prevents accountability.

This re-evaluation should not imply a dismissal of modernism – it was indeed profoundly important – but claims made for it need to be questioned in relation to this broader context. An example is the concept of functionalism, perhaps the central creed of the movement, as represented in the theory and design practice of Walter Gropius.

The early Bauhaus, in the years following the trauma of World War I, was typical of the age in having an escapist emphasis – mediaevalism, craft handwork, and Expressionist utopian visions dominated, a phase culminating in the 1923 Bauhaus Exhibition (fig. 9.01).[3] In 1924, however, Gropius wrote a document, "Breviary for Bauhaus Members," that looked ahead to the further development of the school and introduced the theme of "Art and Technology, a new unity." The goal was to position art as an agent of social change in the mainstream of the age. Despite acknowledging technology, however, art still predominated in the new unity: ". . . every work of art carries the signature of its creator. From the multiplicity of equally economical solutions – for there is not just one in each case – the creative individual selects the one that suits his personal feelings and taste."[4]

This primacy of artists in relationship to technology and industry had been vehemently argued by Gropius in the debates of the Deutsche Werkbund before World War I.[5] At the Bauhaus, he elaborated the idea by proposing the artists' studio as the equivalent of a scientific laboratory, in which creative individuals would develop prototypes suitable for

mass-production, diffusing art to the masses through industry and thereby effecting a transformation of social life.

What did this mean in practice? An example is a design for the bodywork of the Adler "Standard" 8, "Modell Gropius" cabriolet of 1931 (fig. 9.02). An advertising brochure for it stated:

> In purchasing an automobile, the form of the car, its *aesthetic total impression*, plays a decisive role. What then are the means that enable a *beautiful* car to originate? The measure of beauty of an auto depends on harmonizing the form of its external appearance with the logic of its technical function, not on the trimmings of flourishes and ornamentation. The complete technical organization must therefore find its worthy complement in a fully matured, well-proportioned form, that functions in an aesthetic sense exactly as the technical apparatus itself.[6]

The text closely parallels Gropius's "Breviary." Form does not follow, or arise from, function, but from aesthetic choice by the artist. Put another way, the choice of geometric form as most suitable for automobiles stemmed from Gropius's particular artistic theory of the form suitable for technology, not from the technology itself. In fact, it directly contradicted contemporary technical concepts of form such as streamlining. Gropius's design for the bodywork of the Adler, a handbuilt luxury automobile, was therefore symbolic of function, a

Fig. 9.02
**Advertisement for *der neue Adler*
(the new Adler), 1931
Designed by Herbert Bayer**
(American, b. Austria, 1900–85)
Automobile designed by Walter Gropius
(American, b. Germany, 1883–1969)
Published by Adlerwerke vorm. Heinrich Kleyer, A.G.,
Frankfurt am Main, Germany
8 1/4 x 15 5/8 inches (21.0 x 39.7 cm)
XB1991.834

"worthy complement" to the technical function, rather than its direct expression. The difference is important, for although "functionalist" design evolved into a powerful dogma, it was often neither practical, in a technical sense, nor necessarily appropriate to machine production, nor acceptable to customers in commercial markets.

Exaggerated claims for aesthetic theories were not restricted to modernism, however, but were common currency in the atmosphere of the 1920s. In polemics between competing standpoints, objectivity became the first victim of endemic over-statement and assertions of primacy, with attacks on contrary views frequently part of broader political and ideological clashes. Organizations such as the Deutsche Werkbund became a battleground for different factions, and reports in major newspapers and journals brought the debates to the general public.

In this situation, the proponents of modernism sought to appropriate terms such as "functionalism" and "modern" exclusively to their position. Other factions, however, asserted counter-claims, the most vigorous being a diverse group occupying the middle ground of German cultural life. Rather than rejecting the past, they sought to refine and adapt past styles to the present. This attempt to maintain continuity with the past while simultaneously being contemporary has been named Conservative Modernism by Julius Posener.[7] It took many forms. In designs for architecture, furniture, and interiors, Wilhelm Kreis favored stripped Neo-Classicism and Paul Bonatz monumental simplifications of Romanesque, whereas Heinrich Tessenow and Theodor Fischer refined traditional regional forms. Politically, their beliefs were more nationalistic than the cosmopolitan sympathies of modernists. Craft work was highly valued, but tempered by awareness that machines could not be ignored – the problem was to bring them within the compass of cultural and qualitative concerns. Karl Schmidt was a pioneer in this respect, transmuting Arts and Crafts values into terms applicable for mechanized production. Established in 1897, his workshops at Hellerau, near Dresden (later named the Deutsche Werkstätten), employed leading designers such as Richard Riemerschmid and Hans Hartl on an impressive array of serially produced furniture and fittings.

Although Conservative Modernism was too diverse to constitute a coherent movement, it was a clear alternative tradition, the general tenor and purpose of which were summarized in an influential book of 1922, *Das Dritte Reich* (The Third Reich), by Arthur Moeller van den Bruck. Prescribing sweeping change to preserve what was best in German and European life and culture in the chaos following the war, he wrote: "Let us combine revolutionary and conservative ideas till we attain a set of conditions under which we can hope to live again."[8] In a distinction vital to understanding Conservative Modernism, he repeatedly emphasized that it was necessary to distinguish between the reactionary, who wished to restore or preserve a dead past, and the conservative "who creates by giving to phenomena a form in which they can endure."[9] This meant constant adaptation to contemporary needs as they evolved.

An example in practice was the commissioning of Fritz August Breuhaus[10] and Paul Ludwig Troost, respectively, to supervise designs for the interiors of the *Bremen* and *Europa*, the North German Lloyd liners that entered service in 1929 and 1930 (fig. 9.03). Intended for the Blue Riband route to New York, these vessels became symbols of national recovery from the war and were among the most prestigious design projects of the 1920s.

Opinions on the results depended upon the standpoint of the critic. Modernist critics used "steamer style" as a term of derision and Franz Kollman tartly commented on the *Bremen*: "As with the Zeppelin, the beautiful and clear simplicity of the technical form stands in contrast to the frantically emphasized luxury of the social spaces of the interiors."[11]

Fig. 9.04
Corridor of first class shops
on the ocean liner *Bremen*
Designed by F.A. Breuhaus de Groot
(German, 1883–1960)
From *Fritz August Breuhaus de Groot*
(Berlin, Leipzig, Vienna: Friedrich Ernst Hübsch, 1929)
83.2.996

Fig. 9.05

Chandelier, c. 1930

Design attributed to Fritz August Breuhaus de Groot

(German, 1883–1960)

Germany

Silver-plated brass

31 ½ x 26 ⅝ x 26 ¼ inches (95.3 x 67.6 x 66.7 cm)

86.13.42

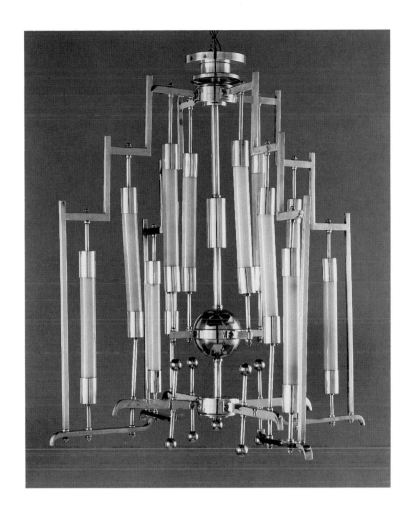

The only spaces to reflect his insistence on functional simplicity, however, were the third class facilities. Max Osborn was more sympathetic in his comments on Breuhaus's designs: "The salons, rooms, and cabins were arranged with an extraordinary gift for organization; their purpose was taken as the point of procedure; . . . at the same time everything gives the impression of comfort, friendliness, and resplendence."[12] A corridor of shops, with clean surfaces and curving radii in bronzed metal, yellow and blue leather (fig. 9.04), does indeed compare favorably to the exotic stylistic mixtures rampant on most contemporary vessels.

That Breuhaus's designs could seem to exemplify modernity is also evident, on a smaller scale, from a chandelier attributed to him (fig. 9.05). With strip electric lighting and finely made in silvered brass using craft techniques, it is a unique piece, contemporary in appearance, but still a reinterpretation of past forms, rather than an attempt at revolutionary redefinition. Evaluations of Conservative Modernism, however, have inevitably been negatively influenced by the roles it continued to play after 1933 and in particular as manifested in the work of Paul Ludwig Troost and Albert Speer, official architects of the Third Reich.

Fig. 9.06 See Cat. 191
Print
Die Bauten der N.S.D.A.P. zu München
**(The buildings of the Nazi Party Headquarters
in Munich; P. L. Troost, architect), c. 1935
C. Hacker**

Based in Munich, Troost joined the Nazi Party in 1924, and converted Hitler from enthusiasm for Baroque to Neo-Classical forms.[13] In his youth, Hitler had unsuccessfully attempted to enroll in the architectural course at the Vienna Academy of Fine Arts and throughout his life he professed a desire to practice architecture. The relationship with Troost obviously gratified this frustrated longing and was described by Speer as "somewhat that of a pupil to his teacher."[14]

When Hitler became Chancellor, Troost was appointed his personal architect, and major commissions rapidly followed. In the Wolfsonian Collection, detailed architectural drawings for the Nazi Party headquarters buildings on Arcisstraße and the House of German Art, both in Munich, together with photographs of major works and events associated with them, demonstrate Troost's technical competence in large-scale projects (figs. 9.06 and 9.07). His work, however, is formulaic in approach with less development of ideas than is evident, for example, in Breuhaus's designs. Symmetry and simplicity based on monumental stripped classical forms dominate both exteriors and interiors, and plain stone facades and columns, marble facing in vestibules and major spaces, and wood-panelling in smaller rooms were repeatedly used with minor variations in all his public buildings. Ceremonial or meeting rooms were invariably symmetrical, usually with Hitler's portrait centrally positioned and emphasized by flanking wall-sconces.

Following Troost's death in 1934, he was succeeded as Hitler's personal architect by Albert Speer, who had studied under Heinrich Tessenow and was later his assistant at the

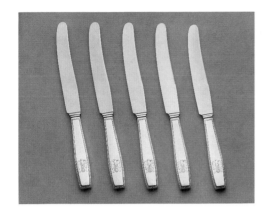

Institute of Technology in Berlin. There, after hearing a speech by Hitler, Speer joined the Nazi Party in 1931. His designs for major projects followed Troost's pattern, though on an even more grandiose scale, as in the new Chancellery building in Berlin completed in January, 1939.[15] In the Third Reich, this style was publicized as "Germany's Modern Architecture" in lavish publications and posters produced in several languages (fig. 9.08).

Furnishings and fittings for such major projects were always by leading designers and manufacturers, such as the dinnerware for the House of German Art designed by Richard Klein and produced by the Nymphenburg Porzellanfabrik, and cutlery with Hitler's monogram by Peter Bruckmann & Söhne of Heilbronn for the Chancellery (fig. 9.09).

Fig. 9.09
Dinner knives, c. 1935
Made by Silberwaren-Fabrik Peter Bruckmann & Söhne,
Heilbronn, Germany
Silver, steel
10 x ⁷⁄₈ x ½ inches (25.4 x 2.2 x 1.3 cm)
Marks: obverse, engraved, on handle monogram "AH";
reverse, stamped, top of handle at base of blade, marks of
crescent, crown, "800" and company mark (eagle)
TD1990.317.1–5

Fig. 9.07
Photograph
Adolf Hitler leading an assembly at the Nazi
Party Headquarters in Munich, c. 1935
(Paul Ludwig Troost [German, 1878–1934],
architect)
Kurt Huhle
(German, dates unknown)
Munich
Marks: reverse, stamped in black, "Fordert Deutsche Arbeit"
encircled/"Copyright by Kurt Huhle Aktuelle
Bilderichterstattung München 250 Erhardstr. 15
Telefon 25010/Professor P.L. Troost Architekt"
15³⁄₈ x 12⅛ inches (39.1 x 30.8 cm)
TD1991.220.24

Fig. 9.08   See Cat. 190

Poster

***Germany's Modern Architecture**, c. 1938*

Designed by R. Klein

Fig. 9.10

Poster

***Auf Zum Reichshandwerkertag**. Frankfurt am Main. 16 Juni 1935.*

(Off to the State Day of the Craftsmen . . .), 1935

Designed by Sepp Semar

(German, b. 1901)

Printed by Sebastian Malz, Berlin

Published by Deutsche Arbeitsfront, Berlin

Commercial color lithograph

33 ½ x 23 ¹/₁₆ inches (85.1 x 58.7 cm)

Marks: obverse, printed in black, upper right corner "SEMAR";

upper left, publisher's mark of a swastika within a gear

XX1990.2762

Fig. 9.11 See Cat. 187
Plaque
Heim der Hitler Jugend
(Home of Hitler Youth), 1933–45

If Conservative Modernism sought a reconciliation of past and present, other attempts to retrieve the past were, in Moeller van den Bruck's terms, reactionary, seeking to turn the clock back and restore the past. This was most true of advocates of folk crafts and traditions, considered the essence of German values – a prime example was the architect Paul Schultze-Naumburg. He became a strident proselytizer for claims that German traditional forms were a manifestation of racial superiority, which closely aligned him with Nazi cultural policies in the late 1920s. Such reactionary arguments appealed to many craftsmen and easily dovetailed into the "blood and soil" ideology of the Nazis.

Craftsmen suffered badly from industrial competition in this period and their grievances made them obvious targets for Nazi political exploitation. Many political promises were made to obtain their support, but few were subsequently fulfilled. Reviving a craft economy was not a priority on Hitler's political agenda. Homage to the crafts in the Third Reich was therefore predominantly symbolic, with frequent festivals and exhibitions, such as the Reichshandwerkertag (State Day of the Craftsman) of 1935 (fig. 9.10). Projects such as hostels for the Hitler Youth did provide some work for local craftsmen, as a large wrought-iron eagle to hang over a hostel entrance attests (fig. 9.11). With their regional styles, designs for the hostels were also considered an important means of educating the young to appreciate their German folk heritage.[16]

The alliance between conservatism and nationalism, although powerful, did not entirely preclude more cosmopolitan influences from penetrating Germany, most notably the style derived from the 1925 Exposition Internationale des Arts Décoratifs et Industriels Modernes held in Paris, now commonly, if inaccurately, known as Art Deco. Although not as widely adopted as in France or the U.S.A., the style was used by German companies seeking a modern, fashionable appeal. With its characteristic fine materials and finishes in stylized decorative patterns, Art Moderne was applied to up-market interior designs, shop-fittings, and personal accessories.[17]

The style that really fired the German public's imagination in this period, however, was streamlining, derived primarily from forms of transportation. In some countries, such as the U.S.A., the streamlined style overlapped and merged with Art Moderne, but in Germany the two had separate origins and remained differentiated. In the 1920s, high-quality black-and-white photographs of sleek new cars, ships, aircraft, and trains, and the mechanisms and structures associated with them, were frequently featured as examples of modern culture in books and magazines. In one such book, *Technische Schönheit* (Technical Beauty), the author Hanns Günther wrote, " . . . the pure functional forms that result from constructive foundations are always the artistically most beautiful forms . . . ."[18]

Fig. 9.12 See Cat. 102
Poster
2 Days to Europe, **1937**
Designed by J. Wiertz

Fig. 9.13 See Cat. 101
Postcard
Lounge of 'A' Deck on the LZ 129 zeppelin,
the *Hindenburg*
Designed by F.A. Breuhaus de Groot, 1936

Here, too, the Nazis appropriated technology as a symbol of national progress to promote pride in the achievements of German industry, under the slogan of "die Schönheit der Technik" (the beauty of technology). The launches of new giant airships, for example, a technology pioneered in Germany, were major national events, and the gigantic LZ 129 *Hindenburg*, completed in 1936, was promoted as "the airship of the German People."[19] It challenged the great Atlantic liners in terms of speed, reducing the crossing from five days to two (fig. 9.12), and designs by Breuhaus set new standards of luxury in airship passenger accommodation. Of the reading room, Rolf Brandt, in a commemorative book, wrote: "This room has nothing more to do with the pioneer days of the Zeppelins."[20] In the interiors, lightweight aluminum and tubular steel furniture and fittings "united the greatest utility with beauty"[21] (fig. 9.13). In a tragic accident, however, the *Hindenburg* was destroyed by a terrible conflagration on arrival at Lakehurst, New Jersey, in 1937. Both the propaganda value of airships and their credibility as a form of transportation were lost. Thereafter, technical imagery in the skies focussed on new aircraft designs.

The most dramatic examples of streamlined forms in transportation were for high-speed performance and were developed in wind-tunnel tests (in which Germany was a pioneer), with supporting scientific calculations to demonstrate the functional efficiency of forms. Only at the upper limits of performance, however, was significant improvement achieved through streamlining, as with high-speed diesel-powered railroad cars for German State Railroad that entered service in 1933, or Grand Prix racing cars.

Fig. 9.14
Booklet
Volkswagen-Werk GmbH, Berlin, c. 1937
Designed by Thomas Abeking
(German, dates unknown)
Printed by Transart Aktiengesellschaft
für Zellglass-Kunstdruck, Berlin
Published by Volkswagen-Werk G.m.b.H.,
Wolfsburg, Germany
8¼ x 11½ inches (21.0 x 30.5 cm)
84.2.612

In most other respects, streamlining was simply used as a contemporary style to suggest speed and modernity. The longest-surviving design of this period, the Volkswagen, with smooth, rounded profile in all dimensions, was not intended for high-speed performance, but stemmed from Hitler's insistence that an affordable small car be made accessible to the bulk of the population. Its introduction was trumpeted as a great achievement of the Nazi regime. Among publicity items for the vehicle was a booklet with acetate overlays, enabling the Volkswagen's structure and uses to be demonstrated on several levels (fig. 9.14).

Within this broader spectrum of trends in form and style, design, as a specialist activity, expanded at all levels of German industry and commerce throughout these years. The emphasis on the heroic figures of Modernism who emigrated, such as Gropius, Mies van der Rohe, Albers and Moholy-Nagy, can imply the dismissal of those who stayed in Germany as untalented Nazi sympathizers. Many able designers did not emigrate and the situation was much less straightforward.

The most obvious example is Wilhelm Wagenfeld. A former student and teacher at the Bauhaus, he later rejected Modernism as too formalistic. After working as consultant for numerous companies, he was appointed in 1935 as artistic director of a large glassware manufacturer, Lausitzer Glasverein. There, the majority of his designs were for pressed glass – everyday, inexpensive wares of a high standard. The "Kubusgeschirr," a range of kitchen storage containers, are perhaps the best-known (fig. 9.15).

Fig. 9.15 See Cat. 141
Containers
***Kubus* (Cube), 1938**
Designed by W. Wagenfeld

Wagenfeld's relationship to the Nazi regime, however, is confusing. Generally, he has been presented as an opponent. In 1934, indeed, he protested publicly when the German Werkbund was incorporated into the Nazi cultural apparatus. In addition, as described in a letter written to Gropius in 1964, he was drafted into the army in 1942 after resisting pressure to join the Party, and was later sent as punishment to the Russian front.[22] Yet his work at Lausitz was widely celebrated in print and frequently exhibited. He was also appointed to the organizing committee for the German pavilion at the 1937 Paris International Exposition, a major propaganda initiative by the Nazi government, with co-members including such luminaries of the Party establishment as Albert Speer and Alfred Ziegler, head of the State Chamber of Art. This fact is not mentioned in a major retrospective catalogue of his life and work.[23] Wagenfeld was no Nazi, that is absolutely clear; but the editing of his career typifies the way the facts of the past can be conveniently circumvented.

An equally outstanding designer, and similarly ambivalent in political terms, was Hermann Gretsch. His work spanned an enormous range of techniques and market levels, with furniture ranging from craft-made pieces through to mass-produced lines using inexpensive materials, such as plywood, for workers' housing. Other products, in a variety of materials and processes, included cast-iron domestic stoves, cutlery, glassware, ceramic ware, and plastic domestic ware. Many high-standard designs were for the Reichsheimstättendienst, a government organization responsible in the Third Reich for workers' housing projects.

However, the Solingen cutlery manufacturer, Carl Pott, who was a close friend, emphatically denied Gretsch was a Nazi.[24]

Another example was the medal engraver Karl Goetz, who was born in Augsburg, apprenticed as an engraver, and later studied at art schools in Germany, before working abroad as an engraver in Holland and Paris. In 1905, he settled in Munich, establishing a high reputation for commemorative medals. Many were bitingly satirical, such as one in 1923 about Hitler's unsuccessful Munich Putsch, showing the Führer in an unflattering light and misspelling his name as "Hittler"(fig. 9.16). Goetz also designed coins; one showing a head of President Hindenburg was adapted for German postage stamps in the Weimar period.

After Hitler assumed power, Goetz's apartment was searched by the Gestapo, who confiscated original casts and models, among them the Hitler Putsch medal. Despite this, he continued to produce a large body of work, including large, flattering images of Hitler and other Nazi leaders, and medals stridently commemorating early German victories in World War II. There is no evidence that he, either, was a Party member.

It is difficult to be certain as to the real views of these talented men about Hitler and the Third Reich. Perhaps, like many nationalists and conservatives, they chose accommodation to the regime in preference to exile. They might also have been so focussed on their work that they found it acceptable to continue despite the consequences of blinding themselves to the evils perpetrated in their country's name. Certainly they were not alone in their reluctance to resist the regime, even if they did not formally embrace its policies by Party membership. In the general silence that has existed on this subject, any conclusions must necessarily be speculative.

Other designers were less ambiguous, however, and openly aligned themselves with the Nazi Party, most notably Ludwig Hohlwein. Before World War I, he had designed posters of a rarely equalled quality. Trained as an architect, he turned to graphic work in 1907 and became a master of lithography, using limited colors in bold, contrasting designs of stunning impact (fig. 9.17). In a thirty-year career, in addition to over three thousand posters, he also designed leaflets, catalogues, labels, letterheads, business cards, and packaging, and was "one of the first professional commercial graphic designers in Munich."[25] In the 1920s, his ability to adapt to clients' requirements brought a continuing flow of work. He also showed, however, a trend toward a coarser, nationalist imagery, as in posters for the Stahlhelm, a veterans organization. For Hohlwein, the transition from nationalism to the Nazi Party was clearly unproblematic, since racial stereotypes and an idealized German past became his stock-in-trade. An example is the image of a racially pure Aryan family on a poster, attributed to Hohlwein, advertising the annual calendar for 1938 of the Racial Policy Office of the Nazi Party (fig. 9.18).

Fig. 9.16 See Cat. 232
Medallion
Hittler Putsch 8 November 1923. National Gen National!!!
(Hitler Putsch . . . National against National!!!), 1923
K. Goetz

Fig. 9.18   See Cat. 213
Poster
Neues Volk
(New People), for the calendar of the Rassenpolitischen
Amtes der N.S.D.A.P.
(Racial Policy Office of the Nazi Party), 1938
Design attributed to L. Hohlwein

Fig. 9.17   See Cat. 58
Poster
Deutsche Kunst und Dekoration, 1911
Designed by L. Hohlwein

The Wolfsonian Collection also provides unusual insights into the work of Hermann Grah, a Leipzig graphic designer. Examples of his work include student exercises in Runic type forms, drawings of modernistic buildings, sketches for commercial advertisements (*e.g.*, a series for an AEG exhibition stand), and work for personalities and political events in the Third Reich (fig. 9.19). Details of his life are otherwise lacking, but he clearly sympathized with the Nazi Party and its aims and profited from the association.

Grah seems to have been a typical, free-lance consultant, a group about whom very little is known. A similar gap also exists regarding designers directly employed by commercial and industrial companies. A glimpse into the nature of in-house product design, however, is provided in an article "Design of Radio Apparatus" that appeared in a 1932 issue of the house magazine of AEG, the giant electrical equipment manufacturer. The author, A. Pfeffer, seems from his title to have been a qualified architect. He wrote on the problems of designing radio

Fig. 9.19 See Cat. 241
Design for poster
Arbeit Siegt
(Work Triumphs), c. 1935
Designed by Hermann Grah
(German, dates unknown)
Germany
Ink, paint, pencil on paper
18³⁄₄ x 13¹⁄₂ inches (47.6 x 34.3 cm)
Marks: obverse, printed in black, lower left artist's mark
"GRAH/ III"
TD1990.330.2.1

housings: "The task of giving a radio apparatus its outer form is more difficult than might at first appear; for it must not be the creation of an aesthetic 'form in itself,' as a covering for the technically determined apparatus, but has a very definite requirement to fulfil, that has proven a difficult obstacle for the creative imagination to overcome."

While the effectiveness of a radio's visual appearance was often reduced by salesmens' attempts to impose "art" ideas or proven formula to meet "so-called general taste," of greater significance, Pfeffer asserted, were manufacturing problems when designing housings in Tenacit, a variant of Bakelite: "This material requires the application of a very rich, small formed detail, such as can be attained with no other material, for smooth surfaces reveal flow-lines from the pressing that would appear as defects. Against that, the execution of relief-work on the surface in small measure produces interesting light-effects and hinders the appearance of flow-lines." He concluded: "It is therefore possible through design to give each type that degree of unity desirable on sales, technical and propaganda grounds, and to make it recognizable as the product of a world company."[26]

Pfeffer covered several themes that did not feature in the theories of modernism: he wrote of designing for commercial markets within the constraints of manufacturing processes; for example, the technical problems of pressing plastic housings did not favor plain forms, but necessitated relief-work. Furthermore, staff in sales and "propaganda" (advertising) clearly tried to impose their concept of what was acceptable to public taste, and giving products what would today be called a recognizable corporate or brand identity was a constant demand. In explaining that all these conflicting factors had to be reconciled, his article has a decidedly contemporary ring.

Designers in many industries experienced similar situations. They were designing new types of products: domestic electrical apparatus and household equipment, office machines and furniture. Materials such as thin-walled tubular steel, light metals, aluminum, and other synthetic materials presented new structural and formal possibilities. Production processes, such as enamelling and chroming, and welding in all its forms, set limits within which forms had to be designed and produced. For example, huge mechanical presses were used to stamp sheet steel into structural forms for automobiles, refrigerators, and other appliances. The sheet steel then used was of a relatively thick gauge and could not be pressed into sharp angles without fracturing. This explains why cars and appliances of the period have wide-radius curves – not out of stylistic choice, but simply because the technology did not permit any other shape.

Another fundamental constraint for designers in industry was the role of standardization and interchangeability, concepts implicit in the nature of mass-production. In World War I, military efficiency was impaired when similar products from different manufacturers were incompatible and their parts not interchangeable. It was therefore considered necessary to establish standards on an industry-wide basis. To achieve this, the Deutsche Normenauschuss (German Standards Commission), which originated in 1916, worked to produce national standards for products of all kinds under the title of Deutsche Industrienormen (DIN or German Industrial Standards). These standards often had a profound influence on visual form. For example, standard dimensions specified for sheet-paper sizes, the "A" format, were extensively adopted by 1930 for stationery, posters, and published material of all kinds. Standards for folders and filing cabinets compatible with the "A" format then followed. Similarly, specifications for three-dimensional standard units, or modules, fixing the height and depth of kitchen units and appliances, enabled different products from various companies to be compatible when used together. Modular systems were also adopted by many leading furniture manufacturers in the 1920s, such as the Wohnkunst Verband, which produced an extensive range of modular shelving and storage units for the home designed by Eugen Buschle.

Another industrial organization, the Reichskuratorium für Wirtschaftlichkeit (State Efficiency Commission) was also established in 1923 to study the rational organization of work, not only in manufacturing, but also in offices, hospitals, and the home. Analyses of work processes led to specifications for standard designs – for example, office and kitchen layouts – that would reduce unnecessary strain and enhance efficiency. Modern design methodologies, such as anthropometrics, the proportions of the human body, and ergonomics, the relationship of people to machines and working environments, originated in such studies.

The standardization inherent in mass-production technology, while reducing costs, at the same time greatly limited possibilities for variation. This created a dilemma for manufacturing companies, which needed to differentiate their own products visually from those of competitors if they were to sell profitably. Reconciling this contradiction was the task assigned to the growing number of designers in industry, who were drawn from a wide range of backgrounds. Some, like Pfeffer, were originally architects, while Hermann Gretsch trained as an engineer; their technical background was a considerable advantage. Others adapted art training to the needs of industry, such as Gerhard Marcks, who taught at the Weimar Bauhaus and later designed products such as a coffee-percolator in fireproof glass for Jenaer Glaswerk, Schott & Genossen (fig. 9.20). A transition from craft work to design for manufacture was also possible. Trude Petri produced craft work such as a series of table lamps with shades,[27] but after graduation in 1928, worked for the Berlin Porzellan-manufaktur. There she designed some of the finest manufactured ceramics of the period, most notably a classically simple set of white porcelain tableware, called "Urbino," which is still in production. Many other designers in industry, however, remain anonymous, and all

Fig. 9.20
Coffeemaker
***Sintrax*, 1925–30**
Designed by Gerhard Marcks
(German, 1889–1981)
Manufactured by Jenaer Glaswerk, Schott & Genossen, Jena, Germany, 1930–39
Glass, wood, rubber
Base: 5 x 8⅜ x 5 inches (12.7 x 21.3 x 12.7 cm)
Filter: 9 x 5 inches dia. (22.9 x 12.7 cm dia.)
Base, marks: underside, etched, in circle with four corners "SCHOTT & GEN. JENAER GLAS ½ LTR."
Filter, marks: frontside, etched, in circle with four corners "JENAER GLAS SINTRAX SCHOTT & GEN. JENA ½ LTR."
84.8.13.1–2

Fig. 9.21
Quartz lamp, c. 1935
Manufactured by Quarzlampen-Gesellschaft m.b.H., Hanau am Main, Germany
Painted metal, chrome-plated metal, glass, plastic
11½ x 11 inches dia. (29.2 x 28.0 cm dia.)
Marks: interior, metal rim around mirror, in high relief "ORIGINAL HANAU"; underside, partial paper label, "ORIGINAL HANAU/200–260V 300 WATT/200–240V/ QUARZLAMPEN GES.m.b.H/ HANAU"
86.13.24

that exists are their products, such as a quartz lamp whose clean, utilitarian form directly reflects its function (fig. 9.21).

Finally, what influence did political policy have on design between the wars? That the government of the new Weimar Republic took its image seriously was made clear in 1919, with the appointment of Dr. Edwin Redslob, a nominee of the German Werkbund to the post of Reichkunstwart (State Art Officer). His responsibilities included the visual appearance of every building, event, publication, or artifact under the authority of the national government, and before his dismissal when the Nazis came to power, he achieved considerable results with limited resources.

Large city governments also undertook major initiatives in the 1920s, such as giant housing projects in Berlin, Hamburg, and Cologne. The most comprehensive scheme was in Frankfurt, where a team under City Architect Ernst May included Ferdinand Kramer, who studied briefly at the Bauhaus in Weimar before graduating as an architect under Theodor Fischer in Munich, Grete Schütte-Lihotsky, who had worked on interiors in mass-housing projects in Vienna after World War I, and the Dutch designer, Mart Stam. They established a set of "Frankfurt Standards," on the basis of which they designed "minimum existence dwellings." These were intended to use scarce resources to create maximum benefit for people moved out of slum housing. They designed rationalized, built-in kitchens, mass-produced furniture, and domestic equipment to fit the dwellings' dimensions and the limited resources of tenants. A magazine publicizing the program claimed: "The 11,000 couples seeking shelter in 1925 and the far more numerous would-be tenants presenting themselves in the meantime, will receive accommodation by 1935 through systematic housing construction." Then the slums could be cleared, since statistics showed "that between 1935 and 1945 there will be no pressing need for new dwellings."[28] Remarkable progress toward meeting these goals was achieved before the program ended, after a Right-wing majority took control of the city council in 1929.

The Third Reich increased initiatives from central government. Hitler's rearmament program meant a policy of autarky (economic self-sufficiency), embodied in the Four Year Plan of 1937. This particularly emphasized light metals, plastics and synthetics, ceramics,

Fig. 9.22
Cover
Great Exhibition of the Reich "Nation at Work,"
1937
Published by Schaffendes Volk, Düsseldorf am Rhein, Germany
7⁷⁄₈ x 7¹⁄₂ inches (20.0 x 19.0 cm)
XB1989.81

and glass as substitutes for heavy metals, to replace imports by home-produced materials. In 1937, a major industrial exhibition, "Schaffendes Volk" (A Nation at Work), opened in Düsseldorf (fig. 9.22) to promote the Four Year Plan, and a model housing development demonstrated innovations of materials in the context of domestic use. Posters exhorted the population to buy only German products (fig. 9.23).

Design in the Third Reich is often dismissed as "Nazi Kitsch,"[29] and indeed there were examples of opportunism that can be included under this imprecise rubric, such as the appropriation during Nazi occupation of Denmark of a neutral trademark registered in 1907 by Carlsberg (fig. 9.24), or the figurines of armed services and Party organization members produced by the ceramic works run by the SS at Allach (fig. 9.25).

Such examples, however, were not typical of average standards of design. The office Schönheit der Arbeit (Beauty of Work) in the German Labor Front, the Nazi organization that replaced trade unions, was responsible for providing good working conditions in offices

Fig. 9.23 See Cat. 240
Poster
Deutsche Kauft. Deutsche Ware. Deutsche
Woche. Deutsche Arbeit.
(German Commerce. German Goods.
German Week. German Work), c. 1937
Designed by H. Keimel

Fig. 9.24
Poster
Carlsberg Apollinaris, **before 1932**
Printed by A/S Kruckow-Waldorff, Copenhagen
Published by Carlsberg A/S, Copenhagen
Commercial color lithograph
16¼ x 12¼ inches (41.3 x 31.1 cm)
XX1990.3950

and factories, the intent being to keep workers content and passive. Under the direction of Albert Speer, its chief designer Karl Nothelfer designed and commissioned a huge range of high-standard products for working environments and workers' housing projects built on new industrial sites. These were manufactured by leading firms, such as the ceramic ware by Hutschenreuter specified as a standard Schönheit der Arbeit model. Numerous publications by the organization also indicated desirable design standards in the new order. The general emphasis was on quiet, simple forms, well made of natural materials and eschewing unnecessary display. In addition, the Kraft durch Freude (Strength through Joy) organization of the Labor Front organized recreational facilities for workers, including cruises on ships specially built for the purpose, such as the *Robert Ley*, named after the Reich leader of the German Labor Front, with interiors that were down-scaled versions of the great liners (fig. 9.26).

The most notable example of design standards in the Third Reich, however, was the publication from 1939 onwards of the Deutsche Warenkunde (Index of German Goods) under the auspices of the State Chamber of Art. This four-volume loose-leaf compendium showed outstanding products in every category: industry, agriculture, the office, and the home, which conformed to the requirements of the Four Year Plan and represented good design and value for money. Primarily intended as a guide to purchasers from abroad and a means of promoting exports, it ironically included designs by leaders of the Modern Movement who had long since emigrated, such as Walter Gropius and Marcel Breuer.

What did the German public make of all these developments? Official material from the period invariably shows unequivocal support for the regime, such as a postcard depicting a family enthusiastically giving the Nazi Party salute to a passing train, with the caption "Our GERMAN railroad" (fig. 9.27). Such printed propaganda is supported, moreover, by large quantities of photographic and newsreel film images testifying to the enthusiasm of many people for the regime, some of whom can be assumed to have also accepted the Party line on design. Once again, however, silence on how people really felt in the period of the Third Reich makes accurate assessment impossible.

Fig. 9.25 See Cat. 216
Figurines
B.D.M. Standard Bearer
and *Hitler Jugend Drummer*, c. 1937
Designed by R. Förster

Fig. 9.26
**Theater and dining room
of the ship E.S. Robert Ley**
From *E.S. Robert Ley*
(Germany, [1938])
XB1991.876

What is certain is that in the inter-war period as a whole, a considerable range of publications aimed at a broad audience vigorously debated the issues of what forms were appropriate for the age. The modernist rejection of nineteenth-century decoration was widely shared, but a constant dilemma was what should replace it. Modernist experiments drew heavy criticism, as from Walter Maria Kersting, an early industrial designer: "Homes cannot be achieved by extreme means. Economically considered, we should not allow extreme experiments."[30] Kersting was no reactionary, but advocated using mass-production for high-quality, affordable products accessible to everyone.

A frequent target for vehement criticism in these debates was Le Corbusier's description of the home as a machine for living. It excluded the possibility of individuality and joy, wrote critic Hans Eckstein in the magazine *Kunst der Nation* in 1934: "What is decisive is always what is human. All functionality has to serve it. Where *Sachlichkeit* [objectivity] becomes an end in itself, it degenerates into commercial art . . . ."[31]

The catalogue introduction to a Werkbund exhibition in Cologne in 1929 expressed a widespread belief in high-quality, simple forms that would not become outmoded: "Better to have a good bed that is not modern and therefore will not be unmodern, than a complete fashionable bedroom that, after a few years, will be unbearable to look at."[32] This too was a theme taken up in the Third Reich, as in a specification by the Beauty of Work organization of the requirements for a worker's home. "No unnecessary luxury and also no cold domestic splendor such as is handed down to us, instead simple furniture, beautiful in form and functional, that requires less attention."[33] When purchasing tableware, Hermann Gretsch recommended: "Pay regard to your way of life and income. Stay genuine and modest also when it concerns your surroundings. If you don't have a villa, your home should not be a salon . . . . Only simple tableware of good form and sound material has lasting value."[34] If there is a mainstream belief with continuity throughout this period, it revolves around such attitudes.

Does continuity mean, however, that essentially no difference existed between work completed under the two regimes? What changed, of course, under Hitler's rule were the reasons why designs were commissioned and the purposes for which they were applied; this, however, does not necessarily imply a fall in design standards, in a formal sense. The assumption that the Nazi regime engendered only work of little value is untenable, I would argue, since it completely underestimates two factors. First, designs of high caliber continued to be produced in the Third Reich: a reprehensible ideology does not necessarily produce inferior design and creativity can flourish in evil conditions. Second, when used for political ends, artifacts serve purposes reaching far beyond the forms, functions, and meanings attributed to them in the processes and practices of design. Ignoring the first may be a convenient self-deception; to ignore the second is highly dangerous.

Fig. 9.27
Postcard
Unsere DEUTSCHE Reichsbahn
(Our GERMAN Railroad), c. 1940
Designed by Franz Th. Würbel
(German, b. 1896)
Printed by Mühlmeister & Johler, Hamburg
Published by W.E.R., Germany
4⅛ x 5⅞ inches (10.5 x 14.9 cm)
XC1991.459

NOTES

1 Herbert Read, *Art and Industry* (London, 1934); Nikolaus Pevsner, *Pioneers of Modern Design* (Harmondsworth, revised edition 1960; original 1936); Siegfried Giedion, *Mechanization Takes Command* (New York, 1948).

2 The Bauhaus Archiv in Berlin is a major repository of material and provides both permanent and rotating exhibitions. A basic documentation on the school is by the late Director of the Archiv, Hans Wingler, *Bauhaus: Weimar, Dessau, Berlin, Chicago* (Cambridge, MA, 1976). A good brief introduction is Gillian Naylor, *The Bauhaus Revisited* (London, 1975).

3 A detailed account of these years is given by Karl-Heinz Hüter, *Das Bauhaus in Weimar* (Berlin, 1976).

4 The phrase is from a draft by Gropius for a "Breviary for Bauhaus Members" in Wingler, *Bauhaus*, p. 76.

5 See John Heskett, *German Design, 1870–1918* (New York, 1986), pp. 135–6.

6 "Der Neue Adler: Adler Schlaf-Kabriolet 'Standard' 8, 'Modell Gropius'," (pamphlet) 1931, Wolfsonian Collection XB1991.834.

7 Various architectural historians have sought to describe this mainstream alternative to modernism. Posener used the term "Conservative Modernism" in an audio tape that he titled "Germany: The Second Tradition of the Twenties," prepared for the Open University course, A305, *History of architecture and design 1890–1939*. Sebastian Müller used the term "Conservative Functionalism" in describing how leading figures of the German Werkbund, such as Hermann Muthesius, sought to define a sense of modernity acceptable to the middle classes in the period before the First World War. See *Kunst und Industrie: Ideologie und Organisation des Funktionalismus in der Architektur* (Munich, 1974), pp. 69–76. Joachim Petsch discusses the continuation of this trend in the Weimar Republic using the term "Conservative Architecture." See his *Baukunst und Stadtplanung im Dritten Reich: Herleitung/Bestandsaufnahme/ Entwicklung/Nachfolge* (Munich, 1976), pp. 39–58.

8 Arthur Moeller van den Bruck (trans. E.O. Lorimer), *The Third Reich* (New York, 1971; original German 1922), p. 38.

9 *Ibid.*, p. 197.

10 His full family name was Breuhaus de Groot, which is sometimes cited in publications, although the more common usage is the shorter form used here.

11 Franz Kollman, "Die Gestaltung moderner Verkehrsmittel, IV: Schiffe," *Das Neue Frankfurt* III Jg. (1929), Heft 7–8: 158.

12 Max Osborn, "Introduction" in *F.A. Breuhaus, Bauen und Räume* (Berlin, 1935), p. XXIII.

13 Robert R. Taylor, *The Word in Stone* (Berkeley and Los Angeles, 1974), pp. 66–8.

14 Albert Speer, *Inside the Third Reich* (London, 1975), p. 77.

15 See Albert Speer, *Die Neue Reichskanzlei* (Berlin, 1939).

16 Paelke, Weimar, "Der Hausrat der Hitler Jugend," *RKW-Nachrichten*, 13 Jg. Heft 2 (May 1939: 41. More sinister insight into the indoctrination of children in this period is provided by an industrially manufactured film-strip projector, with Hitler Jugend plaque, in the Wolfsonian Collection (XX1989.287), that was standard issue in hostels. The accompanying film-strips lauded military virtues, parroted the propaganda of Germany's territorial claims and racial superiority, while asserting the inferiority of peoples such as the Jews and the Slavs.

17   See Paul Maenz, *Art Deco 1920–1940* (Cologne, 1974).

18   Hanns Günther, *Techniche Schönheit* (Zürich-Leipzig, 1929). See also *Das Werk: Technische Lichbildstudien* (Königstein im Taunus, 1931) and other volumes of photographs in this famous Blaue Bücher (Blue Book) series.

19   As in the title of an official book celebrating the maiden voyage: W. von Langsdorff, *LZ 129 "Hindenburg": das Luftschiffe des Deutschen Volkes* (Frankfurt a. Main, 1936).

20   Rolf Brandt, *Mit Luftschiff Hindenburg über den Atlantik* (Berlin, n.d.), p. 11.

21   Langsdorff, *LZ 129 "Hindenburg"*, p. 69.

22   Letter by Wilhelm Wagenfeld to Walter Gropius, August 4, 1964, in Beate Manske and Gudrun Scholz, *Täglich in der Hand: Industrieformen von Wilhelm Wagenfeld aus sechs Jahrzenten* (Bremen: Worpsweder Verlag, 1987), pp. 64–7.

23   See Note 22 above.

24   Taped interview with the author, Solingen, July 1977.

25   *Plakate in München 1840–1940* (Munich: Münchener Stadtmuseum, 1975), p. 69.

26   Pfeffer, Reg. Baumeister A., "Gestaltung von Rundfunkgeräten," AEG-*Mitteilung* (August 1932), pp. 272–4.

27   Wolfsonian Collection TD1990.270.11–15.

28   *Das Neue Frankfurt*, IV Jg., Heft 2/3 (1930): 23.

29   See Rolf Steinberg, ed., *Nazi Kitsch* (Darmstadt, 1975).

30   Walter Maria Kersting, *Die Lebendige Form: Serienmöbel und Massenfabrikation* (Berlin-Tempelhof, 1927), p. 14.

31   Hans Eckstein, "Vom Sinn der Sachlichkeit," *Kunst der Nation*, No. 3 (February 1, 1934), Berlin.

32   Introduction, *Wachsende Wohnung und Einzelgerät* (Cologne: Deutsche Werkbund, Arbeitsgemeinschaft Köln-Rheinland, 1929), p. 11.

33   Introduction, *Ausstellung "Schönheit der Arbeit"* (Munich: Deutsche Arbeitsfront, 1937), p. 14.

34   Hermann Gretsch, *Hausrat, der zu uns passt* (Stuttgart, 1939), p. 47.

Emblems of Production:
Workers in German, Italian, and American Art during the 1930s

Bernard F. Reilly, Jr.

At the end of World War I the industrial worker was poised on the threshold of a new era. *Work for America!* (fig. 10.01), American illustrator Dean Cornwell's heroic 1918 portrait of a metalworker, expresses the optimistic faith in industry and technology held by Americans and Europeans at the opening of the twentieth century.[1] Cornwell's noble, muscular figure embodied the energy and power of the industrial work force, the resource that fueled the industry which in turn underwrote the might of great nations. The accessories of the industrial worker – the leather apron and gloves and metalworker's hammer – identify him as a member of a newly emergent and increasingly visible class.

Evidently created as a design for a poster to be issued by the Division of Pictorial Publicity during World War I, Cornwell's painting was intended to help rally modern industrial workers to maximum production in support of the war effort. Rising boldly behind the metalworker are factory chimneys issuing voluminous clouds of smoke, and the radio towers of several warships which roll off the line by virtue of his labors. Proud, almost defiant, he personifies what home front propagandists of the age referred to as the "sinews of war."

In the radically altered post-war world, Cornwell's worker was soon to be – if he was not already – an anachronism. There occurred a growing disparity between the power and independent spirit with which he was vested and the increasingly dismal realities of modern industrial work. Physical power and manual skills had for some time been ceding ground to machine technology, powered by energy sources such as electricity, steam, and petroleum. Machines, not men, actually drove the foundries, mills, and factories of the time. The British artist C.R.W. Nevinson's *Building Aircraft: Making the Engine* (fig. 10.02) conveys a sense of the grimmer realities of factory work. Workers increasingly served as the operators and attendants of the machines, or were confined to the highly repetitive or menial tasks not yet mechanized, such as assembling machine parts, tending furnaces, and mine excavation. The

Fig. 10.02 See Cat. 239
Print
"Building Aircraft: Making the Engine,"
from *The Great War: Britain's Efforts and Ideals*
series, 1917
C.R.W. Nevinson

author of a *Fortune* magazine essay in December 1932 was prompted to characterize the industrial laborer as a "system of levers and joints."[2]

During the 1920s this decline in the quality and conditions of industrial work combined with massive levels of unemployment to bring about profound and widespread dissatisfaction on the part of workers and intellectuals alike with industrialism. The Stock Market Crash of 1929 and subsequent worldwide depression deepened this crisis of confidence and provoked fundamental disillusionment with the capitalist economic system. A dramatically successful challenge to this system had recently been mounted in the Russian Revolution of 1917. And with the spread of Socialism and Communism among workers in the wake of that revolution, the specter of an international community of the proletariat became a real threat throughout Europe and the U.S.A.

In the early 1930s massive unemployment, a dispirited labor force increasingly drawn toward the orbit of international Communism, and severely constricted industrial and

Fig. 10.03 See Cat. 252
Study
Promote the General Welfare,
possibly for Post Office no. 235, San Jose
mural competition (unknown if realized), c. 1935

agricultural production weighed heavily upon the governments of Europe and the U.S.A. These problems confronted Franklin Delano Roosevelt and Adolf Hitler in 1933, as they took office as President of the United States and Chancellor of Germany respectively, and Italian leader Benito Mussolini as he launched many of his most ambitious economic and military programs. In response, each of these leaders undertook nothing less than a comprehensive rebuilding of their respective societies.

Art was an important instrument in these undertakings. Mural paintings, sculpture, posters, buildings, books, and even ceramics created under their auspices, were used by these regimes to mobilize their citizens for the fulfillment of ambitious national goals, in particular the goal of expanded agricultural and industrial production. At the same time, art was also used for ideological purposes, to undercut the lure of internationalist movements, Communism in particular.

In its rich holdings of works produced under the American New Deal, the Third Reich, and Italian Fascism, the Wolfsonian Collection represents an extraordinary resource for the comparative study of the persuasive strategies of these regimes. This essay will compare a number of such works which address the theme of production. It will show how, and to what extent, the works reflect the economic realities of the era in the three countries and the official policies with regard to industry and labor adopted by the three governments. This comparison will also suggest that despite the profound ideological gulf that separated two militaristic and fascist regimes from a pluralistic, democratic society, a common underlying theme figured in the varying persuasive strategies adopted by all three of them. This theme was the newly assertive role to be taken by the national government in the life and welfare of the individual.

An anonymous maquette in the Wolfsonian Collection, possibly created as a mural design for the U.S. Post Office at San Jose, California, entitled *Promote the General Welfare* (fig. 10.03), typifies much of the art produced under the Works Progress Administration.[3] It glorifies agricultural and industrial production – the twin pillars of New Deal society. The maquette signals the departure from the detached, if not hostile, relationship between government and labor of previous administrations, which Roosevelt's New Deal constituted with its program of immediate and long-term assistance to American workers.

Three workers are prominently featured. At the top stands a farmer, silhouetted against fields of grain and a massive dam. Below him stands a black field hand, beyond whom is visible a cotton field harvested by a team of laborers. Next, a muscular industrial worker with a sledge hammer stands before the dark towers of a factory. While dignified, these workers lack the strong, individualized presence of Cornwell's steelworker. Consistent with the New Deal vision, they are rather the cooperative participants in a highly ordered and regulated

BEALL

FARM WORK

RURAL ELECTRIFICATION ADMINISTRATION

Fig. 10.05
Study
***Scenes from American Life*, c. 1935**
Robert Hallowell
(American, 1886–1939)
New York
Oil on canvas
30¾ x 55⅞ inches (78.1 x 141.9 cm)
Marks: obverse, signed in black, bottom right
"R. HALLOWELL"
87.1137.5.1

Fig. 10.04 *See Cat. 248*
Poster
Farm Work. Rural Electrification
***Administration*, 1937**
Designed by L. Beall

American society. Moreover, the dam, factory, railroad lines, and shipping activity seen in the mural emphasize the technological renewal which New Deal planners envisioned as essential to this society. This same ideal of renewal through technology is presented in more figurative terms in Lester Beall's poster *Farm Work*, designed for the Rural Electrification Administration in 1937 (fig. 10.04).

Another meditation on the importance of technology in New Deal society is Robert Hallowell's mural study of scenes from American life (fig. 10.05), submitted as an entry in a competition for the U.S. Interior Department Building in Washington, D.C. A small nuclear family – father, mother, child, and infant – comprise the focal point of the work. In a series of vertical panels behind them appear five scenes: an Indian in an unspoiled Western wilderness; and four views of men engaged in the construction and operation of the Hoover Dam. An accompanying text reads:

> Power, harnessed and made cheap, controlled democratically and used for the common good, releases man from needless toil and converts "technological unemployment" into mass leisure. Mass leisure means security for all, means individual self-development, means the enrichment of the national culture – the true objective and justification of the democratic experiment.

291

Like *Promote the General Welfare*, Hallowell's work professes an optimistic faith in the benign potential of technology when directed toward the public good. Constructed in 1936, the Hoover Dam was one of many federal projects which, by harnessing the power of large natural waterways, provided electricity, irrigation, drinking water, and transportation for millions. Hallowell's mural asserts a principal tenet of the New Deal, that federal sponsorship of power projects and centralized control of natural resources would be the basis for an improved way of life for Americans.

The art produced under the auspices of the German and Italian governments during the same period shares with American official art this vision of a strong role for government in the sphere of human work and production. Not shared by German and Italian art of the period, however, was the American tendency to spotlight the role of industry and technology in its economic renewal. While industrialization and technological innovation were also central to German and Italian programs of economic recovery, agricultural production was portrayed most often in these regimes' propaganda.

Fig. 10.06
Poster
Schaffendes Landvolk
(Farmers at Work), 1937
Designed by Anto
(Austrian, dates unknown)
Germany
Commercial color lithograph
32⅜ x 23 inches (82.2 x 58.4 cm)
Marks: obverse, printed in gray, bottom right "AN/TO"
TD1991.146.7

The hearty, sun-bronzed Aryan farmers featured on the posters for two 1937 agricultural fairs and expositions, the *Schaffendes Landvolk* (Farmers at Work) and *Vierte Reichsnährstands Ausstellung* (Fourth State Food Producers' Exhibition), were typical of how the German worker was presented to the world in Third Reich propaganda (figs. 10.06 and 10.07). The popularity of the farmer in this context, and in the officially sanctioned painting and sculpture under the Third Reich, must have been due in part to the Reich's efforts to increase agricultural production as part of the Wehrwirtschaft or "war economy." Under Goering's Four Year Plan, Germany sought to achieve self-sufficiency through enhanced food production, and immunity to the threat of economic strangulation which a wartime blockade might pose.[4]

The correspondence between these images and economic realities in Germany, however, was tenuous at best. The Third Reich's enshrinement of the farmer was quite at variance with the economic policies which the regime pursued. In fact, the greatest share of the Reich's efforts and resources went into the buildup of heavy industry, to support manufactures such

Fig. 10.07
Poster
4. Reichsnährstands Ausstellung
(Fourth State Food Producers' Exhibition), 1937
Designed by Ludwig Hohlwein
(German, 1874–1949)
Printed by Deutsche Landwerbung GmbH, Berlin
Commercial color lithograph
32⅞ x 23¼ inches (83.5 x 59.1 cm)
Marka: obverse, printed in blue, bottom right "LUDWIG
HOHLWEIN/ /// MUNCHEN"
XX1990.2850

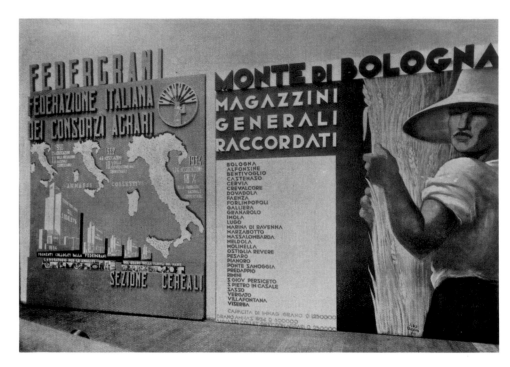

as steel and automotive production which were conducive to the military aims of the government. Meanwhile, the depleted German soil was forcing an increasing number of German peasants to seek industrial work away from the farm in order to subsist. The small farmers who, along with the artisans and rural landowners, composed the traditional base of National Socialist support and had early embraced the Party as a hedge against the growing political unity and power of the urban laborers, actually lost considerable ground during the 1930s as Hitler increasingly courted the large industrial interests.[5]

Despite the Wehrwirtschaft's emphasis on large-scale production, Reich propaganda evoked a curiously anachronistic agrarian ideal. The farmers portrayed in such works often bundle grain by hand and work with scythes and other simple tools, displaying a primitive level of technology out of place in an era of mechanized agriculture. In a similarly disingenuous spirit, a poster advertising a 1933 Bavarian agricultural and crafts festival and exposition, Bayrisches-Central Landwirtschaftsfest (fig. 10.08), features an antiquated plough and oxcart. In stark contrast to New Deal art's emphasis on the importance of technology to the new social order, the official art of the Third Reich presented rural life as simple and unencumbered by the complexities of technology and mechanization.

Fig. 10.08   See Cat. 249
Poster
Bayrisches-Central Landwirtschaftsfest
(Central Bavaria Agricultural Festival), 1933
Designed by Pehns

Fig. 10.09
Exhibition panel
Designed by Aldo Carboni
(Italian, dates unknown)
From *IV Mostra Nazionale dell'Agricoltura – I Mostra Corporativa dell'Agricoltura in Bologna*
(Genoa: S.A.I.G.A. Barabino & Graeve, 1935), p. 40
No. 6017, first commercial edition
83.2.2274

Such images were designed to foster the myth of a pastoral, pre-industrial existence central to German nationalist ideology. The simplicity and moral superiority of agrarian life, as opposed to the decadence and libertarianism of the city, was a notion rooted in the earliest reaction to the industrial revolution in Europe.[6] For the Nazis, the belief was an important component of the German national identity. Nazi theoreticians like Ludwig Ferdinand Clauss saw an ancient and indissoluble spiritual bond which linked the German race and the German land, the union of "Blut und Boden" (Blood and Soil).[7] Whereas urban industrial life was modern and international in character, peasant life was considered enduring and quintessentially German. Similarly, cities were viewed by the Nazis as uncongenial to the temperament of Nordic man, as realms of chaos and anxiety and as incubators of Marxism.[8]

Farm production and the simplicity of rural life were also extolled in Italian Fascist art, and for similar reasons. The frequent agricultural expositions and fairs organized by Mussolini's government served as occasions for the celebration of farm production. One of the most ambitious of these was the Quarta Mostra Nazionale dell'Agricoltura held in Bologna in 1935. The exposition's murals by Marcello Dudovich, Adolfo Busi, Aldo Carboni, and others present an imaginative (and to a large extent imaginary) panorama of peasant life (fig. 10.09). The farmers who appear here are simply dressed, many in traditional local costumes, and possess a quiet grandeur and power. The artists have imparted a timeless quality to these figures and their work, expressing "la nobile fatica dei campi" (the noble toil of the fields) which has endured throughout Italian history.[9]

Considered in isolation, the murals would seem to deny, like the German portrayals, the important role of technology in the nation's modern agricultural program. These simple farmers, in fact, shared the exhibition space with the newest in farm machinery, and were juxtaposed with statistical charts detailing Italy's advances in scientific and mechanized agriculture. Italian propagandists emphasized this archaic image of the farmer, as did their German counterparts, for ideological purposes. The portrayal of the Italian peasant with his rudimentary tools, rather than at the wheel of a tractor or combine, was to link the modern regime to an enduring strength of the nation's past. In this way the Fascists sought to present Mussolini's modern farm programs as a natural extension of a hallowed agricultural tradition which stretched continuously back through Italy's history to the peninsula's first inhabitants, and to invoke the fertility of the earth as an almost mystical source of national strength. This sense of continuity with Italy's rustic past is memorably expressed in Marcello Dudovich's poster for the exhibition (fig. 10.10), a powerful image of simple agricultural tools – shovel, pitchfork, axe, etc. – gathered together to form a *fascio*.

While German propaganda masked the true aims of the regime, Italian propaganda reflected an actual emphasis on agricultural production which was central to the Fascist economic program. Driven by the economic imperatives of his regime's military and territorial ambitions, Mussolini aspired to make Italy economically self-sufficient – a goal to which the expansion of agricultural production was essential. To this end Mussolini instituted massive programs of land reclamation, land drainage, reforestation, and irrigation, invested heavily in improving soil fertility and agricultural technology, and waged several successive national campaigns to enhance agricultural production. And as in Germany, it was those who composed the traditional base of the regime's support – in Italy the rural landowners and tenants, in the words of the newspaper *Giovinezza* the "gentry and the peasants" – who benefited most from those programs. In comparison, the urban proletariat, never considered friendly to the Party, was neglected.[10]

The serene tone of the Bologna murals and other official representations of Italian farmers and farm work, however, belied the actual conditions and hardships of the time. Mussolini's farm programs were designed to counter profound problems in the agricultural

296

Fig. 10.10
Poster
IV Mostra Nazionale dell'Agricoltura Bologna
(Fourth National Agricultural Exhibition . . .),
1935
Designed by Marcello Dudovich
(Italian, 1878–1962)
Printed by Grafiche I.G.A.P. (Impresa Generale Affissione
Pubblicità), Milan and Rome
Commercial color lithograph
55 1/4 x 39 3/8 inches (140.3 x 100.0 cm)
Marks: obverse, printed in black, top right in the stone
"M. DUDOVICH"
87.570.4.1

Fig. 10.11
Figurine
***Pioneer Man*, 1937**
Nils Edwin Hanson
(American, dates unknown)
Cleveland, OH
Glazed earthenware
14⅝ x 5⅝ x 4¾ inches (37.2 x 14.3 x 12.1 cm)
Marks: exterior, impressed on base, "NILS HANSON";
interior, impressed "27"
84.7.103

base of the Italian economy. Mussolini sought to reverse the exodus of workers from the country to the urban industrial centers, an exodus prompted by the poverty and diminishing prospects offered by rural life.

In glorifying rural life, the art of the Fascist and Nazi regimes sought to foster, in the face of a continual erosion of agricultural population, the traditional spiritual bonds of these peoples to their respective lands. In Germany this bond was associated with, and validated, age-old territorial claims asserted by the regime. In both Italy and Germany the land represented a crucial link to the country's history and destiny.

This nostalgia for agrarian life was not unique to German and Italian art in the 1930s. It was a strong current in American art of the period as well. The works of American "region-alist" painters Thomas Hart Benton and John Steuart Curry, and of many of the artists who worked under the aegis of the Works Progress Administration, are also infused with a yearning for a simpler order. Nils Edwin Hanson's 1937 glazed earthenware figure *Pioneer Man* (fig. 10.11), created under the Ohio W.P.A., exudes a simple nobility and strength comparable to that of the Bologna mural peasants. To Americans in the 1930s, pioneers exemplified the heroism and vigor of those who had crossed the Great Plains and opened the West. Their muscular achievements, wrested from the land, were invoked as an example to a dispirited population beset by the overwhelming hardships of the Great Depression. As in Germany and Italy, the traditional values and ways of life associated with pre-industrial times must have been particularly appealing in the face of anxieties about what was perceived as the decaying moral fabric of the country, brought on by urbanization and industrialization. American reformers such as Lewis Mumford were repelled by the excesses of modern industrial capitalism. Mumford's words strike a chord reminiscent of the anti-industrialist rhetoric of the National Socialists:

> . . . our industrialism has been otherworldly: it has blackened and defaced our human environment, in the hope of achieving the abstract felicities of profits and dividends in the industrial hereafter. It is time that we came to terms with the earth, and worked in partnership with the forces that promote life and the traditions that enhance it.[11]

There was, however, an important difference between the rural images in American art and in German and Italian art. While the official art of Germany and Italy obscured the harsh realities of rural existence, American portrayals of farm life frankly acknowledged the poverty and displacement which darkened the countryside. The photographs of Dorothea Lange and Walker Evans, and posters by Ben Shahn, produced for the Resettlement Administration and Farm Security Administration, were created to broadcast to the American public a candid picture of the economic distress of the family farmer.[12] And rather than portraying its revival of production with anachronistic models, as did the propagandists of Germany, the

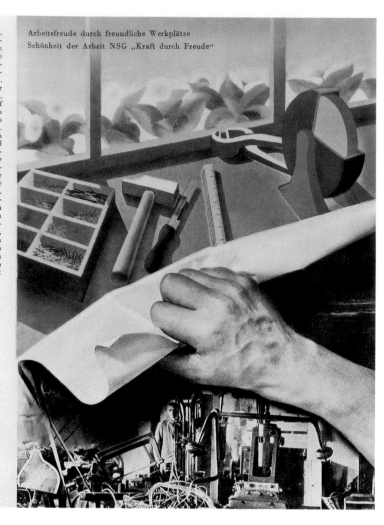

Nichts Zufälliges findet Platz, sondern nur die Spitzenleistung. Keine Luxusgüter zum Gebrauch der ausnahmsweise vom Glück begünstigten, sondern deutsche Wert- und Edelarbeit wird herausgestellt. Keine Katalogisierung oder Warenschau wird geboten, sondern jedes Ding wird auf seinem richtigen Platz und in bezug auf seinen funktionellen Dienst am Menschen gezeigt. Und dann treten dieser großen Darstellung von Heim und Siedlung als der Familienlebensstätte, die „Stätten der Arbeit" zur Seite. Hier gelangen alle Kräfte, die sich für den würdigen Arbeitsplatz der Zukunft einsetzen, zu Wort. Hier wird eine Parade vielfältigster Arbeitsplätze in ihren mustergültigen Formen zum Anschauungsunterricht aufgeboten. Kraftvoll und schön, zukunftsfroh und siegreich schwingt der Rhythmus des ersten deutschen Mai durch diese Hallen. Mit dem Thema „Stätten der Erholung" rundet sich der Ring.

Arbeitsfreude durch freundliche Werkplätze
Schönheit der Arbeit NSG „Kraft durch Freude"

Das Antlitz der Arbeit wandelt sich. Was häßlich war, verschwindet. Eine zweckmäßige Schönheit, eine berechtigte Würde tritt das Erbe an. Arbeit ist für den Deutschen mehr als nur die Möglichkeit seinen Lebensunterhalt zu verdienen. Die Arbeit sollte aber für alle Menschen etwas spüren lassen von dem Segen und der Schönheit dieser Erde: Der Arbeitsplatz, die Würde zweckbedingter Schönheit.

Fig. 10.12

Arbeitsfreude durch freundliche Werkplätze, Schönheit der Arbeit N.S.G. "Kraft durch Freude"
(Worker satisfaction through a congenial workplace, Beauty of Work N.S.G. "Strength through Joy").
Designed by Herbert Bayer
(American, b. Austria, 1900–85)
From *Das Wunder des Lebens* (The Wonder of Life)
(Berlin: Gemeinnützige Berliner Ausstellungshallen, 1935), p. 20
Printed by Messe- und Fremdenverkehrs GmbH, Berlin
TD1989.10.6

art of the New Deal encouraged a forward-looking faith in technology as the foundation for prosperity.

Where industrial workers do appear in German art, one of two persuasive strategies seems to be at work. In some cases the worker is portrayed as a victim of the dehumanizing effects of technology. A photomontage by Herbert Bayer, *Arbeitsfreude durch freundliche Werkplätze* (loosely, Worker satisfaction through a congenial workplace) (fig. 10.12), included in a promotional brochure for the 1935 exhibition *Das Wunder des Lebens* (The Wonder of Life) held in Berlin, offers a frightening image of the industrial worker enmeshed in a tangle of mechanized disorder.[13] This condition was associated in Nazi propaganda with the old order, with the exploitation of the workers under the industrial capitalism of the post-war Weimar period. According to the brochure and exhibition, National Socialism offered a refuge from this nightmare. In the upper portion of Bayer's picture, the claustrophobic complexity of the mechanized factory interior is swept away, giving way to the craftsmanlike simplicity of the workbench – a carpenter's tools are shown – and a view of a cultivated garden beyond. "The face of work changes. What was ugly [*hässlich*] disappears, to be replaced by a purposeful beauty and deserved dignity."[14]

The National Socialists promised to sweep away the grimness and monotony of modern mass production, and to impart to work a new dignity and meaning ("eine berechtigte Würde"). Through government programs like *Die Schönheit der Arbeit* (the Beauty of Work), the redesign of factories and worker housing was to provide more congenial workplaces and domiciles, stressing cleanliness, order, bright natural lighting, and proximity to nature through the provision of gardens and other amenities.[15]

In line with this vision of modern work on a more manageable, human scale, the independent craftsman or artisan was, along with the small farmer, repeatedly invoked as the ideal German worker. In Sepp Semar's 1935 poster for a national craftsmen's day, *Reichshandwerkertag* (see fig. 9.10), a carpenter, armed with tools of his trade, strides purposefully past the quaint facades of northern, seventeenth-century style buildings. He epitomizes an anachronistic ideal that, much like the image of the small farmer, was contrary to the real thrust of Hitler's economic policy, which drove most small handicraft businesses into unprofitability, and their operators into the factories and mills of heavy industry.

In other representations of German labor, a second strategy seems to have been pursued. This was to obscure or undermine the sense of distinct class identity of German industrial workers which the trade unions, abolished by Hitler in 1934, had long worked to build. Prominently featured in the 1937 Schaffendes Volk (A Nation at Work) exhibition in Düsseldorf was a series of portraits of Autobahn workers created by the photographer Erna Lendvai-Dircksen under the auspices of the Institut für Deutsches Wirtschaftspropaganda (Institute for German Economic Propaganda). The photographs were reproduced and published in book form as *Reichsautobahn Mensch und Werk* (State Autobahn Man and Work), a copy of which is in the Wolfsonian. The most ambitious and extensive German public works project, the construction of the Autobahn employed workers from all parts of the nation.

Despite the engineering triumph that the project represented, the text and photographs in the book emphasize not the technological side of the effort, but the workers' spiritual and physical encounter with the German land. Indeed, the refrain of the Autobahn workers, "Wir brechen die ewige Erde auf" ("We plough the eternal earth"), suggests a contact with the elemental forces of nature, and a kinship between these workers and the German farmer far closer than that which they shared with their counterparts in the factories of Berlin, Munich, and Moscow.[16]

ROTES ÖSTERREICH ROTES WIEN

SCHWARZES ÖSTERREICH

Ho-ruck, nach links!

Wählt sozialdemokratisch!

Fig. 10.13 See Cat. 205
Poster (four sheets)
Ho-Ruck! Nach Links! Wählt Sozialdemokratisch!
(Heave-Ho! To the Left! Vote Social
Democratic!), 1930
Designed by V.T. Slama

Aside from the Autobahn workers' intimate attachment to the land (they are all "Erdarbeiter Kind seiner Landschaft" or "laborers born of the soil"), the book's text and images extol their characteristic *Gemütlichkeit* (good-natured disposition) and love of music. By emphasizing such innately German traits, the authors diminish the sense of an international community of interest among workers. This internationalist spirit was fostered in such works produced for the Left as Victor Slama's poster *Ho-Ruck! Nach Links! Wählt Sozialdemokratisch* ("Heave-Ho! To the Left! Vote Social Democratic!") (fig. 10.13), which appeared during the 1930 Austrian elections, and in works produced by Communists in the

U.S.A. and the U.S.S.R., such as the American artist Hugo Gellert's illustrations in *Karl Marx' "Capital" in Lithographs* (fig. 10.14) and a poster for a 1939 Soviet agricultural exhibition (fig. 10.15). Whereas the laborers portrayed in Nazi propaganda display strikingly Nordic features and often wear regional costume, the strapping workers favored by Leftist artists are virtually interchangeable from country to country, and are clad in the plain uniform of the industrial proletariat.[17]

As in Bayer's photomontage in *Das Wunder des Lebens*, the author of *Reichsautobahn Mensch und Werk* emphasizes the workers' dependence upon the state as a source of livelihood. One worker (fig. 10.16) states, "Für sieben Söhne und eine Tochter schaffe ich wieder ehrliches Brot." ("I earn an honest wage again for my seven sons and one daughter.")

In short, the National Socialists aspired, through their propaganda, to generate a sense of the empowerment of the worker under the Nazi economic programs. By their argument, this empowerment stemmed from both the state's programs for workers (such as the Autobahn construction and *Schönheit der Arbeit*) and from the spiritual and racial bonds to the land itself. Images like Bayer's and Lendvai-Dircksen's sought to encourage an allegiance to the state and an acceptance of the central role of the national government in the life of the individual. This was done by projecting an appealing but illusory vision of work under the Nazi system. In reality, this vision masked the real thrust of the Nazi agenda, a program of massive industrialization that ultimately undermined the status and power of the workers.

The Italian Fascists also sought to convey by means of art a sense of worker empowerment through the state. A postcard (fig. 10.17) designed by Giorgio Muggiani shows an aproned, shirt-sleeved factory worker standing before a row of smoking factories in the shadow of a large fasces. Proudly he acknowledges his debt to the system, "Il fascismo mi ha dato tranquillità e lavoro" ("Fascism has given me peace and work"). The contented worker and productive factories in the scene were no doubt meant to offer a sharp contrast to the familiar scenes of unemployment and labor strife which afflicted industrial life in Italy prior to Fascist rule.[18]

Another urban worker is featured in a 1930 design for a plate by Alfredo Gaudenzi, depicting a construction scene (fig. 10.18). Gaudenzi's laborer is engaged in construction of one of the many apartment or office buildings created under the grand national public works programs established by Mussolini between 1927 and 1930. He goes about his task in a dutiful manner, within the carefully ordered framework of the surrounding structures.[19] The image offers an apt metaphor for the order which Fascism imposed, through its rigid reorganization of labor and subsidizing of building projects. Thus Italian propaganda asserted that workers can find order or "tranquillity" only through the state, which has harnessed the enormous economic forces of modern life.

Fig. 10.14
Primary Accumulation
Illustrated by Hugo Gellert
(American, 1892–1985)
From *Karl Marx' "Capital" in Lithographs*
(New York, 1934), p. 19
83.2.811

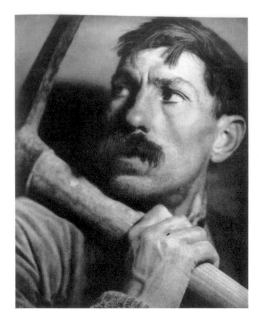

Fig. 10.16
"Nach Jahren der Arbeitslosigkeit schaffe ich für sieben Söhne und eine Tochter wieder ehrliches Brot"
(After years of unemployment, I earn an honest wage again for my seven sons and one daughter)
From Erna Lendvai-Dircksen, *Reichsautobahn Mensch und Werk* (Bayreuth, 1942; first edition 1937), [p. 5]
XB1990.1323

Fig. 10.15
Poster
USSR Agricultural Exhibition, 1939
Designed by Klimaschin
(Russian, dates unknown)
Printed by Mezhdunarodnaja Kniga, Moscow
Commercial color lithograph
40 x 26⅜ inches (101.6 x 67.0 cm)
Marks: obverse, printed in red,
right margin in the stone
"KLIMASCHIN 39"
85.4.108

In Italy agriculture and industry were joined in the centerpiece of the country's economic program, the autarky campaign (see the Doordan and de Guttry/Maino essays for more detail). The *Autarchia* bowl (fig. 10.19), designed by Eugenio Colmo (who signed his work "Golia"), celebrates the regime's drive, intensified after trade sanctions were imposed against Italy in 1935, to make the country self-sufficient by heightening production in certain key areas and by securing colonies which would provide the needed natural resources not available on the Italian mainland. Significantly, a soldier occupies the central position in the bowl's iconographical scheme, indicating that all production activity is subordinated to the national "Difesa" – in actuality the military ambitions of the state. Contributing to this effort are agricultural laborers (representing "Alimentazione" or food production); a miner ("Mineraria") representing the metals industry, whose factories were essential to the military; a textile worker ("Tessile Nazionale"); and a North African laborer ("Colonizzazione").

Fig. 10.17
Postcard
Il Fascismo mi ha dato tranquillità e lavoro
(Fascism has given me peace and work), c. 1925
Designed by Giorgio Muggiani
(Italian, 1887–1938)
Published by Edizioni Muggiani, Milan
3½ x 5½ inches (8.9 x 14.0 cm)
XB1992.1258

Interestingly, the agricultural and metal workers shown in Golia's bowl are engaged not at the processing or industrial stage of production. They are not factory workers, but those that harvest the raw resources. Their tools, like those in Dudovich's poster, are rudimentary – pickaxes, scythes, and shovels – rather than the more modern jackhammers, welding torches, and other powered tools. Inclusion of these primitive tools seems disingenuous in light of the massive scale on which these industries were operating at the time Golia's bowl was fired.

The work uses formal means as well to evoke an earlier era. The reductive classicism of the figures, which appear as dark silhouettes on a contrasting ground, is reminiscent of ancient Etruscan ceramics. Like Dudovich's peasants, Golia's figures are ennobled by their work and by their involvement with the romance and fecundity of the Italian earth. By avoiding quotidian references to modern technology, Golia's bowl, Dudovich's poster, the Bologna exposition murals, and other works glorifying Italian agricultural production evoke a timeless state, linking the modern Fascist nation with Italy's glorious past.

The artistic means used in forging this link echoed the fealty to the past which characterized the *corporazione* system. The figures on the *Autarchia* bowl – farmers, miners, and textile workers – correspond to three of the most prominent *corporazione*. The chief instruments of Fascist manipulation of the economy, the *corporazione* were composed of employers, employees, and Party representatives; these bodies set standards, working conditions, wages, and the policies of the producers. All branches of production were governed by such organizations which, unlike the trade unions they supplanted, were firmly under the control of the state.[20] Manifesting a preference for pre-industrial models which paralleled the Nazis' anti-modernist labor practices, the Italians patterned the *corporazione* upon the medieval guilds in an attempt to reunite all aspects of production within a given industry – from the extraction or cultivation of raw materials to the finished product and its distribution. This "vertical" organization of production was also designed to undermine the class identity of the industrial workers which had been fostered along horizontal lines by Socialism, Communism, and the labor unions. Works of art like Golia's bowl no doubt served this effort to divide and conquer Italian labor. The bowl's iconographic program projects an image of production – and of Italian society – not layered along class lines, but configured as an aggregate of distinct industries all contributing to the national defense.

Two women are prominently featured on the *Autarchia* bowl: a farm hand with a sheaf of grain under one arm and a basket of produce on her head, representing agriculture, and a woman seated at a spindle, representing the national textile industry. Both figures are untainted by any evident involvement with technology, which is incongruous in industries which were highly mechanized at the time. In general, art during this period tended to present and define production, except for agricultural production, as an almost exclusively

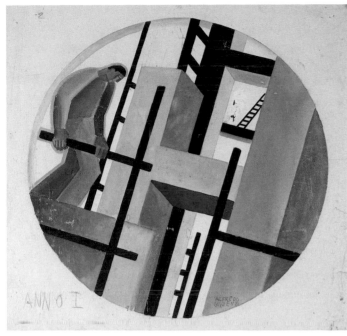

Fig. 10.18
Design for plate, 1930
Alfredo (Alf) Gaudenzi

(Italian, 1908–80)
Albissola, Italy
Gouache over ink on paper
12 x 13 inches (30.5 x 33.0 cm)
Marks: obverse, signed in black, bottom right
"ALFREDO GAUDENZI"
84.5.36

Fig. 10.19   See Cat. 243
Bowl
***Autarchia* (Autarky), 1938**
Designed by Golia

male preserve. With some notable exceptions, portrayals of women emphasized their traditional domestic roles of childbearing and child-rearing. This ignored, or obscured, the fact that in the 1910s and 1920s women had entered the workforce in Europe and the U.S.A. in unprecedented numbers. This trend continued during the Depression, when widespread unemployment among skilled workers drew even more women out of the home and into the sweatshops and factories, particularly in the textile industries.[21]

The portrayal of gender in official art has less to do with real conditions than with the grave concern of the New Deal, Fascist, and Nazi regimes for the cohesion of the family. Industrialization and the exodus of people to the cities in the late nineteenth century and the massive social dislocations of the Depression subjected the traditional family unit to enormous stresses. Problems ranged from rampant epidemics of tuberculosis and syphilis to rising juvenile delinquency. In an effort to preserve and strengthen the family as a basic unit of society, Italy, Germany, and the U.S.A. all sought to train the energies of women on the spheres of child-bearing and -rearing, and the hygiene of the home.

Fig. 10.20 See Cat. 214
Poster
Giornata della Madre e del Fanciullo. Anno XV
(Day of the Mother and Child . . .), 1936
Designed by M. Dudovich

Fig. 10.21
Study (detail)
For the Washington, NJ Post Office
mural competition, c. 1935
Frank Shapiro
(American, 1914–94)
New York
Tempera, gouache on fiberboard
20¼ x 75 inches (51.4 x 190.5 cm)
Marks: obverse, signed in black, lower left corner of right
panel "SHAPIRO"
84.5.104.2

In Italy and Germany, government concern with the family was further intensified by a desire to increase the birth rate in the interest of greater future production and larger armies, and to strengthen the family as the primary unit of a rigidly structured and racially pure society. Italian and German governments offered women powerful inducements to refrain from professional and industrial endeavors and to confine themselves to child care. In both countries financial subsidies were provided for large families. In Italy, the Fascists devoted considerable resources to the care of pregnant women, mothers, and children. These measures were also augmented by statutes banning women from public employment and from numerous occupations in private industry. Marcello Dudovich's poster for the 1936 *Giornata della Madre e del Fanciullo* (Day of the Mother and Child) reflects the Italian ideal of patriotic motherhood (fig. 10.20). The work was produced under the auspices of the Opera Nazionale per la Protezione della Maternità e dell'Infanzia (National Organization for the Protection of Mothers and Infants).

The poster *Neues Volk* (A New People), attributed to Ludwig Hohlwein, was produced for the Racial Policy Office and is similarly emblematic of women's role in German society (see fig. 9.18). In both instances the family is represented as a sacred preserve under the guardianship of the father, and untainted by any reference to the modern urban world. (In Hohlwein's work the protective presence of the German government is suggested by inclusion of an eagle circling overhead.) Whereas in the two countries the highest calling for a woman was to bear children (and to care for the farm in the absence of men who were drawn

307

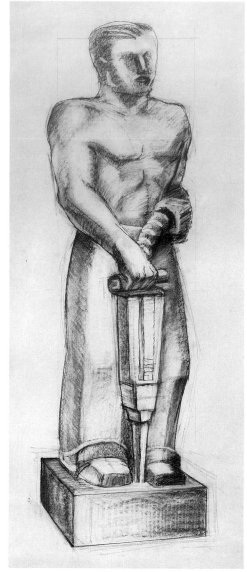

into industrial occupations), this role derived added importance in Germany from the racial program of the Reich. In holding the central role in reproduction, women were the font of Aryan purity and the key to the future of the race.[22]

American works such as Robert Hallowell's *Scenes from American Life* and a series of mural studies by Frank Shapiro (fig. 10.21) express the New Deal's concern for the preservation of the family structure. Again, women are shown as members of a protected class and the center of the family unit, which in turn is subordinated to the larger unit of American society. The central scene in Shapiro's mural studies is a worker's arrival home from the factory, as he is greeted at the threshold of the domestic realm by his wife and children.

Women engaged in industrial production did occasionally appear in American art, however. Beatrice Levy's sculpture bust of a garment industry seamstress, *Factory Worker* (fig. 10.22), attempts to come to grips with the new order of things. The focus of the subject's activity is a sewing machine, with which the woman's shoulders, arms, and upper torso all seem of a piece, suggesting a fluid continuum of human and machine, an ideal espoused by the efficiency experts of the 1920s. While not as anachronistic as the spindle operated by the

Fig. 10.22
Sculpture
***Factory Worker*, c. 1940**
Attributed to Beatrice S. Levy
(American, 1892–1974)
Chicago
Earthenware, wood
13 x 17⅛ x 12 inches (33.0 x 43.5 x 30.5 cm)
XX1990.1006

Fig. 10.23
Drawing
***Workman with Drill*, 1934**
Brents Carlton
(American, 1903–62)
San Francisco
Charcoal, conté crayon on paper
43 x 18⅛ inches (109.2 x 46.0 cm)
TD1991.81.7

woman in Golia's *Autarchia* bowl, the sewing machine here is an ambiguous object, a fixture of either the home or factory. Levy's subject could easily be taken for a wife or mother engaged in traditional home chores. In its ambiguity, the work addresses the intersection of two traditionally separate realms of human endeavor. The subject is situated at the threshold between the timeless domestic role of woman as mother and wife and the modern industrial world of garment manufacturing. In setting up an almost affectionate relationship between woman and machine, the sculptor here softened what was in reality an extremely traumatic social development.

These works of public art from Italy, Germany, and the U.S.A. reflect a wide variety of formal and polemical strategies which, this diversity notwithstanding, pursued a common end. All three countries sought to instill in their citizens a new sense of belonging to an integrated society wherein the individual contributed to large-scale national projects and production programs. Conversely, these works also advocated an acceptance of the strong presence of government in the lives of their citizens. Art thus helped to prepare the three societies for the impending conflict of a second world war.

In Italy and Germany the ultimate military end of production had been clear from early in the decade and informed the art of the 1930s. In the U.S.A. the glorification of production was, until 1941, aimed at achieving economic stability and growth. As it happened, with America's entry into the war, the goals of production and military strength became one, and the New Deal agricultural and industrial programs proved conducive to the transformation to a war economy heavily reliant on such production on a gargantuan scale. Similarly, the mural programs and art projects of the 1930s had introduced the American people to the societal ideals of a collective identity and a strong and pervasive government. This was critical in mobilizing the home front to achieve the rigorous goals of both production and resource conservation during wartime.

It might also be argued that the path from industrial production to warfare was prepared in more specific ways by the official patronage of the federal art projects. In such portrayals of workers produced under the aegis of the P.W.A.P. and W.P.A. as Beatrice Levy's *Factory Worker* and Brents Carlton's *Workman with Drill* (fig. 10.23), the boundary between human and machine has been blurred. The jackhammer operators and riveters in particular operate tools which bear a striking resemblance to machine-guns and other weapons of war. From portraying industrial work in such dynamic, forceful, and impersonalized terms, it was a small step to merging the identities of worker and combatant. The latter was a recurrent motif in works designed for the home front during World War II, such as Jean Carlu's famous *Give 'Em Both Barrels* and even *Women in the War: We Can't Win without Them*, produced by the U.S. Government Printing Office (figs. 10.24 and 10.25).

Works like Carlton's echo the decidedly military tone of New Deal rhetoric, expressed in ringing terms in President Roosevelt's declaration of economic war on the Depression in his 1933 inaugural address, and reflected in the choice of an eagle as the emblem of the National Recovery Act (fig. 10.26).[23] Such treatment of the worker on the eve of war intimated the notion of the interchangeability of worker and soldier. These workers are a long way from Dean Cornwell's metalworker of World War I who, in 1918, stood boldly aloof from the ranks of the battle-ready soldiers who filed past beneath him.

Fig. 10.24
Poster
***Give 'em Both Barrels*, 1941**
Designed by Jean Carlu
(French, 1900–89)
Printed by U.S. Government Printing Office, Washington, D.C.
Published by Division of Information, Office for Emergency Management, Washington, D.C.
Commercial color lithograph
30 x 20¹⁄₁₆ inches (76.2 x 51.0 cm)
Marks: obverse, printed in black, lower left corner
"JEAN/CARLU"
1993.1.11

Fig. 10.25 See Cat. 254
Poster
Women in the War – We Can't Win Without
Them, 1942
Printed by the U.S. Government Printing Office,
Washington, D.C.

Fig. 10.26 See Cat. 186
Poster
NRA Member. U.S. We Do Our Part, 1934
Designed by C.T. Coiner

NOTES

1   Although executed in a format commonly used for posters produced for the Liberty Loan and other U.S. Government campaigns during World War I, Cornwell's painting apparently was never issued as a poster. For posters on the theme of industrial support for the defense which were actually issued, see Walton Rawls, *Wake Up America! World War I and the American Poster* (New York, 1988), pp. 76, 184–5; and Libby Chenault, *Battle Lines: World War I Posters from the Boardman Gray Collection* (Chapel Hill, 1988), p. 46.

2   "Obsolete Men," *Fortune* VI, no. 6 (December 1932): 25ff.

3   The official records of the competition for the murals at the San Jose, CA, Post Office have not come to light. The Wolfsonian Collection maquette is identified by a label on its verso with the inscription: San Jose, California, Post Office no. 235.

4   On the prevalence of the farmer in German official art of the period, see Peter Adam, *Art of the Third Reich* (New York/London, 1992), pp. 129–34. On the Wehrwirtschaft see William L. Shirer, *The Rise and Fall of the Third Reich: a History of Nazi Germany* (New York, 1960), pp. 262–3.

5   For the discrepancy between Hitler's cultivation of the small businessman and farmers and his fueling of German industrialization during the 1930s, see Max H. Kele, *Nazis and Workers: National Socialist Appeals to German Labor, 1919–1933* (Chapel Hill, 1972), pp. 195ff.; Shirer, *Rise and Fall of the Third Reich,*, pp. 259–63; and George L. Mosse, ed., *Nazi Culture: Intellectual, Cultural and Social Life in the Third Reich* (New York, 1966), pp. 345–6.

6   Christiana Payne, in her *Toil and Plenty: Images of the Agricultural Landscape in England, 1780–1890* (New Haven, 1993), traces the genesis and evolution of this notion in eighteenth- and nineteenth-century Britain.

7   Ludwig Ferdinand Clauss, *Die nordische Seele: eine Einführung in die Rassenseelekunde* (Munich, 1932), pp. 19–31, quoted in Mosse, *Nazi Culture*, p. 66.

8   Ludwig Ferdinand Clauss, *Dir nordische Seele*, p. 22; George L. Mosse, *Nazi Culture*, p. xxix. The Third Reich even went so far as to reallocate urban workers to rural areas for farm work in an effort to suppress unrest among the unemployed in the cities.

9   The phrase appears as a caption to a view of a mural in the exhibition by Marcello Dudovich in the pamphlet *IV Mostra dell'Agricoltura* (Bologna, 1935), p. 20. Like the National Socialists in Germany, the Fascist regime also promoted the idea of rural life as conducive to moral and physical health. This idea had some basis in fact, given the recurring epidemics of tuberculosis in the cities.

10 While the Fascists did subsidize certain heavy industries, such as steel, automotives, electricity, and chemicals, they also kept industrial wages artificially low in an effort to curb domestic consumption. For a useful overview of Fascist economic policy, see Alexander De Grand, *Italian Fascism: Its Origins and Development* (Lincoln, NE/London, 1989), pp. 37–41. On the composition of the Italian Fascist Party and the beneficiaries of Mussolini's agricultural program, see Herman Finer, *Mussolini's Italy* (London, 1935), pp. 373–4, 527.

11 Lewis Mumford, *The Culture of Cities* (Westport, CT, 1981), quoted in Marianne Doezema, *American Realism and the Industrial Age* (Cleveland: Cleveland Museum of Art, 1980), p. 92.

12 On the publicity aims of the Farm Security Administration, see Pete Daniel, Merry Foresta, and Sally Stein, *Official Images: New Deal Photography* (Washington, D.C., 1987).

13 In 1938 Bayer left Germany for the U.S.A. in opposition to the Nazi regime.

14 *Das Wunder des Lebens Ausstellung, Berlin 1935, 23. März bis 5. Mai* (unpaginated). The indictment, implicit in this work, of industrial conditions specifically of the Weimar period was pointed out to me by John Heskett, whose comments on a preliminary draft of this essay illuminated for me a number of aspects of Third Reich labor policy.

15 For a particularly clear exposition of the purposes and rationale of the *Schönheit der Arbeit* program, see the guide to two exhibitions held in Munich in 1937, *Führer durch die Ausstellung Schönheit der Arbeit und Die Arbeit in der Kunst* (Munich, 1937), pp. 5–16.

16 Erna Lendvai-Dircksen, *Reichsautobahn Mensch und Werk: Neunundneunzig Aufnahmen* (Bayreuth, 1937), unpaginated.

17 Cecile Whiting's *Antifascism in American Art* (New Haven, 1989) admirably summarizes the quest among Communist artists of the 1920s and early 1930s for an international proletarian style.

18 I am indebted to Dennis Doordan for calling my attention to the frequently cited contrast between pre-Fascist and Fascist labor conditions in Fascist art of the 1920s and 1930s, and for many other thoughtful comments on an early draft of this essay.

19 Another drawing for another plate by Gaudenzi and the finished plate itself are in the Wolfsonian Collection. This depicts marching soldiers, the laborers' military counterparts, who are shown in an equally structured matrix.

20 For the system of *corporazione*, its rationale and structure, see Finer, *Mussolini's Italy*, pp. 502–20, and Philip V. Cannistraro, ed., *Historical Dictionary of Fascist History* (Westport, CT, 1982), p. 138.

21 Although unemployment among working women was high during the Depression, the total number of working women in the United States actually increased during this period. American Social History Project, *Who Built America? Working People and the Nation's Economy, Politics, Culture and Society. Volume Two: From the Gilded Age to the Present* (New York, 1992), pp. 326–7.

22 Mosse's *Nazi Culture*, pp. 39–47, assembles a number of texts which eloquently express the Nazis' rationalization of the role of women in the Third Reich.

23 William Leuchtenberg, "The New Deal and the Analogue of War," reprinted in *Change and Continuity in Twentieth Century America*, ed. John Braeman and others (Columbus, 1964), pp. 81–143.

Checklist of exhibition objects

By Marianne Lamonaca and Donna C. Johnson
(see Explanatory Notes for Captions and Checklist, p. 15)

1

5

Confronting Modernity

Design Reform

Cat. 1
Title pages
Principles of Decorative Design, 1873
Designed and written by Christopher Dresser
(British, 1834–1904)
Published by Cassell, Petter & Galpin, London
Multicolored inks on paper
10¹/₁₆ x 7½ inches (25.6 x 19.0 cm) page
83.2.2073

Cat. 2 [not illustrated]
Plate VIII
Studies in Design, 1874–76
Designed and written by Christopher Dresser
(British, 1834–1904)
Published by Cassell, Petter & Galpin, London
Multicolored inks on paper
16 x 11½ inches (40.6 x 29.2 cm) page
83.2.2097*

Cat. 3 See Fig. 4.08
Soup tureen, model no. 12780, 1885–86
Designed by Christopher Dresser
(British, 1834–1904)
Manufactured by Elkington & Co., Birmingham, England, 1890
Electroplated nickel silver, ebony
8 x 14½ x 8½ inches (20.3 x 36.8 x 21.6 cm)
Marks: underside, stamped "A/12780"/manufacturer's
hallmarks/Birmingham 1899 date-letter "Z/ELKINGTON & CO./
1885–86"/registration number "22866"
83.9.12a,b

Cat. 4 See Fig. 4.07
Sideboard, c. 1867
Designed by Edward William Godwin
(British, 1833–86)
Manufactured by William Watt, London, c. 1876
One of eight sideboards known to exist.
Ebonized mahogany, pine, silver electroplated hardware
73 x 100³/₈ x 20¹/₈ inches (185.4 x 255.6 x 50.9 cm)
TD1989.137.1

Cat. 5
Tea caddy with lid, model no. B2, 1881
Made by Gorham Manufacturing Co., Providence, RI
Silver, copper, bronze
4½ x 3 inches dia. (11.4 x 7.6 cm dia.)
Marks: underside, impressed "GORHAM & CO."/maker's
hallmarks/"STERLING/& OTHER METALS/B2/N"
87.1636.9.2.1a, b

Cat. 6
Furnishing textile
Dove and Rose, 1879
Designed by William Morris
(British, 1834–96) for Morris & Company, London
First woven by Alexander Morton & Co., later by Merton Abbey;
this example acquired by The Silver Studio, 1917
Silk, wool
26³/₄ x 35⁷/₈ inches (68.0 x 91.1 cm)
1993.2.4
Gift of Peter Haxworth.

Cat. 7
Tile, 1872–73
Designed by William Frend De Morgan
(British, 1839–1917)
Chelsea, England
Tin-glazed earthenware
10 x 9½ x ⁵/₈ inches (25.4 x 24.1 x 1.6 cm)
87.1326.7.1

Cat. 8 See Fig. 1.01
Sideboard, c. 1906
Designed by Ernest W. Gimson
(British, 1864–1920)
Made by Daneway Workshops, Sapperton, England
Oak, brass
68⁷/₈ x 54 x 22¼ inches (173.6 x 137.2 x 56.5 cm)
TD1992.142.1

Cat. 9 See Fig. 1.02
Cabinet, c. 1891
Designed by William Richard Lethaby
(British, 1857–1931)
Made by A. Thorn for Kenton & Co., London
Exhibited at the Arts & Crafts Exhibition, London, 1893.
Walnut, walnut veneer, marquetry of palmwood, boxwood
and ebony, ivory, brass
19⁵/₈ x 28¼ x 12½ inches (48.9 x 71.8 x 31.8 cm)
TD1992.112.1

6

7

315

Cat. 10
Bowl, 1913
Decorated by Hugh Thackeray Turner
(British, 1853–1937)
Godalming, England
Glazed porcelain
5⅞ x 14¾ inches dia. (13.6 x 37.5 cm dia.)
Marks: underside, underglaze in blue "AUG/1913/UNDER"
artist's mark "GLAZED/No 254"
TD1990.6.1

Cat. 11
Platter, 1896–97
Gilbert Leigh Marks
(British, 1861–1905)
London
Gold electroplate on sterling silver
1¼ x 17 inches dia. (3.2 x 43.2 cm dia.)
Marks: obverse, incised, inner rim "Gilbert Marks/97"; struck,
inner rim hallmarks for artist, Britannia and London + date
letter stamp for 1896–97
TD1988.31.3

Cat. 12 See Fig. 4.01
Casket
Made for H.M. Queen Victoria on the occasion
of her Diamond Jubilee, 1897
Designed and made by Gwendoline M. Buckler
(British, dates unknown)
For Della Robbia Pottery Ltd., Birkenhead,
Cheshire, England
One of two caskets made; the one presented to Queen Victoria
is in the collection of Osborne House, Isle of Wight.
Lead-glazed earthenware
21¾ x 18⅛ inches dia. (55.3 x 46.4 cm dia.)
Marks: underside of base, etched underglaze "D" + ship mark +
"R"; impressed "<u>D</u>"; underside of lid, etched "VR/1837–97/
Designed and executed by G M Buckler"; interior bottom of
base, etched underglaze flower mark/"POTTERY"/flower mark
+ "DELLA" + ship mark + "ROBBIA" + flower mark/
"BIRKENHEAD"/flower mark
TD1989.49.3a,b

Cat. 13
Color plate
Christ Church (1902–04; W. & S. Owen, architects)
Port Sunlight: A Record of its Artistic & Pictorial
Aspect, c. 1916
Written by Hon. T. Raffles Davison, A.R.I.B.A.
(British, dates unknown)
Published by B.T. Batsford Ltd., London
Multicolored inks on paper
9½ x 7¼ inches (24.2 x 18.4 cm) page
XC1993.743

Cat. 14 See Fig. 4.06
Chandelier, c. 1909
Designed by William Arthur Smith Benson
(British, 1854–1924)
Made by W.A.S. Benson & Co., London
Brass, copper, cordage
28½ x 26½ inches dia. (72.4 x 67.3 cm dia.)
86.13.44

10

11

13

Cat. 15
Hardware display case, c. 1902
Made by C.E. Thompson
(British, dates unknown)
and attributed to
Richard Llewellyn Benson Rathbone
(British, 1864–1939)
Liverpool or London
Brass, copper, iron, pewter, enamel, wood, non-precious stones
19⅝ x 13⅝ x 2¼ inches (48.9 x 33.7 x 5.7 cm)
Marks: impressed on one hinge "THOMPSON 1902"
85.9.26

Cat. 16
Fireplace surround
From the Patrick King residence, now King-Nash
House, Chicago, IL, 1901
Designed by George Washington Maher
(American, 1864–1926)
Maker attributed to Louis J. Millet
(American, 1855–1923)
Chicago, IL
Foil-backed glass, stained glass
39¾ x 74¾ x 2 inches (101.0 x 189.9 x 5.1 cm)
87.746.17.1

Cat. 17
Page 14
The Great Wonder: A Vision of the Apocalypse,
c. 1924
Violet Oakley
(American, 1874–1961)
Philadelphia, PA
This book was made to accompany a seven-panel mural,
designed by Oakley and commissioned by Louise Lawrence
Meigs, for the living room of the Alumnae House at Vassar
College, Poughkeepsie, NY, dedicated June 1924.
Watercolor and ink on vellum
21¼ x 14½ inches (54.1 x 36.8 cm) page
Marks: cover, obverse, engraved in metal, intertwined
monogram "BFH"
Inscription: printed in black and red "Presented to the Alumnae
house/of Vassar College in the/name of the Class of 1891/in
loving memory of/Hester Calowell Oakley Ward"
XC1993.73***

Cat. 18
Shelf clock, c. 1910
Designed by Peter Heinrich Hansen
(American, b. Germany, 1880–1947)
Made by L. & J.G. Stickley Inc., Fayetteville, NY
Oak, copper-plate, clock works
22⅛ x 16⅛ x 6½ inches (56.2 x 41.0 x 16.5 cm)
Marks: obverse, clock face, incised maker's logo of broken
cube at center and at 12, 3, 6 and 9 o'clock positions
TD1988.103.1

15

16

17

18

19

20

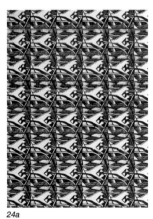

24a

Cat. 19
Secretary, 1901
Designed by Alberto Issel
(Italian, 1848–1926)
Manufactured by Alberto Issel Workshop, Genoa, Italy
Oak, silver electroplate on electro-formed copper
and wrought brass, velveteen, embossed and gilded leather,
almond shells, paint
52¼ x 32½ x 19½ inches (132.7 x 82.6 x 49.5 cm)
Marks: underside of drawer, stenciled in white "AlBERTO/ISSEL/
GENOVA"; underside, stenciled in black "10" + written in black "5"
88.32.11.16.1

Cat. 20
Chair, 1895
Designed by Hendrik Petrus Berlage
(Dutch, 1856–1934)
Amsterdam
Originally designed for a guestroom of the P. van Vlissingen
residence, Helmond, Netherlands.
Wood, brass, cane, steel screws
36½ x 19½ x 22¾ inches (92.7 x 49.5 x 57.8 cm)
TD1991.152.2

Cat. 21   See Fig. 3.08
a) Cover, 1894
Kunst en samenleving. naar Walter Crane . . .
(translation of *Claims of Decorative Art* by
Walter Crane [British, 1845–1915])
Designed by Gerrit Willem Dijsselhof
(Dutch, 1866–1924)
Translated by Jan P. Veth (Dutch, 1864–1925)
Printed by Joh. Enschedé en Zonen, Haarlem, Netherlands
Published by Scheltema en Holkema's Boekhandel,
Amsterdam, 1903
Ink on paper
9 x 7½ x 1 inches (22.9 x 19.4 x 2.5 cm)
XA1993.26

b) Book wrapper [not illustrated]
***Kunst en samenleving.*, c. 1894**
Gerrit Willem Dijsselhof
(Dutch, 1866–1924)
Haarlem, Netherlands
Ink on paper
13½ x 18½ inches (34.3 x 47.0 cm)
XA1993.293

Cat. 22   See Fig. 3.10
Cover
***De Stille Kracht* (The Hidden Force)**
by Louis Couperus
(Dutch, 1863–1923), **1900**
Designed by Joris Johannes Christian Lebeau
(Dutch, 1878–1945)
Printed by G.J. Thieme, Nijmegen, Netherlands
Published by L.J. Veen, Amsterdam
Batik made by Uiterwijk & Co., Batikwerken, Apeldoorn and
The Hague, Netherlands
Binding by J. Brandt & Zoon Boekbinderij, Amsterdam
Batik and gilding on cotton, paperboard
8⅜ x 6¾ x 1½ inches (21.0 x 17.2 x 3.8 cm)
XA1993.8.1

Cat. 23   See Fig. 3.01
Cover
Rembrandt: 26 Photogravures naar de Beste
Schilderijen der Tentoonstellingen te Londen
Jan.–Febr. 1899 en Amsterdam . . .
by C. Hofstede de Groot
(Dutch, 1860–1930), **1901**
Designed by Carel Adolph Lion Cachet
(Dutch, 1864–1945)
Made by Tom Poggenbeek (Dutch, 1872–1942)
Published by Scheltema en Holkema's Boekhandel, Amsterdam
Number 5 in an edition of 25 printed on japonoise paper.
Ink and gold leaf batik on parchment
27 x 21½ x 1½ inches (66.6 x 54.6 x 3.8 cm)
Marks: obverse, printed in gold, five Rembrandt monograms
"RR"; reverse, printed in gold, center monogram "NMvG"
surrounded by four publisher's monograms "SHB"
TD1990.340.132***

Cat. 24
A Specimen Book of Pattern Papers
***designed for & in use at the Curwen Press*, 1928**
Published by Fleuron Ltd., London
Number 151 in an edition of 220.
Multicolored inks on paper, cloth, cardboard
12 x 9 inches (30.5 x 22.8 cm) page
85.2.35

a) Pattern paper, page 23
b) Pattern paper, page 22 [not illustrated]
Designed by Paul Nash
(British, 1889–1946)

Cat. 25   See Fig. 4.16
Print, "The Squire's Tale," from *The Canterbury*
***Tales*, 1930**
Arthur Eric Rowton Gill
(British, 1882–1940)
London
Wood engraving
Proof of block for *The Canterbury Tales* (Golden Cockerel
Press, 1929–31), vol. IV, p.1.
11 x 8¹/₂₅ inches (28.0 x 20.4 cm)
84.4.392

Cat. 26   See Fig. 4.17
Blanket chest, design no. 503, 1927
Designed by Gordon Russell
(British, 1892–1980)
Made by S.G. Gilbert and D. Keen for Russell Workshops, Ltd.,
Broadway, Worcs., England
English oak, wrought iron
28¼ x 65¼ x 13¼ inches (71.8 x 165.7 x 33.7 cm)
Marks: underside, paper label printed in black, "The RUSSELL
WORKSHOPS/BROADWAY. WORCS/. . ./design No./. . ./
Designer: Gordon Russell/Foreman: Edgar Turner/Cabinet
Maker:/Metal Worker:/Timber used:/Date"; variables written in
black ink "503/S G Gilbert/D. Keen/English oak/20/6/27"
TD1991.69.6

Romantic Nationalism

Cat. 27 *See Fig. 1.12*
Design drawing
Bedroom for Villa Bobrinsky
(Gesellius, Lindgren, Saarinen, architects;
unknown if built), Moscow, 1903
Eliel Saarinen
(Finnish, 1873–1950)
Helsinki
Watercolor and ink on paperboard
7⅛ x 8½ inches (18.1 x 21.6 cm)
Marks: obverse, in ink, bottom right "Eliel Saarinen 1903"
TD1992.163.1

Cat. 28 *See Fig. 1.10*
Print
Saarinen's living room, Hvitträsk (1901–03;
Gesellius, Lindgren, Saarinen, architects),
Kirkkonummi, near Helsinki, c.1905
Eliel Saarinen
(Finnish, 1873–1950)
Helsinki
Lithograph
21⅞ x 17⅝ inches (55.6 x 44.8 cm)
Marks: obverse, printed, lower right "HVITTRASK/E. Saarinen"
TD1993.154.1

Cat. 29 *See Fig. 1.04*
Armchair, c.1899
Lars Trondsen Kinsarvik
(Norwegian, 1846–1925)
Hardanger, Norway
Painted wood
37 x 25⅜ x 22¼ inches (94.0 x 64.5 x 56.5 cm)
TD1994.204.4

Cat. 30 *See Fig. 1.06*
Tapestry
The Daughters of the Northern Lights
***(Aurora Borealis)* or *The Suitors*, 1895**
Designed by Gerhard Munthe
(Norwegian, 1849–1929)
Made by Nini Stoltenberg (Norwegian, 1877–1968), Oslo, 1920–30
Based on a Munthe watercolor shown at the Black and White Exhibition, Kristiania (now Oslo), 1893. First commissioned as a tapestry by the Museum für Kunst und Gewerbe, Hamburg, 1895; executed 1896.
Cotton, wool
51 x 64½ inches (129.5 x 163.8 cm)
Marks: obverse, woven in brown, lower right "G MUNTHE"; lower left "NS"
TD1993.132.1

Cat. 31
Design drawing
***Magyar Népi Müveszetek Háza* (Museum of**
Hungarian Folk Art), 1937
Gyula Tálos
(Hungarian, 1887–1975)
Budapest
Ink, gouache, graphite and watercolor on paper
20⅛ x 51½ inches (51.1 x 130.8 cm)
Marks: obverse, signed, lower right corner artist's mark / "938/XII 28"; in black ink, lower left corner "A MAGYAR/NÉPI MÜVESZETEK/HÁZAMAGYAR/TANULMANY"
TD1991.201.48

Cat. 32 *See Fig. 1.15*
Page 4
"He had heard the last girl's pledge/Standing
hid behind the hedge" (translation), *Skazka*
***otsare Saltane* (The Tale of Tsar Saltan) by**
Aleksander Sergeyevich Pushkin
(Russian, 1799–1837), **1905**
Illustrated by Ivan Yakovlevich Bilibin
(Russian, 1876–1942)
Published by the Department for the Production of State Documents, St. Petersburg
Multicolored inks on paper
10¹⁄₁₆ x 12¹³⁄₁₆ (25.5 x 32.8 cm) page
Marks: obverse, printed in black, bottom right artist's signature + "1905"
XB1990.1888

Cat. 33 *See Fig. 1.13*
Mirror, 1903
Made by the furniture workshop at the
Talashkino artists' colony, near Smolensk, Russia
Wood, silvered glass, paint
15⅜ x 11⅛ x 3 inches (38.5 x 28.3 x 7.6 cm)
Marks: reverse, impressed, upper left corner furniture workshop mark of a firebird/"1903"; in ink, "N182"
XX1990.1283

Cat. 34
Teacart, for the *Carretto Siciliano* (Sicilian Cart)
line, 1906
Designed by Ernesto Basile
(Italian, 1857–1932)
Made by Ducrot, Palermo, Sicily, 1906 – c.1925
Polychromed beech, plate glass, brass hardware
29³⁄₁₆ x 44¼ x 22¼ inches (74.1 x 104.8 x 56.5 cm)
84.11.4.1

Cat. 35
Curtain valance (detail), c.1905
Rome(?), Italy
Linen, cotton
21½ x 91¾ inches (54.6 x 233.1 cm)
XX1993.27.5

Cat. 36 *See Fig. 7.09*
Cabinet
Now known as "La Notte" (The Night), 1925
Designed by Duilio Cambellotti
(Italian, 1876–1960)
Rome
Exhibited at Seconda Mostra Internazionale delle Arti Decorative, Monza, 1925.
Walnut, ivory, ebony
21⅔ x 27⁶⁄₁₁ x 15¾ inches (55.0 x 70.0 x 40.0 cm)
GX1993.209

Cat. 37 *See Fig. 2.21*
Armchair, model no. 864, 1908
Designed by Heinrich Vogeler
(German, 1872–1942)
Made by Worpsweder Werkstätte, Worpswede
bei Bremen, Germany
Painted oak, rush
41½ x 23¾ x 17⅛ inches (105.4 x 60.3 x 43.5 cm)
Marks: reverse, incised, back splat "H" + maker's mark + "V/W"
TD1990.268.1

Cat. 38 *See Fig. 2.17*
Stein, model no. 1757, 1902
Designed by Richard Riemerschmid
(German, 1868–1957)
Made by Reinhold Merkelbach, Höhr-Grenzhausen, Rhineland, Germany, c.1903
Salt-glazed stoneware, pewter
6 x 5 x 4 inches (15.2 x 12.7 x 10.2 cm)
Marks: handle, impressed, top left trumpet mark + "0.5L"; underside, impressed "1757/R"
TD1990.298.7

Cat. 39
Portfolio
Ausgeführte Bauten und Entwürfe
(Executed Buildings and Sketches), 1910
Frank Lloyd Wright, architect
(American, 1867–1959)
Published by Ernst Wasmuth, Berlin
Ink on paper
15⅝ x 25⅜ inches (39.5 x 64.4 cm)
XC1991.371***

a) Plate XXXI, *Aussenansicht vom Städtischen Wohnhause für Frau* (Exterior view of city dwelling for Frau Dana) (The Susan Lawrence Dana House, Springfield, IL, 1902–04)
Marks: obverse, in high relief, lower left artist's logo + "FRANK LLOYD WRIGHT"

b) Plate XXXIb, *Inneres des Festsaales für Frau Dana* (Interior of banquet room for Frau Dana) (The Susan Lawrence Dana House, Springfield, IL, 1902–04)
[not illustrated]
Marks: obverse, in high relief, upper left artist's logo + "FRANK LLOYD WRIGHT"

Cat. 40
Drawing
***Alcazar Hotel* (1886–88; James Merven Carrère**
and Thomas Hastings, architects; commissioned
by Henry Flagler), now Lightner Museum, St.
Augustine, FL, 1887
Robert F. Blum
(American, 1857–1903)
New York
Ink on paper
30 x 50 inches (76.2 x 127.1 cm)
Marks: obverse, in ink, bottom right "BLUM/ '87"
Inscription: obverse, center on image "ALCAZAR BUILT IN/ THE YEAR OF OUR/ LORD MDCCCLXXXVIII"
TD1993.140

31

34

35

39

40

41

42

43

44

Nature and the New Art

Cat. 41
Portfolio
Le Castel Béranger: oeuvre de Hector Guimard,
1898
Hector Guimard, architect
(French, 1867–1942)
Published by Librairie Rouam et Cie., Paris
Offset lithograph
Marks: obverse, printed, lower right corner artist's
monogram "HG"
XB1990.1480**/c.1

a) Title page
12⅜ x 17⅛ inches (31.4 x 43.5 cm)
Inscription: obverse, in ink, bottom right "Hommage
respectueux/ de l'auteur/ Hector Guimard"

b) Plate 4, *Entrée principale de l'immeuble* (Main entrance)
[not Illustrated]
17 x 12⁵⁄₁₆ inches (43.1 x 31.2 cm)

Cat. 42
Theater seats
For the Humbert de Romans Concert Hall, Paris,
1897–1901
Designed by Hector Guimard
(French, 1867–1942)
Paris
Cast iron, leatherette, mahogany
36¼ x 48 x 14 inches (92.1 x 121.9 x 35.6 cm)
Inscription: obverse, embossed, chair back monogram "HR"
TD1994.144.1

Cat. 43
Poster
Österreich auf der Weltausstellung Paris 1900
(Austria at the World's Fair . . .), 1900
Designed by Alphonse Mucha
(Czech, 1860–1939)
Published by S. Czeiger, Vienna
Commercial color lithograph
40⅛ x 28⅛ inches (101.9 x 71.4 cm)
Marks: obverse, printed in black, lower left artist's signature
"Mucha/Paris"
TD1990.242.1

Cat. 44
Centerpiece
Presented to Prince and Princess Albert of
Belgium, 1900
Designed by Philippe Wolfers
(Belgian, 1858–1929)
Manufactured by Wolfers Frères, Brussels
Silver
10½ x 12½ inches dia. (26.7 x 31.8 cm dia.)
Marks: underside, impressed "800" in a square and 3 stars in a
triangle
Inscription: "ALL•AA•RR•LE PRINCE ET PRINCESSE/ALBERT
de BELGIQUE/LES MEMBRES DE LA COMMISSION DE LA
BOURSE DE BRUXELLES/. . ./2 OCTOBER 1900"
TD1990.265.1

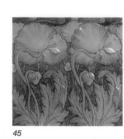

45

46

48

49

52

Cat. 45
Tile, 1898–1902
Galileo Chini
(Italian, 1873–1956)
Made by Arte Della Ceramica, Florence
Tin-glazed earthenware
11½ x 11⅜ x ⅞ inches (29.2 x 28.3 x 2.2 cm)
Marks: reverse, underglaze in blue company mark "DACF";
underglaze in yellow "C"
87.1491.7.1

Cat. 46
Side chair, 1900
Designed by Eugenio Quarti
(Italian, 1867–1929)
Made by Eugenio Quarti Workshop, Milan
Retailed by James Phillips & Sons Ltd., Bristol, England
Mahogany, mother-of-pearl, bronze, copper, silver
36½ x 13 x 14 inches (92.7 x 33.0 x 35.6 cm)
Marks: underside, printed on paper label, rear seat stile
"JAMES/PHILLIPS/& SONS LTD/UNION ST/BRISTOL"
84.11.10.1

Cat. 47   See Fig. 6.08
Incense burners, c. 1925
Modesto Demenego (Italian, 1896–1982)
and Ugo Demenego (Italian, 1900–90)
Cortina d'Ampezzo, Italy
Wrought iron
42½ x 12½ inches dia. ea. (108.0 x 31.8 cm dia. ea.)
Marks: underside on base, incised "M.U.D."
84.9.11.1-2

Cat. 48
Stool, c. 1890
Designed by Carlo Bugatti
(Italian, 1856–1940)
Made by Carlo Bugatti Workshop, Milan
Wood, copper, parchment
17¼ x 41 x 16 inches (48.3 x 104.1 x 40.6 cm)
83.11.11

Cat. 49
Secretary, 1903
Designed by Ernesto Basile
(Italian, 1857–1932)
Metalwork by Antonio Ugo (Italian, 1870–1950)
Painted interior decoration by Ettore de Maria Bergler
(Italian, 1851–1938)
Made by Ducrot, Palermo, Sicily
Exhibited at the V Esposizione Internazionale d'Arte, Venice, 1903.
Mahogany, bronze, leather, paint
67 x 52 x 18½ inches (170.2 x 132.1 x 47.0 cm)
Marks: reverse of drop leaf, printed on inlaid celluloid label,
rear center "DUCROT/ PALERMO"
84.11.17

Cat. 50   See Fig. 1.11
Ryijy rug
***Ruusu*, 1904**
Designed by Eliel Saarinen
(Finnish, 1873–1950)
Made by Suomen Käsityön Ystävät (Friends of Finnish
Handicraft), Helsinki, for the Rose Boudoir, Friends of Finnish
Handicraft's twenty-fifth anniversary exhibition, Helsinki, 1904
Cotton, wool
120 x 73½ inches (304.8 x 186.7 cm)
TD1989.49.1

Cat. 51   See Fig. 2.13
Clock
**From the Dr. Rosenberger residence, Berlin,
c. 1902–05**
Designed by August Endell
(German, 1871–1925)
Berlin
Stained oak, aluminum leaf, clock works
80 x 37¼ x 19¼ inches (203.2 x 94.6 x 48.9 cm)
Marks: reverse, stamped in purple, proper left center illegible
mark
TD1989.82.4

Cat. 52
***January*, from a 12-month calendar, 1898**
Theodoor Willem Nieuwenhuis
(Dutch, 1866–1951)
Printed by L. Kuipers, Amsterdam
Published by Scheltema en Holkema's Boekhandel, Amsterdam
Multicolored inks on paper
14⅛ x 11¼ inches ea. (36.0 x 28.4 cm ea.)
Marks: obverse, printed in black, lower left artist's mark of
overlapping "TN"
TD1989.317.132
Note: Additional months also in exhibition [not illustrated]

Cat. 53   See Fig. 3.15
Door
**From the study of the Ferdinand Kranenburg
residence, Keizersgracht, Amsterdam, c. 1900**
Designed by Theodoor Willem Nieuwenhuis
(Dutch, 1866–1951)
Manufactured by E.J. van Wisselingh & Co., Amsterdam
Oak, fruitwood, brass hardware, gold paint
85 x 40½ x 4⅜ inches (215.9 x 102.2 x 10.5 cm)
TD1990.235.1

Cat. 54   See Fig. 3.11
Napkin, no. 505, *Vlinder* (Butterfly), c. 1906
Designed by Joris Johannes Christian Lebeau
(Dutch, 1878–1945)
Made by E.J.F. van Dissel en Zonen, Eindhoven, Netherlands,
c. 1906–c. 1939
Linen
26¾ x 27¼ inches (68.0 x 69.2 cm)
Inscription: obverse, embroidered in one corner "D"
TD1991.152.4

Cat. 55   See Fig. 3.18
Fireplace
**From the boudoir of the Th. G. Dentz von Schaick
residence, Frederiksplein, Amsterdam,
c. 1911–12**
Designed by Carel Adolph Lion Cachet
(Dutch, 1864–1945)
Relief designed by Lambertus Zijl
(Dutch, 1866–1947)
Amsterdam
Wrought iron, copper, cast and sheet iron firebox
29⁸⁄₁₁ x 29⅝ x 9¼ inches (75.7 x 75.3 x 23.5 cm)
TD1992.23.1a-g

Art and Industry

Cat. 56 *See Fig. 3.26*

Platter, model no. 25, commemorating the twenty-fifth year of the reign of Queen Wilhelmina, 1923
Designed by Theodorus Adriaan Christiaan Colenbrander
(Dutch, 1841–1930)
Decorated by Antoon Muller (Dutch, b. 1899)
Made by Plateelbakkerij Ram, Arnhem, Netherlands, 1924
Number 43 in an edition of 100.
Lead-glazed earthenware
1¾ x 16½ inches dia. (4.5 x 41.9 cm dia.)
Marks: underside, printed, underglaze in black "1898–6 September–1923/RAM" within red circle/"ARNHEM/COLENBRANDER/,RAM'"/mark of ram's head/"ARNHEM-HOLLAND/25/43–100"/decorator's mark "am"/year mark "C.";
impressed "25"
XX1990.1147

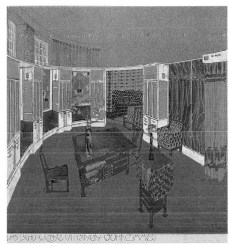

57

61

Cat. 57

a) Plate XI
Das Blau-Weisse-Vitrinen Wohnzimmer
(The Blue-White Vitrine Living Room)
Leopold Bauer, architect
(Austrian, 1872–1938), **1902**
Das Haus eines Kunst-Freundes: ein Entwurf in Zwölf Tafeln von Leopold Bauer (The House of an Art Lover: One plan in twelve plates by Leopold Bauer)
Printed by Emil Hochdanz, Stuttgart, Germany
Published by Alexander Koch, Darmstadt, Germany
Multicolored inks on paper
20⅞ x 15⅝ inches (53.0 x 39.6 cm)
Marks: obverse, printed in black, lower right artist's mark "LD" + "1902"
XC1991.369***

b) Plate IX *(See Fig. 2.11)*
Music Room
Mackay Hugh Baillie Scott, architect
(English, 1865–1945), **1902**
Meister der Innen-Kunst: Haus eines Kunst-Freundes (Masters of Interior Decoration: House of an Art Lover)
Edited by Hermann Muthesius (German, 1861–1927)
Printed by Emil Hochdanz, Stuttgart, Germany
Published by Alexander Koch, Darmstadt, Germany
Multicolored inks on paper
15⅝ x 20⅞ inches (39.6 x 53.0 cm)
XC1991.368***

c) Plate VII *(See Fig. 2.12)*
Empfangs Raum und Musik Zimmer
(Reception Hall and Music Room)
Charles Rennie Mackintosh, architect
(Scottish, 1868–1928), **1901**
Panels designed by Margaret MacDonald Mackintosh (Scottish, 1865–1933)
Charles Rennie Mackintosh, Glasgow: Haus eines Kunst-Freundes (. . . House of an Art Lover), 1902
Edited by Hermann Muthesius (German, 1861–1927)
Printed by Emil Hochdanz, Stuttgart, Germany
Published by Alexander Koch, Darmstadt, Germany
Multicolored inks on paper
15⅝ x 20⅞ inches (39.6 x 53.0 cm)
Marks: obverse, printed in brown, lower right "CHARLES/RENNIE/MACKINTOSH/1901"
XC1991.370***

Cat. 58 *See Fig. 9.17*
Poster
Deutsche Kunst und Dekoration, **1911**
Designed by Ludwig Hohlwein
(German, 1874–1949)
Printed by G. Schuh & Cie., Munich
Published by Vereinigte Druckereien & Kunstanstalten G.m.b.H., Munich
Commercial color lithograph
20⅝ x 9⅞ inches (52.4 x 25.1 cm)
Marks: obverse, printed in black, upper left corner "LUDWIG HOHLWEIN"
TD1991.146.4

Cat. 59 *See Fig. 2.05*
Poster
Darmstadt. Ein Dokument deutscher Kunst. Die Ausstellung der Künstlerkolonie. Mai–Okt. 1901. **(Darmstadt. A Document of German Art. Exhibition of the Artists' Colony . . .), 1901**
Designed by Peter Behrens
(German, 1868–1940)
Printed by Jos. Scholz, Mainz, Germany
Commercial color lithograph
50 x 17⁵⁄₁₆ inches (127.0 x 44.0 cm)
Marks: obverse, printed in gray, lower left corner designer's mark "PB" within square
TD1991.134.2

Cat. 60 *See Fig. 2.07*
Armchair
From the dining room of the Peter Behrens residence, Darmstadt artists' colony, 1900
Designed by Peter Behrens
(German, 1868–1940)
Made by Hofmöbelfabrik J.D. Heymann, Hamburg, Germany
Wood, leather, silverplated brass tacks, paint
41¼ x 22⅜ x 24¼ inches (104.8 x 56.8 x 61.6 cm)
Marks: underside, printed in black, rear seat splat "11257"
TD1988.36.1

Cat. 61
Portfolio
Ideen von Olbrich, Zweite Auflage
(Ideas of Olbrich, Second Edition), 1900
Designed and written by Joseph Maria Olbrich
(German, 1867–1908)
Printed by H.F. Jütte, Kunstanstalt, Leipzig, Germany
Published by Baumgärtners Buchhandlung, Leipzig, Germany, 1904
Multicolored inks on paper
7⁹⁄₁₆ x 9 inches ea. (19.2 x 22.7 cm ea.)
XB1990.19

a) Frontispiece
Marks: obverse, printed in black, lower left of image "OLBRICH"

b) Plate R, *Studie zu Einem Oberlicht* (Study for a skylight)
[not illustrated]

c) Plate Z, *Zinnkanne Studie* (Study for a pewter pitcher)
[not illustrated]

d) Plate a, *Studie für Gruppenhaus Facaden Darmstadt, Architektur Skizze* (Study for the facade of a multiple dwelling . . .)
[not illustrated]
Marks: obverse, printed in black, lower left artist's mark

Cat. 62 *See Fig. 2.08*
Toilette towel, c. 1904
Designed by Joseph Maria Olbrich
(German, 1867–1908)
Made by Joseph Stade, Darmstadt, Germany
Cotton
27½ x 22⅜ inches (69.9 x 56.8 cm)
Inscription: obverse, woven in red, bottom center "G.W./ 24"
TD1991.205.11

Cat. 63 See Fig. 2.09
Sideboard, c. 1902
From the "Hessisches Zimmer"
(also known as the "Blaues Zimmer"),
Prima Esposizione Internazionale d'Arte
Decorativa Moderna, Turin, c. 1902
Designed by Joseph Maria Olbrich
(German, 1867–1908)
Made by Julius Glückert, Darmstadt, Germany
Oak, brass, copper, glass
78³/₄ x 23⁷/₁₁ x 86⁷/₁₁ inches (200.0 x 60.0 x 220.0 cm)
GX1993.46a-e

Cat. 64
Flatware and ladle, 1901
Designed by Joseph Maria Olbrich
(German, 1867–1908)
Manufactured by C.B. Schröder, Alfenidewaren-Fabrik,
Düsseldorf, Germany
Alpacca (electroplated nickel silver)

a) Fish knife
9¹/₄ x 1¹/₈ x ¹/₂ inches (23.5 x 2.9 x 1.3 cm)
Marks: handle, obverse, in high relief designer's monogram;
reverse, struck "CBS 60"
TD1992.9.3.1

b) Fish fork
7¹/₄ x ⁷/₈ x ³/₄ inches (18.4 x 2.2 x 1.9 cm)
Marks: handle, obverse, in high relief designer's monogram;
reverse, struck "CBS 60"
TD1992.9.1.1

c) Ladle
13 x 3 x 3⁵/₈ inches dia. (33.0 x 7.6 x 5.2 cm dia.)
Marks: handle, obverse, in high relief designer's monogram;
reverse, struck "CBS 90"
TD1990.95.2

Cat. 65 See Fig. 2.10
Title pages
***Also sprach Zarathustra* (Thus spoke**
Zarathustra) by Friedrich Nietzsche
(German, 1844–1900), **1908**
Designed by Henry Clemens van de Velde
(Belgian, 1863–1957)
and Georges Lemmen
(Belgian, 1865–1957)
Printed by Offizin W. Drugulin, Leipzig, Germany
Published by Insel-Verlag, Leipzig, Germany
One in an edition of 530.
Gilded and polychromed vellum
14³/₄ x 20¹/₈ inches (37.7 x 51.8 cm)
XB1990.94

Cat. 66
Flatware, 1902
Designed by Henry Clemens van de Velde
(Belgian, 1863–1957)
Made by Koch & Bergfeld, Bremen, Germany for Theodor
Müller, Weimar, Germany
Design originally commissioned by State of Weimar as a
wedding present for Grand Duke of Saxe-Weimar; later put into
production and sold in other countries including Russia.
Silver
Marks: blade, reverse, struck Russian silver-standard mark
"84"/designer's mark/unidentified mark

a) Fish knife
8¹/₄ x 1¹/₄ x ³/₈ inches (21.0 x 3.2 x 1.0 cm)
XX1989.239

b) Fish fork
7¹/₄ x 1 x ³/₄ inches (18.4 x 2.5 x 1.9 cm)
XX1989.247

Cat. 67
Urn, 1911–12
Designed by Karl Klaus
(Austrian, b. 1889)
Manufactured by Ernst Wahliss, Turn-Teplitz, Germany and
Vienna, Austria
Lead-glazed earthenware, silver
32¹/₂ x 8⁵/₈ inches dia. (82.6 x 21.0 cm dia.)
Marks: underside, stamped overglaze "SERAPIS-FAYENCE/
WAHLISS"; underglaze in gold "F.9782 D.9810"; impressed
"9782"
TD1993.148.1

Cat. 68
Punch bowl, model no. 2468, *Bowle*, c. 1906
Made by Reinhold Merkelbach, Höhr-Grenzhausen, Germany
Salt-glazed stoneware
10⁵/₈ x 9¹/₂ inches dia. (26.0 x 24.1 cm dia.)
Marks: underside, impressed "REINHOLD/MERKELBACH/
GRENZHAUSEN/2468"/maker's mark "D3RW/H"
86.7.49a,b

Cat. 69
Laces, c. 1918
Manufactured and retailed by Wiener Werkstätte,
Vienna
Cotton

a) Lace, *Chloe* (4/22004)
10⁷/₈ x 7⁵/₈ inches (27.6 x 19.4 cm)
1994.36.1

b) Lace doily (4/1005) [not illustrated]
23¹/₂ x 19¹/₂ inches (59.7 x 49.5 cm)
1994.33.1

c) Lace doily (4/1006) [not illustrated]
23¹/₂ x 19¹/₂ inches (59.7 x 49.5 cm)
1994.33.2

Cat. 70
Furnishing textile
***Rosenkavalier*, c. 1911–12**
Designed by Dagobert Peche
(Austrian, 1887–1923)
Manufactured and retailed by Wiener Werkstätte,
Vienna
Printed silk
15¹/₄ x 37 inches (38.7 x 94.0 cm)
1994.37.1

64a and b

64c

66

68

67

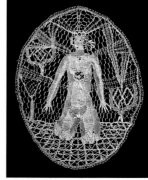

69a

70

71a

72

73

78

Cat. 71 [not exhibited in Miami]
Furnishing textiles
Manufactured by Wiener Werkstätte, Vienna
Printed silk

a) *Lianen* **(Liane), 1910–12**
Designed by Franz von Zülow
(Austrian, 1883–1963)
12⅝ x 8⅛ inches (32.1 x 20.6 cm)
1994.11.1

b) *Hecht* **(Pike), 1910–11** [not illustrated]
Designed by Carl Otto Czeschka
(Austrian, 1878–1960)
9¼ x 8¼ inches (23.5 x 21.0 cm)
1994.18.2

Cat. 72
Chaise, model no. 2, c. 1904
Manufactured by Gebrüder Thonet, Vienna
Beech, wicker
39½ x 20½ x 64½ inches (100.3 x 52.1 x 163.8 cm)
Marks: reverse of back splat, printed on paper label,
manufacturer's monogram + "THONET" + manufacturer's
monogram
1994.6.1
Gift of Roberto Schezen, Miami.

Cat. 73
Poster
II. Kraft- und Arbeits-Maschinen-Ausstellung,
München 1898 **(Second Exhibition of Engines**
and Machinery . . .), 1898
Designed by Adolf Münzer
(German, 1870–1953)
Printed by Karl Stücker's Kunstanstalt, Munich
Commercial color lithograph
43¹/₁₆ x 31¹/₁₆ inches (110.0 x 89.1 cm)
Marks: obverse, printed in black, lower right corner "AM/97"
TD1990.330.7

Cat. 74 See Fig. 2.02
Vitrine cabinet, model no. 2616, 1903–04
Designed by Bruno Paul
(German, 1874–1968)
Made by Vereinigte Werkstätten für Kunst im Handwerk,
Munich
Sycamore, sycamore veneer, oak, marquetry of mahogany
and sycamore, glass, brass
71 x 38½ x 16⅜ inches (180.3 x 97.8 x 41.0 cm)
Marks: reverse, impressed, contor "1108" + "VW" within
rectangle + "2616" + "VW" within rectangle + "16346" + "VW"
within rectangle
TD1001.205.0a–e

Cat. 75 See Fig. 2.03
Side chair, model no. 1555
From the Hermann Obrist residence, Munich,
1899
Designed by Richard Riemerschmid
(German, 1868–1957)
Made by Vereinigte Werkstätten für Kunst im Handwerk,
Munich
Elm, cane
34 x 18¼ x 20½ inches (86.4 x 46.4 x 52.1 cm)
XX1990.795

Cat. 76 See Fig. 2.23
Side chair, model no. 137/2, 1907–08
Designed by Richard Riemerschmid
(German, 1868–1957)
Made by Dresden Werkstätten für Handwerkskunst,
Dresden, Germany
Walnut
35 x 18 x 20 inches (88.9 x 45.7 x 50.8 cm)
TD1993.148.2

Cat. 77 See Fig. 2.16
Side chair, 1902–03
Designed by Peter Behrens
(German, 1868–1940)
Made by Anton Blüggel, Möbelschreinerei, Berlin
Exhibited originally at the Ausstellung für moderne
Wohnungskunst, Wertheim Department Store, Berlin, 1902;
later put into production.
40 x 17⅞ x 17⅞ inches (101.6 x 33.3 x 33.3 cm)
TD1993.44.2

Cat. 78
Wineglass
Aegir, **c. 1901–05**
Designed by Peter Behrens
(German, 1868–1940)
Made by Rheinische Glashütten Aktien-Gesellschaft,
Köln-Ehrenfeld, Germany
Glass
7⅛ x 3¼ inches dia. (18.1 x 8.3 cm dia.)
TD1992.64.3

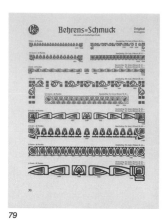

79

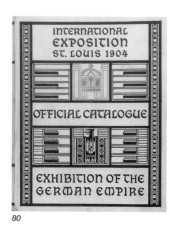

80

83

84

New Directions

Cat. 79
Page 30
Behrens: Schrift und Zierat **(Behrens: Type and**
Ornament), c. 1902
Designed by Peter Behrens
(German, 1868–1940)
Published by Rudhard'sche Giekerei, Offenbach am Main,
Germany
Blue and green inks on paper
11 x 8½ inches (27.9 x 21.5 cm) page
TD1989.116.14

Cat. 80
Cover
International Exposition, St. Louis:
1904 Official Catalogue of the Exhibition
of the German Empire, **1904**
Designed by Peter Behrens
(German, 1868–1940)
Published by Georg Stilke, Berlin
Number 101 in an edition of 300.
Black and gold inks on morocco
9⅜ x 7½ x 1¾ inches (23.8 x 19.0 x 4.3 cm)
85.2.174

Cat. 81   *See Fig. 2.27*
Electric kettle, model no. 3599, 1909
Designed by Peter Behrens
(German, 1868–1940)
Manufactured by Allgemeine Elektricitäts–Gesellschaft (AEG),
Berlin
Brass, wicker
8 x 7⅜ x 5⅞ inches (20.3 x 18.7 x 14.9 cm)
Marks: exterior, impressed on plug cap "200/240v/AEG"
+ manufacturer's logo within circle/"440w"; underside,
stamped manufacturer's logo + "GERMANY"
1994.7.1
Gift of Denis Gallion and Daniel Morris, Historical Design
Collection, New York.

Cat. 82   *See Fig. 8.04*
Cover
Zang Tumb Tuuum: Adrianopoli, ottobre 1912:
parole in libertà **(Zang Tumb Tuuum:**
Adrianopolis, October 1912: Words in Freedom),
1914
Designed and written by Filippo Tommaso
Marinetti
(Italian, 1876–1944)
Published by Edizioni Futuriste di Poesia, Milan
Black ink on paper
8 x 5½ x ¾ inches (20.3 x 14.0 x 2.0 cm)
Inscription: inside front cover on facing flypage, written in
brown ink "A CARLO RESSALET . . . F T MARINETTI"
Collection: Sackner Archive of Concrete and Visual Poetry.
Note: The Wolfsonian's copies of this book 83.2.475 &
GF1993.1.13 will be exhibited after the American tour.

Cat. 83
Cover
"Before Antwerp," *Blast,* **War issue no. 2, 1915**
Designed and edited by Wyndham Lewis
(British, 1882–1957)
Published by John Lane/The Bodley Head, London
Black ink on paper
11⅞ x 9¾ x ¾ inches (30.2 x 24.8 x 1.6 cm)
Marks: obverse, printed in black, bottom center "Wyndham
Lewis"
XB1990.2020

Cat. 84 [exhibited in Miami only]
Armchair
Red Blue, **1918**
Designed and made by Gerrit Rietveld
(Dutch, 1888–1964)
Executed for the Dutch painter Lode Sengers, 1920–21
Utrecht, Netherlands
Painted plywood
33¾ x 26 x 32 inches (85.7 x 66.0 x 81.3 cm)
Collection: The Art Institute of Chicago. Through prior gifts of
Mrs. Albert J. Beveridge, Florence May Schoenborn and
Samuel A. Marx; through prior acquisitions of the Richard T.
Crane, Jr. Memorial and Mary Waller Langhorne funds; Richard
T. Crane, Jr. Endowment, 1988.274.

Cat. 85
Desk with light, 1925–35
Designed by Camillo Cerri
(Swiss, ?–1980)
Made by August Tobler
(Swiss, 1899–1975)
Dornach, Switzerland
Advertised as furniture "stimulated by the art fostered at the
Goetheanum," Rudolf Steiner's Anthroposophical Society in
Dornach, Switzerland.
Plywood, metal hardware, glass
78¼ x 59 x 45 inches (198.8 x 149.9 x 114.3 cm)
Marks: rear cabinet door, impressed, interior latch "VICI/DRGM"
TD1992.67.1

85

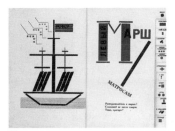

86

87

88

89

91

Cat. 86
Pages 6 and 7
Dlia Golosa (For the Voice)
by Vladimir Mayakovsky
(Russian, 1893–1930), **1923**
Designed by El Lissitzky
(Russian, 1890–1941)
Printed by Lutze & Vogt, Berlin
Published by Soviet Russian State Publishing House, Berlin
One of 3,000 thumb-indexed copies.
Black and red inks on paper
7½ x 5¼ inches (19.1 x 13.3 cm) page
TD1989.284.1

Cat. 87
Title pages
S Lodi Jez Dovazi Caj A Kavu. Poesie 1926–27
**(With the Ship Comes Tea and Coffee. Poetry
1926–27) by Konstantin Biebl**
(Czech, 1898–1951), **1928**
Designed by Karel Teige
(Czech, 1900–51)
Published by Odeon, Prague
Black and pink inks on paper
8 x 11⅛ x ¼ inches (20.2 x 28.0 x 0.6 cm)
83.2.622

Cat. 88
Cover
Depero Futurista (also known as Libro
imbullonato [Nailed book]), 1927
Designed and written by Fortunato Depero
(Italian, 1892–1960)
Published by Dinamo-Azari, Milan
Aluminum nuts and bolts with steel cotter pins, cardboard,
printed paper
9⅝ x 12⅝ x 1⅞ inches (24.5 x 32.2 x 4.8 cm)
83.2.459

Cat. 89
Cover
L'Anguria lirica: lungo poema passionale
**(The Lyric Watermelon: a long passionate poem)
by Tullio d'Albisola**
(Italian, 1899–1971), **1934**
Designed by Bruno Munari
(Italian, b. 1907)
Published by Edizioni Futuriste di Poesia, Rome and Lito-Latta,
Savona, Italy
Tin-plated steel pages, chrome-plated spine, steel wire binding,
silkscreened cover
8¼ x 7 x 1⅛ inches (20.8 x 17.7 x 2.7 cm)
87.1493.2.1

Cat. 90   See Fig. 3.13
Group of postage stamps
Printed by Joh. Enschedé & Zonen, Haarlem, Netherlands

a) *Nederland 2 cent* and *Nederland 4 cent*, **1943–44**
Designed by Pijke Koch
(Dutch, 1901–91)
¹⁵⁄₁₆ x 1¼ inches and 1¼ x ¹⁵⁄₁₆ inches
(2.4 x 3.2 cm and 3.2 x 2.4 cm)
XC1992.429.3–4

b) *Nederland: Luchtpost 40 cent*, **1928**
Designed by Jorio Johannes Christian Lebeau
(Dutch, 1878–1945)
1 x 1 inches (2.5 x 2.5 cm)
XC1992.758.1

c) *Nederland 1½ cent*, *Nederland 5 cent*, *Nederland 6 cent*
and *Nederland 12½ cent*, **1931**
Designed by Gerard Kiljan
(Dutch, 1891–1977)
1 x ¹³⁄₁₆ inches ea. (2.5 x 2.1 cm ea.)
XC1992.759.1-4

d) *Nederland 1 cent* and *Nederland 2 cent*, **1923**
Designed by Michel de Klerk
(Dutch, 1884–1923)
1 x ¹³⁄₁₆ inches ea. (2.5 x 2.1 cm ea.)
XC1992.430.1-2

e) *Nederland 2 cent*, **1923**
Designed by Jan Theodoor Toorop
(Dutch, 1858–1928)
2⅝ x 1½ inches (6.8 x 3.8 cm)
XC1992.421.1

f) *Nederland 1 cent*, *Nederland 1½ cent*
and *Nederland 2½ cent*, **1926**
Designed by Joris Johannes Christian Lebeau
(Dutch, 1878–1945)
⅞ x 1 inches ea. (2.1 x 2.5 cm ea.)
XC1992.423.2,3,6

Cat. 91
Page 13
Het boek van PTT, **1938**
Designed by Piet Zwart
(Dutch, 1885–1977)
Printed by Nederlandsche Rotogravure, Leiden, Netherlands
Published by Posterijen, Telegrafie en Telefonie (PTT), Amsterdam
Multicolored inks on paper
9⅞ x 6¾ inches (25.1 x 17.2 cm) page
Marks: front cover reverse, stamped in green, top left "piet
zwart/ rijksstraatweg 290/wassenaar holland"
TD1989.116.2

Celebrating Modernity

Time and Motion

Cat. 92   See Fig. 4.23
Book
La Prose du Transsibérien et de la Petite
Jehanne de France, 1913
Sonia Delaunay
(French, b. Ukraine, 1885–1979)
Written by Blaise Cendrars (pseudonym for
Frédéric Sauser)
(Swiss, 1887–1961)
Published by Editions des Hommes Nouveaux, Paris
Number 147 in a proposed edition of 150.
Multicolored inks and pochoir gouache on simili japon paper
78⅛ x 14⅛ inches (198.3 x 35.9 cm)
Marks: obverse top, signed in ink, upper left "Blaise Cendrars"
87.799.2.1

[exhibited in Miami only]
Same as above entry except the following:
Number 131 of a proposed edition of 150.
79 x 14 inches (200.1 x 35.5 cm)
Collection: Sackner Archive of Concrete and Visual Poetry,
Miami.

Cat. 93
Painting
Pavillon doré **(Gilded Pavilion), 1922**
Tato (pseudonym for Guglielmo Sansoni)
(Italian, 1896–1974)
Bologna, Italy
Exhibited at the Terza Biennale Romana, Esposizione
Nazionale di Belle Arti, Rome, 1925.
Oil on board
27½ x 34 inches (69.9 x 88.9 cm) unframed
Marks: obverse, signed in black, bottom left "TATO/1922"
TD1989.82.1

Cat. 94   See Fig. 8.13
Painting
Prima crociera atlantica su Rio de Janeiro
(First Atlantic long-distance flight over Rio
de Janeiro), 1933
Alfredo Gauro Ambrosi
(Italian, 1901–45)
Verona, Italy
Oil on canvas
40 x 51 inches (101.6 x 129.5 cm) unframed
Marks: obverse, signed in black, bottom left "AMBROSI"
83.5.16

Cat. 95   See Fig. 8.03
Sculpture
Profilo continuo del Duce
(Continuous profile of Mussolini), 1933
Renato Bertelli
(Italian, 1900–74)
Florence
Later manufactured by Ditta Effeffe, Milan, with Mussolini's
approval, patent no. 1073.
Bronzed terra-cotta
11¾ x 9 inches dia. (28.7 x 22.9 cm dia.)
Marks: interior, incised signature on base "R. Bertelli"
84.6.4

93

103

Cat. 96   See Fig. 5.04
Print
Whence and Whither?, **c. 1932**
Cyril Edward Power
(British, 1872–1951)
London
Number 26 in an edition of 50.
Color linocut
14 x 11¼ inches (35.7 x 28.5 cm)
Marks: obverse, signed in pencil, lower left corner
"Whence & Whither?/Cyril E Power No. 26/50"
83.4.10

Cat. 97   See Fig. 5.06
Poster
Immer Schneller. Deutsche Reichsbahn
(Always Faster. German State Railroad), c. 1935
Designed by H.J. Barschel
(German, dates unknown)
Printed by A. Bagel A.G., Düsseldorf, Germany
Published by W.E.R., Germany
Commercial color lithograph
33⅛ x 23⁵⁄₁₆ inches (84.1 x 59.2 cm)
Marks: obverse, printed in white, lower right corner
"H.J. BARSCHEL"
XX1990.3083

Cat. 98   See Fig. 5.07
Poster
100 Jahre Deutsche Eisenbahnen Ausstellung,
Nürnberg, 1935 **(Centennial Exhibition of the**
German State Railroad . . .), 1935
Designed by Jupp Wiertz
(German, 1888–1959)
Printed by Christian Weiersmüller, Nürnberg, Germany
Commercial color lithograph
42⁷⁄₁₆ x 27⁹⁄₁₆ inches (107.7 x 70.0 cm)
Marks: obverse, printed in black, lower left designer's mark
"JUPP/WIERTZ"
XX1992.187

Cat. 99   See Fig. 5.20
Toy
Burlington Zephyr, **1934**
Manufactured by American Flyer, Chicago, IL,
c. 1934–36
Based on the original Burlington Zephyr, designed by Budd
Manufacturing Company, Philadelphia, PA, 1934.
Cast aluminum, sheet steel, brass, acetate
1) 3½ x 2¾ x 12 inches (8.9 x 7.0 x 30.5 cm)
2) 3 x 2¾ x 10 inches (7.6 x 7.0 x 25.4 cm)
3) 3 x 2¾ x 10¾ inches (7.6 x 7.0 x 27.3 cm)
Marks: underside, in high relief multiple patent numbers
87.1325.18.3.1–3

Cat. 100   See Fig. 5.21
a) Toy
Graf Zeppelin, **1928**
Manufactured by Metalcraft Corporation,
St. Louis, MO
Based on the original Graf Zeppelin, designed by Dr. Hugo
Eckener, Friedrichshafen, Germany, 1928.
Tinned sheet steel
27 x 5½ x 7 inches (68.6 x 14.0 x 17.8 cm)
87.1567.18.1

b) Cover
Instruction Book Zeppelin Construction Set,
1928
Published by Metalcraft Corporation, St. Louis,
MO
8⅝ x 5⅞ inches (22.1 x 14.8 cm)
86.2.191

104

107

108

109

Cat. 101 *See Fig. 9.13*
Postcards
Hindenburg, **1936**
Interiors designed by Fritz August Breuhaus de Groot
(German, 1883–1960)
Published by Luftschiffbau Zeppelin, Friedrichshafen, Germany
Multicolored inks on paper
4³/₁₆ x 5⁷/₈ inches ea. (10.7 x 15.0 cm ea.)
XC1992.441*

a) Postcard No. 1, *Gesellschafts Raum im Luftschiff "Hindenburg"* (Lounge . . .)

b) Postcard No. 4, *Speisesaal im Luftschiff "Hindenburg"* (Dining Room . . .) [not illustrated]

c) Postcard No. 10, *Rauchzimmer im Luftschiff "Hindenburg"* (Smoking Lounge . . .) [not illustrated]

Cat. 102 *See Fig. 9.12*
Poster
2 Days to Europe, **1937**
Designed by Jupp Wiertz
(German, 1888–1939)
Published by Hamburg-American Line, North German Lloyd, Hamburg, Germany
Commercial color lithograph
33⁹/₁₆ x 23⁵/₁₆ inches (85.2 x 59.1 cm)
Marks: obverse, printed in black, lower left designer's mark "JUPP/WIERTZ"
TD1991.174.12

Cat. 103
Poster
A New York in 6¹/₂ Giorni (To New York in 6¹/₂ Days), **1932**
Designed by Giuseppe Patrone
(Italian, 1904–63)
Printed by Barabino & Graeve, Genoa
Published by Edizione Supercartello, Italy
Commercial color lithograph
75¹⁵/₁₆ x 53⁷/₈ inches (192.8 x 136.5 cm)
Marks: obverse, printed in white, lower left "G. Patrone/1932"
84.4.19

Cat. 104
Pitcher
Normandie, **1935**
Designed by Peter Müller-Munk
(American, b. Germany, 1904–67)
Made by Revere Copper and Brass, Inc., Rome, NY, 1935–c.1941
Chromeplated steel
12 x 9³/₄ x 3 inches (30.5 x 24.8 x 7.6 cm)
Marks: underside, impressed "REVERE/ROME/N.Y."
XX1990.1272

Cat. 105 *See Fig. 4.21*
Poster
Aeroshell Lubricating Oil: The Aristocrat of Lubricants, **1932**
Designed by Edward McKnight Kauffer
(American, 1890–1954)
Printed by Chorley & Pickersgill Ltd., Lithographers, Leeds, England
Published by Shell Oil Company, Ltd., London
Commercial color lithograph
29¹⁵/₁₆ x 44³/₈ inches (76.1 x 112.5 cm)
Marks: obverse, printed in black, lower right "E. MCKNIGHT/KAUFFER 1932"
87.818.4.1

Cat. 106 *See Fig. 5.05*
Digital clock, model no. 304-P40, *Zephyr*, **1934**
Designed by Kem (Karl Emanuel Martin) Weber
(American, b. Germany, 1889–1963)
Made by Lawson Time, Inc., Los Angeles, CA, 1934–c.1941
Lacquered copper, chromeplated brass, plastic
3⁵/₈ x 8¹/₄ x 3³/₁₆ inches (10.6 x 21.0 x 7.8 cm)
Marks: rear, impressed "Lawson Time inc/LOS ANGELES, CALIF./W.4.V110 CYC60 MODEL NO. 304/PAT. NO.1.990.645"
1994.8.1

Cat. 107
Painting
6th Ave El, **1937**
Peter Berent
(American, b. 1909)
New York
Oil on fiberboard
63 x 35⁷/₈ inches (160.0 x 91.1 cm) unframed
Marks: obverse, signed, lower left corner artist's mark "PB"
83.5.10

Cat. 108
Painting
Le Vélodrome, **c. 1925**
Marcel Stobbaerts
(Belgian, 1899–1979)
Brussels
Oil on canvas
24⁷/₈ x 32¹/₂ inches (63.1 x 82.6 cm) unframed
Marks: obverse, signed in red, lower left corner "Stobbaerts-Marcel"
XX1989.26

Cat. 109 *[left to right]*
Maquettes
Lecture, News, Advertising **and** *S.O.S.*, **for the Social Science Hall, "A Century of Progress" exposition, Chicago, IL, 1933**
Alfonso Iannelli
(American, b. Italy, 1888–1965)
Chicago
Polychromed fiber-enforced plaster, wood, metal
Left: 26 x 18¹/₈ x 3¹/₄ inches (66.0 x 46.0 x 8.3 cm)
Right: 25⁵/₈ x 15⁹/₁₆ x 3¹/₄ inches (65.1 x 39.5 x 8.3 cm)
83.6.4; 83.6.3

327

110

112

113

114

Cat. 110
Radio, model no. 1186, *Nocturne*, c. 1935
Designed by Walter Dorwin Teague
(American, 1883–1960)
Manufactured by Sparton Corporation, Jackson, MI, c. 1936
Glass, metal, wood
45½ x 43½ x 15½ inches (115.6 x 110.5 x 39.4 cm)
Marks: obverse, face, printed in black "Sparton/JACKSON,
MICHIGAN/MADE IN/U.S.A./A-12231"
XX1990.168

Cat. 111   See Fig. 5.14
Panel
***Radio Broadcasting*, from the Westinghouse**
Pavilion, "A Century of Progress" exposition,
Chicago, IL, 1933
Made by Westinghouse Electric and
Manufacturing Company, Pittsburgh, PA
One of four panels exhibited.
Urea formaldehyde laminate and anodized and dyed aluminum
foil on 14 gauge steel sheet, painted press wood fiberboard,
aluminum foil covered wood
49½ x 97½ x 1¼ inches (125.7 x 247.7 x 3.2 cm)
XX1989.190a-c

Cat. 112
Table
From the Robert Scanlon residence,
San Francisco, CA, c. 1939
Designed by Archibald Taylor
(American, 1900–75)
San Francisco, CA
Maple, birch, glass, metal
22½ x 42 inches dia. (57.2 x 106.7 cm dia.)
83.11.1

Cat. 113
Poster
***Salon Aéronautique*, 1936**
Designed by E. Deloddere
Printed by Léon Beyaert Sioen, Kortrijk (Courtrai), Belgium
Commercial color lithograph
39½ x 24 inches (100.3 x 61.0 cm)
Marks: obverse, printed in white, upper right corner
"e. deloddere./36"
XX1990.2876

Cat. 114
Medal
To the Advancement of Motor Transportation.
Commemorating the 25th anniversary of General
***Motors*, 1933**
Designed by Norman Bel Geddes
(American, 1893–1958)
Made by René Chambellan for Medallic Art Company, New York
Silverplated brass
³⁄₁₆ x 3 inches dia. (0.5 x 7.62 cm dia.)
Marks: obverse, in high relief, bottom center
"NORMAN BEL GEDDES © 1933"
83.1.355
Note: Additional medallions with similar theme also in
exhibition [not illustrated]

Brave New Worlds

Cat. 115
Sculpture
***La Gloire du Fer* (The Glory of Iron), c. 1889**
Waagen
(German, dates unknown)
France(?)
Cast tin, solder, brass
24 x 16⅞ x 10 inches (61.0 x 42.8 x 25.4 cm)
Marks: obverse, signed, proper right of base "Waagen";
impressed, center metal escutcheon "LA GLOiRE DU FER"
84.6.14

Cat. 116
Portfolio
Une cité industrielle: étude pour la construction
***des villes* (An industrial city: studies for the**
construction of towns), 1917
Tony Garnier, architect
(French, 1869–1948)
Printed by Phototypiques Baise, Lyons, France
Drawings first exhibited in Paris, 1904.
Offset lithograph
12⅝ x 16⅝ inches ea. (32.1 x 42.2 cm ea.)
XC1991.480**

a) Plate 76, *Quartier d'Habitation Rue Principale*
(Main street of the residential neighborhood) [not illustrated]

b) Plate 164, *Les Hauts-Fourneaux* (View of the furnaces)

Cat. 117
Cover
***La Nuova Architettura* (New Architecture), 1931**
Edited by Fillia (pseudonym of Luigi Colombo)
(Italian, 1904–36)
Published by Unione Tipografico, Turin
12⅞ x 9⁹⁄₁₆ x 1⅛ inches (32.6 x 24.3 x 2.8 cm)
XB1990.1514

Cat. 118
Poster
5ème Exposition de l'Habitation. XVe Salon des
Arts Ménagers. Grand Palais, Paris.
27 Janvier – 13 Février 1938.
(Fifth Housing Exhibition . . .), 1938
Designed by Geneviève Lecornue
(French, dates unknown)
Printed by Edition de l'Architecture d'Aujourd'hui, Boulogne
(Seine), France
Published by Office National des Recherches et Inventions,
Ministère de l'Education Nationale, Paris
Commercial color lithograph
47¼ x 31⁷⁄₁₆ inches (120.0 x 79.8 cm)
Marks: obverse, printed in white, lower left "GEN. LECORNU"
86.4.46

Cat. 119
Drawing
Perspective view of a building, 1931
Miklos Suba
(American, b. Hungary, 1880–1944)
New York
Graphite, black and red colored pencil, and silver metallic ink
on paper
15¹⁵⁄₁₆ x 12¹⁄₁₆ inches (40.6 x 30.6 cm)
Marks: obverse, signed "MIKLOS SUBA 1931"
86.5.74

115

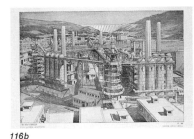

116b

117

118

119

121

120

123

122

124

Cat. 120
Illustration
"Chicago Getreidespeicher 5" (Chicago Grain Elevator 5), *Amerika: Bilderbuch eines Architekten* **(America: Picture Book of Architecture), 1926**
Photographed and written by Erich Mendelsohn
(German, 1887–1953)
Book design by Graphic Artist Studio: Albert Frisch
Published by Rudolf Mosse, Berlin
Black ink on paper
13¾ x 9¼ (34.6 x 23.5 cm) page
85.2.45

Cat. 121
Illustration
"The American Radiator Building"
(1924; Raymond M. Hood, architect),
The Metropolis of Tomorrow, **1929**
Illustrated and edited by Hugh Ferriss
(American, 1889–1962)
Published by Ives Washburn, New York
Black ink on paper
12⅛ x 9 inches (30.6 x 23.0 cm) page
83.2.972

Cat. 122
a) Poster
Rockefeller Center, New York. New York Central Lines, **c. 1939**
Designed by Leslie Darrell Ragan
(American, b. 1897)
Printed by Latham Lithography & Printing Co., Long Island City, NY
Published by New York Central Railway, New York
Commercial color lithograph
39 x 25³⁄₁₆ inches (99.1 x 64.0 cm)
Marks: obverse, printed on image, lower left "LESLIE/RAGAN"
TD1991.174.11

(exhibited in Miami only)
b) Photograph [not illustrated]
RCA Building **(1930–33; Reinhard & Hofmeister; Corbett, Harrison & MacMurray; Hood, Godley & Fouilhoux, architects), c. 1933**
Man Ray (pseudonym of Emmanuel Rudnitsky)
(American, 1890–1976)
Gelatin-silver
Paris
5⁷⁄₁₆ x 3½ inches (13.8 x 9.0 cm)
Marks: reverse, printed "MAN RAY 8 RUE/ DU VAL-DE-GRACE/ PARIS 5° FRANCE/ DANTON 92-25"
XX1990.1059

Cat. 123
Bookcase
Skyscraper, **c. 1926**
Designed by Paul Theodore Frankl
(American, b. Austria, 1886–1958)
Retailed by Frankl Galleries, New York, c. 1926–30
Painted plywood, wood, brass hardware
96¼ x 42 x 15⅝ inches (244.5 x 106.7 x 39.7 cm)
TD1993.42.1

Cat. 124
Pitcher
Skyscraper, **for the Apollo Studio line, 1928**
Designed by Louis Rice
(American, dates unknown)
Manufactured by Bernard Rice's Sons, Inc., New York, 1928–c. 1935
Electroplated nickel silver
9¾ x 8¾ x 5 inches (24.8 x 22.2 x 12.7 cm)
Marks: underside, impressed, within square "APOLLO/E.P.N.S."; "MADE IN U.S.A. BY/BERNARD RICE'S SONS, INC./5258/ Designed by. PAT. PENDING"; "SKY/S/C/R/A/P/E/R"
TD1993.29.3

Cat. 125
Scale, model S, *Height & Weight Meter*, c. 1927
Designed by Joseph Sinel
(American, b. New Zealand, 1889–1975)
Made by International Ticket Scale Corporation, New York,
c. 1929
Painted sheet steel, cast iron, machine-polished stainless steel,
nickelplated brass, chromeplated pot metal, glass, rubber
77½ x 18 x 25½ inches (196.9 x 45.7 x 64.8 cm)
Marks: obverse, impressed in black, last line of metal label
"INTERNATIONAL TICKET SCALE CORPORATION
NEW YORK CITY"
XX1990.24

Cat. 126
Game
***Skyscraper Game*, 1937**
Manufactured by Parker Brothers, Inc., Salem, MA, 1937–40
Wood, paint, printed paper
Box: 11¼ x 13⅝ x 2⅞ inches (28.6 x 34.6 x 7.3 cm)
Game pieces: various sizes
1994.2.1
Gift of John P. Axelrod, Boston.

Cat. 127
Escutcheon
***Post* (Mail slot), c. 1920**
Made under the aegis of the Social Democratic city council
for public housing.
The Netherlands
Bronze
13 x 18½ x 1 inches (33.0 x 47.0 x 2.5 cm)
TD1994.204.3

Cat. 128
Signage
***Numerals 0–8*, c. 1920**
Made under the aegis of the Social Democratic city council
for public housing.
The Netherlands
Plywood, lacquer
Numerals 0, 2–6, 8: 4⅜ x 3 x ¼ inches (10.5 x 7.6 x 0.6 cm)
Numeral 1: 4¼ x 1½ x ¼ inches (10.2 x 3.8 x 0.6 cm)
Numeral 7: 4⅜ x 2¼ x ¼ inches (10.5 x 5.7 x 0.6 cm)
87.693.10.9.1–9

Cat. 129
Poster
**Working-class housing complexes of "Red"
Vienna, c. 1930**
Designed by S. Weyr
Vienna
Photo-lithograph
28⁹⁄₁₆ x 44⅝ inches (72.6 x 113.3 cm)
Marks: obverse, printed, lower left corner
"Photomontage/S. WEYR"
XX1990.3046

Cat. 130
Print
***Construction of Trylon and Perisphere*, c. 1938**
Hugh Ferriss
(American, 1889–1962)
New York
Lithograph, correction fluid
19¾ x 26¾ inches (50.2 x 66.9 cm)
Marks: obverse, signed in black crayon, lower left "Hugh Ferriss"
TD1993.12.1

Cat. 131
Model
***Theme Center – New York World's Fair 1939*, 1937**
Designed by Wallace K. Harrison
(American, 1895–1981)
and J. André Fouilhoux, architects
(French, 1879–1945)
Executed c. 1938
U.S.A.
One of 49 models presented to the U.S. President and state
governors.
Stainless steel, wood, plastic
36¼ x 31 inches dia. (92.1 x 78.7 cm dia.)
Marks: underside, in pencil "20"
86.17.1

Cat. 132
a) Postcard
***Trylon & Perisphere, New York World's Fair*, 1939**
Printed by Paris Art Label Co., Inc., New York
Published by New York World's Fair, New York
5 x 3¹⁄₁₆ inches (12.7 x 8.1 cm)
86.19.237

b) Postcard [not illustrated]
***The Firestone Tire & Rubber Company
Building, New York World's Fair*, 1939**
Printed by C.T. Art-Colortone, Chicago, IL
Published by Firestone Tire and Rubber Company,
Akron, OH, and New York World's Fair, New York
3⁷⁄₁₆ x 5⁹⁄₁₆ inches (9.0 x 14.3 cm)
86.19.72.1

c) Postcard [not illustrated]
***The Glass Centre Building: New York
World's Fair*, 1939**
Printed by Miller Art Co., Brooklyn, NY
Published by New York World's Fair, New York
3⁷⁄₁₆ x 5½ inches (9.0 x 14.0 cm)
86.19.79

125

126

127

128

129

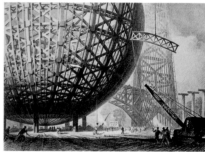

130

131

132

135   136   137   138   139

Design for Industry

Cat. 133 See Fig. 5.02
Print
***New York Breadline*, c. 1932**
Clare Veronica Hope Leighton
(American, b. England, 1901–88)
London
Number 32 in an edition of 100.
Wood engraving
15 1/2 x 10 1/16 inches (39.1 x 25.6 cm)
Marks: obverse, in pencil, lower right corner "Clare Leighton"
83.4.39

Cat. 134 See Fig. 5.03
Drawing
***City with Machines*, c. 1930**
Edmond van Dooren
(Belgian, 1896–1965)
Anvers, Belgium
Charcoal and graphite on paper
20 1/2 x 14 1/2 inches (52.1 x 36.8 cm)
Marks: obverse, in pencil, bottom right "E. Van Dooren"
83.5.6

Cat. 135
Painting
***Suicide with Skyscrapers*, 1940**
Stuyvesant van Veen
(American, 1910–88)
New York
Acrylic on canvas
47 3/4 x 32 inches (121.3 x 81.3 cm) unframed
Marks: obverse, signed, upper right corner "STUyVeSant Van
Veen 40-6"
XX1989.18

Cat. 136
a) Book
***Staatliches Bauhaus Weimar, 1919–1923*, 1923**
Designed by Herbert Bayer
(American, b. Austria, 1900–85)
Written by Walter Gropius (American, b. Germany, 1883–1969)
and Laszlo Moholy-Nagy (American, b. Hungary, 1895–1946)
Published by Bauhausverlag, Weimar, Germany
9 7/8 x 10 x 1 inches (25.0 x 25.4 x 2.5 cm)
TD1988.67.28

[exhibited in Miami only]
b) Postcard [See Fig. 9.01]
Bauhaus Ausstellung: Juli-September 1923
(Bauhaus Exhibition . . .), 1923
Designed by Oskar Schlemmer
(German, 1888–1943)
Published by Staatliches Bauhaus Weimar, Weimar, Germany
Red and blue ink on card
6 x 4 1/8 inches (15.2 x 10.4 cm)
Marks: reverse, printed in black "KARTE 8: OSKAR
SCHLEMMER"
87.19.242

[exhibited in Miami only]
c) Invitation [not illustrated]
Bauhaus-Fasching "Metallisches Fest"
***9 Febr. 1929* (Bauhaus Carnival "Metallic**
Festival" . . .), 1929
Designed by Herbert Bayer
(American, b. Austria, 1900–85)
Published by Staatliches Bauhaus Weimar, Weimar, Germany
Metallic ink on card
4 3/16 x 5 7/8 inches (10.6 x 15.0 cm)
XB1989.76

Cat. 137
Side chair, model no. B-32, 1928
Designed by Marcel Breuer
(American, b. Hungary, 1902–81)
Manufactured by Gebrüder Thonet, Frankenberg, Germany,
c. 1930–32
Chromed tubular steel, solid beech, cane
32 x 18 1/4 x 22 1/2 inches (81.5 x 46.5 x 57.0 cm)
Marks: rear seat rail, impressed on metal disk, center "Thonet"/
manufacturer's chair mark; underside on seat rail, impressed
"Y" + "B" + "X"
Collection: John C. Waddell, New York City

Cat. 138
Side chair, model no. MR-10, 1927
Designed by Ludwig Mies van der Rohe
(American, b. Germany, 1886–1969)
Manufactured by Bamberg Metallwerkstätten, Berlin-Neukölln,
Germany, c. 1931
Nickeled tubular steel, cane, solid steel, wood
31 3/4 x 22 x 33 inches (80.5 x 56.0 x 84.0 cm)
Collection: John C. Waddell, New York City.

Cat. 139 [not exhibited in Miami]
Side chair, model no. 301, 1932
Designed by Marcel Breuer
(American, b. Hungary 1902–81)
Manufactured by Embru-Werk A.G., Rüti, Switzerland for
Wohnbedarf, Zürich
Bent plywood, aluminum
29 x 17 x 18 1/2 inches (73.7 x 43.2 x 47.0 cm)
Marks: reverse of back splat on aluminum label, in black high
relief "wohnbedarf" + impressed in black
"taistr. 11./zurich/typ"
TD1993.81.2

Cat. 140
Teacup, saucer, and teapot, 1930–34
Designed by Wilhelm Wagenfeld
(German, 1900–90)
Manufactured by Jenaer Glaswerk, Schott & Genossen, Jena,
Germany, before 1945
Glass
Cup: 1½ x 4¾ x 4¼ inches (3.8 x 12.1 x 10.8 cm)
Saucer: ½ x 6½ inches dia. (1.3 x 16.5 cm dia.)
Teapot: 4½ x 10½ x 6⅛ inches (11.4 x 26.7 x 15.6 cm)
Cup and saucer marks: underside, etched "Jenaer Glas"/circle
within pentagram/"Tefla"
Teapot marks: underside of base, etched manufacturer's mark
"Schott & Gen./Jena" within circle with four corners; center of
lid, in mold manufacturer's mark circle with four corners
84.8.14.5a,b; 84.8.14.1a-c

Cat. 141   See Fig. 9.15
Containers
Kubus **(Cube), 1938**
Designed by Wilhelm Wagenfeld
(German, 1900–90)
Manufactured by Vereinigte Lausitzer Glaswerke A.G.,
Weisswasser, Germany
Glass
9¼ x 10⅝ x 7 inches (23.5 x 27.0 x 17.8 cm) as illustrated
Marks: all impressed with manufacturer's mark "XX" within
rhomboid
87.521.8.10.1-7

Cat. 142
Tea service, model no. 13944,
*Hallesche Form***, 1929,**
with decoration *Goldringe***, 1930**
Form designed by Marguerite Friedländer-
Wildenhain
(American, b. France, 1896–1985)
Decoration designed by Trude Petri
(German, 1906–68)
Manufactured by Staatliche Porzellanmanufaktur (KPM), Berlin,
1931–38
Glazed porcelain, gold

a) Creamer
2½ x 4 x 2¾ inches (6.4 x 10.2 x 7.0 cm)
Marks: underside, underglaze in blue manufacturer's
sceptor mark; impressed "1"
TD1994.177.3

b) Teapot
4⅞ x 8 x 5 inches (12.4 x 20.3 x 12.7 cm)
Marks: underside, underglaze in blue manufacturer's
sceptor mark; impressed "8" + 3 concentric rings
TD1994.177.1

c) Sugar bowl
3¾ x 4⁹⁄₁₆ inches dia. (9.5 x 11.6 cm dia.)
Marks: underside of base, underglaze in blue
manufacturer's sceptor mark; underglaze in gray castle
mark of the Kunstgewerbeschule Halle at Burg
Giebichenstein; overglaze in red manufacturer's Imperial
orb mark + "KPM"; overglaze in black "84/116"; impressed
"W:" + wavy line; underside of lid, overglaze in black,
interior rim "84/116"
TD1994.177.2

Cat. 143
Armchair
From the dining room of the Diehl residence,
Chicago, IL, c. 1928
Designed by Kem (Karl Emanuel Martin) Weber
(American, b. Germany, 1899–1963)
Manufactured by Grand Rapids Chair Co., Grand Rapids, MI
Spray-lacquered beech, leather upholstery
40½ x 21⁵⁄₁₃ x 20 inches (103.0 x 54.3 x 50.8 cm)
XX1989.25

Cat. 144
Dresser, c. 1934
Designed by Donald Deskey
(American, 1894–1989)
Made by Estey Manufacturing Co., Owosso, MI
Walnut burl and white holly veneer, plywood
34¾ x 48 x 21⅛ inches (88.3 x 121.9 x 53.7 cm)
Marks: reverse, stenciled in black, top center "52056";
impressed, top left "520 98"; interior of top drawer, in high
relief, metal label on right panel "TRADEMARK/REGISTERED"/
ESTEY logo/"OWOSSO, MICH"
87.967.11.4.1a

Cat. 145
Table, c. 1933–34
Designed by Warren McArthur
(American, 1885–1961)
Made by Warren McArthur Corporation, Rome, NY
Aluminum, plastic laminate, plywood
30 x 22½ x 22½ inches (76.2 x 57.2 x 57.2 cm)
86.11.3

Cat. 146
Glassware
*Embassy 4900 Line***, 1939**
Designed by Walter Dorwin Teague
(American, 1883–1960)
and Edwin W. Fuerst
(American, dates unknown)
Manufactured by Libbey Glass Company, Toledo, OH,
c. 1940–42
Designed originally for the State dining room,
Federal Building, New York World's Fair, 1939.
Glass
Marks: acid-etched on base "Libbey" within a circle

a) Champagne glass
6⅝ x 3¾ inches dia. (15.9 x 9.5 cm dia.)
TD1992.146.17

b) Goblet
8¾ x 2⅞ inches dia. (22.2 x 6.0 cm dia.)
TD1992.146.1

c) Liqueur glass
6⅞ x 2¾ inches dia. (16.1 x 7.0 cm dia.)
TD1991.149.3

c) Wineglass
6⅜ x 2¾ inches dia. (15.6 x 7.0 cm dia.)
84.8.12.2

d) Wineglass
6⅞ x 2½ inches dia. (16.1 x 6.4 cm dia.)
TD1992.146.13

140

142

143

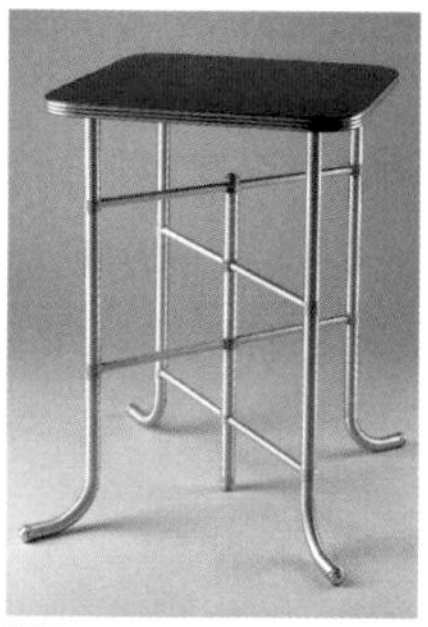

145

144

146

147

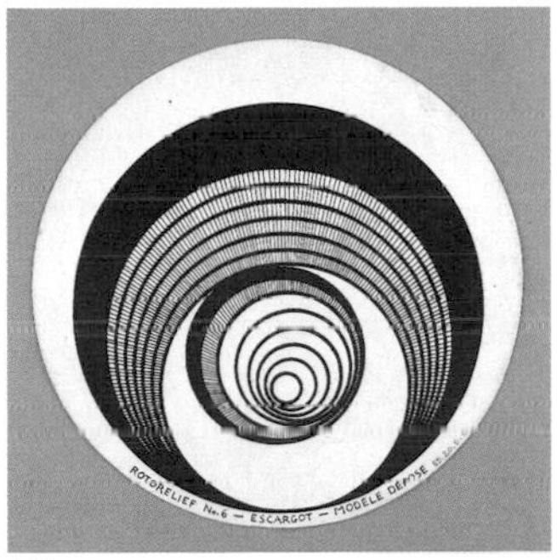

148

149

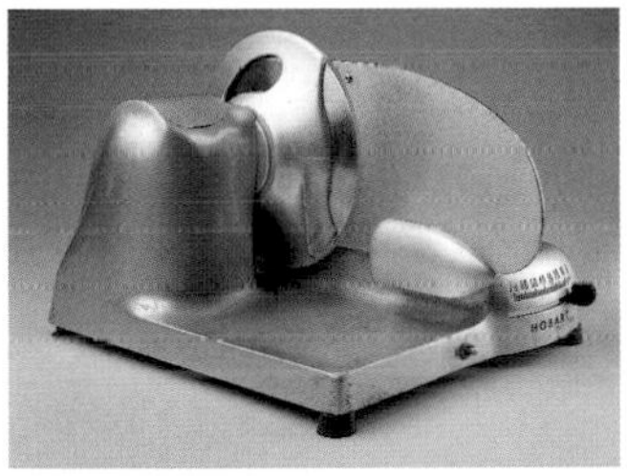

150

151

Cat. 147
Portable phonograph
Model M, *RCA Victor Special*, c. 1937
Design attributed to John Vassos
(American, b. Greece, 1898–1985)
Manufactured by RCA Manufacturing Company, Inc., Camden, NJ, c. 1937
Aluminum, chromeplated steel, velvet, plastic
8 x $17\frac{1}{2}$ x $17\frac{1}{4}$ inches (20.3 x 44.5 x 43.8 cm)
Marks: exterior of case, printed, rear metal label "RCA VICTOR SPECIAL"; interior, under turntable mount multiple U.S. patent numbers
XX1989.415

Cat. 148
Rotoreliefs (Disques optiques)
(Optical discs), first edition, 1935
Designed by Marcel Duchamp
(French, 1887–1968)
Paris
A set from the first edition of 500 was exhibited at the 33rd Concours Lépin, Salon des Inventions, Parc des Expositions, Porte de Versailles, Paris, 1935.
Color offset lithograph
$7\frac{7}{8}$ inches dia. ea. (20.0 cm dia. ea.)
83.20.5a-g

a) No. 6, *Escargot* (Snail)

b) No. 7, *Verre de Bohême* (Bohemian Glass) [not illustrated]

c) No. 12, *Spiral Blanche* (White Spiral) [not illustrated]

Cat. 149
Short-wave radio transmitter
***Radio Nurse*, 1937**
Designed by Isamu Noguchi
(American, 1904–88)
Manufactured by Zenith Radio Corporation, Chicago, IL, 1937–39
Bakelite housing produced by Chicago Molded Products Corporation, Chicago, IL and Kurz-Kasch, Inc., Dayton, OH
Commissioned by Commander E.F. McDonald, Jr., president of Zenith
Bakelite, metal, rubber
$8\frac{1}{4}$ x $6\frac{3}{4}$ x 6 inches (21.0 x 17.2 x 15.2 cm)
Marks: reverse, in high relief manufacturer's mark "Zenith/ RADIO" + SOS logo + "NURSE/ DESIGNED BY NOGUCHI/ PATENT APPLIED FOR/ 117 VOLTS-50/60 CYCLE-25 WATTS/ ZENITH RADIO CORP., CHICAGO"
XX1990.662

Cat. 150
Meat slicer, model no. 410, *Streamliner*, 1941
Designed by Egmont H. Arens
(American, 1889–1966)
and Theodore C. Brookhart
(American, dates unknown)
Manufactured by Hobart Manufacturing Company, Troy, OH
Aluminum, steel, rubber
$13\frac{1}{2}$ x 21 x 15 inches (34.3 x 53.3 x 38.1 cm)
Marks: underside, metal label "THE HOBART MFG. CO./TROY, OHIO/MODEL 410"
XX1990.109

Cat. 151
Camera
***Kodak Bantam Special*, 1933–36**
Designed by Walter Dorwin Teague
(American, 1883–1960),
Joseph Mihalyi and Chester W. Crumrine
Manufactured by Kodak Company, Rochester, NY, 1936 – c. 1940
Painted brass, glass, leather
$3\frac{1}{4}$ x $4\frac{7}{8}$ x $1\frac{3}{4}$ inches (8.3 x 11.0 x 4.5 cm)
Marks: front interior, in high relief "KODAK BANTAM SPECIAL/ MADE IN USA/BY EASTMAN KODAK CO./ROCHESTER NY"; reverse interior, in high relief "DESIGN PATENT 90589/DESIGN PATENT 99906"
83.15.5

Cat. 152 *See Fig. 4.24*
Coffee service, c. 1934
Designed by Keith Day Pearce Murray
(British, b. New Zealand, 1892–1981)
Made by Josiah Wedgwood and Sons, Ltd., Etruria, Staffs., England
Glazed stoneware

a) Sugar bowl with lid
$3\frac{5}{8}$ x $3\frac{3}{8}$ inches dia. (8.3 x 8.0 cm dia.)
Marks: underside, printed, underglaze in green "KM/ WEDGWOOD/MADE IN/ENGLAND"; impressed "E/H"
85.7.55.3a, b

b) Coffeepot with lid
$7\frac{7}{8}$ x $6\frac{1}{4}$ x $3\frac{1}{4}$ inches (18.7 x 15.9 x 8.3 cm)
Marks: underside, printed, underglaze in green "KM/WEDGWOOD/MADE IN/ENGLAND/X"; underside of lid, printed underglaze in green "X"
85.7.55.1a, b

c) Creamer
$2\frac{1}{2}$ x 4 x $2\frac{1}{2}$ inches (6.4 x 10.2 x 6.4 cm)
Marks: underside, printed, underglaze in green "KM/WEDGWOOD/MADE IN/ENGLAND/F"
85.7.55.2

Cat. 153 *See Fig. 5.24*
Travel iron
***Smoothie*, 1946**
Designed by Christopher Kerr, Norman Harry Lucas, Eric Lucas and Harold Thomas Holder
(all British, dates unknown)
Made by Lucas Holder & Co., Coventry, England, c. 1948
Chromeplated steel, bakelite, cordage
$2\frac{3}{8}$ x 2 x $4\frac{1}{2}$ inches (5.5 x 5.1 x 11.4 cm)
Marks: rear, impressed, metal plate "SMOOTHIE/MADE IN ENGLAND/BY LUCAS HOLDER COVENTRY/REG. G.T. BRT. 850220, 848 149/PAT. NO. 607450/75 WAT 100-250 VOL."
83.15.23

154

155

156

157

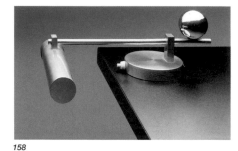

158

Cat. 154
Armchair, c. 1934
Designed by Gerald Summers
(British, 1899–1967)
Made by Makers of Simple Furniture Ltd., London,
1934–c.1939
Retailed by Grange Furnishing Stores, Harrow, Middlesex,
England
Plywood
35 x 30 x 24 inches (88.9 x 76.2 x 61.0 cm)
Marks: underside, printed, plastic label "Grange Furnishing
Stores/(London) Ltd/HARROW-MIDDX."; impressed, metal
label "REG NO/791116"
85.11.16

Cat. 155
Lounge chair, model no. 41, 1931–32
Designed by Alvar Aalto
(Finnish, 1898–1976)
Manufactured by Oy. Huonekaluja Rakennustyötehdas AB,
Turku, Finland, c.1932
Plywood, laminated birch, solid birch
25⅝ x 23¾ x 34½ inches (65.0 x 60.0 x 87.0 cm)
Collection: John C. Waddell, New York City.

Cat. 156
Vase, model no. 3031, 1936
Designed by Alvar Aalto
(Finnish, 1898–1976)
Made by Iittala Lasitehdas, Iittala, Finland, probably 1954–55
Glass
8 x 8¼ x 7¾ inches (20.3 x 21.0 x 19.7 cm)
Marks: underside, engraved "ALVAR AALTO – 3031"
84.8.16

Cat. 157 [left to right]
Glassware
Peer **(Pear), 1926**
Designed by Andries Dirk Copier
(Dutch, 1901–91)
Manufactured by N.V. Glasfabriek Leerdam, Leerdam,
Netherlands
Glass
Marks: underside, etched Copier/Leerdam mark "C•"
+ reverse "L"
Gift of Jan van der Marck in memory of Everand and Anny van
der Marck.

a) Beer beaker
4⅞ x 3⅜ inches dia. (12.4 x 8.6 cm dia.)
1994.45.27

b) Champagne coupe
6⅜ x 3½ inches dia. (16.2 x 8.9 cm dia.)
1994.45.5

c) Wine decanter with stopper
10⅜ x 4⅝ inches dia. (26.4 x 11.7 cm dia.)
1994.45.1 a, b

d) Liqueur glass
4⅞ x 1¾ inches dia. (10.2 x 4.4 cm dia.)
1994.45.56

e) Burgundy glass
5⅞ x 2¾ inches dia. (14.9 x 7.0 cm dia.)
1994.45.16

f) Bitter glass
4½ x 1⅜ inches dia. (11.4 x 3.5 cm dia.)
1994.45.66

g) Lemonade beaker [not illustrated]
4¾ x 3 inches dia. (12.1 x 7.6 cm dia.)
1994.45.37

h) Port glass [not illustrated]
5 x 2⅛ inches dia. (12.7 x 5.4 cm dia.)
1994.45.46

Cat. 158
Piano lamp, model no. 404, *GISO***, 1927**
Designed by Jacobus Johannes Pieter Oud
(Dutch, 1890–1963)
Manufactured by W.H. Gispen & Co., Rotterdam, c.1930
Designed originally as a wedding present for painter and
ceramist Harm Kamerlingh Onnes (Dutch, 1893–1984).
Nickelplated brass, chrome
4⅜ x 7⅝ x 11½ inches (10.5 x 18.4 x 29.2 cm)
86.13.4

159

160

161

163

162

Traditions Transformed

Cat. 159
Desk, 1916
Designed by Emile-Jacques Ruhlmann
(French, 1879–1933)
Paris
Macassar ebony veneer, ivory, brass
28³⁄₄ x 43⁵⁄₁₆ x 19⁵⁄₈ inches (73.0 x 110.0 x 49.9 cm)
Marks: underside, signed "RUHLMANN"
Collection: Virginia Museum of Fine Arts, Richmond.
Gift of Sydney and Frances Lewis.

Cat. 160 [left to right]
Cutlery
Deauville, **1937**
Designed by Jean-Elisée Puiforcat
(French, 1897–1945)
Manufactured by Puiforcat, Paris, c.1940
Silver

a) Salad fork
6¹⁄₂ x 1¹⁄₄ x ³⁄₄ inches (6.5 x 3.2 x 1.9 cm)
Marks: obverse, struck on bowl, at left Puiforcat mark;
at right French Minerva-head export mark
XX1991.472.2

h) Dinner fork
8 x 1¹⁄₈ x ³⁄₄ inches (20.3 x 2.9 x 1.9 cm)
Marks: obverse, struck on bowl, at left Puiforcat mark;
at right French Minerva-head export mark
XX1991.472.1

c) Dinner knife
9¹⁄₄ x 1 x ³⁄₈ inches (23.5 x 2.5 x 1.0 cm)
Marks: reverse, struck on blade "PUIFORCAT"; struck on
top of handle Puiforcat mark/"MADE IN FRANCE"
XX1991.472.6

d) Soup spoon
7⁷⁄₈ x 2¹⁄₈ x 1 inches (18.7 x 5.4 x 2.5 cm)
Marks: obverse, struck on bowl, at left Puiforcat mark;
at right French Minerva-head export mark
XX1991.472.3

e) Teaspoon
4¹⁄₂ x 1¹⁄₄ x ¹⁄₂ inches (11.4 x 3.2 x 1.3 cm)
Marks: obverse, struck on bowl, at left Puiforcat mark;
at right French Minerva-head export mark
XX1991.472.4

f) Butter knife
5¹⁄₄ x ⁷⁄₈ x ³⁄₁₆ inches (13.3 x 2.2 x 0.5 cm)
Marks: reverse, struck on blade, at left Puiforcat hallmark/
French hallmark of Minerva-head export mark
XX1991.472.5

Cat. 161
Cover
L'Homme Traqué
(The Hounded Man) by Francis Carco
(French, 1886–1956), **1929**
Designed by Chas (Charles) Laborde
(French, b. Argentina, 1886–1941)
Published by Libraries des Champs-Elysées, Paris
Leather
10¹⁄₂ x 8 x 1⁷⁄₈ inches (25.4 x 20.4 x 4.8 cm)
XC1994.3000

Cat. 162
Vase, model no. 14594, 1933
Designed by Siegmund Schütz
(German, b. 1906)
Made by Staatliche Porzellanmanufaktur (KPM), Berlin, 1934
Biscuit porcelain with glazed interior
8⁵⁄₈ x 5³⁄₈ inches dia. (21.0 x 13.1 cm dia.)
Marks: underside, underglaze in blue maker's mark; impressed
"SS/34/R"
85.7.29

Cat. 163
Cabinet, 1913–14
Designed by Dagobert Peche
(Austrian, 1887–1923)
Maker attributed to Jakob Soulek, Vienna
Ebonized tropical hardwood (purpleheart?), other hardwood,
gilded wood appliqués, granite
41¹⁄₄ x 38⁵⁄₈ x 19 inches (104.8 x 98.1 x 48.3 cm)
XX1990.45 a, b

Cat. 164 See Fig. 7.11
Vase, c. 1920
Design attributed to Vittorio Zecchin
(Italian, 1878–1947)
Made by Benvenuto Barovier (Italian, 1855–1932) or Giuseppe
Barovier (Italian, 1853–1942) for Vetreria Artistica Barovier,
Murano (Venice), Italy
Retailed by Vetreria Salviati, Venice
Murrhine glass
19³⁄₄ x 7³⁄₄ inches (50.2 x 19.7 cm)
GX1993.271

Cat. 165 See Fig. 7.02
Plate
Le attività gentili. I progenitori
(Noble activities. Our ancestors), 1923
Designed by Gio (Giovanni) Ponti
(Italian, 1891–1979)
Made by Manifattura Ceramica Richard-Ginori, Doccia
(Florence), Italy, 1924
Glazed porcelain, gold
1¹⁄₄ x 12¹⁄₈ inches dia. (3.2 x 31.4 cm dia.)
Marks: underside, overglaze in gold, partially worn plate title
and maker's mark with facsimile signature; overglaze in green
"GINORI/G"; overglaze in gray "GIO PONTI/1924"
84.7.51

Cat. 166 See Fig. 7.15
Sideboard
From the Schejola residence, Milan, c. 1928
Designed by Gio (Giovanni) Ponti
(Italian, 1891–1979)
Maker attributed to S. Turri, Bovisio, Italy
Walnut burl veneer, brass
36³⁄₄ x 59¹⁄₄ x 12¹⁄₈ inches (88.2 x 150.5 x 30.8 cm)
XX1991.503

170

171

172    173

174

Cat. 167
Urns, 1932
Designed by Umberto Bellotto
(Italian, 1882–1940)
Venice
Exhibited at the XVIII Esposizione Internazionale d'Arte, Venice, 1932.
Wrought and cast iron

a) Urn (See Fig. 6.12)
19¾ x 19¼ x 18¼ inches (50.2 x 48.9 x 46.4 cm)
XX1991.273

b) Urn [not illustrated]
21 x 8 x 8 inches (53.4 x 20.3 x 20.3 cm)
XX1991.272

Cat. 168   See Fig. 6.10
Gate, 1925
Designed by Alessandro Mazzucotelli
(Italian, 1865–1938)
Made by A. Mazzucotelli, Milan
Exhibited in the Capellin-Venini, Ravasco, Ravasi installation, Exposition Internationale des Arts Décoratifs et Industriels Modernes, Paris, 1925.
Wrought iron
124 x 141¼ inches (315.0 x 358.8 cm)
Marks: underside of mounting brackets, impressed "MAZZUCOTELL"
XX1989.481

Cat. 169   See Fig. 7.16
Side chair
From the entrance hall of the Fiammetta Sarfatti and Count Livio Gaetani residence, 1933
Designed by Marcello Piacentini
(Italian, 1881–1960)
Rome
Painted wood
35¼ x 17¾ inches dia. (89.5 x 45.1 cm dia.)
GD1993.6.1

Cat. 170
Armchair
From the visitors' waiting room of Crane-Bennett, Ltd., London, 1931
Designed by Sir Edwin Landseer Lutyens
(British, 1869–1944)
London
Walnut, leather
37½ x 27 x 18 inches (95.3 x 68.6 x 45.7 cm)
TD1991.69.7

Cat. 171
Doors
Allegories of Art & Industry, c. 1925
Designed by Oscar Bruno Bach
(American, 1884–1957)
Made by Bach Products, Inc., New York, c. 1930
Silver electroplate on copper, painted cast iron

a) Door
80¼ x 29¼ x 4¼ inches (203.8 x 74.3 x 10.8 cm)
TD1990.144.1

b) Door
80¼ x 35¼ x 4 inches (203.8 x 89.5 x 10.2 cm)
TD1990.144.3

Cat. 172
Candlestand, c. 1925
Designed by Wilhelm Hunt Diederich
(American, b. Hungary, 1884–1953)
New York
Wrought iron
78½ x 18 inches dia. (199.4 x 45.7 cm dia.)
TD1988.153.1

Cat. 173
Coffee service, c. 1935–40
Design attributed to Porter George Blanchard
(American, 1886–1973)
Made by Porter Blanchard, Los Angeles, CA
Marks: underside, struck "PORTER BLANCHARD" encircled/ "STERLING" encircled/"HANDMADE"

a) Creamer
Silver, ivory
3¼ x 8⅝ x 6 inches (8.3 x 21.0 x 15.2 cm)
87.9.1.3

b) Coffeepot with lid
Silver, ivory, bakelite
10¼ x 9¼ x 5¾ inches (26.0 x 23.5 x 14.6 cm)
87.9.1.1 a, b

c) Sugar bowl
Silver
3⅛ x 5¾ inches dia. (7.9 x 14.6 cm dia.)
87.9.1.4

Cat. 174
Bench
Banco, c. 1930
Designed by Jesse Nusbaum
(American, 1877–1975)
Santa Fe, NM
Fir
32 x 56⅜ x 17¼ inches (81.3 x 142.6 x 43.8 cm)
Marks: underside, in pencil "L15"
TD1990.86.6

Cat. 175   See Fig. 1.20
Stained glass window, for the International Labor Building, League of Nations, Geneva, commissioned 1926, completed 1930 (never installed)
Harry Clarke
(Irish, 1889–1931)
Made by Clarke Studios, Dublin
Stained glass, lead cames
71½ x 40 inches (181.6 x 101.6 cm)
Marks: obverse, etched near base, lower right panel "Harry Clarke/Dublin 1930"
TD1988.34.1

Cat. 176
Medal
***Exposition Internationale des Arts Décoratifs et Industriels Modernes, Paris*, 1925**
Pierre Turin
(French, b. 1891)
Made by Paris Mint, Paris
Bronze
³/₁₆ x 3¼ inches dia. (0.5 x 8.3 cm dia.)
Marks: obverse, impressed, lower right "P. TURIN"
83.1.37
Note: Additional medallions with similar theme also in exhibition
[not illustrated]

Cat. 177   See Fig. 3.23
Tea cabinet, 1915
Designed by Michel de Klerk
(Dutch, 1884–1923)
Commissioned by F.J. Zeegers for 't Woonhuys
(The Dwelling), Amsterdam
Manufactured and retailed by 't Woonhuys,
Amsterdam, c.1917
Mahogany, mahogany veneer, plywood, brass hardware
20¾ x 32⅝ x 19½ inches (75.6 x 81.9 x 49.5 cm)
TD1989.328.4

Cat. 178   See Fig. 3.25
Dining chair with armrests, 1915–16
Designed by Michel de Klerk
(Dutch, 1884–1923)
Commissioned by F.J. Zeegers for 't Woonhuys
(The Dwelling), Amsterdam
Manufactured and retailed by 't Woonhuys,
Amsterdam, c. 1917
Mahogany, mohair velvet upholstery, leather straps, brass
44½ x 26⅝ x 22 inches (113.0 x 66.7 x 55.9 cm)
TD1989.328.9

Cat. 179   See Fig. 3.22
Shelf clock and incense burners, c.1920
Designed by Hildo Krop
(Dutch, 1884–1970)
Made by H.J. Winkelman & Van der Bijl, Amsterdam, c.1920–30

a) Burner
Cast bronze
8 x 4½ x 3¾ inches (20.3 x 11.4 x 9.5 cm)
87.653.3.3 a, b

b) Clock
Cast bronze, enamel, metal, paint
14¾ x 12½ x 6 inches (37.5 x 31.8 x 15.2 cm)
87.653.3.1

c) Burner
Cast bronze
7 x 9¾ x 4¾ inches (17.8 x 24.8 x 12.1 cm)
87.653.3.2 a, b

Cat. 180
Cabinet, c.1928
Designed by Gerhard Schliepstein
(German, 1886–1963)
Berlin
Painted hardwoods and softwoods, plywood
64⁷/₁₂ x 46½ x 17¼ inches (164.0 x 118.1 x 43.8 cm)
XX1990.80

Cat. 181
Table, c.1930
Manufactured by A.B. Nordiska Kompaniet, Stockholm
Painted wood, pewter
24¾ x 30½ x 17¼ inches (62.9 x 77.5 x 43.8 cm)
Marks: underside, in high relief, brass plate "A.B. NORDISKA KOMPANIET/R33243-T2130"; stamped in black ink "P"; table top, proper left side rail, impressed company mark + "SVENSKT TENN STOCKHOLM" + "D8"
TD1989.241.2

Cat. 182
Maquette
***Elephant Tower*, for the Portals of the Pacific, 1939 Golden Gate International Exposition, San Francisco, CA, c.1938**
Donald Macky, architect
(American, b. 1913)
U.S.A.
Polychromed plaster
14 x 11 x 11⅜ inches (35.6 x 27.9 x 28.9 cm)
XX1989.399

Cat. 183
Poster
***Portals of the Pacific. 1939 World's Fair on San Francisco Bay*, c.1938–39**
U.S.A.
Photo-lithograph
29⅞ x 39 inches (75.9 x 100.9 cm)
Marks: obverse, printed, bottom left an encircled "G"
XX1990.4500

176

180

181

182

183

Manipulating Modernity – Political Persuasion

Evoking the Past

Cat. 184   See Fig. 4.10
Plate 2
"The Party Fight and the New Party or Liberalism and Toryism disturbed by the appearance of Socialism," 1894
Cartoons for the Cause, 1886–1896
Illustrated and written by Walter Crane
(British, 1845–1915)
Published by Twentieth Century Press, London, 1896
Ink on paper
20 x 12½ inches (50.8 x 31.8 cm)
TD1990.44.25**

Cat. 185
Design drawing
Perspective view of the south elevation of the Viceroy's House (1912–31; Edwin L. Lutyens [British, 1869–1944] and Herbert Baker [British, 1862–1946], architects), now known as Rashtrapati Bhavan, New Delhi, India, 1914
William Walcot
(British, 1874–1943)
London
Watercolor, black ink and wash, over graphite on paper
42¹⁵/₁₆ x 18⅜ inches (109.0 x 46.6 cm)
Marks: obverse, signed, lower right corner
"Edwin L. Lutyens A.R.A./1914"
TD1992.165.1

Cat. 186   See Fig. 10.26
Poster
NRA Member. U.S. We Do Our Part, 1934
Designed by Charles T. Coiner
(American, b. 1898)
Printer attributed to the U.S. Government Printing Office, Washington, D.C.
Published by the National Recovery Administration, Washington, D.C.
Commerical color lithograph
27⅜ x 20¹⁵/₁₆ inches (69.5 x 53.2 cm)
84.4.666

Cat. 187   See Fig. 9.11
Plaque
Heim der Hitler Jugend
(Home of Hitler Youth), 1933–45
Germany
Wrought iron, traces of original polychrome
45½ x 66¾ x 5½ inches (115.6 x 169.6 x 14.0 cm)
TD1992.49.3

185

188

Cat. 188
Flag of the Italian Social Republic, 1943–45
Italy
Wool, cotton, silk(?) appliqué, acrylic(?) embroidery, linen hoist, acrylic halyard
57 x 82 inches (144.8 x 208.3 cm)
Marks: reverse of hoist, " . . . donata dai Paracadutisti – Hardouin G. Principe di Belmonte e Mario Re . . . "
TD1992.135.1

Cat. 189   See Fig. 7.20
Poster
L'Art Italien XIXe-XXe Siècles, Jeu de Paume, Tuileries
(Italian Art 19th-20th Centuries...), 1935
Designed by Umberto Brunelleschi
(Italian, 1879–1949)
Printed by H. Chachoin Imp., Paris
Commercial color lithograph
61⅝ x 46½ inches (156.4 x 117.9 cm)
Marks: obverse, printed in white, upper right corner
"BRUNELLESCHI"
84.4.7

Cat. 190   See Fig. 9.08
Poster
Germany's Modern Architecture, c. 1938
Designed by Richard Klein
(German, 1890–1967)
Published by Reichsbahnzentrale für den Deutschen Reiseverkehr, Berlin
Commercial color lithograph, with gold metallic ink
39³/₁₆ x 24⅞ inches (101.1 x 63.2 cm)
Marks: obverse, printed in red, upper right corner "KLEIN/MÜNCHEN"
XX1990.4073

Cat. 191   See Fig. 9.06
Print
Die Bauten der N.S.D.A.P. zu München
(The buildings of the Nazi Party Headquarters in Munich; Paul Ludwig Troost [German, 1878–1934], architect), c. 1935
Christian Hacker
(German, dates unknown)
Munich
Etching
23⅛ x 48⁷/₁₆ inches (58.9 x 123.0 cm)
Marks: obverse, printed in black, lower right corner
"IN BILD GESETZT CHRISTIAN HACKER"
TD1991.224.1

Cat. 192
Painting
Doppelakt (Double Nude), c. 1940
Ivo Saliger
(German, b. 1894)
Vienna
Oil on canvas
47½ x 55¼ inches (120.7 x 140.3 cm) unframed
Marks: obverse, signed in black "Ivo Saliger"
TD1990.282.1

Cat. 193
Teapot, 1932
Designed by Ljudmila Viktorovna Protopopova
(Russian, 1906–81)
Decorated by the Leningrad Porcelain Factory, Leningrad, on a blank manufactured by the Imperial Porcelain Factory, St. Petersburg, 1897
Glazed porcelain, gold
8¾ x 9¼ x 4⅞ inches (22.2 x 23.5 x 10.5 cm)
Marks: underside, underglaze in black "N=432/no puc."/artist's signature/"Z"; underglaze in green "1932="; underglaze in black on green ground Imperial Porcelain Factory crown mark of Nicholas II/"97"
TD1990.22.2a, b

192

193

194

196

197

Cat. 194
Plate
Iustitia et Pax osculantae sunt
(Justice and Peace are united),
commemorating the Lateran Pacts between the
Holy See and the Fascist government, 1929
Designed by Galileo Chini
(Italian, 1873–1956)
Manufactured by Chini & Co., Borgo S. Lorenzo, Mugello
(Florence), Italy
Tin-glazed earthenware
2⅝ x 11¼ inches dia. (5.7 x 28.6 cm dia.)
Marks: underside, underglaze in blue company mark/"CHINI &
CO./MUGELLO/ITALIA/H"; underglaze in brown 301/ANNO.VII";
impressed "302"
GX1989.54

Cat. 195   See Fig. 7.19
Mural study
Le forze fasciste
(The Fascist forces), for the Padiglione
dell'Architettura (Architecture Pavilion),
VI Triennale, Milan, c. 1935
Designed by Tullio d'Albisola
(Italian, 1899–1971)
Made by Casa Giuseppe Mazzotti, Albisola (Savona), Italy
Glazed earthenware
18⅜ x 35 x 1½ inches (46.1 x 88.9 x 3.8 cm)
84.7.82

Cat. 196
Poster
Fiasta Nazionala 1940. Per Nossa Schuldada
(National Festival 1940. For Our Debts), 1940
Designed by Charles L'Eplattenier
(Swiss, 1874–1946)
Printed by Paul Bender, Zollikon, Switzerland
Commercial color photo-lithograph
49⅝ x 35¼ inches (126.0 x 89.5 cm)
Marks: obverse, printed in black, lower left "C. L'EPLATTENIER"
XX1992.144

Extolling the Modern

Cat. 197
Cover
"Der Sinn von Genf" (The Meaning of Geneva),
Arbeiter-Illustrierte Zeitung: das Illustrierte
Volksblatt **(AIZ), Jahrgang XI, No. 48,**
November 27, 1932
Designed by John Heartfield
(pseudonym for Helmut Herzfeld)
(German, 1891–1968)
Published by Neuer Deutscher Verlag, Berlin
15 x 11⅛ inches (38.1 x 28.2 cm)
Marks: obverse, printed in white, lower right corner
"MONTAGE: JOHN HEARTFIELD"
XB1990.2047

Cat. 198   See Fig. 8.22
Poster
Ente Radio Rurale, Radioprogramma Scolastico
N. 67. La Rivoluzione Fascista, no. 14
(Rural Radio Corporation, Scholastic Radio
Program N. 67. The Fascist Revolution, no. 14),
1938
Designed by Oreste Gasperini
(Italian, dates unknown)
Printed by Tumminelli & Co., Rome
Published by Ente Radio Rurale, Società Anonima Istituto, Rome
Commercial color photo-lithograph
27½ x 39¼ inches (69.9 x 99.7 cm)
Marks: obverse, printed in black, lower right corner
"COMPOSIZIONE DI ORESTE GASPERINI"
XX1990.2982

Cat. 199   See Fig. 8.10
Painting
Sintesi Fascista **(Fascist Synthesis), 1935**
Alessandro Bruschetti
(Italian, 1910–81)
Perugia, Italy
Oil on plywood
61 x 110¹³⁄₁₆ inches (154.9 x 281.6 cm) overall unframed
Marks: obverse, signed in red, lower right corner "Bruschetti XIII"
84.5.43.1-3

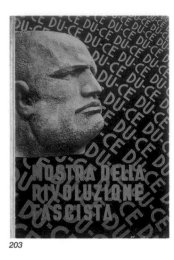

203

206

207

208

Cat. 200   See Fig. 6.16
Center panel
"Cantare Insieme" (To Sing Together),
Trittico dell'Amicizia **(The Friendship Triptych),**
1932
Thayaht (pseudonym for Ernesto Michahelles)
(Italian, 1863–1959)
Florence, Italy
Exhibited at the XVIII Esposizione Internazionale d'Arte, Venice, 1932.
Thayahtite (aluminum alloy)
55 1/8 x 39 inches (140.0 x 99.0 cm)
Marks: obverse, impressed, lower right corner
"THAYAHT 1932"
Private collection, Florence, Italy.
Note: The Wolfsonian Collection contains the original plaster molds for two of the three triptych panels.

Cat. 201
Plates
From the *Vita di Marinetti*
(Life of Marinetti) service, 1939
Designed by Giovanni Acquaviva
(Italian, 1900–71)
Made by Casa Giuseppe Mazzotti, Albisola (Savona), Italy
Glazed earthenware
3/4 x 8 1/4 inches dia. (1.9 x 21.0 cm dia.)

a) *Fascismo Futurismo* (Fascism Futurism) (See Fig. 8.09)
Marks: underside, signed, underglaze in green "ACQUA/VIVA";
underglaze in red "MG/A/1939/XVII"
TD1992.47.4

b) *San Sepolcro Duce Duce Duce* [not illustrated]
Marks: underside, signed, underglaze in blue "ACQUA/VIVA";
underglaze in orange "MG/A/1939/XVII"
TD1992.47.5

Cat. 202   See Fig. 8.11
Tile
XXVIII Ottobre
(also known as *La Marcia su Roma*
[The March on Rome]), 1931–32
Designed by Corrado Cagli
(Italian, 1910–76)
or Dante Baldelli
(Italian, b. 1904)
Made by Ceramiche Rometti, Umbertide, Italy
Glazed earthenware
8 x 8 x 1/2 inches (20.3 x 20.3 x 1.3 cm)
Marks: underside, signed, underglazed in black
"rometti umbertide"
GX1993.366

Cat. 203
Cover
Mostra della Rivoluzione Fascista
(Exhibition of the Fascist Revolution), 1933
Edited by Dino Alfieri
(Italian, 1886–1966)
and Luigi Freddi
(Italian, b. 1895)
Printed by Officine dell'Istituto Italiano d'Arti Grafiche, Bergamo, Italy
Published by Partito Nazionale Fascista, Rome
This book documents a 1932 exhibition of the Fascist revolution commemorating the tenth anniversary of the March on Rome.
9 5/8 x 6 7/8 x 3/4 inches (24.5 x 17.5 x 2.0 cm)
83.2.562/c.1

Cat. 204   See Fig. 8.15
Poster
Crociera Aerea del Decennale 1933
(Decennial of Long-Distance Flight . . .), 1933
Designed by Luigi Martinati
(Italian, 1893–1934)
Printed by Grafiche I.G.A.P. (Impresa Generale Affissione Pubblicità), Milan and Rome
Commercial color lithograph
54 11/16 x 38 9/16 inches (138.9 x 97.9 cm)
Marks: obverse, printed in blue, upper left corner
"L. MARTINATI -"
XX1990.1755

Cat. 205   See Fig. 10.13
Poster (four sheets)
Ho-Ruck! Nach Links! Wählt Sozialdemokratisch!
(Heave-Ho! To the Left! Vote Social Democratic!),
1930
Designed by Victor Th. Slama
(Austrian, 1890–1973)
Printed by Vorwärts, Vienna
Published by Alois Pipergau, Vienna
Commercial color lithograph
73 1/16 x 96 7/8 inches (185.6 x 246.1 cm) approx. overall
Marks: obverse, upper right panel, printed in black, upper right corner "Slama"
XX1990.3050a-d

Cat. 206
Poster
Pozor na Samozvané Prátele Lidu! **(Beware of**
the Self-proclaimed Friends of the People!), 1945
Designed by Návrh Štěpán
Printed by Tisk M. Schulz A.S., Prague
Published by Komunistický, Strana Ceskoslovenksa
(Czech Communist Party), Prague.
Commercial color lithograph
35 x 25 inches (88.9 x 63.5 cm)
Marks: obverse, printed in white, lower left corner
"NÁVRH ŠTĚPÁN"
TD1991.55.13

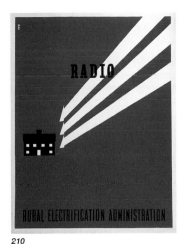

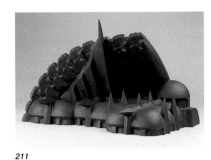

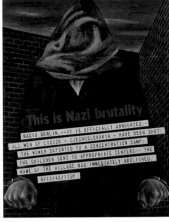

209 210 211 212

Cat. 207
Poster
Vencerem Pel Bé Del Proletariat Mundial
(We Will Triumph for the Good of the World
Proletariat), 1936
Designed by Coves
Printed by I.G. Seix I. Barral, Empresia Collectivitzada, Barcelona
Published by Partit Republicá d'Esquerra, Barcelona
Commercial color lithograph
39⅜ x 27½ inches (100.0 x 69.9 cm)
Marks: obverse, printed in white, lower right corner "-coves-/36"
XX1990.2919

Cat. 208
Plates
Designed by Mikhail M. Adamovich
(Russian, 1844–1947)
Decorated by the State Porcelain Factory, Petrograd, on a
blank manufactured by the Imperial Porcelain Factory,
St. Petersburg
Glazed porcelain

a) "Long Live the Third International" (translation), 1921
Blank dated 1912
1⅜ x 10½ inches dia. (3.5 x 26.7 cm dia.)
Marks: underside, overglaze in blue State Porcelain Factory
hammer and sickle mark/"1921/ Ap."; overglaze in black on
gray ground Imperial Porcelain Factory crown mark of
Nicholas II/"1912"
XX1990.1336

b) "He Who Does Not Work Does Not Eat" (translation), 1924
[not illustrated]
Blank dated 1892
1¼ x 9⅞ inches dia. (3.1 x 23.7 cm dia.)
Marks: underside, overglaze in blue State Porcelain Factory
hammer and sickle mark/"1924/243/92"; underglaze in green
Imperial Porcelain Factory crown mark of Alexander III/"92"
XX1990.1337

Cat. 209
Poster
Ozet Lottery No. 2, **1929**
Designed by Mikhail Dlugach
(Russian, 1893–1968)
Printer and publisher unidentified (in Cyrillic)
Moscow
Commercial color lithograph
29¼ x 43⅝ inches (74.9 x 110.8 cm)
Marks: obverse, printed in blue, lower left artist's name + "29"
Inscription: obverse, printed in black, upper right "Let us finish
with the old to build more quickly if we participate in the Ozet
lottery" (translation); printed in white, bottom "To increase
Jewish toilers to agricultural work" (translation)
TD1990.326.2

Cat. 210
Poster
Radio. Rural Electrification Administration, **1937**
Designed by Lester Beall
(American, 1903–69)
Published by the Rural Electrification Administration,
Washington, D.C.
Silkscreen
40¹⁄₁₆ x 29¼ inches (101.7 x 76.6 cm)
Marks: obverse, printed in white, upper left corner "BEALL"
TD1991.174.3

Cat. 211
Maquette
The Threatening Shadow, c.**1938**
Alfonso Iannelli
(American, b. Italy, 1888–1965)
Chicago, IL
Designed for installation at the New York World's Fair, 1939
(never built).
Monochromed plaster
11¼ x 17 x 16 inches (28.6 x 43.2 x 40.6 cm)
83.6.2

Cat. 212
Poster
This is Nazi Brutality, **1942**
Designed by Ben Shahn
(American, b. Lithuania, 1898–1969)
Printed by the U.S. Government Printing Office, Washington, D.C.
Published by the Office of War Information, Washington, D.C.
Commercial color photo-offset lithograph
37¹⁵⁄₁₆ x 28¹⁵⁄₁₆ inches (96.3 x 71.9 cm)
Marks: obverse, printed in black, lower right corner "Ben Shahn"
86.4.19

Domesticating the Political

Cat. 213 See Fig. 9.18
Poster
Neues Volke 1938 (New People . . .), for the
calendar of the Rassenpolitisches Amtes der
N.S.D.A.P. (Racial Policy Office of the Nazi
Party), 1938
Design attributed to Ludwig Hohlwein
(German, 1874–1949)
Published by Rassenpolitisches Amt der N.S.D.A.P., Berlin
Commercial color lithograph
16½ x 11⅝ inches (43.9 x 29.5 cm)
XX1990.2734

Cat. 214 See Fig. 10.20
Poster
Giornata della Madre e del Fanciullo. Anno XV
(Day of the Mother and Child . . .), 1936
Designed by Marcello Dudovich
(Italian, 1878–1962)
Printed by Grafiche I.G.A.P. (Impresa Generale Affisione
Pubblicità), Milan and Rome
Published by Opera Nazionale per la Protezione della Maternità
e dell'Infanzia, Rome
Commercial color lithograph
54 x 38¼ inches (137.2 x 97.3 cm)
Marks: obverse, printed in black, upper left corner "M. Dudovich"
84.4.11

Cat. 215
Beer stein, c. 1900
Designed by Peter Dümler
(German, 1860–1907)
Retailed by Joh. Korzilius, Köln-Ehrenfeld, Germany
Made by Dümler & Breiden, Höhr, Germany
Glazed stoneware, pewter
8¾ x 5⅜ x 3⅝ inches (22.2 x 13.1 x 82.5 cm)
Marks: underside, incised "MUSTERSCHUTZ"; obverse,
in high relief artist's mark "PD" intertwined; near base of handle
"Joh. Korzilius, Hoflieferant, Köln-Ehrenfeld"
TD1990.294.1

Cat. 216 See Fig. 9.25
Figurines, c. 1937
Designed by Richard Förster
(German, dates unknown)
Made by Porzellan Manufaktur Allach, Allach and Dachau
(Bavaria), Germany
The Porzellan Manufaktur Allach was under the direction of the
Personal Staff Department of the Reichsführer S.S. Heinrich
Himmler.
Glazed porcelain

a) *B.D.M. Standard Bearer*
12 x 3⁷⁄₁₆ x 3⁷⁄₁₆ inches (30.5 x 8.7 x 8.7 cm)
Marks: underside, underglaze, impressed "R. FÖRSTER/59";
written in green Allach double "SS" logo + "Allach"
85.7.274.2

b) *Hitler Jugend Drummer*
10½ x 4⅜ x 5⁵⁄₁₆ inches (26.7 x 11.1 x 13.5 cm)
Marks: underside, underglaze, impressed "R. FÖRSTER";
written in green Allach double "SS" logo + "Allach"
85.7.274.1

Cat. 217
Wall hanging, c. 1935
Manufactured by Münchner Bildteppichmanufaktur, Munich
Linen, cotton, silk
87 x 42½ inches (221.0 x 108.0 cm)
TD1993.142.2

Cat. 218 See Fig. 8.02
Plate
Amate il Pane Cuore della Casa . . . Mussolini
(Love Bread Heart of the Home . . .), c. 1927
Design attributed to Virgilio Retrosi
(Italian, 1892–1975)
Made by Ferruccio Palazzi, Fabbrica Ceramiche d'Arte, Rome
Tin-glazed earthenware
1½ x 14 inches dia. (3.8 x 35.6 cm dia.)
Marks: reverse, written, underglaze in yellow
"•FACE•/ FABBRICA CERAMICHE/ -D'ARTE-/ -ROMA-"
Inscription: obverse, written in black "AMATE IL PANE/CUORE
DELLA CASA/PROFUMO DELLA MENSA/GIOIA DEI
FOCOLARI/-MUSSOLINI-" (Love Bread/ Heart of the Home/
Fragrance of the Table/Joy of the Hearth . . .)
84.7.30

Cat. 219 See Fig. 7.03
Vase
Commemorating the twentieth wedding
anniversary of Ugo and Fernanda Ojetti, 1926
Designed by Guido Maria Balsamo Stella
(Italian, 1882–1941)
Decorated by Franz Pelzel (Czech, 1900–74)
Made by Laboratorio Balsamo, Venice
Glass
11½ x 11¼ inches dia. (29.2 x 28.6 cm dia.)
Marks: obverse of bowl, incised "balsamo inv./1926/pelzel inc."
Inscription: obverse of base, incised
"UGO*FERNANDA**OJETTI*XIV*XII*MCMV*MCMXXV*"
XX1990.1582
Note: One of a pair; the Wolfsonian collection also contains the
other.

Cat. 220 See Fig. 8.06
Wall lamp
Fascio, c. 1940
Italy
Silver electroplate on copper, glass
29½ x 12⅝ x 3½ inches (74.9 x 31.1 x 8.9 cm)
TD1989.78.1

Cat. 221 See Fig. 8.14
Certificate
Opera Nazionale Balilla, Caposquadra
(National Balilla Organization, Squad Captain),
c. 1935
Designed by Attilio Calzavara
(Italian, 1901–52)
Printed by Romano di S. Michele, Rome
Published by Opera Nazionale Balilla (O.N.B.), Rome
Multicolored inks on paper
13⅝ x 19⅛ inches (34.7 x 48.6 cm)
Marks: obverse, printed in white, center right "A. CALZAVARA"
Inscription: obverse, printed in white, center left "IL MODA DI
VITA/FASCISTA DEVE/INCOMINCIARE/DALL'AURORA/
MUSSOLINI" (The Fascist lifestyle must start at the dawn . . .)
TD1989.86.15

215

217

222

223

225

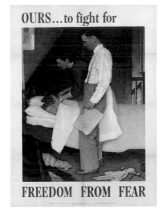
226

228

230

227

229

231a

Cat. 222
"F Fascio," *Italia dall'A alla Z*, **1936**
Designed by Carlo V. Testi
(Italian, dates unknown)
Written by Vincenzo Fraschetti (Italian, dates unknown)
Published by Direzione Generale Italiano all'Estero,
Novara, Italy
Printed by Officine dell'Istituto Geografico de Agostini,
Novara, Italy
Multicolored inks on paper
9¾ x 9 inches (24.6 x 22.9 cm) page
XB1991.103

Cat. 223
"C c c Châtions Les Traitres!" (Punish the Traitors), *Mon Alphabet*, **1940–45**
Designed by F. Touzet
Printed by Impressions ALFA, Lyons, France
Published by Editions Centres d'Information et de
Renseignements (C.I.R.), Vichy, France
Multicolored inks on paper
8½ x 5¾ inches (21.5 x 14.6 cm) page
XC1991.642

Cat. 224 See Fig. 8.23
Board game
La Conquista dell'Abissinia, **1936**
Published by Carlo Erba S.A., Milan
Printed by Istituto Italiano d'Arti, Milan
Multicolored inks on paper
22 x 15⅜ x 1/16 inches (55.9 x 39.1 x 0.2 cm)
XB1992.1787

Cat. 225
Game
Yank thru the lines: Slidem-Solitaire Puzzle,
1942
Made by Electric Corporation of America, Chicago, IL
Multicolored inks on paper
4½ x 6½ inches (11.4 x 16.5 cm) folded
XB1992.2344

Cat. 226
Poster
"Ours . . . to Fight For – Freedom from Fear,"
from the *Four Freedoms* series, **1943**
Designed by Norman Rockwell
(American, 1894–1978)
Printed by the U.S. Government Printing Office, Washington, D.C.
Published by the U.S. Office of War Information, Washington, D.C.
Commercial color photo-lithograph
27¹⁵/₁₆ x 20 inches (71.0 x 50.7 cm)
Marks: obverse, printed in gray, lower left corner
"NORMAN ROCKWELL"
1993.1.24
Gift of the Ringling School of Art and Design, Sarasota, FL.

Social Commentary

Cat. 227
Candleholders, 1876
Designed by Louis Dee
(British, 1831–84)
Made by Louis Dee, London, 1881–82
Design based on a cartoon by Daumier satirizing Louis Philippe
King of France, 1830–48.
Silver
8½ x 4½ inches dia. (21.6 x 11.4 cm dia.)
Marks: underside of foot, struck registration mark for August 30,
1876; obverse, struck, bottoms of base and cap "LD" hallmark
+ hallmarks for Britannia and London + date letter for 1881–82
XX1991.127.1-2 a, b

Cat. 228
Portfolio
Jeu de massacre: 12 personages à la recherche d'une • **(Massacre game. 12 people in search of a •) by Henri Barbusse**
(French, 1873–1946), **1920**
Illustrated by Fred Deltor
Published by Editions Socialistes, Brussels
12⅝ x 9¾ inches ea. (32.1 x 24.5 cm ea.)
XC1993.20

a) Plate 12, *Le Chauvinisme* (Nationalism)

b) Plate 3, *La Philanthropie* (Philanthropy) [not illustrated]

Cat. 229
Collages, c. 1914–17
Bertha Czegka
(Austrian, b. 1880)
Vienna
Colored papers

a) *Flohkönig Nikita* (Flea King Nikita)
8¹/₁₆ x 5⅞ inches (20.5 x 14.9 cm)
Marks: obverse, signed in black ink, lower left "B. CZEGKA"
86.5.113

b) *Il Re* (The King) [not illustrated]
6⅝ x 5¹³/₁₆ inches (16.8 x 14.7 cm)
Marks: obverse, signed in black ink, lower left corner "B. CZEGKA"
86.5.115

Cat. 230
Pincushion
Hotzi Notzi, **1941**
Manufactured by Bassons Dummy Products, Maspeth, NY
Polychromed plaster, cloth
4¾ x 2 x 4⅛ inches (12.1 x 5.1 x 10.5 cm)
XX1990.291

Cat. 231 [exhibited in Miami only]
Puppets, c. 1940
U.S.A.(?)
Printed paper

a) *Adolf Hitler*
12 x 5½ inches (30.5 x 14.0 cm)
XB1992.1604

b) *Joseph Goebbels* [not illustrated]
11¾ x 3¾ inches (29.6 x 9.5 cm)
XB1992.1606

c) *Hermann Göring* [not illustrated]
12½ x 6½ inches (31.7 x 16.5 cm)
XB1992.1605

233

234

235

236

Cat. 232   See Fig. 9.16
Medallion
***Hittler Putsch 8 November 1923. National Gen National!!!, Munchner Theater* (Hitler Putsch. National against National!!!, Munich Theater), 1923**
Karl Goetz
(German, 1875–1950)
Munich
Bronze
³⁄₁₆ x 2³⁄₈ inches dia. (0.5 x 5.5 cm dia.)
Marks: reverse, in high relief, bottom left "K"; bottom right "G"
TD1989.212.20
Note: Additional medallions with similar theme also in exhibition [not illustrated]

Cat. 233
Sketch
***Carne da cannone* (Cannon fodder), c. 1943**
Alberto Bazzoni
(Italian, 1889–1973)
Milan
Charcoal, paper
18¹⁰⁄₁₁ x 26¹⁄₈ inches (48.0 x 66.5 cm)
Marks: obverse, signed in charcoal, lower right corner "A. BAZZONI"
GX1993.524.6

Cat. 234
Poster
***Fool the Axis – Use Prophylaxis*, 1942**
Designed by Arthur Szyk
(American, b. Poland, 1894–1951)
Published by John Wyeth & Brother, Inc., Philadelphia, PA
Commercial color lithograph
17 x 22¹⁄₈ inches (43.3 x 56.2 cm)
Marks: obverse, printed in black, lower right corner "Arthur Szyk / N.Y. 42."
1993.13.1
Gift of Alexandra Braciejowski, Highland Beach, FL.

Cat. 235
Illustration
"Alabama Justice,"
***Scottsboro – A Story in Block Prints*, c. 1932**
Illustrated and written by Lin Shi Khan and Ralph Austin
(American, b. 1912)
California (?), U.S.A.
Ink and pencil on paper
12 x 9¹⁄₈ inches (30.5 x 23.4 cm) page
83.2.2295

Cat. 236
Print
***Civilization A.D. 1935*, c. 1935**
Leo Meissner
(American, 1895–1977)
New York
Number 28 in an edition of 50.
Wood-engraving
15⁵⁄₈ x 12⁹⁄₁₆ inches (39.7 x 31.9 cm)
Marks: obverse, in pencil, lower right corner "Leo Meissner"
TD1988.70.1

Promoting Production

Cat. 237   See Fig. 3.04
Poster
***Loten van de Nationale Tentoonstelling van Vrouwenarbeid* (Lottery of the National Exhibition of Women's Work), 1898**
Designed by Jan Theodoor Toorop
(Dutch, 1858–1928)
Printed by S. Lankhout & Co., The Hague, Netherlands
Published by Nationale Tentoonstelling van Vrouwenarbeid, The Hague, Netherlands
Commercial color lithograph
47¹³⁄₁₆ x 27⁹⁄₁₆ inches (121.4 x 70.0 cm)
Marks: obverse, printed in white, lower left at base of anvil "TOOROP.lith:"
TD1989.317.66

Cat. 238   See Fig. 10.01
Painting
***Work for America!*, 1918**
Dean Cornwell
(American, 1892–1960)
New York
Oil on paper, wood panel
36¹⁄₄ x 25³⁄₄ inches (92.1 x 65.4 cm) unframed
Marks: obverse, signed in yellow, upper right corner "DEAN/CORN•/ WELL/ 1918"
87.5.21

Cat. 239   See Fig. 10.02
Print
"Building Aircraft: Making the Engine,"
from *The Great War: Britain's Efforts and Ideals* series, 1917
Christopher Richard Wynne Nevinson
(British, 1889–1946)
Published by the Ministry of Information, His Majesty's Stationery Office, London, 1918
Number 54 in an edition of 200.
Lithograph
20¹⁄₈ x 15³⁄₁₆ inches (51.1 x 38.6 cm)
Marks: obverse, in pencil, lower right corner "C.R.W.Nevinson"
85.4.64.43

Cat. 240   See Fig. 9.23
Poster
***Deutsche Kauft. Deutsche Ware. Deutsche Woche. Deutsche Arbeit* (German Commerce. German Goods. German Week. German Work), c. 1937**
Designed by Hermann Keimel
(German, 1889–1948)
Printed by Chromolithographische Kunstanstalt A.G., Munich
Commercial color lithograph
32¹¹⁄₁₆ x 23⁵⁄₈ inches (83.0 x 60.0 cm)
Marks: obverse, printed in black, lower left "KEIMEL"
TD1988.30.165

Cat. 241 See Fig. 9.19
Poster (two sheets)
Arbeit Siegt (Work Triumphs), c. 1935
Designed by Hermann Grah
(German, dates unknown)
Published by N.S. Hago Gauamtsleitung and Kreisamtsleitung,
Düsseldorf, Germany
Commercial color lithograph
70 1/16 x 92 10/16 inches (177.8 x 235.4 cm) overall
Marks: obverse, printed in black, bottom panel, lower left
corner "GRAH/III/LEIPZIG/DÜSSELDORF"
TD1990.34.14a,b

Cat. 242
Poster
Work to Keep Free!, 1943
Printed by the U.S. Government Printing Office, Washington, D.C.
Published by the War Production Board, Washington, D.C.
Commercial color lithograph
40 x 28 1/2 inches (101.6 x 72.3 cm)
XX1990.3323

Cat. 243 See Fig. 10.19
Bowl
Autarchia (Autarky), 1938
**Designed by Golia
(pseudonym for Eugenio Colmo)**
(Italian, 1885–1967)
Turin, Italy
Glazed earthenware
3 1/2 x 12 1/4 inches dia. (8.9 x 31.1 cm dia.)
Marks: underside, signed, underglaze in black "Golia/1938 XVII"
XX1990.627

Cat. 244 See Fig. 6.18
**Writing desk, 1935
Designed by Clemente Busiri Vici**
(Italian, 1887–1965)
Made by Ditta Alfredo Papalini, Rome
Aluminum, plate glass, fiberglass mat, wood, steel
32 3/4 x 59 1/4 x 30 1/4 inches (83.2 x 150.5 x 76.8 cm)
84.11.13.1

Cat. 245
**Chair, c. 1939
Designed by Fortunato Depero**
(Italian, 1892–1960)
Made by Sani, Trento, Italy
Buxus manufactured by Cartiere G. Bosso, Turin.
Carved plywood, other soft woods, buxus (resin impregnated
paper veneer)
42 1/2 x 19 3/4 x 18 3/4 inches (108.0 x 50.2 x 47.6 cm)
Marks: underside of seat, signed in red "F Depero";
stamped in red "IRR/SANI/3NTO" encircled
84.11.7

Cat. 246 See Fig. 8.19
Cover
Opere Pubbliche 1922–1932 (Public Works . . .),
**1933
Designed by Attilio Calzavara**
(Italian, 1901–52)
Published by Ministero dei Lavori Pubblici, Rome
13 x 9 1/4 x 1 3/4 inches (33.0 x 23.6 x 4.4 cm)
83.2.979

Cat. 247
Medallion
*République Français Routes Navigation Mines
Electricité. Musée Permanent des Travaux
Publics*, c. 1930
Edouard Pierre Blin
France
Bronze
3/8 x 2 5/8 inches dia. (1.0 x 6.7 cm dia.)
Marks: obverse, struck, bottom right "E.BLIN"; reverse, struck,
center right "EB"
88.47.1.1
Note: Additional medallions with similar theme also in exhibition
[not illustrated]

Cat. 248 See Fig. 10.04
Poster
Farm Work. Rural Electrification Administration,
**1937
Designed by Lester Beall**
(American, 1903–69)
Published by the Rural Electrification Administration,
Washington, D.C.
Silkscreen
39 15/16 x 30 1/4 inches (100.4 x 76.7 cm)
Marks: obverse, printed in white, upper left corner "BEALL"
TD1991.174.1

Cat. 249 See Fig. 10.08
Poster
Bayrisches-Central Landwirtschaftsfest.
16 September – 1 Oktober. München, 1933.
(Central Bavaria Agricultural Festival . . .), 1933
Designed by Pehns
Printed by Kunst im Druck G.m.b.H., Munich
Commercial color lithograph
32 7/8 x 23 1/2 inches (83.5 x 59.8 cm)
Marks: obverse, printed in black, lower right corner "Pehns"
XX1990.3101

Cat. 250
Print
Granaries of Democracy, 1943
Louis Lozowick
(American, b. Ukraine, 1892–1973)
New York
Number 12 in an edition of 25.
Ink on paper
13 x 8 1/2 inches (33.0 x 21.6 cm)
Marks: obverse, signed in pencil, lower right
"LOUIS LOZOWICK '43"
TD1990.192.2

Cat. 251
Study
Rock Quarry, for U.S. Post Office, Westerley, RI
**mural competition, 1941
Leo A. Raiken**
(American, 1914–72)
New York
Oil on canvas
69 x 149 1/4 inches (175.3 x 379.1 cm) unframed
Marks: obverse, signed in brown, lower right
"Leo Raiken 1941"
84.5.125

242

245

247

250

251

345

Cat. 252   See Fig. 10.03
Study
***Promote the General Welfare*, possibly for U.S.
Post Office no. 235, San Jose, CA, mural
competition (unknown if realized), c. 1935**
U.S.A.
Oil on canvas with plywood back
42⅜ x 18⅛ inches (107.6 x 46.0 cm) unframed
TD1989.45.66

Cat. 253
Traction leg splint, 1942
Designed by Charles Eames, Jr.
(American, 1907–78)
and Ray Kaiser Eames
(American, 1913–88)
Manufactured by Evans Products Company, Molded Plywood
Division, Los Angeles, CA
Developed originally for the United States Navy.
Plywood
42 x 8⅛ x 4⅛ inches (106.7 x 20.6 x 10.5 cm)
Marks: obverse, branded, lower leg section "82–1790"; reverse,
printed in green manufacturer's logo + "MOLDED PLYWOOD
DIVISION/LOS ANGELES, CALIF"
XX1990.148

253

Cat. 254   See Fig. 10.25
Poster
***Women in the War – We Can't Win Without Them*,
1942**
Printed by the U.S. Government Printing Office, Washington, D.C.
Published by the War Manpower Commission, Washington, D.C.
Commercial color lithograph
39¹⁵⁄₁₆ x 28¹⁄₁₆ inches (101.4 x 71.3 cm)
1993.1.6
Gift of the Ringling School of Art and Design, Sarasota, FL.

255

Cat. 255
Print
**"Captain Pauline Gower of the Women's Air
Transport Auxiliary," from the *Women's Work in
the War Other Than the Services* series, 1940**
Ethel Leontine Gabain
(British, 1883–1950)
Printed by Curwen Press, London
Published by the Ministry of Information, His Majesty's
Stationery Office, London
Lithograph
22 x 16½ inches (55.8 x 42.0 cm)
Marks: obverse, printed in black, bottom center "E.GABAIN"
XX1990.2168

256

Cat. 256
Poster
***America's Answer! Production*, 1942**
Designed by Jean Carlu
(French, 1900–89)
Printed by the U.S. Government Printing Office, Washington, D.C.
Published by the Division of Information, Office for Emergency
Management, Washington, D.C.
Commercial color lithograph
29⅞ x 40⁵⁄₁₆ inches (75.9 x 102.5 cm)
Marks: obverse, printed in black, lower left corner
"JEAN/CARLU"
XX1990.2977

Contributors

Ellinoor Bergvelt is a lecturer at the University of Amsterdam. Formerly a curator in the Netherlands Office for Fine Arts, she has edited and contributed to a number of exhibition catalogues, among them *The Amsterdam School, Industry and Design*, and *Jan Theodoor Toorop 1858–1928*.

Irene de Guttry and Maria Paola Maino are the co-authors of several books, including *Le arti minori d'autore in Italia dal 1900 al 1930* and *Il mobile deco italiano*. They are the founders of "Archives of Twentieth-Century Applied Arts," a documentation and research center in Rome.

Dennis P. Doordan is an associate professor in the School of Architecture at the University of Notre Dame and an editor of *Design Issues*. He is the author of *Building Modern Italy: Italian Architecture 1914–1936* and has contributed essays to many exhibition catalogues, such as "Rebuilding the House of Man: Italian Architecture 1943–1968" (*The Italian Metamorphosis 1943–1968*), and "Aspects of Architectural Drawings in the Modern Era" (*The Modern Movement*).

Paul Greenhalgh is Director of Research at the Victoria and Albert Museum. He is the author of *Ephemeral Vistas: Expositions Universelles, Great Exhibitions and World's Fairs 1851–1939*, the editor and co-author of *Modernism in Design*, and general editor of a series on the history of design and material culture for Manchester University Press.

John Heskett is a professor at the Institute of Design, Illinois Institute of Technology, Chicago. He is the author of *Industrial Design, Design in Germany 1870–1918*, and *Philips: A Study of the Corporate Management of Design*.

Wendy Kaplan is curator of the Wolfsonian. As research associate at the Museum of Fine Arts, Boston, she organized the exhibition "'The Art that is Life': The Arts and Crafts Movement in America" and was principal author of its catalogue. She is co-author of *The Arts and Crafts Movement*, editor of *Charles Rennie Mackintosh*, and has contributed chapters to many other books on late nineteenth- and early twentieth-century design.

Marianna Lamonaca is associate curator at the Wolfsonian. Formerly assistant curator of decorative arts at The Brooklyn Museum, Ms. Lamonaca organized several collections-related exhibitions, including "Biomorphicism and Organic Abstraction in Twentieth-Century Decorative Arts."

Jeffrey L. Meikle is a professor of American Studies and Art History at the University of Texas at Austin. His publications include *American Plastic: A Cultural History* and *Twentieth Century Limited: Industrial Design in America, 1925–1939*.

Bernard F. Reilly, Jr. is head curator in the Prints and Photographs Division of The Library of Congress, and serves as the Library's specialist in political art and propaganda. He is the author of *American Political Prints, 1766–1876* and *In Good Conscience: The Radical Tradition in American Illustration in the Twentieth Century*, as well as many other publications about graphic art.

Laurie A. Stein is a curator at the Werkbund-Archiv in Berlin. Formerly at the Art Institute of Chicago and The Saint Louis Art Museum, her work on Jugendstil topics includes "Interior Textiles: New Design in the Age of Industry," "Henry van de Velde im Werkbund-Archiv," and "Spurensuche: Friedrich Adler zwischen Jugendstil und Art Deco." She is co-organizing an exhibition and catalogue about the German Museum of Art in Trade and Industry.

Photograph Credits

Unless otherwise noted, all photography by Bruce White Photography, Upper Montclair, New Jersey.

Amsterdam Historical Museum, Amsterdam, Netherlands, *fig. 3.17*

Archivio Storico delle Arti Contemporanee, La Biennale di Venezia, Venice, Italy, *figs. 6.07, 6.16*

The Art Institute of Chicago, Illinois, *cat. 84*

Piero Baguzzi, Milan, Italy, *fig. 2.09*

Mauro Buffoni, Genoa, Italy, *figs. 6.11, 6.14, 7.21, 7.22, 8.21*

George Chillag, Miami, Florida, *fig. 3.10*

Dennis Doordan, Notre Dame, Indiana, *fig. 8.01*

Foto Barsotti, Florence, Italy *fig. 6.01*

Gemeentilijk Archiefdienst Amsterdam, Amsterdam, Netherlands, *figs. 3.05, 3.06, 3.20*

Hessisches Landeshochschule Bibliothek, Darmstadt, Germany, *fig. 2.04, 2.06*

Kaiser Wilhelm Museum, Krefeld, Germany, *figs. 2.14, 2.26*

Kunstindustrimuseet, Oslo, Norway; photo by Teigens Fotoatelier, *fig. 1.05*

Museo Vetrario, Murano, Italy, *fig. 6.09*

Museum of Finnish Architecture, Helsinki, Finland; photo by Studio Granath, *fig. 1.08*

Museum of Folk Art, Moscow, Russia, *fig. 1.14*

Massimo Napoli, Rome, Italy, *fig. 7.09*

National Museum of Ireland, Dublin, Ireland, *fig. 1.03*

Enrico Polidori, Genoa, Italy, *figs. 6.03, 6.13*

Victoria and Albert Museum, London, England, *fig. 4.15*

Virginia Museum of Fine Arts, Richmond, Virginia, *cat. 159*

Werkbund-Archiv, Berlin, Germany, *figs. 2.01, 2.15, 2.22, 2.28*

John C. Waddell, New York, *cats. 137, 138, 155*

Willard Associates, Miami, Florida, *figs. 1.20, 3.01, 4.05, 4.14, 4.23, 5.04, 7.06, 7.08, 9.05, 10.26; cats. 10, 45, 229a*

Zul, Sussex, England, *fig. 4.09*

Index

Page numbers in italics refer to illustrations